D1324590

GCSE MATHS

FOUNDATION LEVEL

Jean Holderness

seway Books

SHEFFIELD HALLAM UNIVERSITY
LEARNING CENTRE
WITHDRAWN FROM STOCK

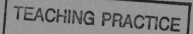
TEACHING PRACTICE

Cover and diagrams by Allen Associates

Published by Causeway Press Ltd.,
P.O. Box 13, Ormskirk, Lancs L39 5HP
First published 1987
Reprinted 1987, 1988, 1989, 1990, 1991

© Jean Holderness, 1987

British Library Cataloguing in Publication Data

Holderness, Jean
    GCSE maths – foundation level.
    1. Mathematics-1961-
    I. Title
    510   QA39.2

ISBN 0-946183-32-5

Other titles in this series:
GCSE Maths: Higher Level
GCSE Maths: Intermediate Level

Typesetting and printing by
The Alden Press, Oxford

Preface

This book is planned for use on a 2 year or 1 year course leading to the Foundation level papers of the GCSE. It is based on the syllabuses of the four English boards plus the Welsh and Northern Ireland boards, as published for use in 1988.

The findings of the Cockcroft Report, and the aims and assessment objectives of the examinations have been guidelines followed in the writing of this book.

Students will have been learning Mathematics from an early age, so they will have already met many of the topics in this book. The earlier chapters will help to review and consolidate the learning of former years. A good understanding of the basic topics, leading to a sense of achievement, will form a firm foundation to build on when progressing through the syllabus. The order of the book has been carefully planned, although, of course, it need not be followed rigidly. As well as the main chapters there are miscellaneous sections which include aural practice exercises, multi-choice exercises, revision exercises which could be used as practice papers, suggestions for practical work and investigational work, and suggestions to students for study, revision and preparation for the examination. In addition there are puzzle questions throughout the book, some traditional and some original.

Many people have encouraged and helped me during the preparation of this series of books. I am grateful to them all. I would especially like to thank my brother Jim for his practical help, Fred and Maureen for reading the scripts and making helpful suggestions, Andrew and Rosemary for their drawings, the staff at Alden Press for their speed and efficiency in typesetting and printing the books, and most of all Mike and Ian at Causeway Press.

Jean Holderness

To Winnie and Tom

Contents

CONTENTS

Topics for Practical Work and Investigations

To the teacher:

This book has been planned for a 2 year course or a 1 year course leading up to the GCSE examination at the Foundation level.

The first few chapters deal with elementary work in Arithmetic, Geometry and Statistics, to give a good start to the course. Students will gain a greater understanding of these topics which they may not have learnt fully at an earlier age, and thus they gain confidence. It is essential for them to have a good basic foundation of elementary work to build on later. Since these topics are used in later chapters there is constant recall.

The bookwork has been kept to a minimum, for simplicity. Explanations are best left for the teacher to include, and will depend on the ability and the previous knowledge of the students. For instance, if the students can already use geometry instruments adequately then they are ready to do the questions involving them, but if they cannot use a protractor or compasses then time must be spent on improving these skills, and they will need more help with the questions.

In the exercises some questions are straightforward enough for most students to work through by themselves, but for other questions it would be helpful to have a preliminary discussion when any uncommon terms can be explained, and different methods of approach can be suggested. The students should be encouraged to contribute to such discussion. It may not be desirable for every student to do every question in an exercise. Some must just attempt the simpler ones, to give them confidence, others need more challenging work.

It is assumed that students have calculators. They eliminate much of the routine work, giving more time for mathematics. They give the less able students confidence, as they take out the worry of having to calculate. Although mental arithmetic is to be encouraged, for some students it might have to be improved slowly, with practice, and the calculator used in the meantime. To encourage more practice in mental arithmetic, decimals are not introduced in Chapter 1, but are left until Chapter 6. Once decimals are used, the calculator is relied on more and mental arithmetic tends to be neglected. Many of the questions in this book can be done without a calculator. The final chapter in the book should give useful revision practice both in mental arithmetic and in using a calculator.

Statistics has been separated into small sections. Although it is an easy subject, if too many ideas are introduced too quickly they tend to get all muddled up. It is desirable to allow time for practical work to be carried out as this aids understanding so the suggestions for practical work in Statistics have been included in the relevant chapters.

The rest of the book has been planned on the same basis, with further work in Arithmetic and Geometry being covered in stages, and work on elementary Algebra and Probability being fitted in. As far as possible the same order has been followed as in the Intermediate Level book, but the earlier chapters contain much less material.

This means that if it becomes apparent that some students have been placed on the wrong course, they could be transferred after a few weeks from the Intermediate to the Foundation course without too much difficulty in adjustment. However, someone transferring from the Foundation to the Intermediate course would probably have to catch up on some of the work.

For graphical questions, graph paper with 2 mm squares is easier to use than that with 1 mm squares, and for some questions, paper ruled in 1 cm squares is better still. In an examination the graph paper would be supplied and in many cases the axes will have already been drawn and labelled. To do the questions from this book, therefore, the students should be given help in drawing and labelling the axes. (Scales have not always been suggested as they depend on the type and size of paper you have available, so you should decide on the scale to be used for each question.)

After every 5 chapters, that is roughly one term's work if using the book over two years, there is a Miscellaneous section. This includes the following:

Aural practice. For some Boards this is already a compulsory part of the examination. Many of the questions in the main parts of the book can be used for further aural practice.

Multi-choice exercises. These are not set in any papers but they have been included because they are useful for revision practice. Occasionally it is better for students to work quickly without having to put down every detail of the answer.

Revision exercises, based on the work of the previous chapters. These could be used as practice papers. In this case, select the most suitable questions, depending on your syllabus, using about 10 of the 12 in each case.

Suggestions for practical work and investigational work. Although at present this is an optional part of the course, time spent on this is invaluable for adding interest and understanding to the subject. A variety of suggestions have been included so that students can choose to work on a topic they enjoy. Some students may need help at the beginning, and you may have to modify some of the suggestions. Some of the ideas are more suitable for group work than individual work, and some students would be happier working in a group than alone. For students to achieve their best with independent work it helps if there is a good supply of lined, squared, graph and plain paper, thick and thin cardboard, safe glue, scissors and a collection of reference books. Note:- The suggestions **may** be suitable to count as a component of the examination but the requirements of the Boards differ and you must check with your own syllabus to see if this is so.

There are puzzle questions fitted in at the ends of chapters. Some of these are traditional and some original. They are there to give interest, and perhaps to develop into further investigations. They are arranged in a miscellaneous order and are not necessarily matched to the work of preceding chapters. The main value of the puzzles would be lost if the answers were too readily available so they have not been included.

Notes on Syllabuses

This book has been written using the following syllabuses as published in 1986 for use in 1988.

London and East Anglian Group	Mathematics A and B	Level X	(L)
Midland Examining Group	Mathematics	Foundation level	(M)
Northern Examining Association	Mathematics Syllabus A	Level P	(N)
Southern Examining Group	Mathematics	Level 1	(S)
Welsh Joint Education Committee	GCSE Mathematics	Level 1	(W)
Northern Ireland Schools Examinations Council	Mathematics Syllabus A and B	Basic level	(NI)

These syllabuses have a great deal in common, but there are a few differences, so there are some sections of the later chapters of the book which you may not need for your particular syllabus. In many cases it is difficult to decide from the wording of a syllabus the depth of study needed for a particular topic. The specimen papers, and later on the actual papers, will help to clarify these points. For this reason, general advice would be to include everything from the earlier chapters in your course, unless you are sure that certain minor topics can be omitted.

For other differences, this list is given as a guide to the topics which **you** do not need, (those marked ×), but syllabuses may be changed from time to time and you are advised to check your own syllabus for the year of the examination and amend this list where necessary.

Chapter	L	M	N	S	W	NI
10 Notation for inequalities	×	×	×	×		×
12 Dispersion: the range	×	×	×		×	×
20 The calendar	×	×		×	×	
21 Bearings: alternative notation	×	×	×	×		×
22 Pythagoras' theorem and approximate square roots	×	×	×	×	×	
23 *Construction* of pie charts	×		×	×	×	×
24 Polygons	×	×	×		×	×
Translation		×		×	×	×
Congruent figures	×	×	×	×	×	

1 Learning Mathematics

Maths is not a new subject since you have been learning it all your life, but in this book are all the topics you need to learn for the Foundation level of the GCSE in Maths.

We hope that you will enjoy studying Maths. Just think of some of the ways in which Maths is linked with our lives, for example:
Shapes in the natural world involving symmetry, curves, spirals, etc.
Shapes in architecture and design.
Management of our money.
Understanding of diagrams, graphs and maps.
Ability to think logically, so as to plan ahead.
You can think of many more examples of how Maths is essential in today's world.

Learn to think for yourself. Do not rely on being told how to do everything. The more things you can work out for yourself the better you will do.

Try to discover things for yourself. Look for patterns in numbers and shapes. From a particular result, could you deduce a general formula? As an example, suppose you have a spare moment waiting for a lesson to begin and you put your ruler down on your exercise book and draw lines on either side of it, then you move the ruler and cross the lines with two others, getting a shape in the middle. Now you can discover many things about that shape:- What is it? Are there any equal lines or angles, or any point or lines of symmetry? What is the sum of the angles? Look at its area. By altering the angle at which the lines cross can you get a different area? At what angle do the lines cross to get the smallest possible area? Join the diagonals of the figure and see what further discoveries you can make.

As you work through this book, try to learn the important facts and methods of each chapter. If you do not understand the main ideas, ask someone to help you, either your teacher, someone else in your class or anyone else who can explain them to you. But when you have to answer an unusual question, before you ask for help, try to use your own commonsense and reason it out.

If you work steadily your standard should improve and you should do well enough to gain a grade E or F in the examination, and if you miss these targets there is a chance of a grade G.

To do this course properly, you will need a calculator. You do not need a complicated one with all kinds of scientific functions on. A simple one which will do addition, subtraction, multiplication and division will be sufficient and will be easier to use, but make sure it has got a square root key $\boxed{\sqrt{}}$ on as well, as you will need that.

About the first 5 chapters

You will probably be able to do most of this work already. This is an opportunity to make sure that you know all about the basic ideas in Arithmetic and Geometry, as you will then use these in future work. The important facts are followed by some worked examples and then there are straightforward exercises to give you practice. The last exercise in each chapter has more challenging questions for you. You may do them at this stage or you may leave them to return to later, to give you more revision practice. Learn the important facts, methods and formulae as you go along. There is a chapter introducing Statistics, including suggestions for practical work. Try to find time to do some practical work even if it is not part of your examination.

After the 5 chapters there is Miscellaneous Section A. This can be used at any time, and mainly includes the material of the previous chapters.

There are puzzle questions fitted in at the ends of some chapters. Try some of these if you are interested. Some of them have a catch in them, so don't be caught out. These questions are clearly headed 'Puzzles' so that you know that they are not part of your examination course.

There are some topics in the book which you do not need to learn. The reason for this is that in different parts of the country people take slightly different examinations, so that whilst everyone needs to understand most of this work there are certain topics which may not apply to your particular examination board. Your teacher can advise you about which these are, and there are some details on page xii.

Now, get started and **enjoy your Maths**.

1 Numbers

Numbers

A calculator is an invaluable tool for saving time and doing accurate calculations, but there are basic arithmetical operations which you should be able to do mentally, quickly and accurately, and for which you should not waste time pressing calculator keys.

There will be many situations in your life when you need to work something out quickly and you will not have your calculator available. So make sure you are mentally alert.

To learn your tables

On squared paper, or with columns drawn on lined paper, copy this chart.

Fill in the results of multiplication so that the first column is the 2 times table and the numbers in the first few squares are 4, 6, 8, . . . from 2×2, 2×3, 2×4, . . . (or 2×2, 3×2, 4×2, . . . if you prefer to think of them that way).

When you have filled in all the squares and made sure they are correct, then you must learn all the results you do not already know.

You can look for some patterns in the table.

Which results are odd numbers?

Which results have a unit figure of 5?

Which number appears most in the table ?

What do the digits add up to in the 9's column?

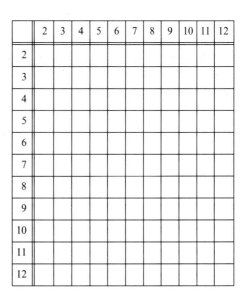

	2	3	4	5	6	7	8	9	10	11	12
2											
3											
4											
5											
6											
7											
8											
9											
10											
11											
12											

What do the digits add up to in the 3's column?

Learn the squares in the table. These are $2 \times 2 = 2^2 = 4$, $3 \times 3 = 3^2 = 9$, $4 \times 4 = 4^2 = 16$, and so on.

If you wish, you can include columns for 0 and 1 in the table. The 1 times table has results such as $1 \times 3 = 3$, $8 \times 1 = 8$. The 0 times table has results such as $0 \times 3 = 0$, $8 \times 0 = 0$.

To check your tables

This time you are going to rearrange the numbers in the headings of the rows and columns. Also leave out one number in each so that there are 10 rows and 10 columns, making 100 spaces to be filled in. Copy this chart.

	2	8	6	9	4	11	3	7	5	12
6										
11										
5										
8										
12										
3										
10										
4										
9										
7										

You are going to fill in the results of multiplication, so the numbers in the first few squares down the first empty column are 12, 22, 10, 16, etc. You will work down each column in turn. Before you begin, note the time. You should complete the chart within 5 minutes. If you take longer, then repeat the exercise, using numbers in a different random order, until you improve. Then check the accuracy of your work, which should be completely correct.

Make a similar chart for addition, so that the numbers down the first empty column are 8, 13, 7, . . .

See how quickly you can complete this.

Now try these questions. They are intended to improve your speed and accuracy so concentrate and do them quickly.

Exercise 1.1

1. 8×7 $30 + 90$ $21 - 6$ 6×12 $100 \div 5$
    6×4 $8 + 7$ $30 \div 5$ 6×0 $99 + 7$
    20×1 11^2 30×20 1×8 99×0
    20×3 $56 \div 7$ $20 - 8$ 13×1 12^2

2. $32 \div 4$ $27 \div 9$ $55 \div 5$ $72 \div 12$ $15 \div 5$
    $42 \div 7$ $132 \div 11$ $72 \div 9$ $30 \div 6$ $49 \div 7$
    $96 \div 12$ $60 \div 6$ $36 \div 3$ $77 \div 11$ $45 \div 5$
    $56 \div 8$ $144 \div 12$ $35 \div 7$ $60 \div 5$ $81 \div 9$

3. What is the remainder when   What must be added to

   1 18 is divided by 5   6 8×7 to make 60

   2 39 is divided by 7   7 4×3 to make 20

   3 68 is divided by 11   8 5×9 to make 50

   4 32 is divided by 4   9 7×11 to make 80

   5 100 is divided by 8   10 9×9 to make 100

4. Write in figures the numbers

   1 Two hundred and sixty-five thousand, three hundred and eighty-four.

   2 Twelve thousand and forty.

   3 One and a half thousand.

   4 Thirty and three-quarters.

   5 Four million, four hundred and forty thousand, four hundred and four.

   6 In 100 567, what do the 1, the 5 and the 6 stand for?

   7 In 2 908 134, what do the 2 and the 8 stand for?

5. Find the value of

   1 $5 \times 3 \times 1$ 4 $10 \times 20 \times 40$ 7 $180 \div 5$

   2 $4 \times 2 \times 0$ 5 $5000 \div 20$ 8 $(8 \times 12) - (7 \times 12)$

   3 $10^2 - 9^2$ 6 $89 + 99$ 9 $(6 \times 9) + (4 \times 9)$

                                                10 $5 \times 2 \times 11$

6.   1 Find two numbers whose sum is 13 and whose product is 36.
    2 Find two numbers whose sum is 11 and whose product is 30.
    3 Find two numbers whose sum is 52 and whose product is 100.
    4 Find two numbers whose sum is 16 and whose product is 15.
    5 Find two numbers whose sum is 16 and whose product is 48.
    6 Find two numbers whose product is 72 and which differ by 1.
    7 Find two numbers whose product is 24 and which differ by 5.
    8 Find two numbers whose product is 77 and which differ by 4.
    9 How many more 4's than 5's are there in 40?
    10 How many more 8's than 12's are there in 96?

7. 1 Start from 100 and count down in 6's until you reach a number less than 10. What number is this?

    2 Start from 1, then 2, then 4, and double the number every time until you reach a number greater than 1000. What number is this?

    3 Start from 25 000 and keep dividing by 5 until you reach a number less than 10. What number is this?

    4 Start with 1 and keep adding 7's until you reach a number greater than 100. What number is this?

    5 Start from 0 and add 1, then 2, then 3, and so on until you reach a number greater than 100. What number is this?

8. 1 Write down any number between 1 and 10, multiply this by 3, then to the result add 8. Double this answer. Now subtract 3, multiply by 5, add 7. Subtract 2 and divide by 10. Add 17, divide by 3 and take away the number you started with. What is your answer?

    2 Write down any number between 1 and 10, add 3 and multiply the result by 6. Then subtract 12, divide by 3, multiply by 10. Add 5, divide by 5 and add 7. Subtract 12 then divide by the number you started with. What is your answer?

    3 Write down any number less than 5, double it and add 3. Square the result, add 3 and divide by 4. Subtract 1 and multiply by 2. Subtract 4, divide by the number your started with, add 14 and halve the result. Take away the number you started with. What is your answer?

9. What are the numbers which follow 199, 9900, 219, 4009, 999?

10. What is the missing number in each of these statements?

    1 $\Box + 11 = 30$ 4 $\Box - 11 = 4$

    2 $\Box \times 11 = 77$ 5 $(11 + 9) - \Box = 4$

    3 $(\Box \times 3) - 11 = 16$

11. 1 I think of a number, divide it by 3 and then add 5. The result is 12. What was the original number?

    2 I think of a number, square it and add 3. The result is 39. What was the original number?

    3 I think of a number, multiply it by 4 and take away 12. The result is 16. What was the original number?

An even number is a number which divides exactly by 2. The units figure is 2, 4, 6, 8 or 0.

An odd number is a number which does not divide exactly by 2. The units figure is 1, 3, 5, 7 or 9.

Tests for dividing by 2, 3 or 5

Dividing by 2

If the units figure is even, i.e. 2, 4, 6, 8, 0, the number divides exactly by 2.

Dividing by 3

Add up the digits in the number, and if the answer is more than 9 you can add up the digits of that answer, and repeat until you get a 1-figure number. If this number divides by 3 then the original number divides by 3. For example, for 2841, $2 + 8 + 4 + 1 = 15$ (and $15 \rightarrow 1 + 5 = 6$). This divides by 3 so 2841 divides by 3.

Dividing by 5

If the units figure is 5 or 0 the number divides by 5.

A prime number is a number which does not divide exactly by any number (except itself and 1).
The first few prime numbers are 2, 3, 5, 7, 11, 13, 17, 19, . . .

To find whether a number is a prime number

Check that it does not divide exactly by any numbers (except itself and 1) by dividing by the first few prime numbers 2, 3, 5, 7, 11, . . .

First, check that it does not divide exactly by 2.
Then check that it does not divide exactly by 3.
Then check that it does not divide exactly by 5. (Since $5 \times 5 = 25$, you do not need to do this or any further checks for numbers less than 25.)
Then check that it does not divide exactly by 7. (Since $7 \times 7 = 49$, you do not need to do this or any further checks for numbers less than 49.)
Then check that it does not divide exactly by 11. (Since $11 \times 11 = 121$, you do not need to do this or any further checks for numbers less than 121.)
You are unlikely to need to check for larger numbers but, if necessary, you would check whether the number divides exactly by 13, 17, 19, . . .

Example 1 Find the prime numbers between 90 and 100.

The even numbers 90, 92, 94, 96, 98, 100 divide by 2 so they are not prime numbers.
This leaves the odd numbers 91, 93, 95, 97, 99 to be checked.
93 and 99 divide by 3 so they are not prime numbers.
This leaves 91, 95, 97 to be checked.
95 divides by 5 so this is not a prime number.
91 divides by 7 so this is not a prime number.
97 does not divide by 2, 3, 5 or 7. Since 97 is less than 121 there is no need to check that it does not divide by 11 or any greater prime number.
97 is a prime number.

Factors

Example 2 Find all the factors of 24.

Factors of 24 are numbers which divide exactly into 24.
All numbers have a factor 1, and 24 has a factor 24.
Also $24 = 2 \times 12 = 3 \times 8 = 4 \times 6$
So the factors of 24 are 1, 2, 3, 4, 6, 8, 12, 24.

Example 3 Find the prime factors of 90.

This means split 90 up into factors which are prime numbers.

$90 = 9 \times 10$ Now turn 9 and 10 into their prime factors
                            $9 = 3 \times 3$, $10 = 2 \times 5$

$90 = 3 \times 3 \times 2 \times 5$
  $= 2 \times 3 \times 3 \times 5$ (putting the factors in order of size)

This is 90 expressed in prime factors.

It can be written as
$90 = 2 \times 3^2 \times 5$ since 3×3 can be written as 3^2

Multiples

e.g. The multiples of 7 are numbers which 7 divides exactly into, including 7 itself.
Some multiples of 7 are 7, 14, 21, 28, 140, 196, 700.

Square numbers

If a number is multiplied by itself, the resulting number is a square number, sometimes called a perfect square.
e.g. $5 \times 5 = 25$ so 25 is a square number and its square root is 5,
$12 \times 12 = 144$ so 144 is a square number and its square root is 12.
You can find square roots on your calculator.
To find the square root of 169 press 169 $\boxed{\sqrt{}}$ and the answer is 13.
If you find the square root of a number on your calculator and the result is not an exact whole number then the original number is not a square number.

Cube numbers

e.g. $5 \times 5 \times 5 = 125$ so 125 is a cube number and its cube root is 5.

5×5 can be written as 5^2 (read as five squared).

$5 \times 5 \times 5$ can be written as 5^3 (read as five cubed).

Use of Brackets

Operations in brackets should be carried out first. If there are no brackets, multiplication and division should be carried out before addition and subtraction.

Examples

$$4 \times 6 - 5 \times 3 = (4 \times 6) - (5 \times 3) = 24 - 15 = 9$$
$$4 \times (6 - 5) \times 3 = 4 \times 1 \times 3 = 12$$
$$4 + 6 \times 5 - 3 = 4 + (6 \times 5) - 3 = 4 + 30 - 3 = 31$$
$$(4 + 6) \times (5 - 3) = 10 \times 2 = 20$$

A fraction line can take the place of a bracket.

$\dfrac{3 + 5}{6 - 2}$ means $(3 + 5) \div (6 - 2)$ which equals $\dfrac{8}{4} = 2$

Numbers to the nearest ten

e.g. For numbers between 50 and 60.
Any number less than 55 is given as 50, to the nearest ten.
Any number from 55 upwards is given as 60, to the nearest ten.
(Actually, 55 is exactly halfway between 50 and 60 but it is usual to round it **up** to 60.)

Numbers to the nearest hundred

e.g. For numbers between 200 and 300.
Any number less than 250 is given as 200, to the nearest hundred.
Any number from 250 upwards is given as 300, to the nearest hundred.

Numbers to the nearest thousand

e.g. For numbers between 7000 and 8000.
Any number less than 7500 is given as 7000, to the nearest thousand.
Any number from 7500 upwards is given as 8000, to the nearest thousand.

Examples

$$64 \quad = 60, \text{ to the nearest ten}$$
$$264 \quad = 300, \text{ to the nearest hundred}$$
$$9264 = 9000, \text{ to the nearest thousand}$$
$$9764 = 10\,000, \text{ to the nearest thousand.}$$

Exercise 1.2

1. Which of these numbers are prime numbers? 21, 23, 25, 27, 29.

2. What are the next two prime numbers after **1** 30   **2** 40?

3. Express these numbers in prime factors.

    1 36   **2** 99   **3** 52   **4** 60   **5** 121

    6 24   **7** 70   **8** 66   **9** 40   **10** 100

4. Which of these numbers are divisible by **1** 2   **2** 5   **3** 3?
    132,   135,   156,   225,   400.

5. Find a number which is a factor of both these numbers. If you can find more
    than one, give the highest one.

    1 88, 99   **5** 28, 16   **8** 48, 40

    2 18, 45   **6** 24, 8   **9** 14, 20

    3 45, 35   **7** 27, 6   **10** 77, 49

    4 18, 21

6. Find a number which is less than 30 and is a multiple of both these numbers. If
    you can find more than one, give the lowest one.

    1 3, 5   **5** 10, 20   **8** 2, 3

    2 8, 12   **6** 11, 22   **9** 2, 10

    3 4, 5   **7** 6, 9   **10** 3, 7

    4 6, 8

7. Find the values of

    1 2^3 **2** $2^3 \times 3^2$ **3** $2^2 \times 5 \times 7$ **4** $2 \times 3^2 \times 5$ **5** $2^3 \times 11$

8. Write the number 30 **1** as the product of three prime numbers   **2** as the
    sum of three prime numbers.

9. Find the value of

    1 $4 \times 7 + 5$ **8** $7^2 - 4^2$

    2 $4 \times (7 + 5)$ **5** $\dfrac{5 + 4}{7 - 4}$ **9** $(7 - 4)^2$

    3 $4 + 7 \times 5$ **6** $4^2 + 7^2$ **10** $(7 + 4) \times (7 - 4)$

    4 $(4 + 7) \times 5$ **7** $(4 + 7)^2$

10. **1** Find the squares of 11, 6, 2, 10, 1.
     2 Find the square roots of 64,   144, 49, 9, 25.
     3 Find two consecutive numbers whose squares differ by 11.
     4 Find two consecutive numbers whose squares add up to 181.
     5 Find three consecutive numbers whose squares add up to 50.

11. Use your calculator to find the square roots of

1 225	**3** 1089	**5** 5625	**7** 441	**9** 4225
2 1764	**4** 256	**6** 196	**8** 1936	**10** 10201

12. **1** Write these numbers correct to the nearest ten.
    46, 7693, 34, 1529, 96

    2 Write these numbers correct to the nearest hundred.
    687, 9716, 323, 3751, 1970

    3 Write these numbers correct to the nearest thousand.
    6501, 3127, 85 800, 12 499, 254 293

13. From the numbers 8, 12, 16, 19, 20

    1 Which number is a prime number?
    2 Which number is a square number?
    3 Which number is a multiple of 5?
    4 Which number is a factor of 84?
    5 Which two numbers have a sum which is a square number?
    6 Which two numbers have a sum which is a cube number?

14. From the numbers 18, 19, 20, 23, 25, 27 write down

    1 the prime numbers
    2 a square number
    3 the numbers which are multiples of 3
    4 a cube number
    5 two numbers whose sum is 44.

15. From the numbers 8, 37, 50, 73, 81, 91, 360

    1 Which number is a square number?
    2 Which number is a cube number?
    3 Which two numbers are prime numbers?
    4 Which number is a multiple of 7?
    5 Which number is a factor of 72?
    6 Which number can be written in index form as $2^3 \times 3^2 \times 5$?
    7 Which number is equal to the sum of two other numbers in the list?
    8 Which number when divided by 9 leaves a remainder of 5?

16. What number is this?

    It is less than 100, it is a prime number, it is one less than a multiple of 7 and its digits add up to 5.

17. What number is this?

    It is less than 100, it is two more than a square number and it is a multiple of 11. When divided by 9 there is a remainder of 3.

18.   What number is this?

It is a factor of 180, it is 4 less than a square number, and when it is divided by 7 there is a remainder of 3.

Exercise 1.3

1. Write down a 3-figure number whose digits are all different and do not include 0. Reverse it, i.e. write it down backwards. Take the smaller number of the two from the larger. Reverse this answer and add this number to the answer. What is your total?

2. What is this number?
   It is less than 100. It is divisible by 11. It is 1 less than a perfect square.

3.

   1 In a knock-out competition there are 32 teams. How many matches must be played altogether to decide the winning team?

   2 In a football competition there are 6 teams. Each team plays each other team twice, once at home and once away. How many matches are played altogether?

4. Extend this number pattern to 65^2.

   $$5^2 = \ 0 \times 10 + 25 = \ \ 25$$
   $$15^2 = 10 \times 20 + 25 = 225$$
   $$25^2 = 20 \times 30 + 25 = 625$$

   Use the pattern to find the value of 85^2.

5. Copy and complete this table.
   (It would be useful to memorise these results.)

   Is there any pattern in the unit figures 1 in the squares column, 2 in the cubes column?

number	square	cube
1	1	1
2	4	8
3	9	
.		
.		
.		
10		

6. Are the answers to the following questions even or odd numbers?
   1 odd number + odd number
   2 odd number × even number
   3 even number − smaller even number
   4 even number × (even number + even number)
   5 odd number × (odd number + even number)

7. Use your calculator to find the answers to these questions.
   1 Which is larger, $\sqrt{225} + \sqrt{64}$ or $\sqrt{225 + 64}$, and by how much?
   2 Find the values of $\sqrt{25 \times 144}$, $\sqrt{25 + 144}$, $\sqrt{25} + \sqrt{144}$
   3 Which of these numbers are perfect squares? 196, 456, 676.

8. At a school election, 320 children voted for Alan, Bob or David. Alan got 60 more votes than Bob, and David got twice as many votes as Bob. Who won the election?

9. Instead of writing down the question $(5 \times 3) + (4 \times 2)$, Andrea wrote down $(5 + 3) \times (4 + 2)$.
   1 What was the answer to the correct question?
   2 What answer would Andrea get if she worked her question out correctly?

10. These numbers follow a pattern. Write down the next two numbers in the sequence.

    1 1, 9, 25, 49,   6 1, 8, 27, 64, 125,
    2 1, 3, 6, 10, 15,   7 80, 70, 61, 53, 46,
    3 2, 4, 8, 16,   8 $\frac{1}{2}, \frac{2}{3}, \frac{3}{4}, \frac{4}{5}$,
    4 100, 93, 86, 79, 72,   9 2, 5, 8, 11,
    5 1, $\frac{1}{2}, \frac{1}{3}, \frac{1}{4}, \frac{1}{5}$,   10 0, 3, 8, 15, 24,

11. A box holds 24 tins. How many boxes must be used to pack 360 tins?

12.

    The attendances at four cricket matches were 3242, 5671, 10470 and 2835.

    Give these attendances

    1 to the nearest hundred,
    2 to the nearest thousand.

13.   What are the missing figures if **1**   62*3 divides exactly by 9,
      2   51*7 divides exactly by 11,   **3**   19*2 divides exactly by 7?

14.   Ashton, Barton, Corton, Dayton and Elton
      are five villages. The distances between each
      are shown on the mileage chart, (for example,
      from Barton to Dayton is 15 miles).
      A cyclist travels from Elton directly to Ashton.
      On his return journey he takes the route via
      Corton. How much further does he travel on
      the return journey?

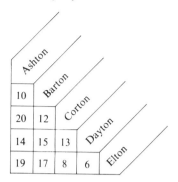

PUZZLES

1.   A man has a wad of £5 notes numbered consecutively from 232426 to 232440. What is
     their total value?

2.   What is the next letter in this sequence?
     N   N   N   E   N   E   E   N   E   E   –   –   –

3.   What is the next prime number after 113?

4.   How many squares can be formed by joining 4 of these points.

5.   Five children were playing a game of cards.
     A set of cards numbered 1 to 10 are dealt so that they get two each. Paul has two cards
     which total 11, Mike has two cards which total 7, Laura has two cards which total 17, Kate
     has two cards which total 4 and Jane has two cards which total 16.
     In this game the winner is the person who has the card numbered 10. Who wins the game?

6.   If $1 m^3$ of earth weighs 1600 kg, how much would there be in a hole 50 cm by 50 cm
     by 50 cm?

7.   Lorraine said 'Two days ago I was 13, next year I shall be 16'. What is the date today and
     when is her birthday?

2 Money and measures

Money

100 pence = £1
65 p can be written as £0.65
£2 and 65 p should be written as £2.65
£2 and 4 p should be written as £2.04
£2 and 40 p should be written as £2.40

Time

60 seconds = 1 minute	52 weeks = 1 year
60 minutes = 1 hour	365 days = 1 year
24 hours = 1 day	366 days = 1 leap year
7 days = 1 week	12 months = 1 year

Recording the time of day can either be by the 12-hour clock, when morning times are denoted by a.m. and afternoon times by p.m., or by the 24-hour clock. To avoid confusion, timetables are often printed with times using the 24-hour clock.

Examples:

	12-hour clock	*24-hour clock*
1 o'clock early morning	1.00 a.m.	1.00 or 01.00
5 past 1 early morning	1.05 a.m.	1.05 or 01.05
Noon	12.00 p.m.	12.00
Quarter-to-1 early afternoon	12.45 p.m.	12.45
1 o'clock early afternoon	1.00 p.m.	13.00
Half-past 8 in the evening	8.30 p.m.	20.30
One minute to midnight	11.59 p.m.	23.59
Midnight	12.00 a.m.	0.00 or 00.00
One minute past midnight	12.01 a.m.	0.01 or 00.01

(The day changes at the instant of midnight so when the time is shown as 12.00 a.m. or 0.00 the date has changed.)

On a timetable the 24-hour times could be printed as 4-figure numbers. The full stop separating the hours and minutes could be left out.
e.g. 1.23 a.m. would be printed as 0123,
     1.23 p.m. would be printed as 1323.

1323 would be pronounced as thirteen twenty-three or thirteen twenty-three hours. But 1300 would be pronounced as thirteen hundred hours.

Units of measurement

The units of measurement in the Metric System are
metre for length, with associated units kilometre, centimetre, millimetre,
gram for weight (or mass), with associated units tonne and kilogram,
litre for capacity, with associated unit centilitre.
These are explained in more detail in Chapter 8.

As Britain is slow to adapt completely to the metric system, you will find the following units in use in some situations.

Length   inch,   foot,   yard,   mile.
There are 12 inches in 1 foot, 3 feet in 1 yard and 1760 yards in 1 mile. (The symbol " is used for inches and ' is used for feet so 3'6" means 3 feet 6 inches.)

Weight   ounce,   pound,   stone.
There are 16 ounces in 1 pound and 14 pounds in 1 stone.
The abbreviation for ounce is oz and for pound is lb.

Capacity   pint,   gallon.
There are 8 pints in 1 gallon.

Temperature

In the Celsius scale (formerly the Centigrade scale) written °C, water freezes at 0°C and boils at 100°C.
In the Fahrenheit scale, written °F, salt water freezes at 0°F, water freezes at 32°F and boils at 212°F.

Use of calculator

If the numbers are large, and you have a calculator available, it is sensible to use it to save time.
Be careful that you do not use your calculator for mixed units not based on ten, such as hours and minutes. For example, to add 14 hours 37 minutes and 15 hours 56 minutes it is no use entering 14.37 + 15.56. You will have to add the minutes first. 37 + 56 = 93. 93 minutes is 1 hour 33 minutes so carry forward 1 hour. 1 + 14 + 15 = 30. The answer is 30 hours 33 minutes.

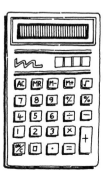

Exercise 2.1

1. 1 How many 5p coins are worth £5?
    2 What is the change from £1 after buying 3 small loaves at 28p each?
    3 If 4 apples cost as much as 5 pears and a pear costs 8 p, how much does an apple cost?
    4 Find the cost of 200 articles at 15p each?
    5 What is the cost of 4 articles at 99p each?

2. Mr Seed bought toys at 5 for 45p and sold them at 4 for 50p. How much profit did he make on each one?

3. What is the total cost of 24 notebooks at 28p each and 24 pens at 22p each?

4. Mr Clark spends £5 on petrol for his car and this takes him 125 miles. What is the cost per mile?

5. Equal numbers of 13p and 15p stamps were bought for £5.60. How many of each kind were there?

6. A bankrupt can only pay his creditors 30 pence in the £. (This means that for each £1 he owes he can only pay 30 p.) How much does a creditor to whom he owes £180 receive?

7. Mrs Davies makes 200 soft toys. The material for each toy costs 48p. Other expenses amount to £5. She sells the toys for £1.25 each. What profit does she make?

8. Find the total cost of 3 bottles of milk at 21p per bottle, 2 packets of tea at 29p per packet, and $\frac{1}{2}$ dozen eggs at 78p per dozen.

9. From a mail-order catalogue Rachel orders 2 items at £6.99 each and 3 items at £11.99 each. What is the total cost?

10. How many articles costing 75 pence each can be bought for £30?

11. Tessa works in a local shop from 1.30 p.m. to 5 p.m. on four afternoons each week. She is paid £2.70 per hour. How much is her weekly wage?

12. Richard has several 2 p and 5 p coins but no more change. On the bus he must pay the exact fare. What coins must he use for a journey costing
    1 13 p, 2 19 p?

13. John is 6 feet 6 inches tall and his son Keith is 5 feet 8 inches tall. How many inches is John taller than Keith?

14. Mary weighed 10 stones 8 lbs on New Year's Day and she decided to lose some weight. Now she weighs 9 stones 10 lbs. How many pounds has she lost?

15. A farmer has 108 gallons of milk to sell. How many pint bottles can he fill with this milk?

16. Fence posts are 3 yards apart. If there are 3 strands of barbed wire nailed to each post, how much wire is needed to stretch between the first and the twentieth posts?

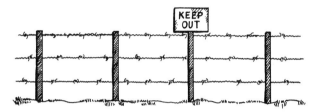

17. Paul runs a race of 1500 metres. (1500 m = 1640 yards.) How many yards short of a mile is this?

18. Alan started school on his 5th birthday in 1984. In which year will he have his 16th birthday?

19. Change these times to the 24-hour clock.

    4.05 a.m.   2.00 p.m.   3.15 p.m.   6.05 p.m.   11.55 p.m.

    Change these times to the 12-hour clock.

    01.10   5.18   10.30   17.05   21.50

20. A train left a station at 9.30 a.m. and arrived at its destination at 2.13 p.m. How long did the journey take?

21. Mike set off on a training ride at 11.50 a.m. and cycled for $4\frac{1}{4}$ hours. At what time did he stop?

22. On a timetable, a plane was due to leave an airport at 20.55 and arrive at its destination at 02.05 the next day. How long should the journey take? It actually arrived 45 minutes early. At what time did it arrive?

23. A school's lessons begin at 9.20 a.m. and end at 3.20 p.m. with an hour's break at lunchtime and 20 minutes break mid-morning. If there are 7 lessons of equal length, how long is a lesson?

24. This flow chart will convert °F into °C.

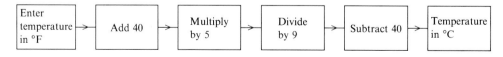

Use this flow chart to change 41°F into °C.
By using the flow chart in reverse, change 40°C into °F.

25.   28 bars of chocolate cost £3.64. What would be the cost of 7 similar bars?

26.   If 20 boxes weigh 36 lb, what is the weight of 40 similar boxes?

27.   If a car travels for 100 miles on fuel costing £4.80, what would the fuel cost be, at the same rate, for a journey of 300 miles?

28.   If a store of emergency food would last 20 men for 36 days, how long would the same food last if there were 40 men?

29.   10 men can build a wall in 9 days. How long would 5 men take, working at the same rate?

30.   A carpet to cover a floor of area 12 square yards costs £150. How much would it cost for a similar carpet to cover a floor of area 24 square yards?

Exercise 2.2

1.   Find the missing item in this bill.

                    £11.29
                    £ 6.09
                    . . . .
                    £20.72

2.   Two packs of bacon weighed 3 lb 2 oz between them. One was 6 oz heavier than the other. What was the weight of the heavier one, in lbs and oz?

3.   If 4 pints of fuel are needed to keep a heater burning for 14 hours, how many gallons are needed to keep it burning continuously, day and night, for a week?

4.   Find the total cost of $1\frac{1}{2}$ lbs of bacon at £1.20 per lb, $\frac{1}{2}$ lb of cheese at £1.40 per lb and 2 loaves at 51 p each. How much change would there be from a £20 note?

5.   This is an evening's programmes on a local TV station.

6.25	Weather
6.30	News
6.50	Entertainment 88
7.20	Sports Today
9.30	The Golden Age (play)
11.05	Local lives
11.45	Closedown

   1 How long was the programme 'The Golden Age'?
   2 If someone switched on at the end of the News and watched TV until closedown, for how long had they been viewing?

6.   This is the **Fares Table** on the local bus. (Fares for Adults)

Town centre	Fares in pence			
25	Pollard Street			
35	30	Victoria Road		
40	37	25	Addison Road	
55	50	40	35	Long Lane

1 What is the total cost for Mr and Mrs Gray to travel from Addison Road to Pollard Street?
2 Make a similar table for the children's fares. Children pay half-price (with $\frac{1}{2}$ penny counted as 1 penny, e.g. half-price for a 25 p fare is 13 p).
3 What is the total cost for 3 children to travel from the Town centre to Long Lane?

7.   Tomatoes at the greengrocer's last week cost 56 p per lb and lettuces were 30 p each. The prices of both these items had risen by 5 p when I went to buy them this week. But cucumbers had remained at 70 p and cabbages had fallen in price by 2 p to 28 p. Find the cost of last week's bill when I bought 2 lb of tomatoes, 2 lettuces, 1 cucumber and 1 cabbage. Find the cost of this week's bill when I bought 1 lb of tomatoes, 1 lettuce, 1 cucumber and 2 cabbages.

8.   If £2.80 is made up of equal numbers of 5p, 10p and 20p coins, how many coins are there?

9.   A car journey takes 42 minutes when the average speed is 56 miles/hour. How long would it take if the average speed was 28 miles/hour?

10. The weekly wages paid by a firm to 5 workmen total £525. What will the weekly wages be if they employ two extra men, and pay them all at the same rate?

11. Here is part of a bus timetable:

Ashmead School	1554	1602	1608	1616	1622	1629
Brook Lane	1604	1612	1618	1626	1632	1639
Carlton Village	1619	1627	––	1641	––	1654
Denham Station	––	––	1640	––	1654	––

   1 Helen finishes school at 4.00 p.m. but it takes her at least 3 minutes to reach
   the bus stop. What is the time of the next bus she can catch to get to her home
   in Carlton Village? How long does the journey take?

   2 Ismail usually catches a train from Denham station at 4.45 p.m. On which
   bus must he travel from school? One day he stays late at school and catches
   the 1622 bus. The next train leaves at 5.30 p.m. How long will Ismail have to
   wait at the station, for that train?

12. This table gives the repayments due when goods are bought from a certain firm
   by hire-purchase. (Amounts are in £.)

Cash price	Hire purchase price		
	Repay over 1 year 12 monthly instalments	Repay over 2 years 24 monthly instalments	Repay over $2\frac{1}{2}$ years 30 monthly instalments
10	0.94	0.53	0.44
20	1.88	1.06	0.88
30	2.82	1.59	1.32
40	3.76	2.12	1.76
50	4.70	2.65	2.20
60	5.64	3.18	2.64
70	6.58	3.71	3.08
80	7.52	4.24	3.52
90	8.46	4.77	3.95
100	9.40	5.30	4.40
200	18.80	10.60	8.80

Mr Jones wants to buy a lawn mower with
cash price £60, and decides to pay on hire
purchase over 1 year. What is the monthly
instalment?

How much will the mower cost him
altogether?

Instead of this he then decides to take longer
to repay so that he will be able to get a better
mower. He finally settles for repayments of
£3.95 per month for 30 months. What is the
cash price of the mower he chooses, and
what will it cost him altogether?

13. Two books together cost £6.50, one being £1.20 more than the other. What did the cheaper one cost?

14. A wheel makes 2500 revolutions per minute. How long will it take to make 50 000 revolutions?

15. An insurance company quotes these rates for travel insurance. (Prices per person.)

	United Kingdom only	Europe	Worldwide
up to 8 days	£3.65	£11.10	£28.60
up to 12 days	£4.00	£11.90	£29.95
up to 17 days	£4.95	£13.25	£31.55
up to 24 days	£5.75	£14.40	£37.10

Winter sports in Europe insured at $2\frac{1}{2}$ times the Europe premium. Double premium for persons aged over 65, Worldwide.

Find the cost of insurance for these people.

1 Next week Mr Stewart is going on a business trip to Scotland for 5 days.
2 For their honeymoon next January Alan and Jayne are going skiing in Switzerland, for 10 days.
3 Mrs Charnley is going to stay with her married daughter in America for 3 weeks. She is looking forward to the trip although at age 70 it will be the first time she has travelled by air.

PUZZLES

8. Copy this long division sum and fill in the missing figures.

```
          2 *
* 3 ) 1 2 4 *
        * 6
      3 * *
      3 * *
```

9. Down the corridor next to the school hall there are five classrooms, numbered from 1 to 5, and these are occupied by the five 1st forms, 1A, 1B, 1C, 1D and 1E.
1A is not in room 1, 1B is not in room 5, 1C is not in room 1 or room 5, 1D is in a room with a lower number than 1B. 1C's room is not next to 1B's room. 1E's room is not next to 1C's room. Which class is in room 1?

10. A group of people on a coach outing went into a cafe for a snack. The party leader ordered a cup of tea and a sandwich for everyone, and the total bill came to £18.49. How many people were on the coach?

3 *Symmetry and angles*

Symmetry

The diagrams show

1   axes of symmetry, marked by dotted lines,

2   points of symmetry, marked ⊙

Rotational symmetry

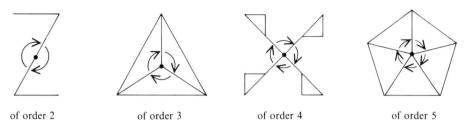

of order 2   of order 3   of order 4   of order 5

Reflection

The dotted lines show the reflections of the triangles in the line *AB*, which is an axis of symmetry of the completed figure.

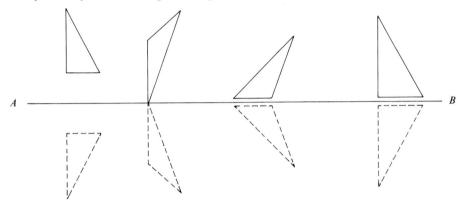

Rotation

The dotted lines show the new positions of the triangles when they have been rotated about the point marked (•) through a half-turn.

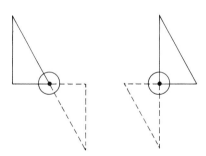

These triangles have been rotated about the point marked (•) through a quarter-turn anticlockwise.

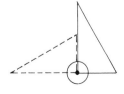
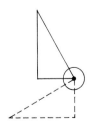

Exercise 3.1

1. Copy these figures onto tracing paper and fold them so that one half fits on top of the other half.
    The fold line is the axis of symmetry.

          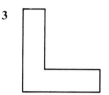

2. Do these figures look the same upside-down? If so, they have a point of symmetry in the centre. Copy the figures and mark the point of symmetry. (These figures also have rotational symmetry of order 2.)

    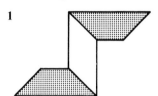   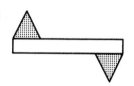   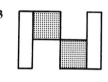

3. From these capital letters

    A B C F H I M N S T U X Y Z

    1 Which have one axis of symmetry which is a vertical line?
    2 Which have one axis of symmety which is a horizontal line?
    3 Which have two axes of symmetry?
    4 Which have a point of symmetry but no axes of symmetry?
    5 Which have a point of symmetry as well as axes of symmetry?

4. Sketch and complete these drawings so that • is a point of symmetry, i.e. they have rotational symmetry of order 2, about the point marked •

    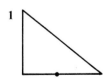   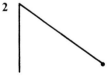   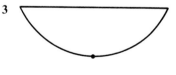

5. Sketch these figures and mark in the axis of symmetry.

6. Sketch these figures and complete them, so that the dotted line is an axis of symmetry.

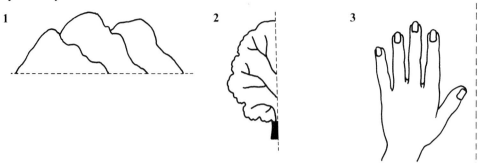

7. Copy these figures and complete them so that they have rotational symmetry of order 3 about the point marked •

8. Copy the figures onto dotted or squared paper and complete them so that they have rotational symmetry of order 4 about the point marked ●

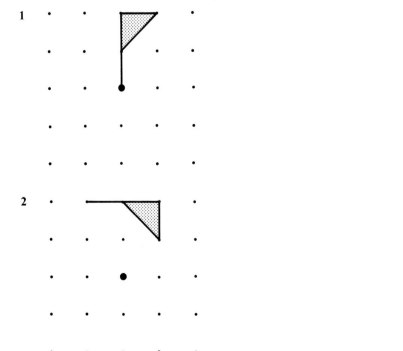

9. This square tile has two axes of symmetry shown by the dotted lines. Copy the figure and complete the rest of the pattern.

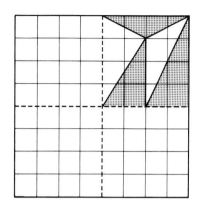

10. The diagram shows a shape and a mirror line. Copy the diagram on squared paper and draw the reflection of the shape.

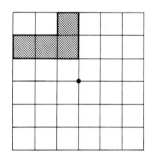

11. The diagram shows a shape and a point ● Copy the diagram on squared paper and draw the shape after it has been rotated a half-turn about the point ●

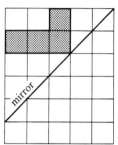

Angles

This is angle ABC (or $\angle ABC$) or angle CBA. If there is no possibility of confusion it can be called $\angle B$.

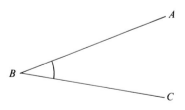

Angles can also be identified by small letters. This angle is b.

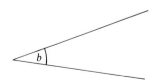

Measurement of angles

A protractor is used to measure angles in degrees.

1 complete turn or revolution is divided into 360°.

1 half-turn is 180°.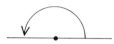

1 quarter-turn is 90°. This is also called a right angle.

The sign for a right angle is

Perpendicular lines are lines which meet each other at right angles.

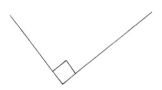  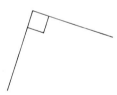

Types of angles

acute angle
less than 90°

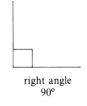

right angle
90°

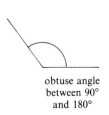

obtuse angle
between 90°
and 180°

Angles at a point	**Adjacent angles** (on a straight line)	**Vertically** **opposite angles**
These add up to 360°	These add up to 180°	These are equal

$$a + b + c + d + e = 360°$$

$$a + b = 180°$$

$$a = c$$
$$b = d$$

Example Calculate the sizes of angles a, b, c, d.

$a + 132° + 155° = 360°$ (they are angles at a point)
$a = 73°$

$b + 130° = 180°$ (they are angles on a straight line)
$b = 50°$
$c = 50°$ (opposite to b)
$d = 130°$ (opposite to 130°)

Exercise 3.2

1. State whether these angles are acute or obtuse angles.

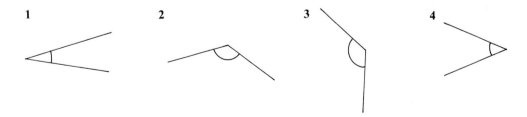

2. Using your protractor, draw angles of **1** 20° **2** 45° **3** 90° **4** 120°.

3. Copy these figures with the angles drawn accurately.

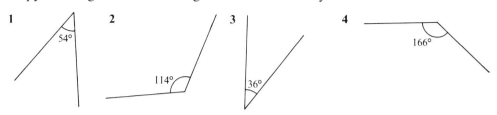

4. Estimate the sizes of these angles, in degrees. Check your estimate by measuring with your protractor.

5. Estimate the sizes of the marked angles, in degrees. Check your estimate by measuring with your protractor. Verify that the angles at a point add up to 360°, adjacent angles on a straight line add up to 180°, and vertically opposite angles are equal.

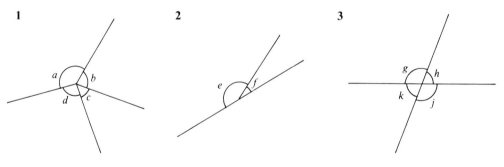

6. Calculate the sizes of angles *a*, *b*, *c*, *d*, *e*.

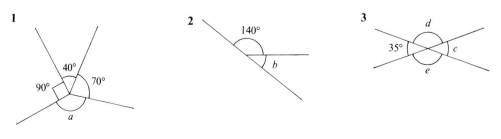

7. Calculate the sizes of angles *a*, *b*, *c*, *d*, *e*.

1

2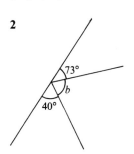

3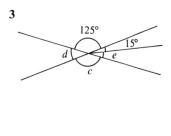

Exercise 3.3

1. From the letters S H A P E, which has
    1 only one axis of symmetry, which is horizontal,
    2 2 axes of symmetry,
    3 a point of symmetry but no axes of symmetry?

2. Sketch these quadrilaterals and mark in any axes and points of symmetry.

1 **2** **3** **4**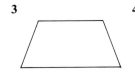

3. Sketch these figures and mark in any axes and points of symmetry.

1 **2** **3** **4**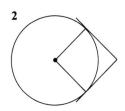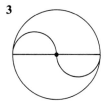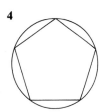

4. Sketch these flags and reflect them in the dotted lines.

1 **2** **3**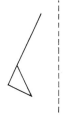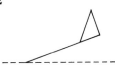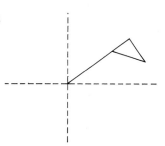

5. Sketch these flags and rotate them about the points marked •

1 through 90°
anticlockwise

2 through 180°

3 through 90°
clockwise

6. Sketch and complete these drawings so that they have rotational symmetry of
   order 4, about the point marked •

1

2

3

7. What is the order of rotational symmetry of these figures?

1

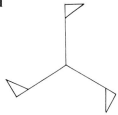

2

3 The outline of a
20 pence coin

8. For each of these diagrams, state how many axes of symmetry there are.

1

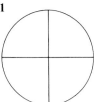

2

3

4

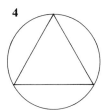

9. Estimate the sizes of the marked angles, in degrees. Check your estimate by measuring with your protractor.

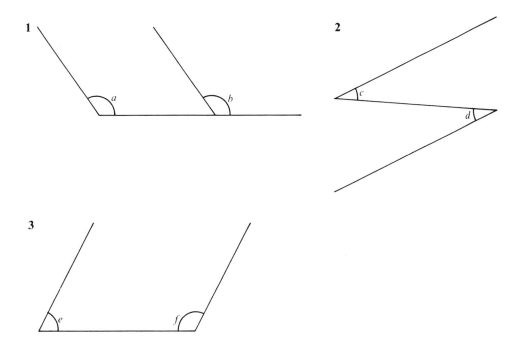

10. In the diagrams measure angle *a* with your protractor and use your answer to calculate the size of angle *b*.

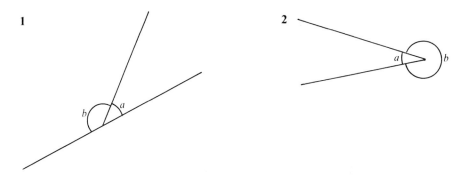

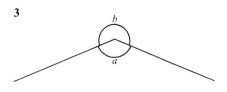

11. Calculate the sizes of angles *a*, *b*, *c*, *d*, *e*.

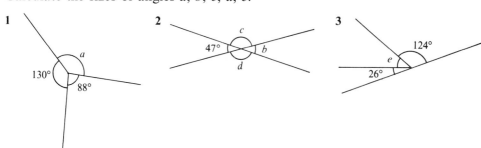

12. In the diagrams the dotted line is an axis of symmetry. Calculate the marked angles.

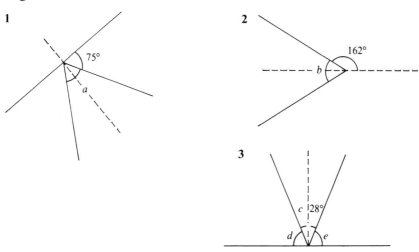

13. **1** If all the angles in the diagram are equal, find the size of angle *a*.
    2 If *a* = 60° and the other angles are all equal, find their size.

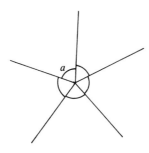

4 Fractions

Fractions are numbers such as $\frac{1}{4}, \frac{1}{3}, \frac{2}{5}, \frac{5}{9}$.

The number on top is called the **numerator** and the number underneath is called the **denominator**.

The shaded part represents $\frac{1}{4}$ (one-quarter) of the circle. (The whole circle is divided into 4 equal parts and 1 part is shaded.)
The unshaded part represents $\frac{3}{4}$ (three-quarters) of the circle.

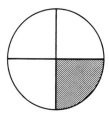

The shaded part represents $\frac{2}{5}$ (two-fifths) of the rectangle.
(The whole rectangle is divided into 5 equal parts and 2 parts are shaded.)
The unshaded part represents $\frac{3}{5}$ of the rectangle.

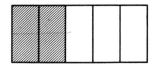

This diagram shows that $\frac{2}{5}$ is equivalent to $\frac{4}{10}$.

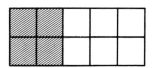

This diagram shows that $\frac{2}{5} + \frac{1}{10} = \frac{4}{10} + \frac{1}{10} = \frac{5}{10} = \frac{1}{2}$.

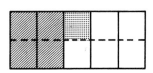

Improper fractions are numbers with a greater numerator than denominator, such as $\frac{6}{5}$ and $\frac{5}{2}$.

Mixed numbers are numbers with a whole number part and a fraction part, such as $1\frac{1}{5}$ and $2\frac{1}{2}$.

This diagram shows that $\frac{6}{5} = 1\frac{1}{5}$.

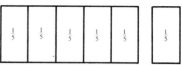

This diagram shows that $\frac{5}{2} = 2\frac{1}{2}$.

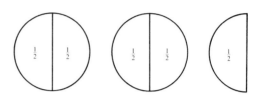

Examples

1   Reduce $\frac{60}{75}$ to its lowest terms.

60 and 75 both divide by 5 so reduce the fraction by dividing the numerator and the denominator both by 5. This process can be called **cancelling**.

$\dfrac{\overset{12}{\cancel{60}}}{\underset{15}{\cancel{75}}}$ This gives the fraction $\frac{12}{15}$ but this is still not in its lowest terms because

12 and 15 both divide by 3.
So divide the numerator and the denominator both by 3.

$\dfrac{\overset{4}{\cancel{\overset{12}{\cancel{60}}}}}{\underset{5}{\cancel{\underset{15}{\cancel{75}}}}} = \dfrac{4}{5}$ This is the fraction in its lowest terms.

2   Change $\frac{5}{6}$ into a fraction with denominator 24.
6 becomes 24 when multiplied by 4, so multiply the numerator and the denominator by 4.

$$\frac{5}{6} = \frac{5 \times 4}{6 \times 4} = \frac{20}{24}$$

3   Change $3\frac{7}{8}$ into an improper fraction.

(Multiply the whole number 3 by 8 to change it into eighths. This is 24 eighths and another 7 eighths makes 31 eighths.)
$3\frac{7}{8} = \frac{24}{8} + \frac{7}{8} = \frac{31}{8}$

4   Change $\frac{45}{7}$ to a mixed number.

(Divide 7 into 45. It goes 6 times so there are 6 whole ones. $6 \times 7 = 42$ and the remainder is 3 so there is also $\frac{3}{7}$.)

$$\frac{45}{7} = \frac{42 + 3}{7} = 6\frac{3}{7}$$

5   Addition

$\frac{5}{6} + \frac{3}{4}$

(Change $\frac{5}{6}$ and $\frac{3}{4}$ into fractions with denominator 12 because 12 is the smallest number into which the denominators 6 and 4 both divide.

$\frac{5}{6} = \frac{10}{12}$ and $\frac{3}{4} = \frac{9}{12}$)

$\frac{5}{6} + \frac{3}{4} = \frac{10}{12} + \frac{9}{12} = \frac{19}{12} = 1\frac{7}{12}$

(The stage $\frac{10}{12} + \frac{9}{12}$ can be written as $\frac{10 + 9}{12}$)

6   Subtraction

$\frac{5}{6} - \frac{7}{12} = \frac{10 - 7}{12} = \frac{3}{12} = \frac{1}{4}$

$1 - \frac{4}{9} = \frac{9 - 4}{9} = \frac{5}{9}$

7   In addition and subtraction questions with **mixed numbers** do the whole number part and the fraction part separately.

$3\frac{5}{6} + 2\frac{3}{4} = 5\frac{10 + 9}{12} = 5\frac{19}{12} = 5 + 1 + \frac{7}{12} = 6\frac{7}{12}$

$3\frac{5}{6} - 1\frac{7}{12} = 2\frac{10 - 7}{12} = 2\frac{3}{12} = 2\frac{1}{4}$

$3\frac{5}{8} - 1\frac{3}{4} = 2\frac{5 - 6}{8} = 1\frac{8 + 5 - 6}{8} = 1\frac{7}{8}$ (Since we cannot take 6 from 5, one of the whole numbers was changed into 8 eighths)

8   Multiplication of a fraction by a whole number

$\frac{5}{6} \times 4 = \frac{20}{6} = \frac{10}{3} = 3\frac{1}{3}$ (5 sixths multiplied by 4 is 20 sixths)

(You can cancel by 2 before multiplying.

$\frac{5}{\underset{3}{\cancel{6}}} \times \overset{2}{4} = \frac{10}{3} = 3\frac{1}{3}$)

9   Multiplication of a mixed number by a whole number

1st Method Turn the mixed number into an improper fraction.

$$2\tfrac{2}{3} \times 5 = \frac{8}{3} \times 5 = \frac{40}{3} = 13\tfrac{1}{3}$$

$$5\tfrac{3}{4} \times 8 = \frac{23}{\overset{}{\underset{1}{4}}} \times \overset{2}{8} = \frac{46}{1} = 46$$

2nd Method Multiply the fractions first, carry forward any whole numbers. Multiply the whole numbers and add on the numbers carried forward.

$2\tfrac{2}{3} \times 5.$ $\tfrac{2}{3} \times 5 = \tfrac{10}{3} = 3\tfrac{1}{3}$. Write down $\tfrac{1}{3}$ and carry forward 3.

   $2 \times 5 = 10$, and adding the 3 carried forward makes 13.
   The answer is $13\tfrac{1}{3}$.

$5\tfrac{3}{4} \times 8.$ $\dfrac{3}{\underset{1}{4}} \times \overset{2}{8} = \dfrac{6}{1} = 6$. Carry 6 forward.

   $5 \times 8 = 40$, and adding the 6 carried forward makes 46.
   The answer is 46.

Note. To multiply two mixed numbers, turn them both into improper fractions.

e.g. $1\tfrac{3}{4} \times 2\tfrac{2}{5} = \dfrac{7}{\underset{1}{4}} \times \dfrac{\overset{3}{12}}{5} = \dfrac{21}{5} = 4\tfrac{1}{5}$

10   Express 24 pence as a fraction of £3.

$$\frac{24\,\text{p}}{£3} = \frac{24\,\text{p}}{300\,\text{p}} = \frac{\overset{2}{24}}{\underset{25}{300}} = \frac{2}{25}$$

11   Find $\tfrac{2}{3}$ of £2.40

$\tfrac{1}{3}$ of £2.40 = 80 pence

So $\tfrac{2}{3}$ of £2.40 = £1.60

12   Which is greater, $\tfrac{5}{6}$ or $\tfrac{7}{8}$?

$\dfrac{5}{6} = \dfrac{20}{24}$, $\dfrac{7}{8} = \dfrac{21}{24}$,   so $\dfrac{7}{8}$ is greater.

Exercise 4.1

1. What fraction of the shape is shaded?

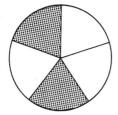

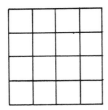   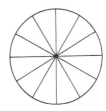

Copy these figures and shade the fraction stated.

6 $\frac{3}{8}$ 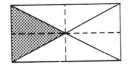   7 $\frac{5}{12}$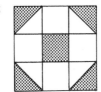

8 $\frac{1}{2}$ 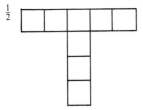   9 $\frac{2}{3}$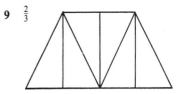

10 $\frac{1}{4}$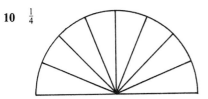

2. **1** Find one-half of each of these numbers
       88   18   8   14   60   24   42   52   90   96

   2 Find one-third of each of these numbers
       18   99   60   24   45   27   3   21   39   75

   3 Find one-quarter of each of these numbers
       8   28   80   100   52   44   4   24   160   36

   4 Find one-fifth of each of these numbers
       60   20   45   10   100   15   35   75   55   200

   5 Find two-thirds of each of these numbers
       6   15   24   9   30   60   33   90   75   18

3. Reduce these fractions to their lowest terms.

   1 $\dfrac{6}{9}$ **2** $\dfrac{10}{12}$ **3** $\dfrac{5}{30}$ **4** $\dfrac{30}{100}$ **5** $\dfrac{24}{80}$

   6 $\dfrac{18}{45}$ **7** $\dfrac{35}{56}$ **8** $\dfrac{21}{36}$ **9** $\dfrac{24}{54}$ **10** $\dfrac{15}{20}$

4. **1** Change $\dfrac{7}{9}$ into a fraction with denominator 18.

   2 Change $\dfrac{3}{5}$ into a fraction with denominator 20.

   3 Change $\dfrac{5}{6}$ into a fraction with denominator 18.

   4 Change $\dfrac{7}{8}$ into a fraction with denominator 24.

   5 Change $\dfrac{3}{10}$ into a fraction with denominator 20.

5. Change these mixed numbers to improper fractions.

   1 $1\frac{3}{4}$ **5** $2\frac{7}{8}$ **8** $7\frac{1}{2}$

   2 $2\frac{1}{3}$ **6** $4\frac{2}{5}$ **9** $3\frac{1}{3}$

   3 $3\frac{7}{10}$ **7** $1\frac{1}{8}$ **10** $2\frac{3}{10}$

   4 $1\frac{5}{6}$

6. Change these improper fractions to mixed numbers.

1 $\frac{23}{5}$		**5** $\frac{11}{4}$		**8** $\frac{17}{4}$	
2 $\frac{17}{6}$		**6** $\frac{20}{3}$		**9** $\frac{25}{3}$	
3 $\frac{31}{10}$		**7** $\frac{13}{5}$		**10** $\frac{13}{4}$	
4 $\frac{21}{8}$					

7. **1** $\frac{1}{2} + \frac{1}{3}$ **5** $\frac{5}{12} + \frac{1}{3}$ **8** $2\frac{1}{2} + 2\frac{5}{6}$

2 $\frac{5}{8} + \frac{1}{6}$ **6** $4\frac{3}{8} + 3\frac{2}{3}$ **9** $2\frac{3}{4} + 1\frac{2}{3}$

3 $\frac{7}{10} + \frac{3}{5}$ **7** $5\frac{1}{3} + 1\frac{1}{6}$ **10** $4\frac{1}{2} + 1\frac{7}{10}$

4 $\frac{3}{4} + \frac{4}{5}$

8. **1** $\frac{5}{8} - \frac{1}{4}$ **5** $1 - \frac{7}{10}$ **8** $2\frac{1}{2} - \frac{7}{8}$

2 $\frac{17}{20} - \frac{3}{5}$ **6** $2 - \frac{3}{8}$ **9** $3\frac{3}{4} - 1\frac{2}{3}$

3 $\frac{2}{3} - \frac{5}{9}$ **7** $1\frac{7}{20} - \frac{4}{5}$ **10** $5\frac{1}{2} - 3\frac{5}{6}$

4 $\frac{2}{3} - \frac{1}{6}$

9. **1** $\frac{3}{8} \times 2$ **5** $2 \times \frac{9}{10}$ **8** $6 \times 1\frac{3}{4}$

2 $\frac{5}{6} \times 5$ **6** $3\frac{1}{2} \times 3$ **9** $8 \times 2\frac{1}{2}$

3 $\frac{2}{3} \times 9$ **7** $2\frac{2}{3} \times 4$ **10** $4 \times 1\frac{3}{5}$

4 $\frac{3}{4} \times 5$

10. **1** Express 8 hours as a fraction of 1 day.
   2 Express 20° as a fraction of 1 right angle.
   3 Express 6 inches as a fraction of 1 yard.
   4 Express 45 seconds as a fraction of 1 minute.
   5 Express 60 p as a fraction of £1.
   6 Express £1.60 as a fraction of £2.40.
   7 Express 10 oz as a fraction of $2\frac{1}{2}$ lb.
   8 Express 50 p as a fraction of £4.50.
   9 Express 12 minutes as a fraction of 1 hour.
   10 Express 120° as a fraction of 1 complete turn.

11. **1** Find $\frac{3}{4}$ of £3.60.   **6** Find $\frac{1}{6}$ of 1 right angle.

     2 Find $\frac{2}{3}$ of 1 foot.   **7** Find $\frac{3}{8}$ of 2 gallons.

     3 Find $\frac{3}{10}$ of £2.   **8** Find $\frac{1}{9}$ of 1 yard.

     4 Find $\frac{3}{5}$ of 1 hour 40 minutes.   **9** Find $\frac{1}{4}$ of 2 stones 8 lb.

     5 Find $\frac{5}{8}$ of 1 lb 8 oz.   **10** Find $\frac{7}{10}$ of 4 feet 2 inches.

12. Which is greater?

     1 $\frac{5}{6}$ or $\frac{7}{9}$ **2** $\frac{1}{3}$ or $\frac{3}{10}$ **3** $\frac{2}{3}$ or $\frac{3}{5}$ **4** $\frac{3}{4}$ or $\frac{5}{6}$ **5** $\frac{7}{10}$ or $\frac{3}{4}$

13. ├────────────────────┼──────────┤
     A   B   C

     Pauline's ruler measures in inches and twelfths. From A to B is $3\frac{5}{12}$ inches and from B to C is $2\frac{1}{12}$ inches. What is the distance from A to C?

14. Michael had a box of chocolates. He put aside $\frac{1}{4}$ of them for his sister and $\frac{1}{3}$ of them for his brother. What fraction had he left?

15. Mr Brown decided to dig his garden. On the first fine day he dug $\frac{1}{2}$ of it. On the next day he dug $\frac{1}{6}$ of it, then he stopped because it was raining. What fraction remained to be dug?

16. Mrs Jenkins has a roll of ribbon which is 10 feet long. She cuts 5 pieces off it, each of length $1\frac{1}{4}$ feet. What length remains on the roll?

17. In a club, two-fifths of the members are Junior members. The remaining 90 members are Senior members. How many members are there altogether?

18. There are 144 eggs in a crate. One-eighth of them are cracked. How many are whole?

19. There were two candidates, Mr A and Mr B, in an election. Mr A got $\frac{7}{12}$ of the votes.

    What fraction did Mr B get? Who won the election?
    If 2400 people altogether voted, how many extra votes did the winner get more than the loser?

20. A farmer had 240 animals on his farm. $\frac{5}{8}$ of them were sheep, $\frac{1}{10}$ of them were pigs, he had 2 horses, 4 dogs and the rest were cows. How many cows had he? What fraction of the total were cows?

21. I think of a number. Two-thirds of this number is 18. What is the number?

22. Maureen was trying to save £7. For 6 weeks she saved 70 p a week. What fraction of the £7 had she still to save?

23. A tank containing liquid is two-thirds full. When 60 more gallons of liquid are put in the tank is full. How many gallons does the tank hold altogether?

Exercise 4.2

1. How many half-pint glasses of fruit juice can be filled from a container which holds 2 gallons?

2. 1 Through what fraction of a revolution does the hour hand of a clock turn in 1 hour? How many degrees is this?

   2 Through how many degrees does the hour hand of a clock turn between 1 p.m. and 4.30 p.m.?

   3 What is the size of the obtuse angle between the hands of a clock at half-past two?

3. Mrs Carr won £750 in a competition. She gave $\frac{1}{3}$ of it to her husband and $\frac{2}{5}$ of the remainder to her daughter. She kept the remaining money for herself. How much did she keep?

4. An engine turns at 1200 revolutions per minute. Find, as a fraction of a second, how long it takes to turn through one revolution?

5. Eric spends half his pocket money on the day he gets it, and one-third on the following day. This leaves him with 50 p. How much pocket money does he get?

6. 2 pints of milk are poured into an urn containing 10 pints of coffee. What fraction of the mixture is milk?

7. A cinema is $\frac{1}{4}$ full. After another 90 people come in it is $\frac{1}{2}$ full. How many people does the cinema hold?

8. $3\frac{1}{4}$ metres of material is needed for a loose cover for an armchair and $\frac{3}{4}$ metre for a small chair. Find the cost of the material for covering a suite of 2 armchairs and 6 small chairs with material costing £5.50 per metre.

9. Mrs Khan earns £3.40 per hour for a basic week of 40 hours. Overtime is paid at time-and-a-half. If she works 42 hours one week, what will she earn? If one week she earns £176.80, how many hours altogether did she work?

10. Mr Taylor's weekly wage is £120. He reckons that $\frac{1}{4}$ of his wages go in tax and insurance. Of the remainder, $\frac{1}{5}$ pays the rent and $\frac{1}{10}$ is put aside to pay the household fuel bills. How much has he left to spend?

PUZZLES

11. Practical maths. Fold a piece of paper in half, then in half again, and again, . . . , 9 times altogether.

12. How many triangles are there in this figure?

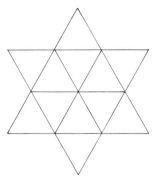

13. Barry was given a box containing 125 small bars of chocolate. On the wrapper of each bar there was a token, and Barry could exchange 5 tokens at the local shop for a similar bar of chocolate. How many extra bars of chocolate did he get?

14. Robert has to saw a 10-metre pole into 1-metre lengths. How long will it take him if he cuts one length every 3 minutes?

15. If 1000 + 1 + 50 + 500 spells MILD, what does 100 + 1 + 5 + 1 + 50 spell?

16. A bag contains several discs, some red and some yellow. I have to take some out of the bag without looking. If I want to be sure that I pick at least 4 discs of the same colour, what is the least number of discs that I should take out of the bag?

5 Statistics

Statistics involves numerical data.
Firstly, the data must be collected.
Secondly, it is displayed in the form of a list, a table or a graph.
Thirdly, it is studied, in order to make conclusions from it, often involving decisions for the future.

Tally tables

Example 1

The type of vehicle passing along a road gave the following data: Lorry, bus, car, lorry, lorry, lorry, car, lorry, bus, bus, lorry, car, car, van, car, car, bus, car, car, lorry, car, lorry, car, car, lorry, car, van, lorry, lorry, car, van, car, bus, van, lorry, car, bus, car.

The items are entered in a tally chart as they occur.

		Total
		Total
Car	ЖЖ ЖЖ ЖЖ I	16
Van	IIII	4
Bus	ЖЖ I	6
Lorry	ЖЖ ЖЖ II	12
		38

Notice that the numbers are grouped in fives, the fifth number going diagonally through the first four. ЖЖ

The groups of 5 are kept in neat columns.
This makes the totals easy to count.

Presenting the data in a table

Example 2

Method of transport to and from school

Copy the table and fill in the figures to satisfy this information.

Of the 50 boys, 10 walk to school, 5 cycle, 3 come on their motorbikes, 8 come by car and 4 come by train. The rest come by bus. All go home by the same method except that 2 who walk to school go home by car and 3 who come by car go home by bus.

	Morning			Afternoon		
	Boys	Girls	Total	Boys	Girls	Total
Walk						
Cycle						
Motorbike						
Car						
Bus						
Train						
Total						

Of the girls, 12 walk to school, 8 cycle, 1 comes on her motorbike, 3 come by car and 16 come by bus. No-one comes by train. 4 of the girls who come by bus walk home and 2 others go home by car instead of by bus.
Fill in the remaining spaces in the table.
What fraction of the pupils come to school by public transport (bus or train)?
What fraction of the pupils go home by public transport?

Diagrams

Pictograms

Example 3

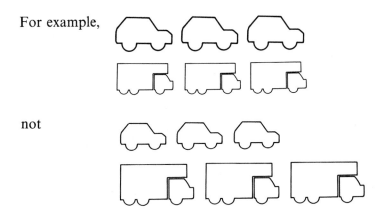

Unless you are spending time on a special project, do not draw elaborate symbols.
Use simple ones, such as used here.

If you make pictures of different kinds, for example, cars, vans and buses, make them of equal length or you will not be able to compare the frequencies by looking at the diagram.

For example,

not

Bar chart

Example 4

Favourite sports of 20 children

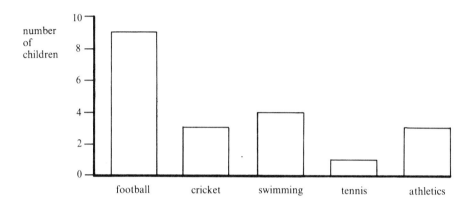

(The rectangles should all have the same width.)

Bar charts could be horizontal instead of vertical.

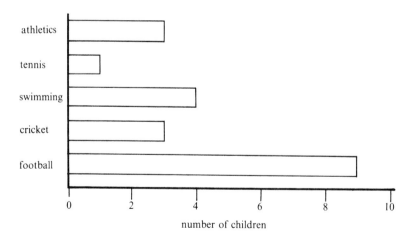

Statistical diagrams and graphs should have headings to describe them. Scales should be clearly marked. Axes should be labelled.

Draw a pictogram and a bar chart to illustrate the data given in the tally chart on page 45.

Straight line graph

Example 5

These figures show the numbers attending a youth-club over the past ten weeks.

20, 35, 28, 25, 33, 41, 37, 46, 48, 42.

We can plot these figures on a graph, putting time on the horizontal axis and attendance on the vertical axis.

Youth club attendance

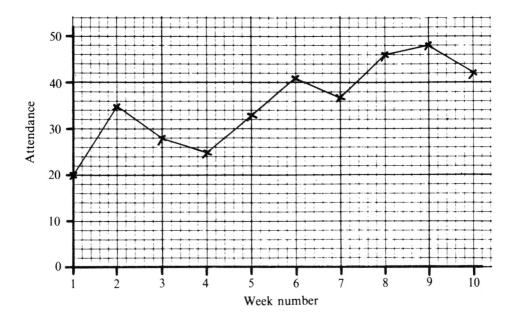

The points are joined from one to the next by straight lines, because this shows increases and decreases more easily, but in this graph the lines have no other meaning. We cannot use the graph to find the attendance at in-between times, because that would be meaningless. The graph does show an upward trend in attendance and we might use this to make a very cautious prediction for future attendances.

From the graph find
1   in which week the attendance was greatest,
2   between which weeks there was the greatest increase in attendance.

Exercise 5.1

1. The numbers of livestock in Britain in a certain year included the following:

    Sheep   44 million
    Cattle   14 million
    Pigs   8 million

      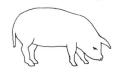

    (Figures are given to the nearest million.)
    Represent the data on a pictogram or bar chart.

2. A family's income of £120 in a particular week was spent as follows:
    Food   £36
    Rent   £21
    Car expenses   £18
    Clothes   £9
    Fuel   £12
    Miscellaneous   £24
    Represent the data on a bar chart.
    What fraction of the total income is spent on food?

3. An arable farm of 90 hectares grows four main crops.
    Barley   56 hectares
    Potatoes   11 hectares
    Carrots   9 hectares
    Green vegetables   14 hectares
    (1 hectare = $10\,000\,\text{m}^2$)
    Represent the data on a bar chart.

4. The U.K. population figures are given in this list. (Figures to the nearest million.)

Year	1901	1911	1921	1931	1941	1951	1961	1971
Population (in millions)	38	42	44	46	48	51	53	56

    Draw a bar chart to represent the data.

5. Each £1 collected in rates was used by a Council as follows:
    Education   52 p
    Social services   10 p
    Police   9 p
    Highways and transport   9 p
    Fire Service   2 p
    Other expenses   5 p
    The rest was kept in reserve. How much per £1 was this?
    Represent this information on a pictogram.

6. The assets of a building society for 7 consecutive years (to the nearest million £'s) were

Year number	1	2	3	4	5	6	7
Assets (in £1 000 000)	19	21	25	29	34	39	47

Draw a bar chart to represent the data.

7. The graph shows the number of passengers carried by a bus company on 14 consecutive days.

   1 On which day were least passengers carried, and how many were there?
   2 On which day were most passengers carried, and how many were there?
   3 On one weekday there are usually less passengers because many of the shops close in the afternoons. Which day do you think this is?

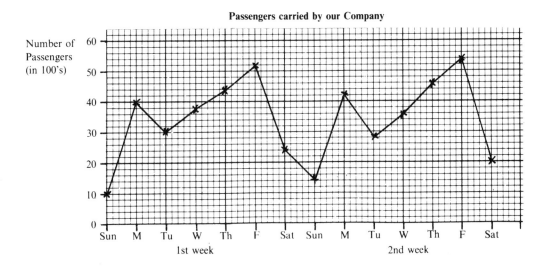

Passengers carried by our Company

8. In a particular year, the destinations of British holidaymakers travelling to other European countries were as follows:
    Spain 30%, France 14%, Italy 8%, Greece 7%, Eire 5%, Other countries 36%
    Represent the data on a pictogram or a bar chart.

9. The temperature in a classroom was recorded at the same time each day for 3 weeks. The results are shown on this graph.

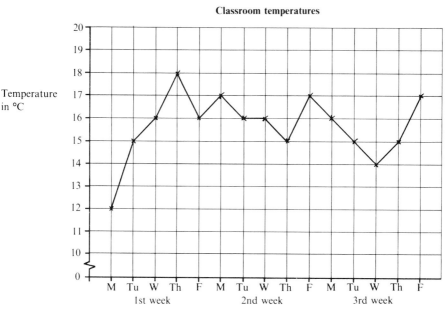

1   On which day was it very cold in the classroom? Give a possible reason for this.
2   How many degrees warmer was it on the next day?
3   On which day was it warmest?
4   On how many days was the temperature below 16°C?

10. Attendances at an exhibition.

	Wed	Thur	Fri	Sat	Sun	Total
Adults	83	120	176	216	313	
Children	104	185	287	384	529	
Total						

Copy the table and complete it.

1   How many children altogether attended the exhibition?
2   On which day was there the greatest attendance?
3   The organisers had been hoping for a total attendance of 200 on the first day. How many visitors were they short of that target?

11. The bar chart shows how a family spent its weekly income of £110.

The rest of the income was saved for the holiday fund. How much was saved that week? The following week the income was increased by a bonus to £130, so £12 extra was spent on food, £3 extra on other expenses and the rest of the increase went into the holiday fund. Draw a bar chart showing the spending and saving for this second week.

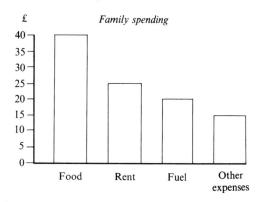

12. A firm made a table showing sales of a product.

	Standard model	De-luxe model	Total
Red			
Green			
Blue			
Total			

Copy the table and fill in the details.
In the standard model there were 60 sold altogether of which $\frac{1}{2}$ were red and $\frac{1}{5}$ were green. For sales in the de-luxe range, 5 more red ones were sold than of the standard model and 4 less blue ones than of the standard model. Altogether 31 green items were sold.
What fraction of the total items sold were blue ones?

13. In a shopping survey, 4 different brands of butter, which we will call brands A, B, C and D, were on sale. The first 50 customers' choices were as follows:

C   C   A   D   D   D   C   C   D   C
C   A   D   D   C   C   A   D   C   A
C   A   B   C   C   A   A   A   A   C
C   C   A   A   A   A   A   C   C   C
B   B   D   C   D   C   C   C   B   D

Tally this information. Draw a bar chart to illustrate the results.

14. Make a tally chart of the number of times the letters a, e, i, o, u occur in this question. Draw a pictogram or a bar chart to illustrate the data.

Statistics is a branch of Mathematics which has a wide variety of uses. The Government collects many kinds of statistics which are often published in journals. Scientists use statistics in their research. Industry uses statistics to plan future action. Insurance companies use statistics to fix the premiums they must charge. Most sports' associations keep statistical records.
(You will notice that the word 'Statistics' can mean the subject (the study of numerical data), or it can simply mean the data.)

Look for examples of statistical tables or diagrams in newspapers, magazines, books or on television.

You can make an attractive poster or scrapbook using cuttings from newspapers and magazines, showing a variety of statistical data and different types of statistical diagrams.

Collecting data

There are several ways in which you could collect data. Having collected it, present it in a list or a table, or in a statistical diagram. Then study it to see if you can find any interesting conclusions from it.
(The ideas of this section are also relevant to the further Statistics chapters in the book. Keep all collected data as you may be able to use it again later.)

1. Data you can collect from yourself, your friends or your family.
    Examples:
    1   Make a list of how you spend your time on an average weekday, e.g. hours sleeping, eating, at school, on homework, watching TV, etc. Draw a bar chart of the results. Compare this with how you spend your time on Saturday or Sunday, or compare with a friend's results.
    2   Make a list of how you spend or save your weekly pocket money. Draw a bar chart of the results. Compare this with the results from a different week.
        If your parents will tell you the amounts, make a list of how the family's weekly income is used, e.g. rent and rates, fuel, food, clothing, fares or car expenses, etc.
        A more detailed project is to find how much money is spent on you each year, e.g. food, clothing, fares to school, school meals, pocket money, presents, etc.

2. Data you can find from books, newspapers and other sources.
    Examples:
    1   Collect the football results of the main leagues from the newspaper. There are many ways in which you can study these.
    2   From the TV timetables in the newspaper or magazines, find how much time in a day is devoted to news, current affairs, sport, nature, comedy, etc. Compare the results for different TV channels.

3 Find out how the Council spends the money they collect in rates. They will give this information with the rates bill. For every £1 collected, find how much goes on Education, Health, Housing, etc. and show this in a bar chart.

4 Make a temperature chart showing the daily temperature outdoors (in the shade) for several days. It is interesting if you can do this in the summer and then in the winter. If you made a rain gauge you could also collect rainfall figures.

5 If you do experiments in Science or other subjects you can use the results to do a statistical study.

6 You can do traffic surveys. Find the number of cars passing your home or school or some other point in a given time. You can repeat this at different times of the day. Estimate the ages of cars by noting the single letter in the registration number. Classify the traffic into categories such as cars, buses, heavy goods vehicles, etc. You could do a survey of the different makes of cars.

Sampling

When we need data about a certain population we often just take a sample. If you wanted to know the favourite meal of pupils in your school you would not be able to ask everyone so you would select certain people and ask them.

If a farmer wanted to know how well his potatoes were growing he would not uproot the whole crop, he would just dig up a sample. (Here the population is the whole crop of potatoes. In statistics the word 'Population' does not need to refer to people.)

It is no use choosing a sample if it is biased, that is, likely to give unfair results. The best kind of sample to take is a **random sample**. In this, every member of the population has the same chance of being chosen. It is not always possible or easy to get a random sample so we have to compromise.

The sample should represent fairly each group in the population, and it should be large enough to give proper results.

If you wanted the views of pupils in your school, for a random sample you would put all their names in a hat and draw out names for the people in your sample. You could use numbers instead of names and use a computer to list some random numbers instead of drawing them out of a hat. There are also lists of random numbers available.

It might be more sensible to decide to choose two members from each class, and these could then be chosen randomly from each class register. If there are equal numbers of boys and girls in your school, it might be better to choose one boy and one girl from each class, so that boys and girls are fairly represented in the sample.

You would have to decide how many people you need in your sample. If there are 1000 pupils in your school a 10% sample would mean a sample of 100, a 5% sample would mean a sample of 50. A smaller sample might not accurately represent the views of the whole school, and too large a sample would make the data collection take too long.

Questionnaires

To conduct a survey amongst a group of people one way is to ask them to answer a questionnaire. You can either give them the questionnaire to fill in themselves or you can ask the questions and write down their answers.

Decide exactly what information you want and how you are planning to use the answers. Keep the questionnaire as short as possible, and keep the questions short, clear and precise. Avoid questions which people may not be willing to answer because they are embarrassing or offensive. The best questions can be answered by Yes/No, or categories such as

strongly agree	agree	don't know/ no opinion	disagree	strongly disagree

where you can put a tick in one of the boxes.

'How long do you spend watching TV?' is a very vague question, and will produce equally vague answers, so you will find it difficult to analyse the data.

'How long did you spend watching TV yesterday? Tick one of the following.'

not at all	up to 1 hour	between 1 and 3 hours	between 3 and 5 hours	over 5 hours

is much more precise, and you have only to count the ticks in each category to have some useful data about viewing habits.

It is a good idea to try out your questionnaire on a few people first to see if it is clear enough and likely to give you the data you need, or whether it needs improving. This is called a **Pilot survey**.

If you are asking members of the public for their views, you have not the resources, time or authority to make a proper sample. You will probably have to question people in the street or shopping area, and your sample will have to consist of people in that area at that time. (But a survey on where people shop could be biased if you select your sample from outside the largest supermarket in the area.) You can try to make your sample representative by including people of different ages, and equal numbers of men and women. Be very polite when you approach people, and thank them afterwards for their help. Remember that some people will be in too much of a hurry to stop to talk to you. Before you do such a survey, discuss your plans with your teacher and with your parents.

———————————————————————————————————————

PUZZLE

17.   The rail journey from Ashfield to Beechgrove takes exactly 4 hours and trains leave each way on the hour and on the half-hour. If you were on a train going from Ashfield to Beechgrove, how many trains going from Beechgrove to Ashfield would you pass during the journey?

Miscellaneous section A

Exercise A1   Aural Practice

If possible find someone to read these questions to you.
You should do questions 1 to 15 within 10 minutes.
Do not use your calculator.
Write down the answers only.

1.   Andrew had 27 marbles. The next day he won 14 more. How many had he then?

2.   How many hours are there from 8 a.m. to 2 p.m.?

3.   If £9 was equally divided among 6 children, how much would they each receive?

4.   There were 8563 spectators at a football match. What is this number to the nearest 100?

5.   It is Mrs Wilson's birthday today. She was born in 1920. How old is she?

6.   In one carton there are 50 packets of sweets. How many packets are there altogether in 8 cartons?

7.   What fraction of an hour is 10 minutes?

8.   What will 250 lollipops cost at 2 pence each?

9.   If the time is 'a quarter past two in the afternoon', write this in figures using the 24-hour clock system.

10.   What do you get when you take 8 from 80 and divide the result by 9?

11.   What change shall I have from £1 after buying 2 magazines, one for 35 pence and the other for 25 pence?

12.   Write in figures the number 'three thousand, four hundred and six'.

13.   Write down the prime numbers between 12 and 20.

14.   Pat's mother is 27, and is three times as old as Pat. How old will Pat be next year?

15.   What is $\frac{1}{2} + \frac{1}{4}$?

Additional aural questions using data from other pages.

16.   Turn to page 21. Use the table of question 12.

   If I buy something costing £20 and repay over 2 years, what is the monthly payment?

17. Also on page 21, use the timetable of question 11.

    If I want to be in Carlton Village by 4.30 p.m., what is the time of the latest bus I can catch from Brook Lane, and how long does the journey take?

18. Use the rectangle drawn round the same table as in the previous question. This rectangle has a width (height) of 2 cm. Estimate its length.

19. Turn to page 50. Use the population data, of question 4.

    What was the approximate increase in the U.K. population between 1901 and 1911?

20. Turn to page 63. Use the table about national savings certificates, of question 10.

    Jayne has 2 savings certificates. What will they be worth, together, at the end of 3 years?

21. Turn to page 142. Use the chart showing sales, of question 12. Approximately how many items of product D were sold last year?

22. Turn to page 121. Use the 2nd diagram of question 1. Estimate the size of angle A in the triangle.

Exercise A2 Multi-choice Exercise

Select the correct answer to each question.

1. Which of these numbers does not divide exactly by 9?

    A 702   **B** 800   **C** 891   **D** 900   **E** 1161

2. The number of seconds in 1 hour is

    A 60   **B** 360   **C** 600   **D** 1440   **E** 3600

3. In a school of 800 pupils, 440 are girls. What fraction of the school is girls?

    A $\frac{9}{20}$ **B** $\frac{1}{12}$ **C** $\frac{11}{20}$ **D** $\frac{9}{11}$ **E** $\frac{11}{9}$

4. If $a = 80°$ and all the other angles are equal, what size are they?

    A 56°   **B** 60°   **C** 70°

    D 72°   **E** 80°

5. If 800 articles which should cost 85 p each are bought at a reduced price of 55 p each, the total saving is

A £240 B £440 C £680 D £24 000 E £44 000

6. The number of insects in a colony doubles each week. If there were 100 insects initially, how many would there be after 5 weeks?

A 500 B 800 C 1600 D 3200 E 6400

7. In the diagram, $\angle DBC$ is cut in half by BE. The value of x is

A 32 · B 58 C 61

D 122 E 151

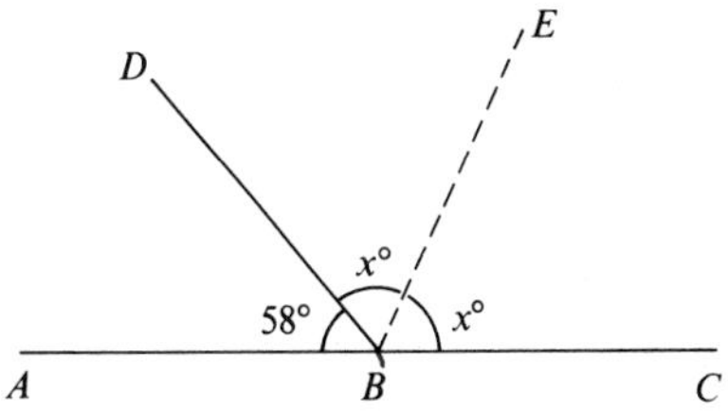

8. The bar chart shows how some money is divided among 3 departments A, B, C. The bar A is 11 cm long, B is 10 cm and C is 4 cm. If the total amount is £125, how much is B's share?

A £20 B £41$\frac{2}{3}$ C £50

D £55 E £114

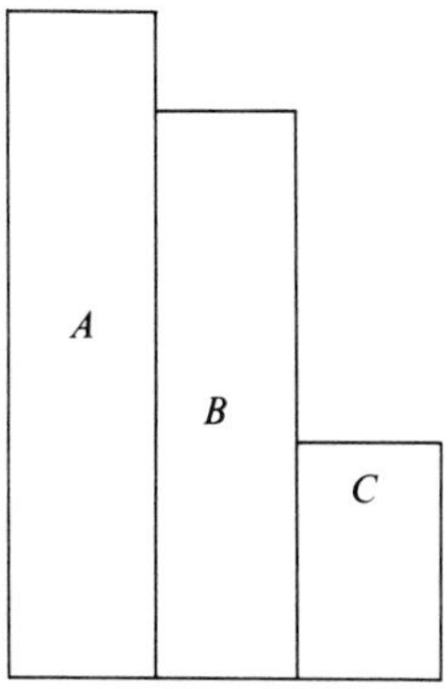

9. A man buys a television set which costs £378. He pays an initial payment of $\frac{1}{3}$ of the cost and arranges to pay the rest in 20 equal monthly instalments. The monthly instalment is

A £5.40 B £12.60 C £17.40 D £18 E £20

10. $2\frac{1}{2} - 1\frac{1}{3} + \frac{1}{4}$ is equal to

A $\frac{2}{3}$ B $\frac{11}{12}$ C $1\frac{1}{3}$ D $1\frac{5}{12}$ E $2\frac{1}{12}$

11. Which of the numbers 61, 63, 65, 67, 69 are prime?

A 61 only B 61 and 67 C 61 and 69

D 61, 63, 67 and 69 E 61, 67 and 69

12. It is 5.15 p.m. and my train is due at 1850 according to the timetable. How long have I to wait?

A 25 min B 35 min C 1 hr 25 min D 1 hr 35 min E 2 hr 35 min

13.   Which of these numbers has a value nearest to 30?

   A $2^2 \times 7$ **B** 3^3 **C** 4^3 **D** 5^2 **E** 6^2

14.   Which amount is nearest to £1?

   A   £0.89   **B**   £1.11   **C**   eleven 10 p coins   **D**   forty-four 2 p coins

   E   four 20 p coins and eleven pence

15.   A watch loses 5 seconds every hour. It is correct on Monday at 9.00 a.m. What
       time does it show at 9.00 a.m. on Tuesday?

   A   8.58   **B**   8.59   **C**   9.00   **D**   9.01   **E**   9.02

16.   When boxes are stacked in piles of 5 there are 2 left over. When they are stacked
       in piles of 8 there are still 2 left over.

       How many boxes are there, if there are between 50 and 100?

   A   52   **B**   57   **C**   58   **D**   80   **E**   82

17. $(1\frac{5}{8} \times 4) + 3\frac{1}{2}$ is equal to

   A $5\frac{9}{10}$ **B** $8\frac{1}{8}$ **C**   9   **D**   10   **E**   11

18.   The opening hours of a shop are shown on this
       poster.
       For how many hours per week is the shop
       open?

   A   48   **B** $48\frac{1}{2}$ **C**   53

   D $53\frac{1}{2}$ **E**   54

Mon	9.30–5.30
Tues	9.30–5.30
Wed	9.30–5.30
Thurs	9.30–8.00
Fri	9.30–8.00
Sat	9.00–5.30
Sun	– – –

19.   The prime factors of 300 are

   A $2^2 \times 3 \times 5^2$ **B** 3×10^2 **C** $3 \times 4 \times 5^2$

   D $2^2 \times 3^2 \times 5$ **E** 10×30

20.   From a plank of wood which is 9 ft 9 ins long, Bill cuts off 5 lengths of 1 ft 3 ins
       each. He then cuts the remaining piece in half. How long is each half?
       (12 inches = 1 foot.)

   A   1 ft 3 ins   **B**   1 ft 7 ins   **C**   1 ft 8 ins

   D   1 ft 9 ins   **E**   4 ft 3 ins

Exercise A3   Revision

1.   The distance by sea from Marseilles to Port Said is one thousand, five hundred and six miles. Write this distance in figures.

2.   If 20 fence-posts cost £48, what would be the cost of 30 posts?

3.

The average prices of semi-detached houses in five districts is given in this table.

District	A	B	C	D	E
Price in £1000's to nearest £1000	23	25	30	38	51

Draw a bar chart to illustrate the data.

4.   Here is one quarter of a symmetrical pattern. Copy it and complete the other three quarters to match, so that the dotted lines are axes of symmetry.

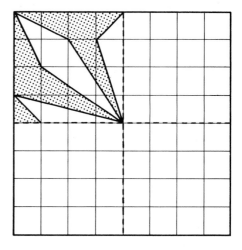

5.   1   Express 36 in its prime factors.
     2   A number expressed in its prime factors is $2 \times 3 \times 5^2$. What is this number?
     3   Which numbers between 40 and 50 are prime?

6.   If you have to pay 83 p, what is the least number of coins you can use, and what are they?
     If instead you pay with a £1 coin, what is the least number of coins you can receive in change, and what are they?

7. These flags have been rotated with ● as centre of rotation. In each case 1 is rotated into 2. Estimate, then measure, the angle through which it has been rotated, and say whether it has been turned clockwise or anticlockwise.

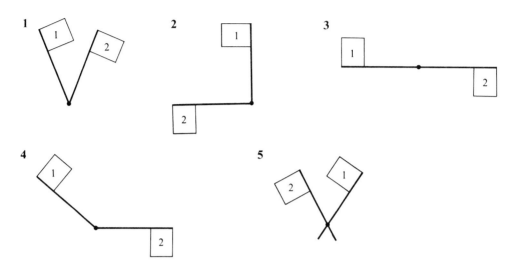

8. A householder paid £360 in rates last year. This compound bar chart shows how this money is used by the County.

   1 How much goes into the Reserve Fund?
   2 What fraction of the rate is spent on 'Fire Service and other services'?

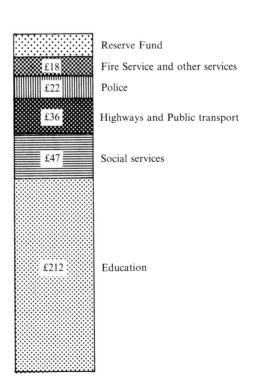

9. The rainfall records for a town in England for one year were as given in this bar diagram.

1 Which was the wettest month and how much rain fell then?
2 Which was the driest month and how much rain fell then?
3 In which month was the rainfall double that of the preceding month?

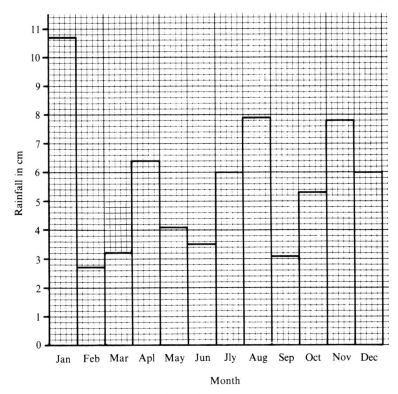

10. A national savings certificate bought in January 1987 cost £25 and gains in value according to this table.

Years after purchase	Value at end of year
1	£26.63
2	£28.63
3	£31.11
4	£34.19
5	£38.03

(The rates are for the 32nd issue. The rates will vary for other issues.)

Margaret invested £500 in these savings certificates. How many certificates did she buy?
She planned to keep the certificates for 5 years. How much would they be worth then altogether?

11. **1** If $a = 35°$ and $b = 51°$, find the sizes of
         c, d, e.

     2 If $a = b$ and c is a right angle, find the sizes
         of a, d, e.

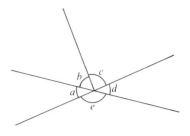

12. This is a timetable of the bus service on market days.

Picton Village	dep.	10.50
Renton Green	dep.	11.30
Suntown	arr.	12.15
Suntown	dep.	3.30
Renton Green	arr.	4.25
Picton Village	arr.	5.05

1 What is the time taken for the journey from Picton Village to Suntown?

2 How much longer does the return journey take?

3 Mrs Lloyd uses this service from Picton Village to visit her mother in Renton
     Green. How long can she spend with her mother, if her mother lives 10
     minutes walk from the bus stop in Renton Green?

Exercise A4   Revision

1. Write down any number less than 10, add 3 to it and square the result. Then add
    1 and multiply by 10. Subtract 100 and divide by the number you started with.
    Add 5 and then divide by 5. Subtract 9 and halve the result. Subtract the number
    your started with. What is your answer?

2. Estimate, then measure, the angles a, b, c, d, e.

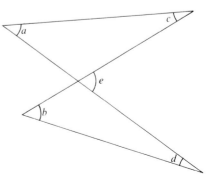

3. The table shows the dinners ordered for the 1st year forms at a school, for a week in September.

	1P	1Q	1R	1S	Total
Mon	35	28	22	25	110
Tues	34	28	18	26	
Wed	33		21	26	104
Thur	33	21			
Fri		26	22		106
Total for week	166		105	131	

Copy the table and fill in the missing figures, including the total number of dinners ordered for the week by all the 1st year forms.

1 On which day were the least dinners ordered?
2 If the dinners cost 60 p each, what was the total cost of the dinners ordered for the week by form 1Q?

4. One parcel weighed 14 lb 7 oz and a second one weighed 6 lb 12 oz.

1 What was the total weight?
2 How much heavier was the first parcel than the second one?
    (16 oz = 1 lb.)

5. Copy the diagrams and

    1 reflect *A* in line 1,
    2 reflect *B* in line 2,
    3 rotate *C* through 180° about point 3,
    4 rotate *D* through 90° anticlockwise about point 4.

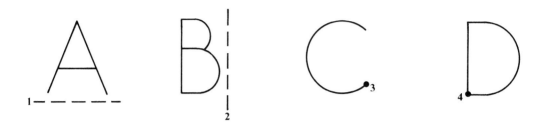

6. A new road is being paid for by four towns *A*, *B*, *C* and *D*. Town *A* pays $\frac{1}{3}$ of the cost and *B* and *C* each pay $\frac{1}{4}$ of the cost. What fraction of the cost does *D* pay? What does the road cost if *D* pays £40 000?

7. Copy and complete this number pattern to the line which begins with 123456789.

    $$0 \times 9 + 1 = \ \ 1$$
    $$1 \times 9 + 2 = 11$$
    $$12 \times 9 + 3 =$$
    $$123 \times 9 + 4 =$$

8. From the letters N U M B E R S, write down

    1 the letters which have a vertical axis of symmetry,
    2 the letters which have a horizontal axis of symmetry,
    3 the letters which have a point of symmetry.

9. Work through this flowchart. What does your answer represent?

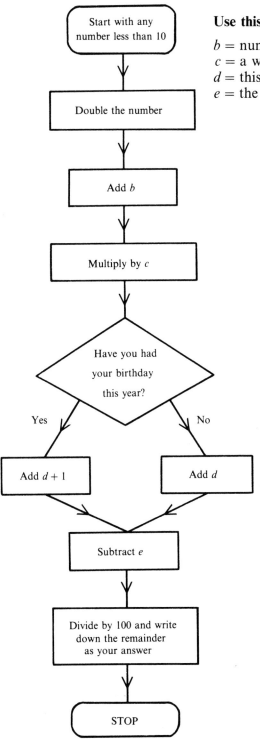

Use this information

b = number of days in a week
c = a whole number between 49 and 51
d = this year's date + 9
e = the year in which you were born − 40

10.   A man worked 48 hours in a week. For the first 40 hours he was paid £2.50 an
       hour. For the rest he was paid at the overtime rate of £3.75 an hour.

       1 What were the man's wages that week?
       2 How many hours altogether had he worked in a week when he earned
          £137.50?

11.   The following information is given by a travel-agent for holidays in Spain.

Prices in £ per person from London	Departure commencing between			Single room supplements per person per night
	1 May–18 Jun	19 Jun–9 Jly	10 Jly–26 Aug	
Hotel Marti 11 days (10 nights)	155	181	213	
12 days (11 nights)	162	189	223	£1.20
15 days (14 nights)	184	214	251	
Hotel Parki 15 days (14 nights)	202	234	274	£1
Supplements for flights from:	11 days	12 days	15 days (dep. Mon)	15 days (dep. Sat)
Glasgow	£49	£47	£39	£57
Manchester	£31	£33	£23	£39

       1 Mr and Mrs Dee are going on their honeymoon for 12 days, departing
          Saturday, 4th July, flying from Manchester. They want a double room.
          Which hotel must they stay at? Find the total cost.
       2 Three friends are going for 15 days holiday, flying from Glasgow, departing
          on Saturday, 13th June. They each want single rooms and will stay at the
          Hotel Parki. Find the cost for each person, and the total cost.
       3 Mr and Mrs Ede and their 7-year old daughter Mary want an 11-days
          holiday, flying from London and departing on Saturday, 8th August. (Mary
          will occupy a bed in her parents' room and there is a $\frac{1}{5}$ reduction in cost
          for her.) Find the total cost.

12. A group of people were asked how they prefer to spend their leisure time, choosing from reading (R), playing sports (S), watching television (T), other activities (U). The results were as follows:

```
R  T  T  S  T  R  T  R  T  S  R  T  R  S  T
U  T  R  U  R  T  S  U  U  S  S  T  U  T  T
T  T  T  T  R  R  T  R  S  U  S  T  R  U  S
T  R  T  U  R  T  R  R  U  T  R  T  U  S  U
```

Tally these results and show them on a bar chart or pictogram.

To the student:

2   Independent work

The next exercise, and the similar exercises in the other Miscellaneous Sections give several suggestions for projects, practical work or investigations which could be done either individually or by a group working together. It is not intended that anyone should do all of them, so a choice should be made, depending on your interests.
Some ideas **may** be suitable for the practical work or investigational work needed for the school-based part of the examination but it is advisable to check first with your own Examination Board's regulations if you wish any work to count towards your final grade.
Only brief details have been given here because too much detail would reduce the value of independent work. Financial information can be found from newspapers, magazines, catalogues, brochures, and by asking family and friends. Mathematical facts can be found from maths magazines and books in the library.
These lists are only suggestions, and you should think of other ideas for other investigations.

Making a booklet about a topic

Present your work in an attractive way. Use file paper of a suitable size. Use unlined paper for pages which include drawings or plans. Squared paper or graph paper may also be appropriate for some sections. Use thin cardboard to strengthen the covers, and design the front cover with a neat title and possibly some illustration. Keep the pages in the booklet with file tags or ribbon.

A Maths Scrapbook

Smaller topics could go all together in a Maths Scrapbook which can have different pages for different investigations. It can be a ready-made book where you stick your writings onto the background, or it can be a made-up booklet as before. Make a suitable mathematical design for the front cover. Look out for any mathematical articles, jokes or cartoons you find in magazines, etc. and put these in your book.

Planning an investigation

Plan ahead to decide what you are going to do. Keep a proper record of your progress and include a summary of it.
These points are useful guidelines:

1   Before you begin, say what you are trying to find.
2   Then say what you actually do to find it.
3   Give your results. (If there is a long list of data, record it separately at the end. Summarise your results here in a table.)
4   Say what you can deduce from your results.
5   If you have used any books, give their titles and authors. If you have had ideas or help from anyone, say what this help was.

Exercise A5 Practical work and Investigations

1. **A holiday abroad.**

   Plan a holiday abroad for your family. (It is an imaginary holiday so you can decide for yourself the type of holiday you want and how much you want to spend on it.)

   Get details of costs from travel agents' brochures. (The old ones for last year that they no longer want will do.) Don't forget costs of things such as passports, travel to the airport, excursions, extras like postcards and presents, money for snacks and drinks. Make a list of all the costs.

   Plan a timetable for the holiday, starting from the time you must leave home. Find your destination in an atlas. How far from home is it, and in roughly what direction? What sort of weather do you expect? What is the usual temperature at the time of year when you will be going?

   Plan the list of things to take. Find out the weight of luggage you are allowed, and whether you are limited to 1 suitcase. Give some idea of the things you plan to do while on holiday. Is it to be a lazy fortnight on the beach or a more energetic holiday? Are you going sightseeing, and if so, where?

   Find out the rate of exchange and make a conversion table for use while you are away, e.g. 10 pesetas = 5 p, 20 pesetas = 10 p, and so on.

   There are other details you can add to make your booklet more interesting. Illustrate it with pictures and a map.

2. Banking

Many people have a bank account nowadays. Many firms pay wages directly into the employees' bank accounts as this is safer and quicker than paying by cash.

Find out

1 the names of the biggest banks in the country, and which of them have branches in your district.
2 The types of bank account they offer, and the advantages and disadvantages of each, e.g. which accounts include a cheque book, and which pay interest. Do the banks charge you for having an account?
3 How to write a cheque, and what a cheque stub is.
4 The procedure for paying money into your account.
5 What a bank statement is.
6 What a cheque card is, and the conditions of use. What you should do if you lose it.
7 What a credit card is, and the conditions of use.
8 How to use an autobank machine.
9 The usual banking hours in your district.
10 What other services the banks offer.
11 Some banks offer special terms for students. Find out about these.
12 When you have decided which bank to choose, what is the procedure for opening an account?

3. **Tests for dividing by small numbers**

The tests for prime numbers 2, 3 and 5 have been given earlier. It is useful to know the checks for other small numbers.

Investigate dividing by 4. Do these numbers divide exactly by 4?
34, 134, 234, 48, 148, 248. Can you find a test for checking if a number greater than 100 can be divided by 4?

Investigate dividing by 6. Do these numbers divide by 2, 3, 6?
22, 27, 30, 134, 135, 138. Can you find a test for checking if a number can be divided by 6?

Here are some numbers which divide by 9. Add up their digits.
738, 2007, 53415, 87651. Can you find a test for checking if a number can be divided by 9?

Dividing by 11

Alternate figures add up to the same total or there is a difference of 11 (or 22, 33, . . .) between the totals. For example; for 28 413, alternate figures are 2, 4, 3 with total 9; and 8, 1 also with total 9; so the number is divisible by 11. For 616, the totals of alternate figures are 12 and 1. There is a difference of 11 so the number is divisible by 11.

Test this rule with other numbers.

What is the test for checking if a number can be divided by 10?

Write down the 25-times table from 1×25 to 12×25. What do you notice about the answers? How can you tell if a number divides by 25?

A number will divide by 12 if it will divide by 3 and by 4.
A number will divide by 15 if it will divide by 3 and by 5.
Test these rules with several numbers.

For dividing by 7, there is no simple test. Here is one method which can be used for 3-figure numbers. Use your calculator to find several numbers which are multiples of 7.
For each number, e.g. 469,

1	add all the figures together	$4 + 6 + 9 = 19$
2	add the first two figures together	$4 + 6 = 10$
3	write down the middle figure	$\underline{6}$
4	add all these totals together	$\underline{35}$

Repeat for other numbers. What do you notice? Can you investigate for 4-figure numbers, or larger numbers?

4. **The Sieve of Eratosthenes**

Write down the numbers 2 to 50 inclusive. Draw a circle round 2 and then cross out every other number which divides by 2. The 1st number not circled or crossed out is 3. Draw a circle round 3 and then cross out every other number which divides by 3. The next number not crossed out or circled is 5. Draw a circle round 5 and then cross out every other number which divides by 5. The next number not crossed out is 7. Draw a circle round 7 and then cross out every other number which divides by 7. Now draw a circle round all the remaining numbers which are not crossed out. The circled numbers are the prime numbers. Write them down in a list.

Why was it sufficient to stop at 7? If we had made a list up to 125 what other number would need to be crossed out?

This method can be used to find the prime numbers up to any large number. It is useful to set the numbers down on squared paper in neat columns and then a pattern can be seen as you cross out the numbers.

Set out in columns of 10,   1   2   3   4   5   6   7   8   9   10
                              11   12   13   14   15   16   17   18   19   20
                              21   22   ·   ·   ·

or try other columns, especially columns of 6.   1   2   3   4   5   6
                                                    7   8   9   10   11   12
                                                   13   14   15   16   17   18
                                                   19   20   ·   ·   ·

1 is a special number, so mark it in a different way. It is not counted as a prime number although it has no factors other than itself. This method is known as 'The Sieve of Eratosthenes'. See if you can find out anything about Eratosthenes (or Erathostenes), who lived a long time ago.

5. **'Russian multiplication' or 'Peasants' multiplication'**

e.g. To multiply 1653 by 937. This method only uses the 2 times table.

	937	1653	
Halve the 1st number each time, ignore $\frac{1}{2}$'s	468	3306	
	234	6612	
	117	13224	
Double the 2nd number each time.	58	26440	
	29	52896	
	14	105792	
Cross out the rows where the number in the 1st column is even	7	211584	
	3	423168	
	1	846336	
		1548861	Add up this column, ignoring the crossed-out numbers. This gives the answer.

Stop when you reach 1

Try using this method with other numbers.

6. **'Casting out nines'**

This is an extra check for a multiplication or addition sum. It is not a foolproof check but it will often indicate an error, and it is an interesting method to learn. First, we must learn how to reduce a number to a 1-figure number by adding its digits, and if necessary adding again.

e.g.   for $5813 \rightarrow 5 + 8 + 1 + 3 = 17 \rightarrow 1 + 7 = 8$

$492567 \rightarrow 4 + 9 + 2 + 5 + 6 + 7 = 33 \rightarrow 3 + 3 = 6$

To save time, any 9 or figures which add up to 9 can be crossed out first without affecting the result, as long as we leave the last 9 if there is no other number, so as not to be left with nothing.

e.g. for 5813, cross out 8 and 1 which make 9.

$5813 \rightarrow 5 + 3 = 8$, (or we could have crossed out 5 and 3 and 1 instead, leaving 8).

492567. Cross out 9, 4 and 5, 2 and 7, leaving 6.

918. Cross out 9, **or** 1 and 8, but not both, leaving 9, because we don't want to be left with 0.

Now, to check multiplication, e.g. $5813 \times 1967 = 11634171$

Reduce the numbers to single figures. 8   5   6

Make a cross

Put the two figures of the question in a and b.
Put the answer figure in c.
Multiply the figures in a and b, reduce this answer and put it in d.
$8 \times 5 = 40 \rightarrow 4 + 0 = 4$

If the numbers in c and d are not the same, as here, the answer is wrong. It should have been 11434171, so $c = 4$. This gives

and here $c = d$, so the answer satisfies the check. (However this does not definitely prove that the answer is correct, as other answers could also satisfy the check.)

Practise using this method with other numbers.

How can this method be used to check addition?

7. **Symmetry**

Write down the alphabet in capital letters and find out which letters have:

1   a horizontal axis of symmetry,
2   a vertical axis of symmetry,
3   an axis of symmetry which is not horizontal or vertical,
4   two axes of symmetry,
5   a point of symmetry.

(Sometimes you have to ignore slight differences in the printing. What about

where the letters have been adjusted slightly?)

Find words which have a vertical axis of symmetry, e.g. M U M, or words which have a horizontal axis of symmetry, e.g. B E D, or a point of symmetry, e.g. N O N, or words which have a vertical axis of symmetry when written downwards, e.g. M
       A
       T

Which 1-figure numbers have an axis or a point of symmetry?
Which 2 or 3-figure numbers have an axis or a point of symmetry?
Which years, within the last 400 years, have an axis or a point of symmetry?

Make a 'butterfly' by putting a blob of wet paint on a piece of paper and folding the paper.
Make a doyley by folding a square piece of paper into half, half again, and then cornerways into half again. Cut the edge to make a curve and then cut bits out of all three edges. Then open out.

Look for examples of symmetry in nature or architecture. Make a collection of pictures, photographs or drawings.
Look at pictures in a kaleidoscope.
Draw your own symmetrical patterns.
Has the Union Jack got a symmetrical pattern?

8. **Moebius bands**

These are long strips of paper glued together at the ends to form a loop. Some of the strips have a twist, or several twists, put in them before they are glued. Make one each with 0 twists, 1 twist, 2 twists, etc. For each loop, investigate whether it is one-sided or two-sided, and how many edges it has. Continue your investigations by seeing what happens when you cut each strip lengthways down a centre line. It is interesting to try to predict the result in advance. Investigate sides and edges again, and the lengths of the new strips in comparison with the original. Finally, make new strips which you can cut lengthways by a cut which is $\frac{1}{3}$ of the width across. Investigate the results.

Moebius (or Mobius) was a Mathematician who lived in the 19th century. Can you find out anything about him?

9. **Experimental Probability**

Probability is the likelihood of an event happening, for example, a trial being successful. It is measured on a numerical scale from 0 to 1 and can either be given as a fraction, e.g. $\frac{3}{4}$, or as a decimal, e.g. 0.75.

If we have a number of beads in a bag, some red and some blue, but otherwise identical, and we pick one out at random (i.e. without looking), record its colour, replace it in the bag and give the bag a shake to mix the beads up again, and keep repeating this, then after a few trials (say 10) we can work out the fraction

$$\frac{\text{number of trials giving a red bead}}{\text{total number of trials}}.$$

These are the results from one such experiment when the bag contained more red beads than blue ones.

number of trials (n)	number of red beads (r)	fraction $\frac{r}{n}$	$\frac{r}{n}$ to 2 decimal places
10	5	$\frac{5}{10}$	0.50
25	16	$\frac{16}{25}$	0.64
50	29	$\frac{29}{50}$	0.58
100	62	$\frac{62}{100}$	0.62
200	120	$\frac{120}{200}$	0.60
300	182	$\frac{182}{300}$	0.61
500	305	$\frac{305}{500}$	0.61
1000	596	$\frac{596}{1000}$	0.60

Here are the first 100 results, worked out after every 10 trials, plotted on a graph.

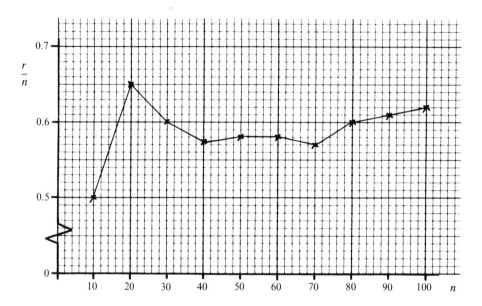

Although the results may be erratic after only a few trials they settle down around 0.6 so that in the long run red appears in 0.6 of the trials.

The probability of a red bead $= \dfrac{\text{number of red beads drawn out}}{\text{total number of beads drawn out}} = 0.6$

We can only use this definition of probability if we do enough trials to show that the fraction is settling down to a steady value. If the event was unpredictable the fraction would not settle down and we could not find a value for the probability.

When we know the probability of an event happening we can use its value to predict the likelihood of a future result. That is why Probability is linked to Statistics. Government departments, business firms, industrialists, scientists, medical researchers and many other people and organisations use the figures from past events to predict what is likely to happen in the future, and thus they can plan ahead. For example, Insurance Companies use their knowledge of past claims to predict future ones, and they can then decide what premiums they must charge. If you want to gamble on a sporting event it is useful to estimate the probability of winning. You might then realise that you are unlikely to win in the long run and decide not to waste your money on the bet.

In many cases we can find the probability by common-sense reasoning. For instance, if we had said that the bag of beads contained 60 red and 40 blue beads you could have reasoned that since $\frac{60}{100}$ of the beads were red, the probability of a red bead $= 0.6$, without doing the experiment.

In Chapter 7 we shall **calculate** probabilities, but before doing that it is interesting to do a few experiments, and later on you can compare the results with calculated probabilities and see how close they are.

Here are some suggestions for experiments. All the trials should be done randomly and fairly. Toss a coin properly. Give a die (dice) a good shake before rolling it out onto a flat surface. Shuffle a pack of cards properly, for most experiments you should take out the jokers first so that the pack contains the 52 cards of the 4 suits. If you have not got proper equipment it is often possible to think of a substitute. If you can combine other people's results with yours to give more trials, do so. Keep a record of your results to use again later.

Experiments

1   Toss a coin 200 times. Record your results in order, in a grid of 10 columns by 20 rows. Put H for head and T for tail.

The grid starts like this:

H	H	T	H	T	T	H			

Before you begin, estimate how many heads you are likely to get.
Make a table similar to this one and fill it in.

number of tosses (n)	number of heads (h)	fraction $\dfrac{h}{n}$	$\dfrac{h}{n}$ to 2 decimal places
1			
2			
3			
4			
5			
10			
20			
50			
100			
150			
200			

From your results, what value would you give for the probability of a toss showing a head?

2 Throw a die 400 times. Record the number which lands face upwards, in a grid of 20 columns by 20 rows.

Make a table similar to this and fill it in.

number of throws (n)	number of 6's (s)	fraction $\dfrac{s}{n}$	$\dfrac{s}{n}$ to 2 decimal places
10			
20			
50			
100			
200			
300			
400			

From your results, what value would you give for the probability of a throw showing a six?

3 Put 10 similar drawing-pins into a cup and holding it approximately 20 cm above a table, gently tip the drawing-pins out so that they land on the table. They come to rest point upwards, like this ⚲, or on their side, like this ⚲ . Count and record how many land point upwards. Repeat the experiment 50 times. Find the total number point upwards after 1, 5, 10, 20, 30, 40 and 50 goes.

Make a table similar to this and fill it in.

total number tipped out (n)	number point upwards (s)	fraction $\dfrac{s}{n}$	$\dfrac{s}{n}$ to 2 decimal places
10			
50			
100			
200			
300			
400			
500			

If the results are settling down to a certain value this gives the value of the probability that a drawing-pin in this type of experiment will land point upwards. (There is no theoretical way of checking this result.)

The height through which the drawing-pins fall may affect the result. You could investigate this by repeating the experiment from different heights. Different makes of drawing-pins may also give different results.

4 Shuffle a pack of cards and pick out 3 cards. Record as *P* if they contain at least one picture-card (i.e. Jack, Queen or King). Record as *N* if there is no picture card. Replace the cards, shuffle and repeat 100 times altogether.

Before you begin, estimate how many times *P* will occur.

Find the fraction $\dfrac{\text{number of times } P \text{ occurs}}{\text{total number of trials}}$ as

a decimal to 2 decimal places.

From your results, what value would you give for the probability that of three cards drawn at random, at least one card is a picture-card?

5 Collect 200 single-figure random numbers by taking the last figure of a list of phone numbers out of a random page of a directory. (If a firm has consecutive numbers listed, only use the first one.) Record these numbers in a grid, as in question 1.

Before you begin, estimate how many of each number 0 to 9 you expect to get.

Count up your results and give them in a table. (The frequency is the number of times that number occurs.)

Now add up the frequencies of the odd numbers.

Find the fraction $\dfrac{\text{number of odd numbers}}{\text{total number of numbers}}$ as a

decimal to 2 decimal places.

From your results, what value would you give for the probability that a number picked at random from the numbers 0 to 9 is odd?

number	frequency
0	
1	
2	
3	
4	
5	
6	
7	
8	
9	

6 Instead of tossing coins again, use the results of question 1 in pairs, as if you had tossed two coins together, so that the possible results are *HH, HT, TH, TT*.

If you had 200 single results you will have 100 results for pairs. Count the number of heads in each pair and put your results on a tally chart. Before you begin estimate how many of each you will get.

heads	tally marks	frequency (f)
0		
1		
2		
		100

What is the most likely result? What are your estimates for the probabilities of 0 heads, 1 head, 2 heads?

7   Use a set of dominoes going up to double six. (If you have no dominoes, label cards 0–0, 0–1, up to 0–6; then 1–1, 1–2, up to 1–6; then 2–2, etc, ending 6–6. There are 28 cards altogether.)

Pick out a domino at random and record the total score. Replace and repeat 200 times. The scores range from 0 to 12. Make a tally chart of the results.

What is the estimated probability of getting a score of 6 if a domino is picked at random?

8   Ask as many people as you can on what day of the week their birthday falls this year. Tally the results. What is the estimated probability that if a person is chosen at random, his/her birthday is on a Saturday?

10. **For the Computer Programmer**

If you have the use of a computer at home or at school, and have learnt how to make programs for it, then you may like to make some programs to link with mathematical ideas.

If you are a beginner, start with simple programs. e.g. You could make a program to improve your mental arithmetic.

Get the computer to display $\boxed{A \times B =}$, where A and B are random numbers between 1 and 12. You input the answer. The computer checks whether the answer equals $A \times B$ and tells you whether you are right or wrong. Then you can improve the program so that a score is kept of how many you get right, or by adding a time limit within which you must answer, or by changing $\times$ to $+$ or $-$ in a random order.

Having made one program you will then think of ideas for other programs. Keep the listings of all programs. As your skill develops you may be able to improve your earlier work.

Here are some suggestions for programs linking with the work of previous chapters:

1   To test whether any number is a prime number.
2   To find all prime numbers up to a fixed number.
3   To find the prime factors of any number.
4   To find all the factors of any number.
5   To draw a bar chart for given data.
6   To draw a straight line graph for given data.
7   To make a simple questionnaire and summarise the results.
8   To plot shapes and reflections or rotations of these shapes.

About Chapters 6 to 10

The Arithmetic is continued with Decimals and the Metric System.

There is a chapter on Probability, which is an interesting branch of Mathematics. You will understand it better if you do some of the experimental work first (from exercise A5), so try to find time for this, even if it is not part of your examination.

Further easy Geometry, on lines and triangles, comes in Chapter 9.

In Chapter 10 are the basic ideas of Algebra, together with the use of directed numbers.

As before, you will find a more challenging exercise at the end of each chapter, and a Miscellaneous Section B after Chapter 10.

6 Decimals

In the number 234.567 the figure 5 represents five-tenths because it is in the first decimal place, the 6 represents six-hundredths and the 7 represents seven-thousandths. It is usual to write a nought before the decimal point if there is no other number there, e.g. 0.51, not just .51, and 0.02, not just .02.

Addition, subtraction, easy multiplication and division

When adding, subtracting, or when multiplying or dividing by whole numbers, keep the figures in their correct positions relative to the decimal point.

Examples

1. $1.5 + 14.83$

$$\begin{array}{r} 1.5 \\ 14.83 \\ \hline 16.33 \end{array}$$

2. $12.1 - 3.02$

$$\begin{array}{r} 12.10 \\ 3.02 \\ \hline 9.08 \end{array}$$

3. 12.6×4

$$\begin{array}{r} 12.6 \\ 4 \\ \hline 50.4 \end{array}$$

4. $27.6 \div 8$

$$\begin{array}{r} 8)\overline{27.60} \\ \hline 3.45 \end{array}$$

Powers of 10

When multiplying by 10, 100, 1000, . . . the numbers grow larger, so the figures move upwards (to the left), 1, 2, 3, . . . places, assuming that the decimal point is fixed. Add 0's to fill any empty places between the figures and the decimal point.

Example 5

$$2.56 \times 10 = 25.6$$
$$3.5 \times 100 = 350$$
$$0.0041 \times 1000 = 4.1$$

When dividing by 10, 100, 1000, . . . the numbers become smaller, so the figures move downwards (to the right), 1, 2, 3, . . . places, assuming that the decimal point is fixed. Add 0's to fill any empty places between the decimal point and the figures.

Example 6

$$31.8 \div 10 = 3.18$$
$$23 \div 100 = 0.23$$
$$5.6 \div 1000 = 0.0056$$

To multiply by 20, multiply by 10 and then multiply that answer by 2. To divide by 20, divide by 10 and then divide that answer by 2.

Example 7

$$2.89 \times 20 = 28.9 \times 2 = 57.8$$
$$4.54 \div 20 = 0.454 \div 2 = 0.227$$

Multiplication

To multiply two (or more) decimal numbers, first ignore the decimal points and multiply, then restore the decimals in the answer keeping as many decimal places in the answer as there were altogether in the question.

Example 8

2.31×0.7 (3 decimal places altogether)
$(231 \times 7 = 1617)$
$2.31 \times 0.7 = 1.617$ (restoring 3 decimal places)

Example 9

0.004×0.3 (4 decimal places)
$(4 \times 3 = 12)$
$0.004 \times 0.3 = 0.0012$ (including two 0's to restore 4 decimal places)

Division

Instead of dividing by a decimal, multiply both numerator and denominator by 10, 100, 1000, . . . as necessary, to make the denominator into a whole number.

Example 10

$$0.07 \div 0.2 = \frac{0.07}{0.2} = \frac{0.7}{2}$$ (multiplying both numerator and denominator by 10 to make 0.2 into 2)

$$= 0.35$$

Example 11

$$3.6 \div 0.04 = \frac{3.6}{0.04} = \frac{360}{4}$$ (multiplying both numerator and denominator by 100 to make 0.04 into 4)

$$= 90$$

If the division is not exact, it will be necessary to stop after a suitable number of decimal places.

Example 12

Find the value of 24 ÷ 7, correct to 2 decimal places.

7)24.000
  3.428

Since the figure in the 3rd decimal place is 8, the figure in the 2nd decimal place must be corrected up from 2 to 3.

24 ÷ 7 = 3.43, correct to 2 decimal places.

The rule for decimal places is:
Work to one more place than you need. If this extra figure is 5 or more, add 1 to the final figure of your answer.

Example 13

3.2976	= 3.3	to 1 decimal place
	= 3.30	to 2 decimal places
0.8692	= 0.9	to 1 decimal place
	= 0.87	to 2 decimal places
0.0827	= 0.1	to 1 decimal place
	= 0.08	to 2 decimal places

Decimals in order of size

To compare 0.56 and 0.6, write 0.6 as 0.60 so that both numbers have the same number of decimal places.
Then 0.56 is 5 tenths and 6 hundredths, which is 56 hundredths, and 0.60 is 60 hundredths.
0.56 is smaller than 0.6.

To compare 0.24 and 0.231 write 0.24 as 0.240.
Then 0.240 is 240 thousandths, and 0.231 is 231 thousandths.
0.231 is smaller than 0.24.

To compare 0.77, 0.769 and 0.7, write all three numbers with 3 decimal places.
0.77 = 0.770 and this is 770 thousandths.
0.769 is 769 thousandths.
0.7 = 0.700 and this is 700 thousandths.
In order of size, smallest first, the numbers are 0.7, 0.769, 0.77.

Use of a calculator

A calculator will save you time in doing routine calculations but do not use it for simple arithmetic which you can do more quickly in your head. You can use it for the functions addition, subtraction, multiplication and division, and there may be other function keys.

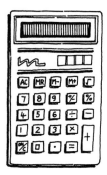

If you are using your calculator for division, and the answer is not exact, then do not write down all the figures which are shown on your calculator. Make a sensible approximation, depending on the question and the accuracy of the original data. For instance, if the question concerns money, decide whether you want an answer correct to the nearest £ or to the nearest penny. If the question concerns length, decide whether you want an answer correct to the nearest metre, cm or mm.

To convert fractions into decimals

$\frac{3}{5}$ means $3 \div 5$ so you can do this calculation on your calculator, getting 0.6.

$\frac{5}{7}$ means $5 \div 7$ so you can do this calculation on your calculator.
The result is 0.7142... so you must correct this to a sensible number of decimal places. If you need 2 decimal places, the next figure (in the 3rd decimal place) is 4 so you do not correct up.
$\frac{5}{7} = 0.71$, correct to 2 decimal places.

$\frac{7}{9} = 0.7777...$
The figure in the 3rd decimal place is 7 so you correct up the 2nd decimal place from 7 to 8.
$\frac{7}{9} = 0.78$, correct to 2 decimal places.

It is useful to turn fractions into decimals if you need to compare their sizes.

Example 14

Write $3\frac{3}{8}$, $3\frac{1}{3}$, $3\frac{2}{5}$ in order of size.

$3\frac{3}{8} = 3.375$
$3\frac{1}{3} = 3.333...$
$3\frac{2}{5} = 3.4$
In order of size, smallest first, they are $3\frac{1}{3}$, $3\frac{3}{8}$, $3\frac{2}{5}$.

Checking calculator answers

It is easy to get a wrong answer from a calculator by pressing the wrong keys, so look at the answer and see if it seems right.

You could also do the calculation twice, possibly entering the numbers in reverse order, to see if you get the same result.

Check the size of the answer

$5813 + 1967$
The numbers are approximately 6000 and 2000.
The answer should be approximately $6000 + 2000 = 8000$.
(The exact answer is 7780.)

5813×2
The answer should be approximately $6000 \times 2 = 12\,000$.
(The exact answer is 11 626.)

$5813 - 1967$
The answer should be approximately $6000 - 2000 = 4000$.
(The exact answer is 3846.)

$5813 \div 2$
The answer should be approximately $6000 \div 2 = 3000$
(The exact answer is 2906.5.)

Check the units figure

$5813 + 1967$
The unit figures are 3 and 7.
$3 + 7 = 10$ so the units figure in the answer is 0.
(The answer is 7780.)

13×67
$3 \times 7 = 21$ so the units figure in the answer is 1.
(The answer is 871.)

$5813 - 1967$
You cannot use $3 - 7$ so use $13 - 7 = 6$ and the units figure in the answer is 6.
(The answer is 3846.)

(You cannot do a similar check for division.)

Check by doing the reverse operation

To check $5813 - 1967 = 3846$, do the calculation $3846 + 1967$ and you will get 5813.
To check $5813 \div 2 = 2906.5$, do the calculation 2906.5×2 and you will get 5813.
To check $\sqrt{121} = 11$, do the calculation 11×11 and you will get 121.

Money

Since there are 100 pence in £1, our money calculations use the decimal system.

£2 and 48 pence is £2.48
£3 and 5 pence is £3.05
£3 and 50 pence is £3.50. On a calculator this may be recorded as 3.5   Remember
this means £3.50, not £3.05.

Examples

15   **Addition**   £2.84 + £3.96
      £
      2.84
      3.96
      6.80   Answer £6.80.   (On a calculator this will be recorded as 6.8)

16   **Subtraction**   £10 − £7.56

      £
      10.00
      7.56
      2.44   Answer £2.44

(On a calculator there is no need to enter 10.00 for £10.00.   10 will do.)

17   **Multiplication**   £3.75 × 8

      £
      3.75
      8
      30.00   Answer £30 or £30.00 (whichever is more appropriate).
               (A calculator will just show 30)

18   **Division**   £75 ÷ 6

      £
      6) 75.0
      12.5   Answer £12.50
              (A calculator will just show 12.5)

19   **Division**   How many books at £5.60 can bought for £50?

      This is £50 ÷ £5.60
      On your calculator do 50 ÷ 5.6
      The answer is 8.92...   showing that 8 books can be bought and there is some
      money left over.
      To find how much is left, multiply £5.60 by 8 and subtract the total from £50.
      50 − (8 × 5.6) = 5.2, so there is £5.20 left.

Amounts to the nearest penny

If you are working in pence,
29.3 pence = 29 p, to the nearest penny.
12.62 pence = 13 p, to the nearest penny.
(If the figure in the 1st decimal place is 5 or more, round up to the next penny.)

If you are working in £'s,
£3.776 = £3.78, to the nearest penny.
£2.494 = £2.49, to the nearest penny.
(The figures in the first two decimal places give the pence. If the figure in the 3rd decimal place is 5 or more, round the pence up to the next penny.)

(There are more details about using a calculator in Chapter 25.)

Approximations and estimations

When you go shopping, it is useful to make an approximate calculation of any bill so that you can see if you have enough money, and you can check that you do not get the wrong change.
For example, in a shop suppose you select 3 articles at £1.99 each, 2 at £2.95 each and 1 at £4.90. Before you go to the cash desk you could do an approximate calculation to see if you had enough money to pay for them. It is nearly 3 at £2, 2 at £3 and 1 at £5 so you would need nearly £17. You also expect to get just over £3 in change if you pay with a £20 note.
(When the exact amount is shown on the till you can check your exact change.)

Exercise 6.1

Try to do questions 1 to 9 without using your calculator, then use your calculator to check your answers.

1.	1	$1.32 + 2.5 + 3.79$	2.	1	$21.03 - 0.07$
	2	$5.87 + 1.03 + 0.1$		2	$7.92 - 0.97$
	3	$0.4 + 0.08 + 0.15$		3	$0.5 - 0.13$
	4	$9.99 + 0.03$		4	$10 - 0.91$
	5	$2.05 + 4.93 + 0.88$		5	$5.82 + 2.19 - 3.13$
3.	1	3.87×4	4.	4	$3.88 \div 4$
	2	0.05×12		2	$0.056 \div 8$
	3	0.8×7		3	$0.8 \div 5$
	4	3.14×3		4	$19.8 \div 9$
	5	1.92×5		5	$35.4 \div 6$

5. Write as decimals

   1 $\frac{3}{4}$ **2** $\frac{2}{5}$ **3** $\frac{7}{10}$ **4** $\frac{37}{100}$ **5** $\frac{3}{5}$

6. **1** 1.32×10 7. **1** $3.79 \div 10$

   2 2.5×100 **2** $0.15 \div 100$

   3 1.03×1000 **3** $21.3 \div 1000$

   4 0.027×100 **4** $3.1 \div 1000$

   5 3.1×20 **5** $3.4 \div 20$

8. **1** 0.8×0.09

   2 0.05×0.06

   3 0.12×0.1

   4 0.9×0.7

   5 0.04×0.5

9. **1** If $314 \times 28 = 8792$, find 3.14×2.8

   2 If $57 \times 14 = 798$, find 0.57×0.14

   3 If $218 \times 91 = 19\,838$, find 21.8×9.1

   4 If $15 \times 16 = 240$, find 1.5×0.16

   5 If $31 \times 41 = 1271$, find 0.31×0.0041

10. **1** $15.6 \div 0.4$

   2 $2.49 \div 0.03$

   3 $21.7 \div 0.7$

   4 $270 \div 0.9$

   5 $0.032 \div 0.04$

11. Find the values of the following, correct to 2 decimal places.

   1 $20 \div 7$

   2 $15.5 \div 0.3$

   3 $0.052 \div 0.6$

   4 $8.74 \div 9$

   5 $0.91 \div 0.8$

12. Write these fractions as decimals, correct to 2 decimal places.

   1 $\frac{2}{3}$ **2** $\frac{5}{7}$ **3** $\frac{4}{9}$ **4** $\frac{1}{6}$ **5** $\frac{8}{11}$

13. Write these numbers correct to 2 decimal places.

    1 29.7122   **2** 1.62815   **3** 202.9157   **4** 4.6798   **5** 0.03527

14. Write these numbers in order of size, smallest first.

    0.8,   0.75,   0.81,   0.7,   0.778

15. Write these numbers in order of size, smallest first.

    62.5,   63.7,   60.9   62.49,   63.72

16. By using approximate values, estimate answers for these questions.

    1 3.99×5.01 **4** $29.12 \div 2.9$

    2 $17.82 \div 5.82$ **5** 395×0.103

    3 3.9^2

17. Use your calculator to find answers to question 16, correct to the nearest whole number.

18. Use your calculator to find answers to the following, correct to the nearest whole number.

    1 $2 \times 3.14 \times 17$ **4** $\dfrac{3.14 \times 78.2}{22.4 - 15.5}$

    2 $\dfrac{219}{0.7 \times 11}$ **5** $7.36^2 - 2.64^2$

    3 $(81.7 + 1.52) \div 6.28$

19. Mrs Martin spent £6.36 on meat and £3.84 on vegetables. How much was this altogether? What change did she get from a £20 note?

20. What is the price of a bar of chocolate if 9 of them cost £1.80?

21. How many 18 p stamps can be bought for £10, and how much change is there?

22. Petrol costs 175.4 p per gallon. What is the cost of 9 gallons, to the nearest penny?

23. Mrs Rija buys 12 yards of curtain material at £4.65 per yard. What is the total cost?

Exercise 6.2

1. Divide 1720 by 0.8.

2. What is the square of 1.2?

3. Simplify $0.1 \times 0.2 \times 0.3$.

4. 0.035×100.

5. Express $\frac{5}{8}$ as an exact decimal.

6. Subtract 0.006 from 0.06.

7. Find the exact value of $4.2752 \div 0.4$.

8. Find the exact value of $\dfrac{1.4 \times 0.05}{0.07}$.

9. Write these numbers in order of size, smallest first.

   0.35,   0.3,   0.299

10. If $A = 5.14$, $B = 3.709$ and $C = 13.3$, find

    1 $A + B + C$ **2** $A \div 100$ **3** $10 \times (C - A)$

11. Write down any even number between 1 and 11. Add 1.83 and multiply the total by 5. Now subtract 10.9 and then divide by 10. Add 0.675 and double the result. Subtract the number you started with. What is your answer?

12. Express 9876.524 correct to

    1 the nearest whole number,

    2 2 decimal places.

13. By turning these fractions into decimals, or otherwise, write them in order of size, smallest first.

    $\frac{7}{10}$, $\frac{3}{4}$, $\frac{5}{6}$, $\frac{5}{8}$, $\frac{7}{9}$.

14. Mrs Sharples wants to buy 2 curtains size 108 by 66, and 4 curtains size 54 by 46. (The measurements are in inches.)

    1 Show how she can find a quick estimate of the cost, and give the estimated total.

    2 Use your calculator, or another method, to find the exact cost.

Very good value! Price per pair			
54 × 46	£29.99	54 × 66	£49.99
72 × 46	£42.99	72 × 66	£59.99
90 × 46	£49.99	90 × 66	£74.99
108 × 46	£59.99	108 × 66	£89.99
54 × 90	£68.99	90 × 90	£99.99
72 × 90	£86.99	108 × 90	£124.99

Curtains Special Offer

15. A shop's takings during the week were Monday £591.17, Tuesday £629.80, Wednesday £212.14, Thursday £859.75, Friday £905.22, Saturday £1028.60. What were the total takings for the week, to the nearest £1? The shopkeeper was hoping for total takings of £5000. How many £'s was he short of his target?

16. 13 people win a competition and share the prize money of £500 equally. How much do they each get, to the nearest penny?

17. Mr Rigby has a £20 voucher to spend at the garden centre. He decides to buy 4 bushes for £1.85 each and spend the rest on bulbs at 21 p each. How many bulbs can he buy?

PUZZLES

18. How many squares are there in this figure, and how many contain the dot?

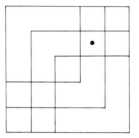

19. Copy the diagram and starting in the top left-hand square, draw a continuous line passing through each square once only, so that the sum of the numbers in each group of four squares is 24.

6	6	3	15	5	3
6	9	3	10	6	3
3	3	3	8	8	5
5	10	4	2	3	10
3	6	11	2	3	9
5	8	4	7	10	9

20. If it takes 5 men 5 days to plough 5 fields, how long does it take 1 man to plough 1 field, working at the same rate?

21. Mine cost 52p, my neighbour's cost 26p and I got some for my friend who lives at the far end of the road, and they cost 78p. What was I buying in the hardware shop?

22. Nine people, Andrew, Bilkish, Craig, Dhiren, Edith, Faruk, Graham, Helen and Iqbal share a prize of £450 amongst themselves.
Bilkish gets £1 more than Andrew, Craig gets £1 more than Bilkish, Dhiren gets £1 more than Craig, and so on. How much does Iqbal get?

7 Probability

There is an introduction to this chapter in exercise A5, question 9.

Probability or chance is the likelihood of an event happening.
A probability of 0 means that there is no chance of the event happening.
A probability of 1 means that it is certain that the event will happen.
A probability of $\frac{1}{2}$ means that there is a 50-50 chance of the event happening. In the long run, $\frac{1}{2}$ of the trials will give successful results.
A probability of $\frac{2}{3}$ means that in the long run $\frac{2}{3}$ of the trials will give successful results.
The nearer the value of the probability is to 1, the more chance there is of a successful outcome.
The nearer the value of the probability is to 0, the less chance there is of a successful outcome.

If a trial has a number of **equally likely outcomes** and of these certain ones are successful then

$$\text{Probability (or chance) of a successful outcome} = \frac{\text{number of successful outcomes}}{\text{total possible outcomes}} = \frac{s}{n}$$

The result can be expressed as a fraction in its lowest terms, or as a decimal.

Example 1

Find the probability of a tossed coin showing heads.

There are 2 equally likely outcomes, heads or tails, and of these 1 outcome, heads, is successful.

Probability of heads $= \dfrac{s}{n} = \dfrac{1}{2}$

Example 2

Find the probability of a number picked at random from the numbers 1 to 10 being divisible by 4.

There are ten equally likely outcomes of which two (4 and 8) are successful.

Probability of picking a number divisible by $4 = \dfrac{s}{n} = \dfrac{2}{10} = \dfrac{1}{5}$

Example 3

In a pack of 52 cards one card is drawn at random. What is the probability that it is **1** a heart   **2** an ace   **3** an ace or a heart?

1 P(heart) $= \frac{13}{52} = \frac{1}{4}$ (P(heart) means 'probability of a heart'.)

2 P(ace) $= \frac{4}{52} = \frac{1}{13}$

3 There are 13 hearts, including the ace, and the other 3 aces, making 16 successful outcomes altogether.

$$\text{P(ace or heart)} = \frac{s}{n} = \frac{16}{52} = \frac{4}{13}$$

Use of Sample spaces

Example 4

Five discs numbered 1 to 5 are placed in a bag and one is drawn out at random and not replaced. A second disc is then drawn out at random.

What is the probability that the second disc has a number higher by at least 2 than the first disc?

Set down the possible equally likely results in a diagram called a sample space.

		1st disc				
		1	2	3	4	5
2nd disc	1		.	.	.	.
	2	.		.	.	.
	3	.	.		.	.
	4	.	(a)	.		.
	5	.	.	.	.	

A dot represents one of the equally likely outcomes, e.g. dot (a) represents the outcome that the first disc is 2 and the second disc is 4. There are 20 dots so there are 20 equally likely outcomes. (It might be more useful to write the actual outcomes e.g. (2, 4), or the total score, instead of just dots.)

We will mark in some way all the outcomes where the second disc has a number higher by at least 2 than the first disc.

(Normally this would go on the original diagram but here to make it clearer we have a new diagram.)

		1st disc				
		1	2	3	4	5
2nd disc	1		.	.	.	.
	2	.		.	.	.
	3	⊡	.		.	.
	4	⊡	⊡	.		.
	5	⊡	⊡	⊡	.	

There are 6 successful outcomes.
The probability that the 2nd disc has a number higher by at least 2 than the first

$$\text{disc} = \frac{s}{n} = \frac{6}{20} = 0.3$$

⊡ represents a successful outcome.

Example 5

Doing the same experiment as in example 4, what is the probability that the total of the two numbers is 6?

Here is the sample space, with the totals shown. Those showing a total of 6 have been circled.
There are 4 successful outcomes.
The probability that the total of the two numbers is 6 is $\dfrac{s}{n} = \dfrac{4}{20} = 0.2$

		1st disc				
		1	2	3	4	5
	1		3	4	5	⑥
2nd	2	3		5	⑥	7
disc	3	4	5		7	8
	4	5	⑥	7		9
	5	⑥	7	8	9	

◯ represents a successful outcome.

If the probability of an event happening is p, then the probability of it not happening is $1 - p$.
e.g. If the probability of an event happening is $\frac{4}{5}$, then the probability of it not happening is $1 - \frac{4}{5} = \frac{1}{5}$.

A coin or die has no memory so the probabilities are not affected by any previous tosses. Suppose a fairly-tossed coin has come down heads 5 times in succession. The 6th toss is not affected by the previous results and the probability of it being a head is still $\frac{1}{2}$.

Exercise 7.1

1. A fair die is thrown once. What is the probability of getting

    1 a three,
    2 a square number?

2. 20 discs, numbered from 1 to 20, are placed in a bag and one is drawn out at random. What is the probability of getting a disc with

    1 a number greater than 15,
    2 a number which includes the digit 1,
    3 a number which is divisible by 3?

3. In a fairground game a pointer is spun and
    you win the amount shown in the sector where
    it comes to rest. Assuming that the pointer is
    equally likely to come to rest in any sector,
    what is the probability that

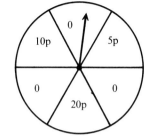

    1 you win some money,
    2 you win 20 p?

4. In a tombola game, $\frac{7}{8}$ of the counters are blank. The rest have a number on them
    and they win a prize. If you take a counter out of the drum at random what is
    the probability that you win a prize?

5. If you choose a card at random from a pack of 52 playing-cards, what is the
    probability that it is

    1 an ace,
    2 a diamond,
    3 a red card with an even number?

6. A letter is chosen at random from the 11 letters of the word MATHEMATICS.
    What is the probability that it is

    1 the letter M,
    2 a vowel,
    3 a letter from the second half of the alphabet?

7. The students in a school club belong to two forms 5X and 5Y.

	5X	5Y
girls	12	16
boys	8	14

    If from this club one member is chosen at random, what
    is the probability that it is

    1 a boy,
    2 a member of 5Y,
    3 a girl from 5X?
    4 If a girl has to be chosen at random what is the
           probability that she is from 5X?

8. In a pack of playing-cards, the 2 of diamonds and the 2 of hearts have been removed. If you choose a card at random from the remaining cards, what is the probability that it is

   1 a diamond,
   2 a two,
   3 the 2 of diamonds?

9. There are 7 beads in a bag, 4 red, 1 white, 2 blue. One is taken out at random and replaced, and then another one is taken out. What is the probability that

   1 the 1st one is red,
   2 the 2nd one is blue?

10. 60 raffle tickets are sold from books of three different colours, blue, green and pink. 20 blue ones and 24 green ones are sold. What is the probability that the winning ticket is pink?

11. A bag contains 120 coloured discs, red, yellow and blue. If one is drawn out without looking, the probability of getting a yellow one is $\frac{1}{3}$ and the probability of getting a blue one is $\frac{1}{2}$.

   1 How many yellow discs are there?
   2 How many blue discs are there?
   3 What is the probability of getting a red disc?

12. Farida can go home from work by train or by bus. The probability that she will go home by train is 0.7. What is the probability that she will go home by bus?

13. In a dice game, you are trying to throw a six, because you cannot start until you get a six. You have already thrown five times, unsuccessfully. What is the probability that on the next throw you will get a six?

14. In Mr Wright's job if extra work comes in during the afternoon he has to work late. The probability that he has to work late on any one evening is $\frac{1}{8}$. What is the probability that he will not have to work late this Friday?

15. Ronnie's bus ticket always has a different 4-figure number on it.
    What is the probability that the number on this morning's ticket has a unit figure of 7?

16. A large batch of red tulip bulbs has been accidentally mixed with some yellow tulip bulbs, so that the probability of picking a red bulb is $\frac{2}{3}$.
    What is the probability of picking a yellow one?

17. A coin is tossed three times in succession. Here are some of the possible outcomes where H stands for head and T for tail.
    HHH, HHT, HTH, . . .
    Copy these and write down the other outcomes.
    What is the probability of getting at least one head?

18. Two dice are thrown together. Copy and complete the sample space showing the total scores.

    1 List in a table the probability of scoring each total from 2 to 12.
    2 What is the most likely total score?

		1st die					
		1	2	3	4	5	6
2nd die	1	2	3	4	.	.	.
	2	3	.	.	.	.	.
	3	.	.	.	.	.	.
	4	.	.	.	.	.	.
	5	.	.	.	.	.	.
	6	.	.	.	.	.	.

Score	2	3	4	5	6	7	8	9	10	11	12
Probability	$\frac{1}{36}$										

19. The probability of Ernie winning a race is 0.21, the probability of Francis winning the race is 0.25 and the probability of Graham winning the race is 0.3.

    1 Who is the most likely of the 3 boys to win it?
    2 What is the probability that none of them will win it?

Exercise 7.2.

1. 120 discs numbered 1 to 120 are placed in a bag and one is drawn out at random. What is the probability of getting a disc with a number which is a square number?

2. In a bag there are 5 red sweets and 3 green ones.

    1 If a sweet is picked out at random what is the probability that it is red?
    2 If the first sweet is red, and it is not replaced, what is the probability that if a second sweet is picked out, it is also red?

3. The caretaker has 5 keys of a similar type on a key-ring. When he has to unlock a particular door, if instead of looking at the numbers on the keys, he picks a key at random to try, what is the probability that it is the correct key?
If it is not the correct one, he then picks a key at random from the remaining ones. What is the probability that this is the correct key?

4. A regular triangular pyramid (tetrahedron) has its four faces numbered 1, 2, 3, 4 and it is used as a die by counting as the score the number on the bottom face.

   Copy and complete a sample space diagram showing the outcomes when this die is thown twice.

   Find the probability that

   1   in each of the two throws the score is 4,
   2   in the two throws the sum of the scores is 4,
   3   in the two throws the product of the scores is 4.

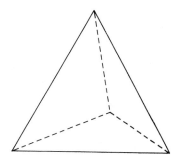

		1st throw			
		1	2	3	4
	1	1, 1	2, 1	.	.
2nd	2	1, 2	2, 2	.	.
throw	3	1, 3	.	.	.
	4	.	.	.	.

5. The following numbers were written on pieces of paper, put into a box and drawn out at random.

   10,   13,   16,   17,   21,   30,   36,   49,   50,   59,   60.

   What is the probability that a number drawn out

   1   is even,
   2   is a square number,
   3   is a prime number?
   4   If an odd number is drawn out and not replaced, what is the probability of drawing out a second odd number?

6. On this spinner, the probability of getting any number from 1 to 5 is equally likely.

   Show in a sample space diagram the results when the spinner is spun twice.

   1   If Betty spins twice, what is the probability that she scores a 5 and then a 4?
   2   What is the probability that she scores the same number twice in succession?

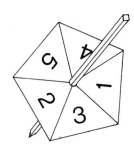

7. A pack of 52 cards is split into two piles with the Kings, Queens and Jacks in the first pile and the rest of the cards in the second pile.

   1 If a card is drawn at random from the 1st pile what is the probability that it is the Queen of hearts?
   2 If a card is drawn at random from the 2nd pile what is the probability that it is an ace?

8. A box contains 2 red, 3 yellow and 5 green sweets. One is taken out at random, and eaten. A second sweet is then taken out.

   1 If the 1st sweet was green, what is the probability that the 2nd sweet is also green?
   2 If the 1st sweet was not red, what is the probability that the 2nd sweet is red?

9. Two dice are thrown together. Make a sample space diagram of the equally likely results. What is the probability
   1 that the sum of the two numbers is greater than 10,
   2 that the sum of the two numbers is 7,
   3 of a double (the two dice showing the same number),
   4 of both dice showing numbers less than 3?

10. There are six cards numbered 1 to 6. One card is selected at random and not replaced, and then a second card is selected. Make a sample space diagram of the equally likely results. What is the probability
    1 that the sum of the two numbers is greater than 10,
    2 that the sum of the two numbers is 7,
    3 that the product of the two numbers is odd?

11. Two cards are drawn from a pack of 52 cards. The first card is a diamond. What is the probability that the second card is also a diamond,
    1 if the 1st card is replaced before the 2nd card is drawn,
    2 if the 1st card is not replaced before the 2nd card is drawn?

12. Write down a list of all possible results if a coin is tossed 4 times in succession, e.g. *HHHH, HTHH, HHHT, . . .*
    What is the probability of getting
    1 4 heads,
    2 3 or more tails,
    3 exactly 2 heads and 2 tails?

PUZZLES

23. If it takes a clock 6 seconds to strike 6, how long does it take to strike 12?

24. A Cross-figure

Across

Copy this diagram and fill in the answers on your copy.

1 Number of miles I can travel in 24 minutes at 60 m.p.h.
3 Number of diagonals of a parallelogram.
4 Number of mm in 1 cm.
5 Three angles of a quadrilateral are 16°, 27° and 150°. What is the 4th angle?
7 $\sqrt{\text{LXIV}}$
8 75% of (11 across) − 40% of (4 across)
9 $(1\frac{3}{4} - 1\frac{1}{3}) \times 7.2$
10 The base of a triangle, in cm, if its height is 8 cm and its area is 20 cm^2.
11 A is south-west of C, B is on a bearing of 273° from C. What is the size of angle ACB, in degrees?
12 Christine bought 2 tins of meat at 47 p each. How much change, in pence, did she get from £1?
13 Number of days in a leap year + number of degrees in the angles of a triangle − number of sides of a triangle.
15 $3^2 + 4^2 + 5^2$
16 If the numbers 4 to 12 are placed in a magic square so that each row, column and diagonal add up to 24, what is the number in the centre square?
17 An article cost £1.80 plus tax at 15%. What was the tax, in pence?

Down

1 If 5 pumps all working together can empty the water out of a tank in 36 minutes, how long would it take if there were 9 pumps working?
2 A circular running-track has diameter 70 yards. How many times must an athlete run round it to run $\frac{1}{2}$ mile? (Take π as $\frac{22}{7}$)
3 In a cuboid, number of faces + number of edges + number of vertices.
4 If 'THE LOVELY FIRE' is coded as 'pug cksgcz bang', decode 'puanpz-basg' and 'babpz-pungg' and write down their product.
5 The next number in the sequence 8, 16, 32, 64.
6 The number of metres in 8 km − the number of cm in 8 metres + the number of articles in 8 score.
8 One number in this sequence is incorrect. What should it be?
1, 8, 27, 64, 125, 216, 333, 512, 729, 1000.
14 A lawn is 12 m long and 8 m wide. There is a path 1 m wide all the way round. How many metres of fencing would be needed to go all round the outer edge of the path?
15 125 equal cubes are placed on the table to form a solid cube. The top and the four side faces of this large cube are then painted red. How many of the original cubes have just one face painted red?
17 Write down any number less than 6. Double it and to the result add 2. Then square the total, subtract 4 and then divide by 4. Divide then by the number you started with, and finally subtract the number you started with. What is your answer?

8 The metric system

Weights and measures in the Metric System

In the metric system the main units are metre (length), gram (weight) and litre (capacity). The main prefixes are milli-($\frac{1}{1000}$), centi-($\frac{1}{100}$) and kilo-(1000).

Length

1000 millimetres (mm) = 1 metre (m)
100 centimetres (cm)   = 1 metre   (so 10 mm = 1 cm)
1000 metres   = 1 kilometre (km)

Weight

1000 milligrams (mg) = 1 gram (g)
100 centigrams (cg) = 1 gram
1000 grams   = 1 kilogram (kg)
1000 kilograms   = 1 tonne

Capacity

1000 millilitres (ml) = 1 litre (l)
100 centilitres (cl) = 1 litre
1000 litres   = 1 kilolitre (kl)

The area and volume tables are derived from the length table.

Area

$100 \, mm^2$ $= 1 \, cm^2$ since $(10 \, mm)^2 = (1 \, cm)^2$
$10\,000 \, cm^2$ $= 1 \, m^2$ since $(100 \, cm)^2 = (1 \, m)^2$
$1\,000\,000 \, m^2$ $= 1 \, km^2$ since $(1000 \, m)^2 = (1 \, km)^2$
(Also $10\,000 \, m^2 = 1$ hectare)

Volume

$1000 \, mm^3$ $= 1 \, cm^3$ since $(10 \, mm)^3 = (1 \, cm)^3$
$1\,000\,000 \, cm^3$ $= 1 \, m^3$ since $(100 \, cm)^3 = (1 \, m)^3$

Volume and Capacity are connected because 1 litre = $1000 \, cm^3$
Volume, weight and capacity are connected because
$1 \, cm^3$ of water weighs 1 g,
1 litre of water weighs 1 kg.

Some approximate comparisons

1 inch	...	$2\frac{1}{2}$ cm	1 cm	...	0.4 inches
1 foot	...	30 cm	1 m	...	40 inches
1 yard	...	0.9 m	1 km	...	$\frac{5}{8}$ mile
1 mile	...	1.6 km	1 kg	...	2.2 lbs
1 lb	...	450 g	1 tonne	...	1 ton
1 gallon	...	$4\frac{1}{2}$ litres	1 litre	...	$1\frac{3}{4}$ pints

Reading numbers on clocks, dials and scales

Example

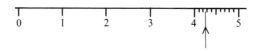

Decide between which two whole numbers the reading lies. This one lies between 4 and 5 so starts 4.

Here is an enlargement of the part of the scale between 4 and 5.
Decide between which two tenths the reading lies. This one lies between 2 and 3 so it is 4.2.
If you have to answer correct to 1 decimal place decide whether it is nearer 2 or 3. This one is nearer 3 so give the answer as 4.3.

If you have to estimate the answer to 2 decimal places, imagine an enlargement of the part of the scale between 4.2 and 4.3. The reading is nearer 4.3 than 4.2 so it is bigger than 4.25. It is approximately 4.27.

Dials on Gas and Electricity Meters

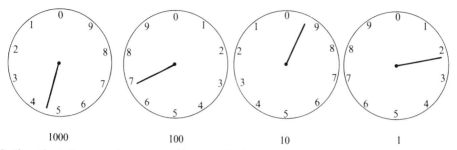

(Notice that the numbers on adjacent dials go in different directions.)

The 1000's figure is between 4 and 5 so the reading is 4000.
The 100's figure is between 6 and 7 so the reading is 600.
The 10's figure is between 9 and 0 so the reading is 90. (The pointer on this dial is turning anticlockwise and the reading has passed 9.)
The units figure is between 2 and 3 so the reading is 2.
The complete reading is 4692.
(There may also be a dial marked $\frac{1}{10}$ which you can ignore.)

Note: In this example you can see that the reading on the 10's dial is 9, and so the pointer will soon go to 0 and start a new revolution. That is why the pointer on the 100's dial is nearly at 7. If you were unable to tell whether its reading was 6 or 7, you could deduce from this that it is still 6, until the 10's pointer reaches 0.

Exercise 8.1

1. How many

    1 mm in 5 cm   **11** cm² in 1 m²

    2 g in 3 kg   **12** degrees in $1\frac{1}{2}$ right angles

    3 pence in £10   **13** minutes in $2\frac{1}{2}$ hours

    4 cm in $\frac{1}{2}$ m   **14** mm in 2 m

    5 days in a year   **15** kg in 3 tonnes

    6 m in 4 km   **16** weeks in a year

    7 hours in 2 days   **17** mm³ in 1 cm³

    8 mg in 6 g   **18** seconds in $\frac{1}{2}$ minute

    9 cm³ in 8 litres   **19** m² in 1 km²

    10 days in 3 weeks   **20** m*l* in 1 litre?

2. **1** How many mm is 80 mm short of 1 metre?

    2 Add together the number of grams in 3 kg, the number of seconds in 4 minutes and the number of mm in 8 cm, then divide the total by the number of pence in £8.30. What is the answer?

    3 A caterer uses 300 g of potatoes per day for each person. Find the cost of providing potatoes for 40 people for 5 days at 25 p per kg.

2. **4** If 40 equal packets weigh 100 kg, what does one weigh?

   5 Equal pieces 20 cm long are cut from a ball of string containing 10 metres. How many pieces can be cut?

3. How many packets of sweets, each containing 110 g, can be made up from $5\frac{1}{2}$ kg of sweets?

4. How many lengths of wood 0.4 m long can be cut from a piece 2.8 m long?

5. 1 stone is 14 lbs. Marie weighs 8 stones 8 lbs. What is her weight in kg, to the nearest kg, taking 1 lb as equivalent to 454 g?

6. The speed limit in a town is 30 miles per hour. What is this in km/hour, taking 1 mile as equivalent to 1.6 km?

7. If a car travels 12 km on a litre of petrol, how much will petrol cost for a journey of 270 km, if the price is 40 p per litre?

8. 500 sheets of paper weigh 3 kg. What is the weight, in g, of 1 sheet? The pile of sheets is 7 cm thick. What is the thickness, in mm, of 1 sheet?

9. Give the readings shown on these instruments.

   1 Weight in kg.

   2 Temperature in °F.

   3 Weighing scale in kg and g   **4** Measuring glass

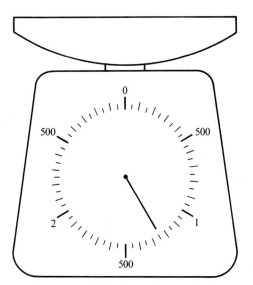

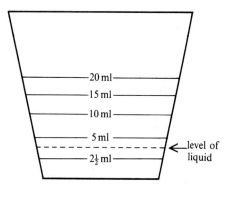

10. Give the readings shown on these meter dials.

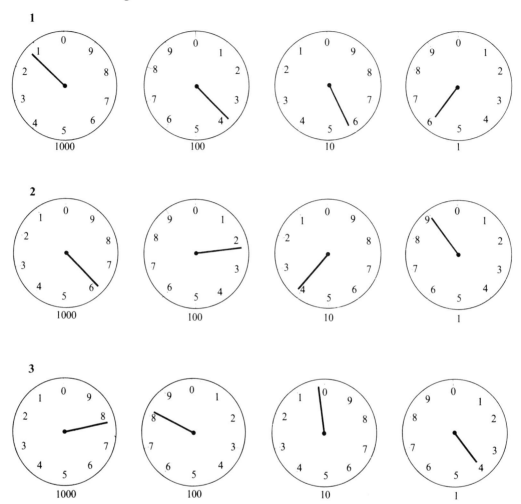

11. Copy and complete this electricity bill.

Meter reading		Units used	Pence per unit	Amount
Present 41527	Previous 40342	— — —	5.4	— — —
			Quarterly charge	£6.50
			Total now due	

12. This distance chart gives distances in km.

Bristol						
299	Dover					
122	400	Exeter				
185	114	277	LONDON			
119	206	208	92	Oxford		
298	568	179	452	402	Penzance	
122	230	169	124	105	349	Southampton

  1 Which two places on the list are 400 km apart?
  2 How far is it from London to Southampton, in km?
  3 How far is it in miles from London to Southampton?
     (1 km = 0.62 miles. Give the answer to the nearest mile.)

Exercise 8.2

1. **1** Write 2380 g in kg   **6** Write 3.1 kg in g

   2 Write 20 cm in m   **7** Write 28 mm in cm

   3 Write 5 litres in ml   **8** Write 512 cm in m

   4 Write 12 cm in mm   **9** Write 3200 cl in litres

   5 Write 2.6 m in cm   **10** Write 0.25 kg in g

2. Equal pieces of ribbon 28 cm long are cut from a strip 5 m long. How many pieces are there, and how many cm are left over?

3. An old knitting pattern for a child's jumper requires 8 oz of wool. How many 50 g balls of wool should Mrs Walsh buy to have enough to knit the jumper? (1 oz = 28 g)

4. Tea is sold in packets of 125 g for 45 p, or packets of 250 g for 85 p. Which size of packet represents the better value for money?

5. The sign shows the price in pence for a gallon
    of petrol. Find the cost of a litre of 2 star
    petrol, if 1 litre is equivalent to 0.22 gallons.
    Give your answer to the nearest penny.

6. Jane has a recipe which gives the quantities in grams. Her old scales, however,
    only give the weight in lbs and ounces. If the recipe uses 350 g of flour, how
    much should she weigh, to the nearest ounce? (1 g = 0.035 oz)

7. Here is a list of costs for Parcel Post.

    1 A parcel weighs 4.7 kg. How much
       does it cost to send it by post if it is
       going a short distance so that it can
       be sent at the Area rate?

    2 How much extra would it have cost
       if it was being sent to a distant
       address, so that it had to go at
       National rate?

    3 Two parcels each weighing 2.7 kg
       are to be sent to the same address.
       (They can go for the Area rate.)
       How much would be saved by tying
       them together to go as one parcel?

Weight in kg (not over)	Area rate	National rate
	£	£
1	1.30	1.50
2	1.70	1.90
3	2.15	2.35
4	2.35	2.55
5	2.55	2.75
6	2.75	2.95

Note that these rates may not be
up-to-date.

8. **Approximations and estimations for a million**. First make a quick estimate, using
    the answers as a guide. Then, if necessary, use your calculator to make a more
    accurate answer.

    1 What is a million?

       A 10 000   **B** 100 000   **C** 1 000 000

       D 10 000 000   **E** 1 000 000 000

    2 What distance is a million mm?

       A 1 m   **B** 10 m   **C** 100 m   **D** 1 km   **E** 10 km

    3 If a million small squares of side 1 cm are put together to make a large
       square, how long is each side of the large square?

       A 10 cm   **B** 1 m   **C** 10 m   **D** 100 m   **E** 1000 m

    4 If a million small cubes of edge 1 cm are put together to make a large cube,
       how large is each edge of the large cube?

       A 1 m   **B** 10 m   **C** 100 m   **D** 1000 m   **E** 10 000 m

5 What weight is a million grams?

   A 1 kg   **B** 10 kg   **C** 100 kg   **D** 1000 kg   **E** 10 000 kg

6 If a tank holds a million cm³, how many litres is this?

   A 1   **B** 10   **C** 100   **D** 1000   **E** 10 000

7 How long is a million seconds?

   A 1 day   **B** 12 days   **C** 100 days   **D** 3 years   **E** 30 years

8 When was a million days ago (approximately)?

   A 750 B.C. **B** 750 A.D. **C** 1066   **D** 1666   **E** 1815

9 If a million pennies are collected for charity, how much is raised?

   A £100   **B** £1000   **C** £10 000   **D** £100 000   **E** £1 000 000

10 If the million pennies are placed side-by-side along a line, each one touching the next, how long is the line?

   A 100 m   **B** 200 m   **C** 1 km   **D** 10 km   **E** 20 km

9. 1250 cm³ of a liquid weighs 1 kg. What is the weight of 5 litres of the liquid?

10. The distance all round the equator is approximately 24 900 miles. Taking 1 mile as equivalent to 1.61 km, find this distance in kilometres, to the nearest 100 km.

11. The diagram shows a thermometer marked in degrees Celsius and degrees Fahrenheit.

   1 What temperature does the thermometer show in °F, and in °C?

   2 What would be the temperature in °F if it was 35°C?

   3 In cold weather, elderly people are advised to heat their living rooms to 68°F. What is this temperature in °C?

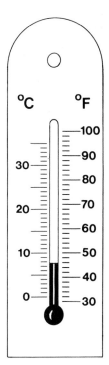

12.

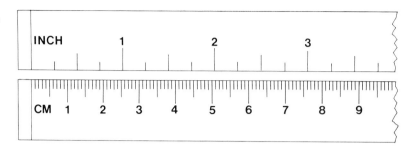

The two rulers show measurements in inches and in centimetres. The top ruler has inches and is divided into quarter inches. The other ruler has centimetres and is divided into millimetres.

1 What measurement in cm is equivalent to $2\frac{3}{4}$ inches?

2 What measurement in inches is equivalent to 3.8 cm?

13. 1 Find the reading on this gas meter.

2 The previous reading was 8350 units. How many units have been used since then?

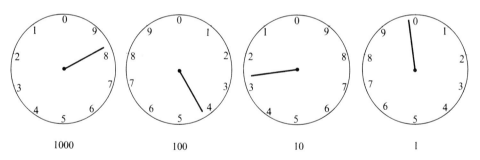

14. Write down the time shown on this clock when it is in the afternoon,

1 in the 12-hour system,
2 in the 24-hour system.

15. Copy and complete this gas bill. (Use the notes below.)

Meter reading		Gas used	Therms	Pence per therm	£
Present	Previous				
5798	5548	. . . (a)	. . . (b)	37	. . . (c)
				Standing charge	9.50
				Amount due	. . . (d)

(a) is the difference in the meter readings
(b) is (a) multiplied by 1.032
(c) is (b) multiplied by the price per therm
(d) is (c) plus the standing charge.

(The amount of heat in the gas being supplied is calculated by the Gas Company and that is why they are using the multiplier 1.032 in this case to calculate the number of therms used.)

PUZZLE

25. In the 'Tower of Hanoi' puzzle, there are 8 discs of different sizes on 1 peg, with two empty pegs.

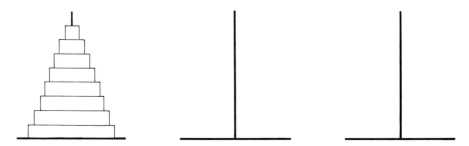

The game is to transfer all the discs to one of the empty pegs.
Only one disc can be moved at a time. A disc can only be placed on an empty peg or onto a larger disc, never onto a smaller one.
Make your own version of this game using circles of cardboard, and see how many moves are needed. You may prefer to discover the pattern of moves by starting with less than 8 discs. Notice the moves of the smallest disc.
The legend has it that there is such a peg with 64 discs on it. At the rate of 1 move per second, how long will it take to move all 64 discs?

9 Lines and triangles

This is the line *AB*

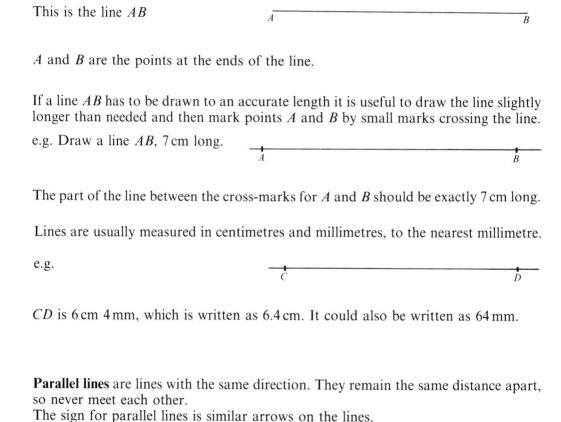

A and B are the points at the ends of the line.

If a line *AB* has to be drawn to an accurate length it is useful to draw the line slightly longer than needed and then mark points *A* and *B* by small marks crossing the line.

e.g. Draw a line *AB*, 7 cm long.

The part of the line between the cross-marks for *A* and *B* should be exactly 7 cm long.

Lines are usually measured in centimetres and millimetres, to the nearest millimetre.

e.g.

CD is 6 cm 4 mm, which is written as 6.4 cm. It could also be written as 64 mm.

Parallel lines are lines with the same direction. They remain the same distance apart, so never meet each other.
The sign for parallel lines is similar arrows on the lines.

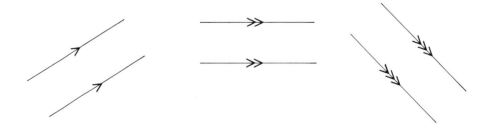

To draw parallel lines with a set-square

Example

Draw a line through C, parallel to AB.

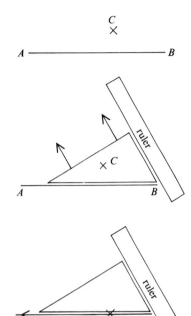

Place the longest side of the set-square on AB so that, if possible, the set-square is placed over C.
Place a ruler along one of the other sides of the set-square.

Keeping the ruler fixed, slide the set-square along the ruler until its longest side passes through C. Draw a line along this edge.

Exercise 9.1

1. Draw a line of length 1 cm, a line of 5 cm and a line of 10 cm. Estimate the lengths of other lines by comparing them with these lengths.

2. Estimate the lengths of the lines AB, CD, EF, GH and check your estimates by measuring them to the nearest mm.

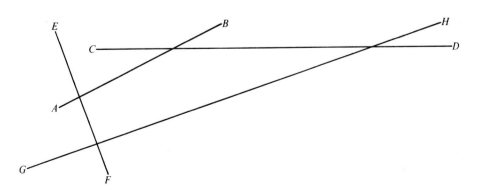

3. Draw a line *AB* 10 cm long.
    Measure an angle of 57° at *A* and
    measure off a length of 6 cm along
    this line to give the point *D*.
    Through *D* draw a line parallel to
    AB.
    Through *B* draw a line parallel to
    AD, and let this line meet the other
    line at *C*.
    Measure *BC*, *DC* and angle *C*.

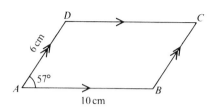

Triangles

Kinds of triangle

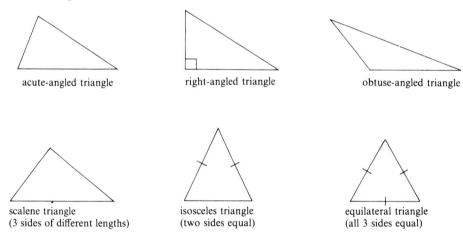

acute-angled triangle

right-angled triangle

obtuse-angled triangle

scalene triangle
(3 sides of different lengths)

isosceles triangle
(two sides equal)

equilateral triangle
(all 3 sides equal)

(The sign for lines of equal length is similar small marks crossing the lines.)

Angle sum of a triangle

The sum of the angles of a triangle is
180°

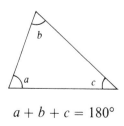

$$a + b + c = 180°$$

Exterior angle of a triangle

If a side is produced, the exterior angle
is equal to the sum of the two opposite
interior angles

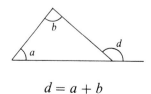

$$d = a + b$$

Isosceles triangle

The angles opposite the equal sides are equal

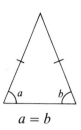

$$a = b$$

Equilateral triangle

All angles are 60°

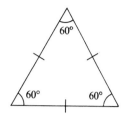

The perimeter of a figure is the total length of all its boundary.

The perimeter of a triangle = the sum of the lengths of its 3 sides.

Example 1 Find the sizes of angles b and c.

$b + c + 42° = 180°$ (sum of angles of a
                                        triangle = 180°)

$b + c = 138°$

$\triangle ABC$ is isosceles, so $b = c$

$b = 69°$
$c = 69°$

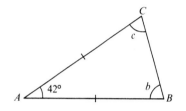

Example 2 Find the sizes of angles d and e.

$d = 73°$ (isosceles triangle,
                                  equal angles)

$e = d + 73°$ (exterior angle of
                                  triangle)

$e = 146°$

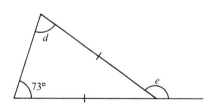

Example 3 Find the perimeter of $\triangle ABC$.

Perimeter $= AB + BC + CA$
               $= (6 + 5 + 9)\,\text{cm}$
               $= 20\,\text{cm}$

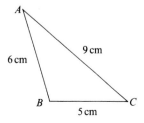

Exercise 9.2

1. Estimate the sizes of the angles in these triangles. Check your estimate by measuring with your protractor. Verify that the sum of the angles is 180°.

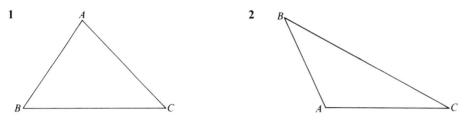

2. Estimate, then measure, the lengths of the sides of the triangles in question 1. Find the perimeters of the triangles.

3. Estimate the sizes of the angles in these isosceles triangles. Check your estimate by measuring with your protractor. Verify that the angles opposite the equal sides are equal.

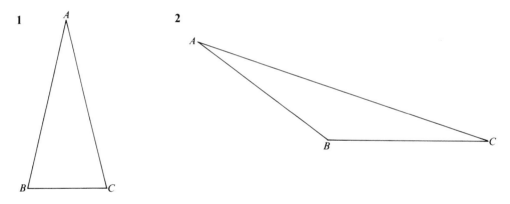

4. Estimate, then measure, the lengths of the sides of the triangles in question 3. Find the perimeters of the triangles.

5. Calculate the sizes of the 3rd angles in these triangles.

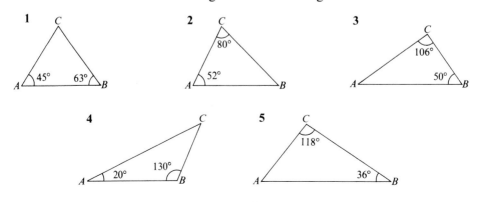

6. Calculate the 3rd angle in these triangles and say whether the triangle is acute-angled, right-angled or obtuse-angled, or if it is isosceles or equilateral.

   1 Two angles are 130°, 36°.   **4** Two angles are 60°, 60°.

   2 Two angles are 72°, 36°.   **5** Two angles are 24°, 36°.

   3 Two angles are 54°, 36°.

7. An isosceles triangle has one axis of symmetry. Sketch the triangles of question 3 or draw them on tracing paper and mark on the diagrams the axes of symmetry.

8. An equilateral triangle has 3 axes of symmetry. Sketch these triangles or draw them on tracing paper and mark on the diagrams the axes of symmetry. They also have rotational symmetry of order 3. On your diagrams mark the points about which there is rotational symmetry.

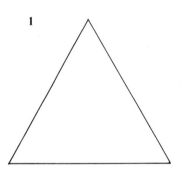

9. Draw a triangle on paper and cut it out. Colour the 3 angles and mark the corner of each, then tear them off. Arrange them together with the points and edges touching. Which diagram shows the result? What does this demonstrate?

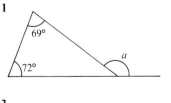

10. Calculate the sizes of the marked angles in these figures.

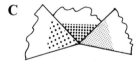

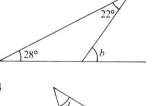

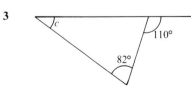

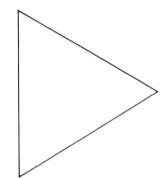

11. Find the sizes of $\angle ACB$ and $\angle DCB$.

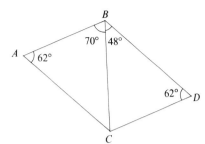

12. **1** Find the sizes of a and b.
     What sort of triangle is it?

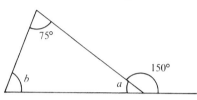

     2 Find the size of angle c.

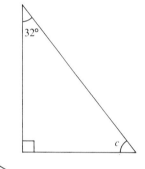

13. Find the sizes of a, b, c.

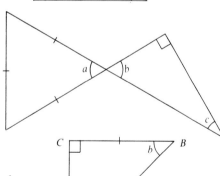

14. $\triangle ABC$ is an isosceles right-angled triangle.
     Find the sizes of a and b.

15. Find the sizes of b and c.
     What sort of triangle is $\triangle ABC$?
     If $AB = 6.8$ cm, what is the perimeter
     of $\triangle ABC$?

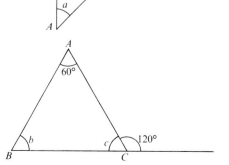

Constructing Triangles

Exercise 9.3

1. **To draw a triangle, given 3 sides**

   Example

   Draw a triangle ABC with $AB = 9$ cm, $BC = 8$ cm and $AC = 7$ cm.

   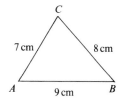

   Draw AB, 9 cm long.
   With compasses, centre A, radius 7 cm, draw an arc.
   With centre B, radius 8 cm, draw an arc to cut the first arc at C.
   Join AC and CB.

   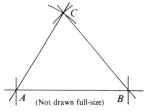

2. **To draw a triangle, given 1 side and 2 angles**

   Example

   Draw a triangle ABC with $AB = 9$ cm, $\angle A = 48°$ and $\angle B = 79°$.

   Draw AB, 9 cm long.
   Measure an angle of 48° at A and an angle of 79° at B. Continue these lines until they meet at C.

   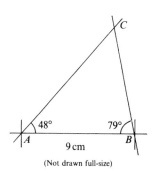

   (If instead of being given the size of $\angle B$ you had been told that $\angle C = 53°$, you could have calculated the size of $\angle B$, since the 3 angles of a triangle have a sum of 180°, and then you could continue as above.)

3. **To draw a triangle, given 2 sides and the angle included between these sides**

   Example

   Draw a triangle ABC with $AB = 9$ cm, $\angle A = 48°$ and $AC = 7$ cm.

   Draw AB, 9 cm long.
   Measure an angle of 48° at A and measure off a distance of 7 cm along this angle line, to give the point C.
   Join BC.

4. **To draw a triangle, given two sides and a non-included angle**

Example

Draw a triangle *ABC* with
AB = 5 cm,   ∠*A* = 48°   and
BC = 6 cm.

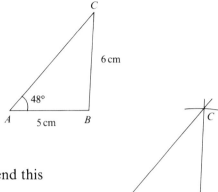

Draw *AB*, 5 cm long.
Measure an angle of 48° at *A* and extend this
angle line onwards.
With compasses, centre *B*, radius 6 cm, draw
an arc to meet this extended line at *C*.
Join *BC*.

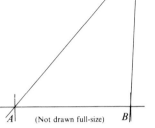

(Not drawn full-size)

(In some cases there could be two points where the arc meets the line, so there
would be two possible triangles of different shapes satisfying the given data.)

Questions 5 to 9. Construct these triangles full-size.

5.

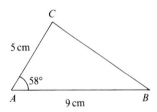

Estimate the length of *BC* and the sizes of ∠*B* and
∠*C*. Check your estimates by measurement.
Find the perimeter of the triangle.

6.

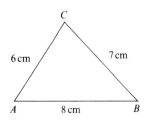

Estimate the sizes of the angles *A*, *B* and *C*, and then
check by measuring them with your protractor.

7.

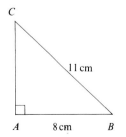

Estimate the length of *AC* and the sizes of angles *B*
and *C*. Check your estimates by measurement.
Find the perimeter of the triangle.

8. 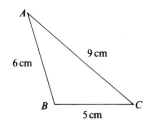 *D* is the mid-point of *AB*. Mark *D* on your diagram. Join *CD*. Estimate, then measure, the length of *CD*.

9. 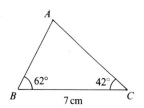 *D* is the mid-point of *AB* and *E* is the mid-point of *AC*. Mark these points on your diagram. Join *DE* and measure *DE*.

Exercise 9.4

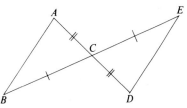

1. In this figure, *C* is a point of symmetry.

   1 Name a length equal to *AB*.

   2 Name an angle equal to ∠*BAC*

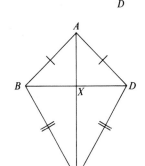

2. In this figure, *AC* is an axis of symmetry.

   1 Name an angle equal to ∠*ABC*.

   2 Name a line equal to *BX*.

3. Calculate the sizes of angles *a*, *b*, *c*, *d*.

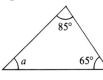 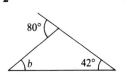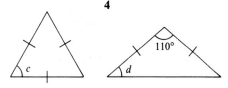

4. Calculate the sizes of
   ∠*ACD*, ∠*CDB*, ∠*DBC*, ∠*BCD*.

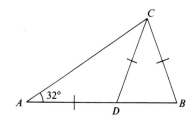

5. Make a rough copy of this map of 'treasure island' and find the place where the treasure is hidden. 'Halve the distance in a straight line from *A* to *B*, and from this halfway point proceed in a straight line at right angles to the line *AB* until you reach the river. Having crossed the river, march North to the coast. Here you will find a cave where the treasure lies hidden.'

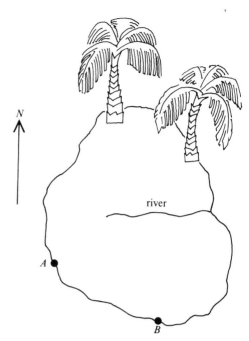

6. If $AB = AC$, which two angles are equal?
   Find the sizes of $\angle ACD$, $\angle CDB$, $\angle DBC$, $\angle BCD$.

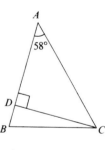

7. Find the size of $\angle A$ and then find the value of d.

8. Construct $\triangle ABC$ with the measurements given.
   Measure $\angle A$.
   Let D be the mid-point of BC. Join AD.
   Measure AD to the nearest mm.

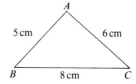

9. In $\triangle ABC$, $AB = AC$, and the bisectors of $\angle B$ and $\angle C$ meet at I. (Bisectors are lines which cut the angles in half.)
   Find the sizes of
   1 $\angle ABC$,
   2 $\angle IBC$,
   3 $\angle BIC$.

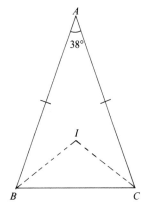

10. Draw accurately a triangle ABC with $AB = 8$ cm, $\angle A = 56°$ and $\angle B = 64°$. From D, the mid-point of BC, draw a line to E, the mid-point of AC. Measure the angles CED and CDE.

11. Draw accurately a triangle ABC with $AB = 7$ cm, $\angle A = 90°$ and $BC = 10$ cm. Measure AC. Find the perimeter of the triangle.

PUZZLES

26. Seasonal greetings. On graph paper, label the x-axis from 0 to 12 and the y-axis from 0 to 8, using the same scale on both axes. Mark these points. Join each point to the next one with a straight line, except where there is a cross after the point.
   (5, 6)   (4, 6)   (4, 8)   (5, 8)×   (8, 6)   (8, 8)   (8.8, 8)   (9, 7.8)
   (9, 7.2)   (8.8, 7)   (8, 7)   (9, 6)×   (1, 2)   (3, 4)×   (1, 6)   (1, 8)
   (2, 7)   (3, 8)   (3, 6)×   (11, 7)   (12, 8)×   (6, 6)   (6, 8)   (6.8, 8)
   (7, 7.8)   (7, 7.2)   (6.8, 7)   (6, 7)   (7, 6)×   (10, 8)   (11, 7)   (11, 6)×
   (4, 7)   (4.8, 7)×   (3, 2)   (1, 4)×
   Complete the diagram.

27. Start from ∗, going horizontally or vertically (not diagonally), and spell out the names of 7 plane figures.

T	A	N	T	R	I	X	A
N	G	O	R	T	A	E	G
E	G	O	A	E	N	H	O
P	R	L	P	L	G	M	N
M	A	E	E	Z	I	U	Q
A	L	L	A	R	E	A	U
R	A	*P	L	S	T	D	R
E	R	A	U	Q	A	L	I

10 *Formulae and directed numbers*

Expressions

If apples cost 15 pence per lb, the cost of 10 lb of apples is 10×15 pence.
If apples cost a pence per lb, the cost of 10 lb of apples is $10 \times a$ pence $= 10a$ pence
($10 \times a$ or $a \times 10$ are written as $10a$)

If a girl is 10 years old and her younger brother is 3 years old, then the girl is $(10 - 3)$
years older than her brother.
If a girl is g years old and her younger brother is b years old, then the girl is $(g - b)$
years older than her brother.

The total weight of 8 parcels of 3 kg each and 6 parcels of 5 kg each is
$[(8 \times 3) + (6 \times 5)]$ kg.
The total weight of 8 parcels of b kg each and 6 parcels of c kg each is $(8b + 6c)$ kg.

If 20 people share £300 equally they each get $£\frac{300}{20}$.

If x people share £300 equally they each get $£\frac{300}{x}$.

Simplifying expressions

Addition and subtraction

$a + a = 2a$
$2a + 4a = 6a$
$8b - 5b = 3b$
$5b - 4b = b$
$3c - 3c = 0$
$3d + 4e + d - e = 4d + 3e$

Multiplication and division

$5 \times a = 5a$
$1 \times b = b$
$c \times 3 = 3c$
$d \times 0 = 0$

$a \times a = a^2$
$2 \times b \times c = 2bc$
$d \times d \times d = d^3$

$e \div f = \frac{e}{f}$

$g \div g = 1$

Removing brackets

$$3(a + 4b) = 3a + 12b$$
$$2(3c - 5d) = 6c - 10d$$

Substitution

If $a = 2$, $b = 5$ and $c = 0$ then
$$3a + b^2 = (3 \times 2) + 5^2 = 6 + 25 = 31$$
$$4abc = 4 \times 2 \times 5 \times 0 = 0$$
$$a^3 + 2b^2 = 2^3 + (2 \times 5^2) = 8 + 50 = 58$$

Note that $2b^2$ means $2 \times b^2 = 2 \times 5^2 = 2 \times 25 = 50$. It does **not** mean $(2b)^2$ which is 10^2 and equals 100.

Formulae

Examples

1   A formula used to find the area of a right-angled isosceles triangle is $A = \dfrac{x^2}{2}$.

If $A = \dfrac{x^2}{2}$, find A when $x = 10$.

$$A = \frac{10^2}{2} = \frac{100}{2} = 50$$

2   A formula used to find Simple Interest is $I = \dfrac{PRT}{100}$.

If $I = \dfrac{PRT}{100}$, find I when $P = 800$, $R = 7$ and $T = 5$.

$$I = \frac{800 \times 7 \times 5}{100} = 280$$

3   A formula used to convert temperatures from the Celsius to the Fahrenheit scale is $F = 1.8C + 32$.
If $F = 1.8C + 32$, find F when $C = 40$.
$$F = (1.8 \times 40) + 32 = 72 + 32 = 104$$

Exercise 10.1

1.   **1**   What is the cost, in pence, of 5 kg of butter at a pence per kg?

     2   How many minutes are there in $2b$ hours?

     3   If a man goes abroad with c francs, and spends d francs, how many francs has he left?

     4   What is the total cost, in pence, of 3 lb of apples at e pence per lb and 2 lb of pears at f pence per lb?

     5   What is the change from 50 p, after buying g packets of sweets at h pence each?

     6   If a pencil costs k pence, what is the cost of 12 pencils?

     7   What is the cost in pence of 4 eggs, if they cost m pence per dozen?

     8   How many seconds are there in $3n$ minutes?

     9   If x pence is shared equally among q children, how much do they each receive?

     10   If a clock gains s seconds per hour, and it is set to the right time, how many seconds fast will it be t hours later?

2.   Simplify these expressions

     1 $3c + 2c - 4c$

     2 $6d - 4d - 2d$

     3 $5e + f + 3e - f$

     4 $2g - 3h + g - h$

     5 $4j + k + 2j + 3k$

     6 $6m - 7m + 2m$

     7 $a \times a$

     8 $b \times b \times b$

     9 $c \div c$

     10 $8d \div 2$

3.   Remove the brackets in these expressions

     1 $2(a + 3b)$

     2 $5(3c - d)$

     3 $10(2e - 3f)$

4. If $p = 6$, $q = 2$, find the value of

1	$2p + 3q$	**5**	$p - 2q$	**9**	$2(p + q)$
2	$3p - 4q$	**6**	p^2	**10**	$\dfrac{p + 2q}{5}$
3	pq	**7**	$3q^2$		
4	$\dfrac{4p}{q}$	**8**	$\sqrt{8q}$		

5. If $x = 4$ and $y = 3$, find the value of

1	$2x^2$			**8**	$4y - 3x$
2	$x^2 + y^2$	**5**	$\dfrac{x + 2}{y}$	**9**	$\dfrac{y^2 + 1}{x}$
3	$2x - y$	**6**	$2y^2$		
4	$2xy$	**7**	y^3	**10**	$\sqrt{x + 4y}$

6. If $a = 5$, $b = 3$ and $c = 1$, find the value of x if

1	$x = 4a + b$	**4**	$x = 2a - 3b - c$
2	$x = a^2 + b^2$	**5**	$x = \dfrac{a}{c}$
3	$x = 2a^2$		

7. **1** If *distance* = *speed* × *time*, what is *distance* when *speed* = 70 and *time* = 3?

2 If *paint* = $\dfrac{area}{18}$, what is *paint* when *area* = 45?

3 If *amount* = *principal* + *interest*, what is *amount* when *principal* = 800 and *interest* = 80?

4 If *weight* = 6 × (*length*)^2, what is *weight* when *length* = 5?

5 If *radius* = $\sqrt{\dfrac{7 \times area}{22}}$, what is *radius* when *area* = 616?

8. **1** If $a = 180n + 360$, find a when $n = 3$

2 If $s = a + ar$, find s when $a = 4$ and $r = \frac{1}{2}$

3 If $b = 2\sqrt{x}$, find b when $x = 25$

4 If $C = \dfrac{5}{9}(F - 32)$, find C when $F = 50$

5 If $s = \dfrac{n}{2}(a + l)$, find s when $n = 20$, $a = 6$ and $l = 24$.

9. Mr West's weekly wage is calculated according to the hours he has worked using this rule:
    If the number of hours is less than 40, wage in £ = (3 × number of hours) + 10.
    If the number of hours is 40 or more, wage in £ = (5 × number of hours) − 70.
    Find how much he will earn in a week when he works for

    1 30 hours,   **2** 50 hours.

Directed Numbers

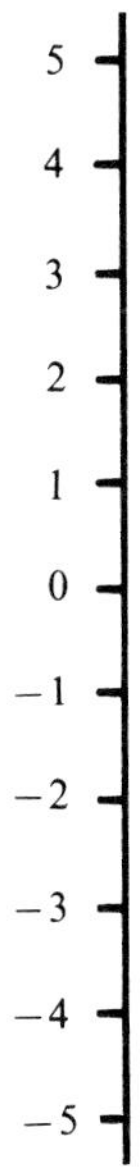

The diagram shows a number scale where the numbers go below 0. This can happen, for example, on a temperature scale where 0°C is the temperature at which water freezes, and the temperature can drop below this.
Temperatures below zero are given as − 1°, − 2°, − 3°, etc.
Temperatures above zero are given as ordinary numbers, 1°, 2°, 3°, etc, or they can be given as plus numbers, + 1°, + 2°, + 3°, etc. + 3° is the same as 3°.

Draw your own number scale diagram, extending it further in both directions than this one.
Follow these examples on your number scale, counting up or down.

Start at 2 and go up 4. You get to 6.
Start at − 5 and go up 4. You get to − 1.
Start at − 5 and go up 7. You get to 2.
Start at 5 and go down 2. You get to 3.
Start at 5 and go down 8. You get to − 3.
Start at − 3 and go down 1. You get to − 4.

These questions can be written as follows:

$2 + 4 = 6$
$(-5) + 4 = -1$
$(-5) + 7 = 2$
$5 - 2 = 3$
$5 - 8 = -3$
$(-3) - 1 = -4$

The difference between two numbers

To get from 3 to 2, go down 1.
To get from 3 to − 5, go down 8. (You go down 3 to 0 then down another 5 to − 5.)
To get from − 2 to 5, go up 7.
To get from − 1 to − 5, go down 4.
To get from − 2 to 0, go up 2.

Exercise 10.2

1. Find the new temperature in the following cases.

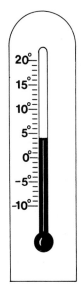

    1 The temperature is $+4°$ and it falls $3°$.
    2 The temperature is $-5°$ and it falls $2°$.
    3 The temperature is $+3°$ and it rises $6°$.
    4 The temperature is $-1°$ and it rises $1°$.
    5 The temperature is $-4°$ and it rises $2°$.
    6 The temperature is $0°$ and it falls $5°$.
    7 The temperature is $-3°$ and it falls $4°$.
    8 The temperature is $+2°$ and it falls $5°$.
    9 The temperature is $+6°$ and it falls $7°$.
    10 The temperature is $-2°$ and it rises $8°$.

2. Say how many degrees the temperature has risen or fallen in the following cases.

    1 It was $+8°$ and is now $+11°$.   **6** It was $+10°$ and is now $-17°$.
    2 It was $+6°$ and is now $-3°$.   **7** It was $-8°$ and is now $+2°$.
    3 It was $-4°$ and is now $+2°$.   **8** It was $-3°$ and is now $0°$.
    4 It was $-9°$ and is now $-7°$.   **9** It was $+5°$ and is now $+1°$.
    5 It was $0°$ and is now $-6°$.   **10** It was $-1°$ and is now $-4°$.

3. (Give the answer in the form '10 minutes to 1' or '10 minutes past 1'.)

    1 If the time is 13 minutes to 1 o'clock, what will be the time in 20 minutes?
    2 If the time is 7 minutes to 2 o'clock, what was the time 5 minutes ago?
    3 If the time is 4 minutes past 3 o'clock, what was the time 10 minutes ago?

4. **1** If the time is 12 minutes past 4 o'clock, how many minutes have passed since it was 5 minutes to 4 o'clock?

    2 If the time is 5 minutes to 5 o'clock, in how many minutes will it be 5.15?

    3 If the time is 20 minutes to 6, in how many minutes will it be 5 minutes to 6?

5. Mr Bramwell has an agreement with his bank to overdraw money, that is, to spend more money than is in his account.

    1 If he has £300 in his account and writes a cheque for £450, how much will his account be overdrawn?

    2 If his account is overdrawn by £200 and he takes out another £60, how much is he overdrawn now?

    3 If his account is overdrawn by £150 and he puts £80 into the account, how much is he overdrawn now?

    4 If his account is overdrawn by £100 and he puts £130 into the account, how much is his account in credit?

6.

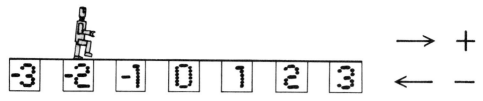

Steve is playing a computer game. To make the robot go to the right he presses
the + key. To make the robot go to the left he presses the − key.

e.g. To get from −2 to 0 he would press +2,
    to get from −1 to −3 he would press −2.

What must he press to move the robot

1 from −3 to 3,

2 from 0 to 3,

3 from 1 to −1,

4 from 2 to −2,

5 from −2 to 1?

Where does the robot end up if

6 it was at −1 and Steve pressed −2,

7 it was at 0 and Steve pressed +2,

8 it was at 3 and Steve pressed −6,

9 it was at −2 and Steve pressed +4,

10 it was at −1 and Steve pressed +1?

7. Find the value of

1 $4 - 6$	**5** $(-2) + 2$	**8** $0 - 8$
2 $(-5) - 3$	**6** $(-10) - 10$	**9** $2 - 3$
3 $(-5) + 7$	**7** $7 - 12$	**10** $(-3) + 1$
4 $6 - 4$		

Inequalities

$<$ is the symbol for 'is less than', so $3 < 4$ means '3 is less than 4'.
$>$ is the symbol for 'is greater than', so $1 > -2$ means '1 is greater than -2'.
Also $\neq$ is the symbol for 'is not equal to', e.g. $3.3 \neq 3\frac{1}{3}$

Example

If x is a whole number, what are the possible values of x if $-1 < x < 5$?

x is greater than -1
x is less than 5

The possible values of x are 0, 1, 2, 3, 4

Inequalities on the number line

Examples

$x > 1$
x is greater than 1

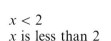

$x < 2$
x is less than 2

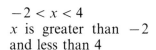

$-2 < x < 4$
x is greater than -2
and less than 4

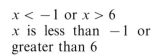

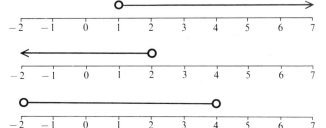

$x < -1$ or $x > 6$
x is less than -1 or
greater than 6

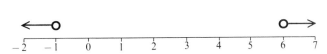

Exercise 10.3

1. Describe these statements in words.

   1 $x > 7$ **4** $1 < x < 4$

   2 $x < 8$ **5** $x > -5$

   3 $x \neq 1$

2. Write these statements in symbols.

   1 x is less than 6.
   2 x is greater than -2.
   3 x is not equal to 0.
   4 x is less than 10 but greater than -3
   5 x is less than 5.

3. Show these inequalities on the number line.

   1 $x > -3$ **6** $-2 < x < -1$

   2 $x < -1$ **7** $-3 < x < 4$

   3 $x > 0$ **8** $x < -3$ or $x > 2$

   4 $x < 3$ **9** $x < 1$ or $x > 2$

   5 $x > 2$ **10** $-1 < x < 1$

4. Write a statement linking a, b, c by $<$ signs, e.g. $b < a < c$, if

   1 $a = -2$, $b = 4$, $c = -1$ **4** $a = -3$, $b = 1\frac{1}{2}$, $c = 1\frac{3}{4}$

   2 $a = 3$, $b = 0$, $c = -4$ **5** $a = 4$, $b = -4\frac{1}{2}$, $c = -3\frac{1}{2}$

   3 $a = -1$, $b = 5$, $c = -6$

5. If x is a whole number, what are the possible values of x if

   1 $3 < x < 7$ **4** $-8 < x < -4$

   2 $4 < x < 6$ **5** $0 < x < 5$

   3 $-2 < x < 2$

Exercise 10.4

1.   **1** Simplify $a + a$, $a - a$, $a \times a$, $a \div a$.

    2 Simplify $3a + 4a$, $4a - 3a$.

    3 Simplify $2(5x - 6) + 3(2x + 4)$

2. If $a = 2$, $b = 5$ and $c = 3$, find the values of

    1 $5c - (a + b)$ **2** $a^2 + b^2$ **3** $a(b - c)$

3.   **1** If 20 lb of apples are bought for x pence per lb, and sold for y pence per lb, what is the profit?

    2 A man is paid £8 per hour for doing a job. What does he earn for x hours work?

    3 How many grams are there in x kg?

    4 There are x children in a Youth club. If 5 of them leave, how many remain?

4.   **1** If $ax - b = c$, find c when $a = 6$, $b = 10$ and $x = 4$.

    2 If $E = 3v^2$, find E when $v = 10$.

    3 If $v = u + at$, find v when $u = 30$, $a = 10$ and $t = 2$.

    4 If $s = t^2 - t$, find s when $t = 8$.

    5 If $area = length \times breadth$, find $area$ when $length = 12$ and $breadth = 7$.

    6 If $A = P + PR$, find A when $P = 700$ and $R = 0.1$

    7 If $t = 180n - 360$, find t when $n = 4$.

    8 If $speed = \dfrac{distance}{time}$, find $speed$ when $distance = 120$ and $time = 4$.

    9 If $3y = 2x - 4$, find y when $x = 17$.

    10 If $P = \dfrac{V^2}{R}$, find P when $V = 10$ and $R = 20$.

5.   If $x = 2y$ and $z = 3x$, find z when $y = 5$.

6.   If $x = 3$ and $y = 5$, find the values of

   1 $\dfrac{2y + 2}{4x}$ **2** $2x^2 - y$ **3** $\sqrt{y^2 - x^2}$

7.   If $y = 3x + 2$, find the value of y when $x = 6$. For what value of x is $y = 11$? For what value of x is $y = 2$?

8.   If $xy = 24$ and $y = 8$, what is the value of x?

9.   The formula for the sum of the numbers from 1 to n is $\frac{1}{2}n(n + 1)$.
     Put $n = 12$ in this formula to find the value of
     $1 + 2 + 3 + \ldots + 11 + 12$.

10. A video recorder costs £60 deposit and then £25 per month for 12 months.

     How much has been paid after
     1 month, 2 months, 3 months?
     Find a formula for the amount paid after
     n months, where n is less than or equal
     to 12. What is the total amount paid for
     the recorder?

11. The time taken to cook a chicken is given as 20 minutes per lb plus 20 minutes extra. How long does it take for a chicken weighing 1 lb, 2 lb, 3 lb?
     Find a formula for the time needed for a chicken weighing c lb.

12. Trixie and Marian are playing a game with cards marked with $+$ numbers or $-$ numbers. At the end of the game they score according to the numbers on their cards.
     e.g. For $\boxed{+8}$ $\boxed{-6}$ $\boxed{-3}$ Trixie scores $8 - 6 - 3 = -1$
     What do they score with these cards?

   1 $\boxed{-1}$ $\boxed{-3}$ $\boxed{+4}$

   2 $\boxed{+2}$ $\boxed{-7}$ $\boxed{+9}$

   3 $\boxed{-3}$ $\boxed{-5}$ $\boxed{-4}$

   4 $\boxed{+5}$ $\boxed{-3}$ $\boxed{-3}$

   5 $\boxed{-3}$ $\boxed{-1}$ $\boxed{+7}$

13. Find the whole number x satisfying these conditions:

   1 $x > 3$, $x < 10$, $x \neq 6$ and x is a multiple of 3.
   2 $20 < x < 40$, $x \neq 25$ and x is a square number.

14. **1** If the temperature is $+3°$ and it falls by $10°$, what is the new temperature?

    2 If the temperature is $-6°$, by how many degrees must it rise to become $+7°$?

    3 If the temperature is $+10°$ and it falls to $-5°$ overnight, through how many degrees has it fallen?

    4 After rising 9 degrees the temperature is $+1°$. What was it originally?

    5 After falling 4 degrees the temperature is $-9°$. What was it originally?

PUZZLES

28. Alan, Bob and Charles are allowed to pick apples in an orchard. Alan picks 7 sackfuls containing 16 kg each, Bob picks 7 sackfuls containing 14 kg each, Charles has smaller sacks and he picks 10 sackfuls holding 9 kg each. They had agreed beforehand that they would share the fruit equally. How can they do this without opening any of the sacks?

29. This map shows the roads where Jenny lives. How many different routes are there for her to cycle from home to school, (never going Northwards, of course)?

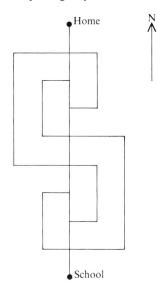

30. There are three married couples having dinner together.
George is older than Michelle's husband.
Frank's wife is older than Nadia.
Lynnette's husband is older than George.
Michelle is not Edward's wife.
The oldest man is married to the youngest woman.
The oldest woman paid the bill. Who was this?

31. Write in figures: eleven thousand, eleven hundred and eleven.

Miscellaneous section B

Exercise B1 Aural Practice

If possible find someone to read these questions to you.
You should do questions 1 to 15 within 10 minutes.
Do not use your calculator.
Write down the answers only.

1. A class of 30 children is split into 6 equal groups for practical work.
    How many children are there in each group?
2. How many 5 pence coins are worth £1?
3. A man is normally paid £5 per hour. How much does he earn for 2 hours work
    on a Sunday when he is paid at 'double time'?
4. How many hundreds are there in a thousand?
5. What is the total cost of 30 textbooks at £6 each?
6. Give an approximate answer to 21×39.
7. Desmond arrived at the station 12 minutes before the train was due. The train
    was 9 minutes late. How long had Desmond to wait?
8. If 10 cm was cut from 1 metre of ribbon, how much was left?
9. Trees are to be planted 10 metres apart along a driveway of length 300 m. If there
    are to be trees at both ends of the driveway, how many are needed altogether?
10. What is the cost of a dozen teacakes if they are sold at 30 pence for 4?
11. A boy jogs $2\frac{1}{2}$ km every evening. How far does he go altogether in 3 evenings?
12. 4 cups of tea and a cake cost 90 pence. If the cake cost 30 pence, what was the
    cost of a cup of tea?
13. A water-tank holding 32 litres of water lost one-quarter of it through a leak.
    How much was left?
14. If my digital clock shows the time as nineteen eleven, what time is this in the
    a.m./p.m. system?
15. Which is the larger fraction, one-third or one-quarter?

Additional aural questions using data from other pages.

16. Turn to page 14. Use the mileage chart, of question 14.

    A cyclist travels from Barton to Corton and then on to Elton. How far is this
    altogether?
17. Turn to page 105. Use the list of approximate comparisons.

    How many pints are approximately equal to 4 litres?

18. Turn to page 68. Use the table of travel information, of question 11.
     What is the basic cost of a 12 days holiday at the Hotel Marti, in May, flying
     from London?

19. Turn to page 19. Use the table of TV programmes, of question 5.
     How long is the 'Sports Today' programme?

20. Use the rectangle drawn round the same table as in the last question.
     The rectangle enclosing the data has a height of 5.4 cm. Estimate its length.

21. Turn to page 52. Use the graph of temperatures, of question 9.
     What was the temperature reading on Tuesday of the 2nd week?

22. Turn to page 115. Use the diagram of question 2.
     Estimate the acute angle at which the lines *DC* and *HG* cross each other.

Exercise B2   Multi-choice Exercise

Select the correct answer to each question.

1. What is the value of $(0.3)^2$?

    A 0.009   **B** 0.09   **C** 0.06   **D** 0.6   **E** 0.9

2. A simplified form of $\frac{77}{49}$ is

    A $\frac{7}{11}$ **B** $1\frac{4}{11}$ **C** $1\frac{4}{7}$ **D** $1\frac{2}{3}$ **E** $2\frac{1}{5}$

3. If $y = mx + c$, the value of y when $x = 9$, $m = \frac{1}{4}$ and $c = 2$ is

    A $2\frac{1}{4}$ **B** $2\frac{3}{4}$ **C** $4\frac{1}{4}$ **D** 11   **E** $11\frac{1}{4}$

4. The size of $\angle DAB$ is

    A 10°   **B** 44°   **C** 52°

    D 56°   **E** 72°

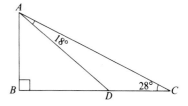

5. The number of centimetres in 1 kilometre is

    A 100 000   **B** 10 000   **C** 1000   **D** 100   **E** 10

6. A medicine spoon holds 5 ml. How many spoonfuls are there in a bottle
    containing $\frac{1}{4}$ litre of medicine?

    A 5   **B** 20   **C** 50   **D** 200   **E** 500

7. In the diagram, *b* equals

    A 40°   **B** 70°   **C** 100°

    D 110°   **E** 140°

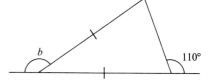

8. A bag of sugar contained 1 kg and after using some to bake a cake it contained 0.85 kg. How many grams of sugar had been used?

   A 0.015   **B** 0.15   **C** 1.5   **D** 15   **E** 150

9. How many axes of symmetry has an equilateral triangle?

   A 0   **B** 1   **C** 2   **D** 3   **E** 6

10. Mr Sumner's car will run for about 40 miles on one gallon of petrol, and petrol costs £1.60 per gallon. For a journey of 450 miles the cost of the petrol will be approximately

   A £6.40   **B** £18   **C** £44   **D** £64   **E** £72

11. If oranges are packed 150 to a box, 12 boxes are needed. How many boxes are needed if they are packed 200 to a box?

   A 6   **B** 9   **C** 12   **D** 15   **E** 16

12. Which of the following is the closest approximation to $\dfrac{15.9 \times 20.1}{3.95}$?

   A 8   **B** 10   **C** 80   **D** 100   **E** 800

13. 50 metres, as a fraction of $1\frac{1}{2}$ km, is

   A $\frac{1}{3}$ **B** $\frac{1}{10}$ **C** $\frac{1}{30}$ **D** $\frac{1}{50}$ **E** $\frac{3}{100}$

14. The value of x is

   A 19   **B** 26   **C** 32

   D 52   **E** 64

15. The weight of 1 cm^3 of water is 1 g. What is the weight, in kg, of 5 litres of water?

   A 0.005   **B** 0.05   **C** 0.5   **D** 5   **E** 50

16. If Denise travels to work by train it is quicker, but costs her three times as much as if she travelled by bus. She decides that she could save £300 a year by going by bus. The cost of travel by bus for the year would be

   A £100   **B** £150   **C** £200   **D** £300   **E** £600

17. A stallholder had 200 kg of potatoes to sell but $\frac{1}{4}$ were bad and $\frac{1}{5}$ of the remainder were too small for sale. What quantity were fit for sale?

   A 30 kg   **B** 40 kg   **C** 110 kg   **D** 120 kg

   E 160 kg

18. If $V = \frac{1}{3}x^2 h$, what is the value of V when $x = 9$ and $h = 10$?

   A   37   **B**   60   **C**   90   **D** $91\frac{1}{3}$ **E**   270

19. There are a lot of coloured beads in a bag, and some of them are green ones. When picking a bead at random the probability that it is green is 0.64. The probability of picking a bead that is not green is

   A   0.32   **B**   0.36   **C** $\dfrac{1}{0.64}$ **D**   0.64   **E** 0.64^2

20. If the temperature one morning is $-2°$, and it rises by 8 degrees during the day and then falls by 11 degrees at night, what is that night's temperature?

   A $-5°$ **B** $-3°$ **C** $-2°$ **D** $-1°$ **E** $1°$

Exercise B3   Revision

1. From this list of numbers:

   15   21   24   27   31   34   44   47   51   57

   1 Find the largest prime number.
   2 Find two numbers whose product is 765.
   3 Find two numbers whose sum is 104.
   4 Find two numbers which as numerator and denominator of a fraction reduce to $\frac{7}{8}$.
   5 Find two numbers which as numerator and denominator of a fraction simplify to 1.8.

2. Express these numbers to the nearest ten.

   1 687   **2** 528   **3** 274.9

3. One of the numbers 5, 6, 7, 8, 9, 10, 11, 12 is drawn at random. What is the probability that it is a factor of 60?

4. Find the total cost of 4 kg of sugar at 48 p per kg, $\frac{1}{4}$ kg of cheese at £3.52 per kg, $\frac{1}{2}$ kg of apples at 54 p per kg and 2 dozen eggs at 85 p per dozen. How much change would there be from a £10 note?

5. How many

   1 cm in 1 metre   **6** pence in £1

   2 m in 1 km   **7** mm in 1 metre

   3 seconds in 1 minute   **8** minutes in 1 hour

   4 g in 1 kg   **9** mm^2 in 1 cm^2

   5 cm^3 in 1 litre   **10** cm^3 in 1 m^3?

6. **1** If 1 franc is worth p pence, how many pence will f francs be worth?
   2 If x kg of potatoes are bought for y pence, what is the price per kg?
   3 The sum of two numbers is 12. One of them is x. What is the other? What is their product?
   4 Elaine is 3 years younger than Eric. If Eric is x years old, how old will Elaine be next year?
   5 A man earned £x per month and his wife earned £y per week. What were their total earnings in a year?

7. Simplify

   1 $5 - 0.27$ **6** $3.6 \div 40$

   2 0.49×1000 **7** $0.56 \div 0.7$

   3 $0.63 \div 100$ **8** $\dfrac{0.3 \times 0.42}{0.7}$

   4 0.6×0.04

   5 0.3^2 **9** 4.6×0.11

                                      10 $4.83 \div 2.1$

8. The diagram shows a thermometer marked in °C.
   What temperature does it show?
   If the temperature rises 10 degrees, what will it be then?

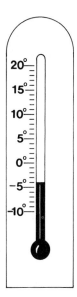

9. Calculate the sizes of the angles a, b, c, d, e.

1

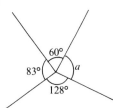

2

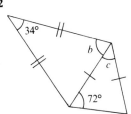

3

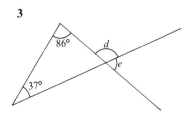

10.   If $a = 3$, $b = 4$ and $c = 0$, find the values of

1 $ab + 2bc$

2 $2b^2 + a^3$ **4** $\dfrac{2a + 3b + 4c}{2a - b}$

3 $3c(a + b)$ **5** $\sqrt{a^2 + b^2}$

11.   Construct a triangle ABC with $BC = 7$ cm, $\angle B = 95°$ and $\angle C = 40°$. Bisect $\angle A$, letting the bisector cut BC at D. Measure the length of BD, to the nearest mm.

12.   The bar chart shows sales of 5 products A, B, C, D and E, by a manufacturing company in two years, this year and last year.

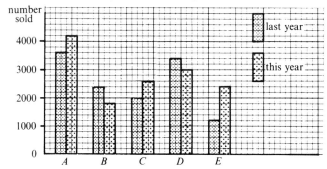

1   How many items of product A were sold last year?

2   Which products sold less this year than last year?

3   Of which product were approximately 2000 sold last year?

4   Find the total sales of all 5 products this year, to the nearest 1000.

Exercise B4   Revision

1.   What fraction is £4.80 of £6.40?

2.   A baby was weighed at the Health Clinic every month and the results for the first 8 months were as follows:

Age in months	1	2	3	4
Weight in kg	4.5	5.0	6.0	6.5

Age in months	5	6	7	8
Weight in kg	7.0	7.5	8.0	8.5

Show this information on a bar chart.

3. Alan plays a game where he can either win, draw or lose. The probability of him winning is $\frac{1}{3}$, the probability of him drawing is $\frac{1}{2}$. What is the probability of him losing?

4. Write these numbers correct to the nearest whole number.

   1 562.8   **2** 322.96   **3** 3728.3   **4** 9.76   **5** 6.512

5. $\triangle ABC$ is equilateral. Find the sizes of angles a, b and d.

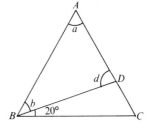

6. A newspaper advertisement to sell a car is charged at £1.80 per line, with a minimum charge of £5.40.

   1 What is the cost of an advert which takes 5 lines?
   2 Mrs Barker decided to sell her car. The advert cost her £14.40. How many lines long was it?

7. Construct $\triangle ABC$ with each side 8 cm long.
   D is the mid-point of BC. Join AD.
   Estimate the length of AD, then measure it, to the nearest mm.

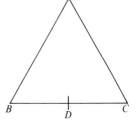

8. Find the approximate value (to the nearest whole number) of 3.92×9.08. Use your calculator to find a value correct to 1 decimal place.

9. The electricity bill for a certain householder was worked out as follows:-
   a standing charge of £5.50 per quarter plus a cost of 4.6 pence per unit used. The meter reading was 32340, and the previous reading was 31740. How many units had been used, and what was the total cost for that quarter?

10. **1** If $s = ut + \frac{1}{2}ft^2$, what is the value of s when $u = 9$, $f = 10$, $t = 4$?

   2 If $I = \dfrac{PRT}{100}$, what is the value of I when $P = 750$, $R = 8$, $T = 4$?

   3 If $g = \dfrac{v - u}{t}$, find g when $v = 90$, $u = 20$ and $t = 7$.

   4 If $S = 90(2n - 4)$, find S when $n = 6$.

   5 If $a = \dfrac{b(100 + c)}{100 - c}$, find a when $b = 6$ and $c = 20$.

11. **1** Draw a line *AB*, 8.4 cm long. By calculation and measurement, or otherwise, divide it into 4 equal parts.

   2 Draw an angle *ABC* of 84°. By calculation and measurement, divide it into 3 equal parts.

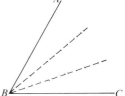

12. The design shows 8 isosceles right-angled triangles arranged in a square.
State which triangle results if

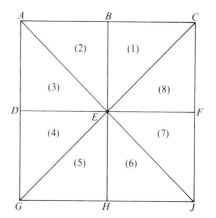

   1 triangle (1) is reflected in the line *DF*,
   2 triangle (2) is rotated through 90° anticlockwise about *E*.
   3 triangle (3) is rotated through 180° about *E*.

   State the transformation (reflection or rotation), which would map

   4 triangle (4) into triangle (7),
   5 triangle (5) into triangle (1),
   6 triangle (6) into triangle (3).

Exercise B5   Practical work and Investigations

1. **Sevenths**

   Work out the recurring sequence of decimals for $\frac{1}{7}$, $\frac{2}{7}$, $\frac{3}{7}$, $\frac{4}{7}$, $\frac{5}{7}$, $\frac{6}{7}$.
   Investigate the patterns formed.
   Also try adding the 1st and 4th figures, the 2nd and 5th, the 3rd and 6th.
   Add the 1st 2 figures as a 2-figure number, with the 3rd and 4th, and 5th and 6th.
   Add the 1st 3 figures as a 3-figure number with the last 3 figures as a 3-figure number.
   Investigate the decimals for the thirteenths, $\frac{1}{13}$, $\frac{2}{13}$, etc.
   You could also investigate the seventeenths, but the sequence is too long to get it all displayed on your calculator. You can find it in stages, however.

2. **Motoring**

How much does it cost to run a car?

Imagine that you are planning to buy a car and want to see how much it will cost you.

Decide what make of car you want, and whether you will buy a new one or a secondhand one. Find the cost of the car, or of a bank loan to buy the car, or the hire-purchase payments. Find other costs, such as road tax, insurance. For the cost of petrol, find out how many miles per gallon your car should do on average, decide how many miles you will travel in a year, (ask other drivers how many miles they do), and work out the cost of the petrol. There are other costs such as oil, car cleaning, repairs and replacements, garage rent, parking fees, membership of a motoring association, MOT if the car is over 3 years old, and so on. Make an estimate of these. Find the estimated total cost for a year, and see from this how much you will need per week.

Illustrate your booklet with a picture of the car.

If you prefer you can imagine you are buying a motor bike instead of a car.

Other ideas:

Find a list of 'stopping distances' from the highway code booklet and plot these on a graph, drawing 2 curves, one for dry conditions and one for wet conditions. Look at second-hand values for cars as advertised in the local newspaper, and for different makes draw graphs showing the average prices of cars 1 year old, 2 years old, and so on. After a few years you may want to sell your car. Do some models seem to retain their values more than others?

3. Probability of winning in competitions

There are many competitions in newspapers, magazines and leaflets available in shops. Other competitions such as raffles are organised to raise money for Charities. Examples:

1   If there are 8 items which you have to put in order of merit, find how many different entries are possible. Often the winning entry depends on the judge's opinion, so assume that all entries are equally likely to win. What is the probability that your entry is the correct one?

2   If there are 8 questions each with possible answers A, B, C, D, how many possible combinations of answers are there? If you choose answers at random, what is the probability that your entry is the correct one?
    (Investigate the number of possible answers if there are 2 questions, 3 questions, . . . , and find the pattern in your answers.)

3   Premium Bonds are a form of gambling where you do not lose your original investment, but instead of earning interest on it the interest is paid out in prizes to the winners. You can get a leaflet from the Post Office which gives details about how the scheme works, and from this you can work out your chances of winning a prize.

4   You may like to try to work out the probability of winning on various 'fairground' games, or other forms of gambling such as the football pools, poker or roulette. But note that the promoter arranges things so that he makes a profit in the long run.

4. History of numbers and calculation

Counting can be traced back to very ancient times, and yet it is only a few years ago that modern calculators and computers were invented. You could make a topic booklet about this, including early methods of writing numbers in different parts of the world, and methods of calculation such as the abacus, Napier's bones and logarithms, and ending with a section on the development of the computer.

5. **History of measurement**

It is interesting to find out about the measures which were used long ago in Britain. Land is still measured in acres. An acre is the area of land that could be ploughed in a day, in the days when oxen were used for ploughing.

If you have an interest in another country, maybe you could find out about how its system developed.

In France at the time of the Revolution, the old measures were abolished and the Metric System adopted. This is now used worldwide for scientific work and is being introduced gradually into Britain.

You could make a topic booklet about measurements. You could include weights as well. You could also find out about the measurement of time, and about coinage, or these could be topics in themselves.

6. **Shapes in Everyday Life**

Make a booklet about these, illustrated with drawings, pictures, postcards and photographs.

Ideas:

symmetry in nature, and in man-made objects,

triangles—pylons, etc.

circles—wheels, drainpipes,

shapes in nature—spirals in snails, jellyfish, pattern on a sunflower centre, cone of a volcano,

shapes in building—unusual modern designs, bridges, the Pyramids, radio telescopes (paraboloid), cooling towers (hyperboloid), spheres of the early warning system.

Your booklet can include all of these, arranged in different sections, or you may choose to concentrate on one aspect such as circles.

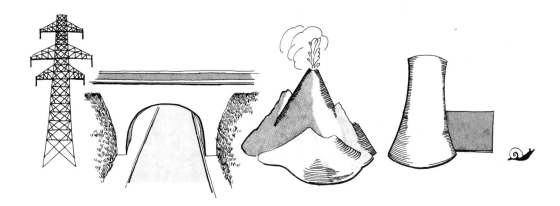

7. **Constructions**

1 To find the mid-point of a line *AB* or the perpendicular bisector of *AB*

(1) **By measurement.** Find the length of *AB*, divide this by 2 and measure this distance from *A* to get the mid-point.
If you need the perpendicular bisector also, use your protractor to draw a line through this mid-point at right-angles to *AB*.

(2) **By paper folding.** You need to use thin paper such as tracing paper. Fold the paper so that *B* lies on top of *A* and make a firm crease. This crease is the perpendicular bisector of *AB* and cuts *AB* at its mid-point.

(3) **Using ruler and compasses.**
With centre *A* and a radius more than half of *AB*, draw two arcs.

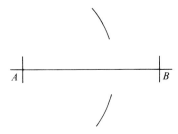

With centre *B* and the same radius, draw two arcs to cut the first two arcs at *X* and *Y*.

Join *XY*, cutting *AB* at *Z*.

Then *Z* is the mid-point of *AB*, and *XZY* is the perpendicular bisector of *AB*.

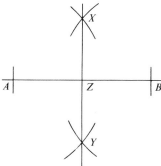

2 To bisect an angle *ACB*

(1) **By measurement.** Find the size of ∠*ACB* with your protractor, divide this by 2 and measure this angle from *A*, turning towards *B*.

(2) **By paper folding.** Fold the paper so that the line CA fits along the line CB. Make a firm crease (which goes through C). This crease is the bisector of $\angle ACB$.

(3) **Using a ruler.** Place the edge of the ruler along AC with the ruler on the side of the line nearer B. Draw a line along the opposite edge. Then place the edge of the ruler along BC with the ruler on the side of the line nearer A. Draw a line along the opposite edge.

If the two lines you have drawn cross each other at Z, join CZ, which is the bisector of $\angle ACB$.

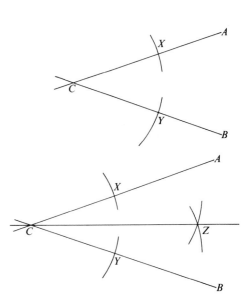

(4) **Using ruler and compasses.**

With centre C, draw arcs to cut CA and CB at X and Y.

With centres X and Y in turn, and a suitable radius, draw arcs to cut at Z. Join CZ, which is the bisector of angle ACB.

3   To draw a perpendicular to a line AB from a point C

(1) **Using a protractor.**
Place your protractor so that the $0°$ line passes through C and the $90°$ line lies along AB. Mark the point where the $180°$ mark is and after moving the protractor join this point to C. Then this line through C is perpendicular to AB.

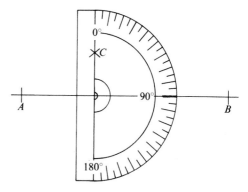

(2) **By paper folding.** Fold the paper so that *AB* lies along itself and the crease passes through *C*. This crease is the perpendicular from *C* to *AB*.

(3) **Using ruler and compasses.**
With centre *C* and a suitable radius, draw arcs to cut *AB* at *X* and *Y*.

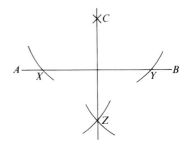

With centres *X* and *Y* in turn, draw arcs, with the same radius for both, to cut at *Z*. Join *CZ*, which is perpendicular to *AB*.

4 To make an angle of 60°, at *P*, on the line *PQ*, using ruler and compasses.

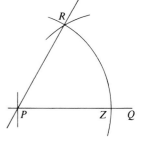

With centre *P* draw a large arc, to cut *PQ* at *Z*.
With centre *Z* and the same radius, draw an arc to cut the other arc at *R*.
Join *PR*.
Then angle *RPQ* = 60°

5 To make an angle of 90°, at *C*, on the line *AB*, using ruler and compasses.

i.e. **To draw a perpendicular to a line *AB* from a point *C* on *AB***

With centre *C*, draw arcs to cut *AB* at *X* and *Y*.

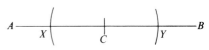

With centres *X* and *Y* in turn, and radius slightly larger than before, draw arcs to cut at *Z*. Join *CZ*, which is perpendicular to *AB*.

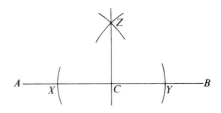

6 Using ruler and compasses, construct an angle of 60°, and then bisect it to make an angle of 30°.

7 Using ruler and compasses, construct an angle of 90°, and then bisect it to make an angle of 45°.

8 **To construct the circumscribed circle of a triangle**
Draw an acute-angled triangle *ABC*.
Draw the perpendicular bisectors of *AC* and *BC* to meet at *O*.
With centre *O*, radius *OA*, draw the circle.
(This circle is also called the circumcircle of the triangle.)

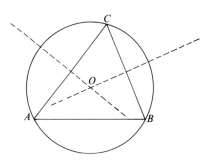

9 **To construct the inscribed circle of a triangle**
Draw an acute-angled triangle *ABC*.
Draw the bisectors of angles *A* and *B* to meet at *I*.
Draw a line from *I*, perpendicular to *AB*, meeting *AB* at *X*.
With centre *I* radius *IX*, draw the circle.
(This circle is also called the in-circle of the triangle.)

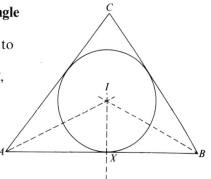

8. **Pentominoes and hexominoes**

Pentominoes are arrangements of 5 equal squares which join together with edges of adjacent squares fitting exactly together, such as

Pieces which would be identical if turned round or turned over are counted as the same. Thus ⬜⬜⬜⬜ is the same as ⬜

There are 12 different pieces. Find them. Some of them will form the net of an 'open' cube. Which ones? The 12 pieces can be fitted together to form various rectangles. Make some cardboard pieces and investigate.
Hexominoes consist of 6 squares joined together. Investigate these shapes and see how many you can find. Some of them will form the net of a cube. Which ones? Which pieces can be used to make tessellations? (Tessellations are explained on pages 315 and 316.)

9. **Areas**

When we measure area we compare it with a unit area.
We can use the area of a square of side 1 cm for the unit.
This is called 1 square centimetre and written $1\,\text{cm}^2$.

1 cm

1 cm

Cut out 12 such squares out of cardboard. Together they make an area of
$12\,\text{cm}^2$. By arranging them together, find some shapes which have an area of
$12\,\text{cm}^2$. You can cut up some of the squares to make more interesting shapes.
Three of these shapes are rectangles. What are the measurements of rectangles
which have an area of $12\,\text{cm}^2$? If you had more squares, say 20 squares, what
sizes of rectangles could you make? Can you find the formula for the area of a
rectangle?

Cut out a rectangle 2 cm long by 1 cm wide. Its area is $2\,\text{cm}^2$. Divide it into 2
triangles by cutting along a diagonal. What is the area of each triangle?
Put the 2 triangles together. What other shapes can be made, as well as the
original rectangle? What are the areas of these shapes? Can you find the
formulae for the areas of these shapes, by seeing how they are made from the
right-angled triangles?

To find the area of a general triangle, enclose it in
a rectangle, then cut out the two extra triangles and
rearrange them to fit on the top of the original
triangle. Thus the original triangle is half the area of
the enclosing rectangle. Will this help you to find
the formula for the area of a triangle?

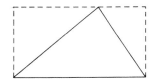

To find the area of a parallelogram, cut off one end,
put it onto the other end, and what shape do you
get? Will this help you to find the formula for the
area of a parallelogram?

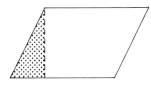

If we are measuring larger areas we will compare them with $1\,\text{m}^2$ or $1\,\text{km}^2$.
Imagine you are making a square with edge 1 m with your squares of edge 1 cm.
How many will you need? This tells you how many cm^2 make $1\,\text{m}^2$. Similarly,
how many m^2 are there in $1\,\text{km}^2$? How many mm^2 are there in $1\,\text{cm}^2$?

Areas of irregular shapes

One way to estimate these areas is to
draw them on a squared grid and
count the squares.
For those squares on the boundary,
where more than half the square is
included in the area, count it as a
whole one, and where less than half the
square is included, do not count it at
all. This method will give an
approximate value for the area.

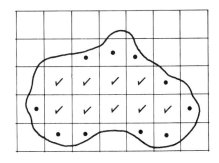

In the diagram,

Whole squares . . . 9

Boundary squares counted . . . 10

Other boundary squares not counted.

Total area 19 squares.

If each square has edge 1 cm, area = 19 cm^2.

If the squares are larger, e.g. edge 5 cm, their areas are 25 cm^2, so area = 19 × 25 cm^2 = 475 cm^2.

If the squares are smaller, e.g. edge 2 mm, their areas are 4 mm^2, so area = 19 × 4 mm^2 = 76 mm^2 = 0.76 cm^2.

Can you think of other ways to estimate such areas?

10. **For the Computer Programmer**

More suggestions for programs:

1 To make a conversion table, e.g. to convert gallons into litres.

2 To generate random numbers instead of throwing dice, tossing coins, etc. in statistics experiments.

3 To use various formulae when you input the data.

4 To do calculations involving directed numbers.

5 To put a set of numbers in order of size.

To the student:

3   Improving your work

Check your handwriting and if necessary, improve it. It must be legible even when you are working quickly. Badly written work means that you confuse 6 with 0, 1 with 7, and so on. Show minus signs clearly. Do not alter figures, e.g. a 2 into a 3, by overwriting. Cross the 2 out and write the 3 nearby. Do not change $+$ into $-$ except by crossing it out and re-writing clearly. $+$ which might mean either $+$ or $-$ cannot be marked as correct because you have not made it clear which it is. Altered figures cannot be marked as correct. So always make clear alterations.

Try to work at a reasonable speed. If you tend to work slowly, try to speed up, because in an examination you must give yourself a reasonable chance of completing the paper to gain good marks. When you are doing a question, concentrate completely on it so that you immediately think about the method, start it quickly, and continue working it out without a pause until you finish it. Work out any simple arithmetic in your head so that you do not break your concentration, and waste time, by pressing calculator keys. (You could do a check later, using the calculator, if you want to.)

Make sure that you use brackets correctly. $180 - 30 + 40$ is not the same as $180 - (30 + 40)$. The first expression equals 190, the second one equals 110. Be careful when you work out such expressions.

Sketch diagrams, or rough plans of what you are going to do, are very useful even if they are not required as part of the answer.

When you have found an answer, consider if it is reasonable, especially if you have pressed calculator keys to get it. Look at the relative sizes of lengths or angles on the diagram, which should give a general idea even if the diagram is not drawn to an exact scale. A man earning £12 000 per year would not pay £30 000 per year in tax! If a triangle has an angle of over 90°, then a second angle cannot also be over 90°. (why?) If the answer to a simple question is an awkward number such as $3\frac{10}{71}$, this **could** be correct, but it is more likely that you have made a mistake.
When you have found an answer, give it correct to a suitable degree of accuracy, e.g. to the nearest whole number, and don't forget the units, e.g. £, cm, m^2, kg, where necessary.

About Chapters 11 to 15

There is Geometry of quadrilaterals in Chapter 11 and of circles in Chapter 13. This chapter also includes calculations of circumferences. There is more statistics, finding averages, in Chapter 12. Areas of plane figures are calculated in Chapter 14 (and there is an introduction to this topic in Exercise B5). Percentages are introduced in Chapter 15. Percentages are used so much in our lives that this is a very important chapter with interesting and useful applications.

11 *Quadrilaterals*

A **quadrilateral** is a figure with 4 sides.

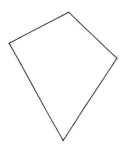

The sum of the angles of a quadrilateral is 360°.

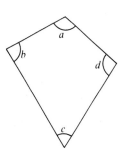

$$a + b + c + d = 360°$$

The perimeter of a quadrilateral is the sum of the lengths of its 4 sides.

Perimeter $= AB + BC + CD + DA$

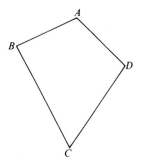

Special sorts of quadrilaterals

Trapezium

One pair of parallel sides

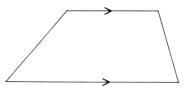

If the other 2 sides are equal it is an isosceles trapezium.

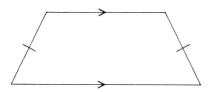

Kite

Two adjacent sides are equal and the other two adjacent sides are equal.

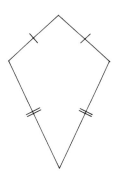

Parallelogram

Opposite sides are parallel

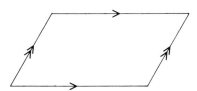

Opposite sides are equal
Opposite angles are equal

Rectangle

It is a parallelogram with one angle a right angle

Opposite sides are parallel and equal
All angles are right angles

Rhombus

It is a parallelogram with one pair of adjacent sides equal

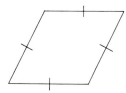

Opposite sides are parallel
All sides are equal
Opposite angles are equal

Square

It is a rectangle and a rhombus

Opposite sides are parallel
All sides are equal
All angles are right angles

Perimeter of a rectangle = sum of lengths of its 4 sides

$$= 2 \times (\text{length} + \text{breadth}) = 2(l + b)$$

Example

Find the perimeter of the rectangle.

Perimeter $= 2(l + b)$

$\qquad = 2 \times (10 + 8)\,\text{cm}$

$\qquad = 2 \times 18\,\text{cm} = 36\,\text{cm}$

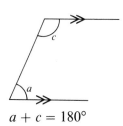

8 cm

10 cm

Interior angles between parallel lines
(in trapeziums, parallelograms, rhombuses.)

These add up to 180°.

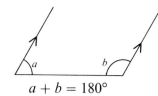

$a + b = 180°$

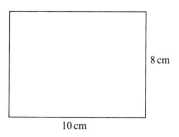

$a + c = 180°$

Diagonals

A diagonal is a line which joins opposite points.

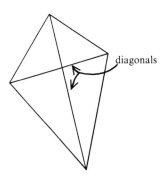

diagonals

Symmetry

An isosceles trapezium has one axis of symmetry.
A kite has one axis of symmetry. (It is a diagonal of the kite.)
A parallelogram has no axes of symmetry.
A rectangle has 2 axes of symmetry.
A rhombus has 2 axes of symmetry. (They are the diagonals of the rhombus.)
A square has 4 axes of symmetry. (Two of them are the diagonals of the square.)

The parallelogram, rectangle, rhombus and square have a point of symmetry at the
point where the diagonals cross each other.
The parallelogram, rectangle and rhombus have rotational symmetry of order 2.
The square has rotational symmetry of order 4.

Exercise 11.1

1. Draw sketch diagrams of these figures and mark on your drawings any lines or points of symmetry.

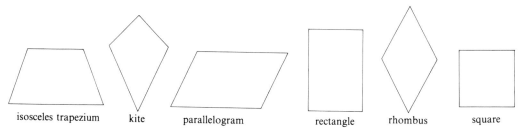

isosceles trapezium   kite   parallelogram   rectangle   rhombus   square

2. Estimate the sizes of the angles in these figures, in degrees. Check your estimates by measuring with your protractor. For each figure, find the sum of the 4 angles. Notice which angles are equal.

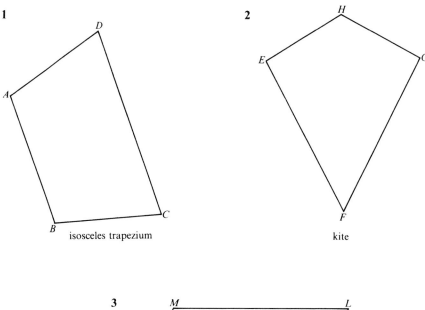

1   isosceles trapezium

2   kite

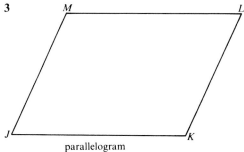

3   parallelogram

3. Estimate, then measure, the lengths of the sides of the figures of question 2. Notice which sides are equal.
   Find the perimeters of the quadrilaterals.

4. Three angles of a quadrilateral are 50°, 75° and 123°. Find the size of the 4th angle.

5. Two angles of a quadrilateral are 72° and 118° and the other two angles are equal. What size are they?

6. *ABCD* is a rectangle and *ABX* is an equilateral triangle.
   1 Find the sizes of angles *a* and *b*.
   2 Find the perimeters of the rectangle *ABCD* and the triangle *ABX*.

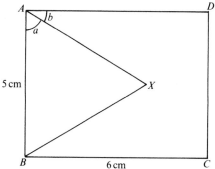

7. Find the sizes of the marked angles.

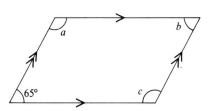

8. *ABCD* is a kite with *AB* = *BC* and *AD* = *DC* = diagonal *AC*. ∠*ABC* = 80°. Find the size of ∠*BAD*.

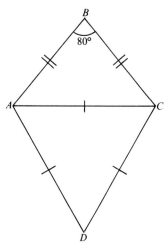

9. Sketch a rectangle, a square and a rhombus.

 What sort of triangles are these?

 1   $\triangle ABC$, where $ABCD$ is a rectangle.

 2   $\triangle PQR$, where $PQRS$ is a square.

 3   $\triangle XYZ$, where $WXYZ$ is a rhombus.

10. Draw an accurate, full-size drawing of this figure.
 (If you cannot draw parallel lines, make $\angle C = (180 - 58)° = 122°$)
 Join AD and measure it to the nearest mm.
 What sort of figure is $ABCD$?

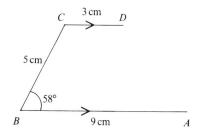

11. Four rods are placed together to make the outline of a plane shape.

 1   If the rods are, in order, 4 cm, 6 cm, 4 cm and 6 cm, what two possible shapes can be made?

 2   If the rods are, in order, 4 cm, 4 cm, 6 cm and 6 cm, what shape is made?

 3   If all the rods are 8 cm long, what two possible shapes can be made?

Constructions and diagonals

12. Construct the parallelogram $ABCD$, as follows:
 Draw $BC = 9$ cm.
 Make an angle of 62° at B.
 Measure off 6 cm to get point A.
 Draw AD parallel to BC, and CD parallel to BA.
 These lines meet at D.
 (If you cannot draw parallel lines, make $\angle A$ and $\angle C$ both $(180 - 62)° = 118°$.)

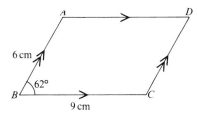

 Draw the diagonals of the parallelogram and let them meet at X.

 1   Measure AC and BD. Are the diagonals equal?
 2   Measure AX and CX, BX and DX. Do the diagonals bisect each other (cut each other in half)?
 3   Measure $\angle BXC$. Do the diagonals intersect each other at right angles?

 These facts about diagonals are true for any parallelogram. (Keep the results to use in question 16.)

13. Repeat question 12 with a rectangle *ABCD*.
    Make ∠*B* = 90° instead of 62°.
    The facts about diagonals are true for any rectangle.

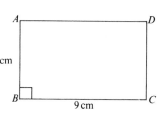

14. Repeat question 12 for a rhombus *ABCD*.
    Make *BC* = 6 cm instead of 9 cm.
    The facts about diagonals are true for any rhombus.

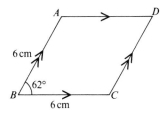

15. Repeat question 12 for a square *ABCD*.
    In addition,

    4 Measure the size of ∠*DBC*.
    The facts about diagonals are true for any square.

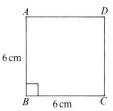

16. Use your results from questions 12 to 15 for this question. Of the figures parallelogram, rectangle, rhombus and square,

    1 which have diagonals which bisect each other,
    2 which have diagonals which cut each other at right angles,
    3 which have diagonals which are equal?

    Write your results in a table, putting 'yes' or 'no' in the columns.

	Diagonals bisect each other	Diagonals cut each other at right angles	Diagonals are equal
Parallelogram			
Rectangle			
Rhombus			
Square			

Exercise 11.2

1. What is the order of rotational symmetry of

   1 a rectangle,   **2** a square?

2. In the diagrams, find the sizes of angles *a, b, c, d, e, f*.

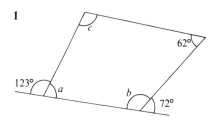

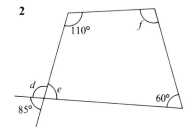

3. *ABCD* is a parallelogram.

   1 What is the size of ∠ *A*?
   2 Find the size of ∠ *AYX*.
   3 What sort of triangle is Δ*AYX*?

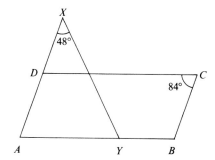

4. In the rectangle, find the size of angle *a*.

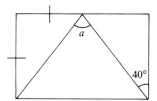

5. *ABCD* is a square.
   Δ*CDE* is an equilateral triangle.

   1 Explain why *AD = DE*.
   2 What sort of triangle is Δ*ADE*?
   3 Find the sizes of angles *g, h, j* and *k*.

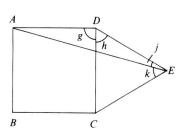

6. **1** Draw 2 right-angled triangles of the same size and shape, on paper, and cut them out.
       Put the 2 triangles together so that they meet exactly along one edge. (The triangles can be turned over.)
       Sketch the shapes which can be made and give their names.
    2 Repeat this with 2 equilateral triangles of the same size.

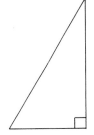

7. **1** In this parallelogram, name the point of symmetry.
    2 Name an angle equal to $\angle DAB$.
    3 Name lengths equal to AX, and BX.

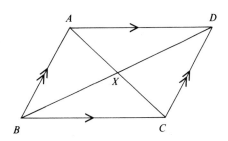

8. If $\triangle ABC$ is reflected in the line BC, with A reflected into a point D, what sort of quadrilateral is $ABDC$?

1

2
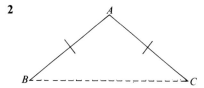

3
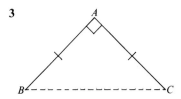

9. Construct a parallelogram $ABCD$ with $AB = 7\,$cm, $AD = 4\,$cm and $\angle A = 60°$. Join AC and estimate, then measure, its length.

10. Draw a triangle ABC with $BC = 6\,$cm, $\angle B = 70°$, $\angle C = 55°$.
    Find, using compasses, a point D to complete the quadrilateral $ABCD$ such that $AD = CD = 8\,$cm.
    Measure the length of AC and the angle ADC.
    If the quadrilateral has a line of symmetry show it on your diagram by a dotted line.

11.   Construct the quadrilateral $ABCD$ in which $AB = 4\,\text{cm}$, $BC = 6\,\text{cm}$, $CD = 5\,\text{cm}$, $\angle B = 60°$ and $\angle C = 90°$. Measure $\angle A$, and the length of AD. Find the perimeter of $ABCD$.

12.   Construct a square $ABCD$ with side $AB = 5\,\text{cm}$. Join its diagonals and let them meet at X. Measure AC and BD, and also measure the sizes of the angles at X.

PUZZLES

32.   **Tangrams.** Use thin cardboard to make this. Start with two equal squares and cut into 7 pieces as shown.
Rearrange these 7 pieces to make one large square.
This is an ancient puzzle. The pieces make many more shapes, using all 7 pieces each time. The pieces can be turned over.

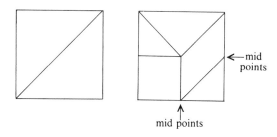

←— mid points

mid points

Make a parallelogram, an isosceles trapezium, a rectangle, an isosceles right-angled triangle and a trapezium with 2 adjacent right angles. Here are some other designs to make, and you can invent others.

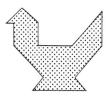
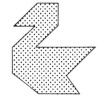
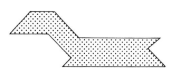

33.   In a dress shop there were six dresses in the window, marked for sale at £15, £22, £30, £26, £16 and £31. Five of the dresses were sold to two customers, the second customer spending twice as much as the first one. Which dress was unsold?

34.   When Katie and Roger were married, they hadn't much money, and on their first wedding anniversary Roger was unable to buy his wife a decent present. So he gave her 1p, and said that it was all he could afford, but he would try to double the amount each year from then on. Sure enough, the next year he gave her 2p, and the following year 4p. Katie was quite pleased to get £5.12 this year, and says she is looking forward to their Silver Wedding anniversary when they will have been happily married for 25 years. Roger, however, doesn't seem quite so enthusiastic about this. Why?

35.   How many times in 12 hours do the hands of a clock point in the same direction?

36.   A ship in the harbour has a ladder with 12 rungs, each 30 cm apart, hanging over the side. At low tide 4 rungs are covered by the sea. If the tide rises at 40 cm per hour, how many rungs will be covered 3 hours later?

12 Averages

When statistical data has been collected, we often need to find an average measurement. There are several kinds of average. Here we will use the mean, the median and the mode.

1   **The mean** $= \dfrac{\text{the total of the items}}{\text{the number of items}}$

2   **The median.** When the items are arranged in order of size, the median is the value of the middle item, or the value halfway between the middle two if there is an even number of items.

3   **The mode** is the value which occurs most often. (Sometimes a set of values will not have a mode, as there may not be any value which occurs more often than any of the others.)

Example 1

Numbers of members of a club attending the meetings

Week number	1	2	3	4	5	6	7	8	9	10	Total
Attendance	20	19	24	22	20	23	20	28	24	20	220

The mean attendance $= \dfrac{\text{the total of the attendances}}{\text{the number of attendances}} = \dfrac{220}{10} = 22$

The median

(Arrange the items in order of size.)

19   20   20   20   20   22   23   24   24   28
                              ↑
                           middle

The median is halfway between 20 and 22, i.e. 21.
(Half the values are less than 21 and half are greater than 21.)

The mode

The value which occurs most often is 20 (as there were 4 weeks when 20 members were present), so the mode is 20.
Summary:- Mean = 22, median = 21, mode = 20.

All these averages can be used in different circumstances, although the most usual one is the mean, as this is the one which involves all the values. If one of the values is very high or low compared to the others, this will affect the mean and in this case the median might be a better average to use. The mode is the simplest average to find, but generally it is not as useful as the other two. However, if a trader was selling, for instance, women's slippers, he would find it useful to know the mode size of women's feet, as he could then stock most of that size and less of other sizes.

Example 2

In a class test, the marks were

5   10   25   25   25   30   30   30   30   35

$$\text{The mean mark} = \frac{\text{total of marks}}{\text{number of marks}} = \frac{245}{10} = 24.5$$

The halfway mark is 27.5. (This is the median mark.)
The most frequent mark is 30. (This is the mode mark.)
The fairest average to quote here is the median. Half the students have less than 27.5 and half have more. The mean has been distorted by the two low values, and only two students have marks less than the mean. The mode is not a representative average, as only 1 student has a better mark.

If you are using your calculator to find the total and then the mean, do a check in case you miss some out. Does the answer **look** right? With the numbers above you would expect the average mark to be about 25, but in any case it must be somewhere between 5 and 35.

It can sometimes be misleading if an average is used without saying which one it is. For instance, in a wages dispute, the workers could quote the lowest of the mean, median or mode wage as the 'average' wage, to support their case for better wages. The management could reply by quoting one of the other averages.
As a simple example, suppose a child got £1 pocket money and he did a survey with another 7 of his friends and the 8 amounts were £1, £1, £1, £1, £2, £2, £2, £10.

The mean amount $= \dfrac{£20}{8} = £2.50$. The child could quote this to his parents as the

'average' amount when he asked for a bit more. But the mean has been distorted by the high value of £10, so it is not very representative. In fact his parents could point out that he was getting the 'average' amount already, as the mode is £1. But the median amount is £1.50, (half get more, half get less,) and this seems the fairest average to use in this case.

If the word 'average' is used without specifying which one in an arithmetical question, it refers to the mean.

Example 3

Find the mean and median of these ages:

12y 4m,   5y 7m,   4y 3m,   8y 5m,   7y 9m.   (Ages in years and months.)

y	m
12	4
5	7
4	3
8	5
7	9
38	4

Mean age $= \dfrac{\text{total of ages}}{\text{number of ages}}$

$= \dfrac{38y\ 4m}{5} = 7$ years 8 months

(If using a calculator remember to deal with the months and years separately.)

For the median, arrange the ages in order of size.

4y 3m,   5y 7m,   7y 9m,   8y 5m,   12y 4m.

↑
middle

The median age is 7 years 9 months.

In your answers, remember to give the unit of measurement. Here the ages are in years and months. Check that your answer seems to be reasonable. Do not give too many decimal places. If the data is accurate to the nearest whole number then it is reasonable to give the averages to 1 decimal place.

Example 4

After 5 tests Kevin has an average of 13 marks. In a 6th test he scores 19 marks. What is his new average mark?

(Do **not** just find the average of 13 and 19 as this is wrong. You must find the total of the marks first, before finding the average.)

In the 1st 5 tests Kevin scored 13 × 5 = 65 marks
In the 6th test he scored   19 marks
Total of marks   = 84 marks

Average mark $= \dfrac{\text{total of marks}}{\text{number of marks}} = \dfrac{84}{6} = 14$ marks

Combining means

Example 5

> If the mean amount spent on travelling to work by 6 girls was 40 p, and the mean amount spent on travelling to work by another 4 girls was 50 p, what was the mean amount for the 10 girls together?
>
> Do **not** just average 40 p and 50 p, because 45 p is not the correct answer. Always find the total amount, then find the mean.
> The total amount for the 1st 6 girls is   40 p × 6 = 240 p
> The total amount for the other 4 girls is 50 p × 4 = 200 p
> The total amount for the 10 girls is   440 p
> The mean amount is $\frac{440}{10}$ p = 44 p

Example 6

> There are 100 workers in a firm and their mean wage was £115 per week. If everyone received a £5 per week pay-rise what would the new mean wage be? (You would probably guess that it would be £120 and this is correct.)
> The previous total of wages was £115 × 100 = £11 500
> The extra total of wages is   £5 × 100 =   £500
> The new total is   £12 000
>
> The new mean wage $= \dfrac{£12\,000}{100} = £120$

Dispersion

The average (mean, median or mode) gives us a general idea of the size of the data, but two sets of numbers can have the same mean but be very different in other ways. The other main statistic we find is a measure of dispersion (or spread).
There are several measures of dispersion, of which we will consider the range.

The range is the simplest measure of dispersion to find.

Range = highest value − lowest value

The range only uses the extreme values so it is not always very representative.

Example 7

> The numbers of members of a club attending a meeting in different weeks. The numbers have been arranged in order of size.
> Case (a).   19, 20, 20, 20, 20, 22, 23, 24, 24, 28.
> Case (b).   8, 11, 13, 15, 18, 23, 30, 32, 34, 36.
>
> The mean in each case is 22 but there is a much bigger dispersion in case (b).
>
> Range in (a) = 28 − 19 = 9
> Range in (b) = 36 − 8 = 28

Exercise 12.1

1. Find the mean (average) of these sets of numbers.

   1   4   5   5   7   7   8   9   10   12   15   17

   2   12   20   31   35   39   48   55   71   85

   3   2   14   5   12   7

   4   25   53   37   17   62   93   41   27   33   19

   5   1.5   1.7   1.8   1.9   2.0   2.0   2.1   2.2

2. Find the median (halfway value) of the sets of numbers in question 1.

3. Find the median (halfway value) of these sets of numbers.

   1   4   5   5   7   7   7   8   9   9   10   12   12   12   12   13

   2   26   27   29   25   31   33   27   32   28   27   33

   3   3   5   1   6   2   5   4   8   1   5   2   5

       7   2   1   5   4   3   6   9   4   1   6   7

4. Find the mode (most frequent value) of the sets of numbers in question 3.

5. Find the mean (average) of

   1   59.2,   90.0,   75.8,   32.6.

   2   £985,   £863,   £904,   £967,   £868.

   3   1 hr 20 min,   2 hr 30 min,   1 hr 45 min,   3 hr 10 min,   2 hr 8 min,
       1 hr 13 min.

   4   1.2 cm,   2.6 cm,   3.7 cm.

   5   2.5 kg,   3.4 kg,   2.7 kg,   1.9 kg,   4.0 kg.

6. 1   The weights in kg of 10 children are

       54,   52,   62,   49,   61,   56,   51,   64,   54,   67.

       Find the mean (average) and the median (halfway value) of the weights.

   2   The ages of 5 boys are

       12 y 1 m,   12 y 5 m,   13 y 7 m,   11 y 2 m,   11 y 7 m.

       Find the mean (average) age.

   3   The weights of 10 helpings of potatoes (to the nearest 10 g) are

       150 g,   170 g,   190 g,   160 g,   180 g,   140 g,   170 g,   170 g,   150 g,
       160 g.

       Find the mean (average) weight.

6. 4   The temperature in a city each day of a summer week was (in °C)

22   22   23   24   23   20   20

Find the mean (average) temperature.

5   The times taken by 6 girls on a training run were

10 min 20 sec,   9 min 5 sec,   11 min 45 sec,   12 min 0 sec,   8 min 30 sec

10 min 50 sec.

Find the mean (average) time taken.

7. Find the range for the sets of numbers in question 1 on the previous page.

8. Find the range of the data in question 5 on the previous page.

9. A cricketer had an average of 30 runs (per innings) after playing 10 innings. In his next innings he was out after scoring 52 runs. What is the total number of runs he has scored? What is his new average?

10. The average age of 6 boys is 8 years 2 months, and the average age of 5 others is 9 years 1 month. What is the total of the ages of the 11 boys? Find the average age.

11. The average weight of 5 packages is 8.6 kg. What is the total weight? The average weight of 4 of them is 9.6 kg. What is the total weight of these 4? What does the 5th package weigh?

12. 12 kg of pet food at 7 p per kg are mixed with 18 kg of pet food at 10 p per kg. What is the total cost of the mixture? What is the cost of 1 kg of the mixture?

13. In a class there are 8 boys in set 1 and 12 boys in set 2. In a test the set 1 boys' average mark is 65 and the set 2 boys' average mark is 60. Find the total of the marks for the whole class. Find the average mark for the class.

14. A dealer bought 90 cases of goods at £10 per case and a second lot of 70 cases at £6 per case. What is the total price? What was the average price per case?

Exercise 12.2

1. In one group of children (group A) the marks in a test were 2, 3, 4, 4, 5, 5, 5, 6, 7, 8.

   In a second group (group B) the marks in the same test were 3, 5, 5, 5, 6, 6, 6, 6, 7, 7.

   1 Find the mean (average), median (halfway value) and mode (most frequent value) of the marks in group A.
   2 Find the mean, median and mode of the marks of group B.
   3 Find the range of marks for each of the two groups.
   4 Which group had the greater mean mark?
   5 Which group had the greater range of marks?

2. The 1971 census recorded 7.45 million people living in Greater London in 2.65 million households.

   Find the mean (average) number of people per household.

   The figures for the North-west region of England were 6.74 million people and 2.27 million households.

   Find the mean (average) number of people per household in the North-west region. Were there more people per household in London or in the North-west region?

3. At a seaside resort there was a mean amount of 3 hours of sunshine per day for the 6 days Monday to Saturday of a certain week. On the Sunday there were 10 hours of sunshine.

   What were the total hours of sunshine for the week? What was the mean (average) amount of sunshine per day for the week?

4. If 6 bars of chocolate cost 15 pence each, and 4 bars of chocolate cost 20 pence each, what was the total price? What was the average price per bar?

5. 7 men earn £120 per week each, 4 men earn £100 per week each, and one man earns £80. What is the total of the weekly wages? What is the average wage for all these men?

6. The average age of 12 girls is 8 years and the average age of 8 boys is 10 years 6 months. What is the total of the ages of all the children together? What is the average age of all the children together?

7. A school had 1050 pupils and 70 teachers. What was the average number of pupils per teacher? The next year the school increased its intake and had an extra 110 pupils and 10 extra teachers. What was the average number of pupils per teacher then?

8. The goals scored by 20 football teams were as follows:
    8 teams scored no goals, 4 teams scored 1 goal, 3 teams scored 2 goals, 1 team scored 3 goals, 3 teams scored 4 goals, 1 team scored 5 goals.

    1   What was the total number of goals scored by the 20 teams?
    2   What was the average number of goals scored by the 20 teams?

9. Here is a flow chart.

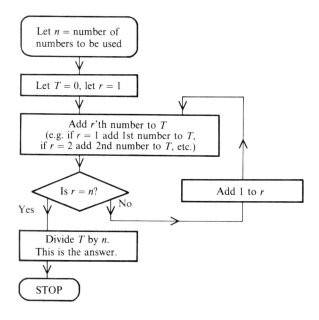

Use the set of numbers 6, 8, 12, 15, 17 in this flow chart.
What is the answer?
What does the answer represent?

10. Repeat question 9 using the numbers 1.2, 3.6, 2.8, 4.4.

11. **Collect other data** suitable for finding averages.
    Some suggestions are:
    The shoe sizes of boys or girls in your class.
    The number of pets kept by a sample of children.
    The number of children in a sample of families.
    The number of goals scored in football matches by home teams, compared with the number of goals scored by away teams.
    The number of passengers in cars.
    The number of customers entering a shop in 1-minute intervals, compared at different times of the day.
    The heights of students in your year-group.
    The times students spend on their homework.
    The ages of cars in a car park. (Estimates based on the registration letter.)
    The weekly amounts spent by students on snacks, sweets, drinks, etc.
    The distances people travel to work.
    The length of time of phone calls.
    Guesses from people of the length of a line, the weight of an object or the number of sweets in a jar.

PUZZLES

37. How many mathematical words can you find reading horizontally, vertically or diagonally, in both directions?

T	S	P	H	E	R	E	R	T	I	L
I	E	Q	U	M	S	I	R	P	A	A
M	S	L	U	E	N	I	L	R	E	C
D	A	O	G	A	A	R	E	A	T	I
I	I	R	S	N	R	T	C	T	U	T
S	O	C	G	C	A	E	M	I	C	R
T	R	L	E	L	E	T	R	O	A	E
A	E	T	I	K	M	L	C	T	D	V
N	E	U	P	R	I	M	E	E	E	E
C	Q	U	A	R	T	E	R	S	R	M
E	S	T	A	T	I	S	T	I	C	S

13 *Circles*

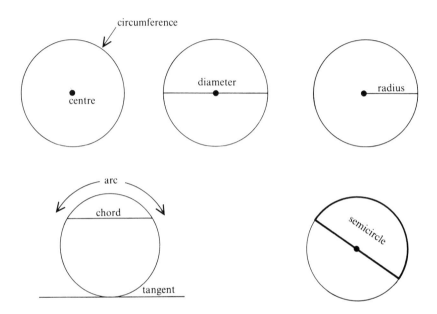

circumference

centre

diameter

radius

arc

chord

tangent

semicircle

Length of Circumference

Circumference = $\pi \times$ diameter = $2\pi \times$ radius

$C = \pi d$

$C = 2\pi r$

π (pi) is a number which cannot be written as an exact decimal. It is approximately 3.14159 but for normal calculations we use 3, 3.1, 3.14 or 3.142 depending on how accurate we need to be. A useful fraction to estimate π is $3\frac{1}{7}(=\frac{22}{7})$. If you use 3.14 or $\frac{22}{7}$ for π, your answer should normally be given corrected to 3 figures. Even if you use a more accurate value for π it would be sensible to give a final answer to 3 or 4 figures. There may be a special key labelled π on your calculator.

Measure the circumference C and diameter D of circles of different sizes from

a penny to a large wheel and find the value of π from $\dfrac{C}{D}$.

Examples

1   Find the circumference of a circle with diameter 8 cm. Take π as 3.14

$C = \pi d$

$\quad = 3.14 \times 8\,\text{cm}$

$\quad = 25.12\,\text{cm}$

$\quad = 25.1\,\text{cm}$ (to 3 figures)

(If the answer is needed in mm it is 251 mm)

2   Find the circumference of a circle with radius 12 cm. Take π as 3.14

$C = 2\pi r$

$\quad = 2 \times 3.14 \times 12\,\text{cm}$

$\quad = 75.36\,\text{cm}$

$\quad = 75.4\,\text{cm}$ (to 3 figures)

(If the answer is needed in mm it is 754 mm)

3   Find the circumference of a circle with radius 28 cm. Take π as $\frac{22}{7}$.

$C = 2\pi r$

$\quad = 2 \times \dfrac{22}{\cancel{7}} \times \overset{4}{\cancel{28}}\,\text{cm} = 176\,\text{cm}$

Axes of symmetry

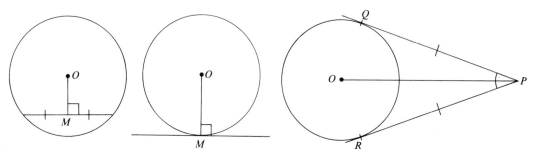

OM is an axis of symmetry.   OP is an axis of symmetry.

In a circle every diameter is an axis of symmetry. There is an infinite number of diagonals so there is an infinite number of axes of symmetry.

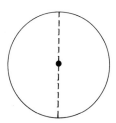

Exercise 13.1

1. Find the circumference of these circles. Take π as 3.14. After you have found an exact answer, when necessary give it corrected to 3 figures.

   1 radius = 5 cm   **4** radius = 20 cm

   2 radius = 9 cm   **5** diameter = 15 cm

   3 diameter = 11 cm

2. Find the circumference of these circles. Take π as $\frac{22}{7}$.

   1 diameter = 14 cm

   2 radius = 35 cm

   3 diameter = 42 cm

3. Find the circumference of these circles. Take π as 3.1. Give your answers correct to the nearest metre.

   1 radius = 8 m   **4** radius = 13 m

   2 diameter = 4 m   **5** diameter = 18 m

   3 diameter = 7 m

4. Sketch these diagrams and mark in the axes of symmetry.

   1 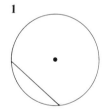   **2** 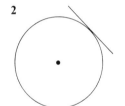   **3** 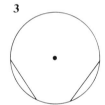   **4**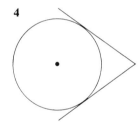

5. TP and TQ are tangents, touching the circle centre O at P and Q.

   1 Name the axis of symmetry.

   2 Name an angle equal to $\angle TOP$.

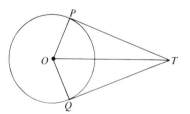

6. AB and CD are equal chords in a circle centre O.

   1 Copy the figure and draw in an axis of symmetry.

   2 Name an angle equal to $\angle AOB$.

   3 Can $\triangle AOB$ be rotated into the position of $\triangle COD$?

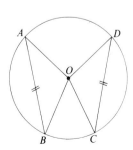

7. **1** Explain why $OA = OB$.
    2 What sort of triangle is $\triangle OAB$?
    3 Find the sizes of angles e and f.

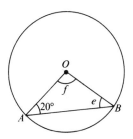

8. Draw a line AB of length 14 cm, and find its mid-point O.
    Through O draw a line crossing AB at right angles.
    With centre O, radius 7 cm, draw a circle. Let the points where it cuts the second line be C and D.
    Join AC, BC, AD, BD. Measure AC to the nearest mm.
    What sort of figure is $ACBD$?

9. Copy these diagrams.
    Invent other designs of your own.

1

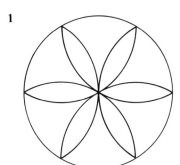

2

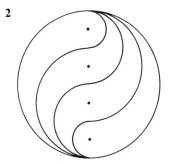

3

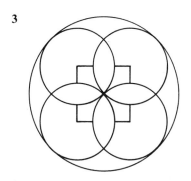

10. Measure the diameters of these circles in cm, to the nearest cm.
Calculate the lengths of their circumferences, taking π as 3.1. Give the answers to the nearest cm, and write them in order of size, smallest first.

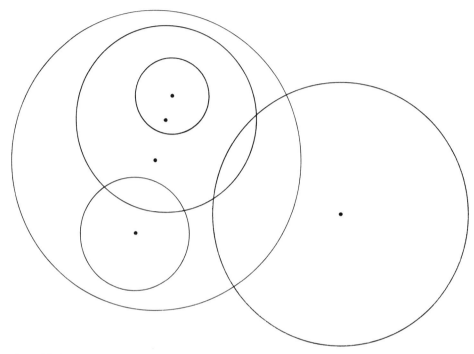

Exercise 13.2

1. Find the circumferences of these circles, giving answers corrected to 3 figures.
   1 Radius 14 cm. Take π as $\frac{22}{7}$
   2 Radius 6 cm. Take π as 3.14
   3 Diameter 2 m. Take π as 3.14

2. The circle is inscribed in a square of side 6 cm.
   1 What is the diameter of the circle?
   2 Find the circumference of the circle, taking π as 3.14 and giving the answer to the nearest mm.

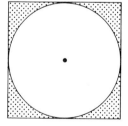

3. A circular pond of radius 18 metres is surrounded by a circular path of width 2 metres.

   1 Find the distance round the inner edge of the path, to the nearest metre.
   2 What is the radius of the circle of the outer edge of the path?
   3 Find the distance round the outer edge of the path, to the nearest metre.
   Take π as 3.14.

4. There is a circular running-track with diameter 35 m. How far has Peter run when he has made 10 complete circuits? Take π as $\frac{22}{7}$.

5. A cotton reel has diameter 3 cm. The cotton is wound round 500 times. What is the length of cotton, to the nearest metre? Take $\pi = 3.14$

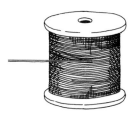

6. This rug is in the shape of a semicircle with radius 80 cm. A strip of tape is sewn all round the edge of the rug. How much tape is needed, to the nearest cm? Take π as 3.14

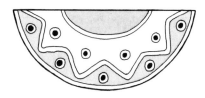

7. A car wheel has a diameter of 50 cm. What is its circumference? When the wheel has rotated 1000 times, what distance has the car travelled, to the nearest 100 metres? Take π as 3.14

8. It is planned to plant a bush with a circle of flowering plants round it.
   The plants have to be 5 feet from the bush so the radius of the circle for the plants is 5 feet. (5 feet = 60 inches)
   What is the circumference of this circle? (Take $\pi = 3.14$ and give the result in inches to the nearest inch.)
   A box of 25 plants is bought.
   Approximately how far apart should they be planted around the circle? (Give the answer in inches to the nearest inch.)

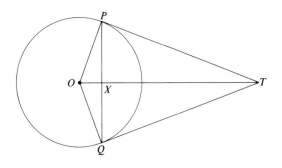

9. *TP* and *TQ* are tangents touching the circle centre *O* at *P* and *Q*.

   1 Name the axis of symmetry.
   2 Name a line equal to *PX*.
   3 Name an angle equal to $\angle PXT$.
   4 What is the size of $\angle PXT$?

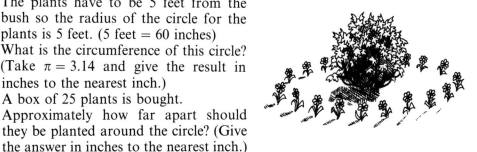

10. In the diagram, O is the centre of the circle.
     What kind of triangles are $\triangle OBC$ and $\triangle OAC$?
     Find the sizes of the angles at point C in these triangles.
     Hence find the size of $\angle ACB$.

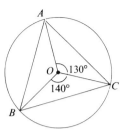

<hr>

PUZZLES

38. Draw 7 regular hexagons of the same size on cardboard and cut them out.
     Join the 3 pairs of opposite points on each hexagon to divide the hexagon into 6 equal triangles.
     Colour these triangles as follows, going in clockwise order round the hexagon.
     1st hexagon: Red, orange, yellow, green, blue, purple.
     2nd hexagon: Red, orange, yellow, green, purple, blue.
     3rd hexagon: Red, orange, purple, yellow, green, blue.
     4th hexagon: Red, green, purple, orange, yellow, blue.
     5th hexagon: Red, green, orange, yellow, blue, purple.
     6th hexagon: Red, green, orange, blue, purple, yellow.
     7th hexagon: Red, blue, green, orange, purple, yellow.
     Now arrange the hexagons with one in the centre and the other six around it, so that all hexagons meet each other edge to edge. Where two edges meet, their triangles should have the same colour.

39. A shop sells one brand of chocolate bars which are priced at, small, 16p; medium, 23p and large 39p; and a second brand where the prices are, small, 17p; medium, 24p and large 40p. A customer buys some of these bars of chocolate and they cost him exactly £1. What does he buy?

40. In this sentence, each letter of the alphabet has been substituted by another letter chosen at random (the same one each time that letter occurs). Can you decode the sentence, and say whether it is a true statement?

     I JMSIYV WJ I MSIQYWDIOVYID FWOE IDD JWQVJ VMSID
     IKQ IDD IKRDVJ YWREO IKRDVJ, JA WOJ QWIRAKIDJ
     IYV VMSID IKQ WO EIJ NASY IPVJ AN JCBBVOYC.

41. A weighty problem. Which would you rather have, half a tonne of 10 pence coins or a tonne of 5 pence coins?

42. How many squares are there on a chessboard?

14 *Areas*

(Areas are introduced in Exercise B5, question 9.)

Area of a rectangle = length × breadth = lb

Area of a square = (length)^2 = l^2

Area of a triangle = $\frac{1}{2}$ × base × perpendicular height = $\frac{1}{2}bh$

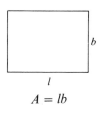

$A = lb$

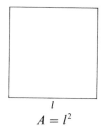

$A = l^2$

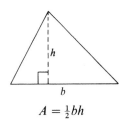

$A = \frac{1}{2}bh$

Examples

1 Rectangle

Area $= lb$

$\quad = 10 \times 8\,\text{cm}^2$

$\quad = 80\,\text{cm}^2$

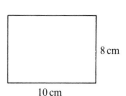

2 Square

Area $= l^2$

$\quad = 8^2\,\text{cm}^2$

$\quad = 64\,\text{cm}^2$

3 Triangle

Area $= \frac{1}{2}bh$

$\quad = \frac{1}{2} \times 10 \times 6\,\text{cm}^2$

$\quad = 30\,\text{cm}^2$

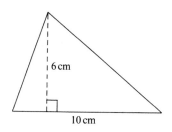

4   Find the area of this figure, which represents the side of a shed.

Area of rectangle $= lb$
$$= 8 \times 6\,\text{m}^2$$
$$= 48\,\text{m}^2$$
Area of triangle $= \frac{1}{2}bh$
$$= \frac{1}{2} \times 8 \times 3\,\text{m}^2$$
$$= 12\,\text{m}^2$$
Total area $= (48 + 12)\,\text{m}^2$
$$= 60\,\text{m}^2$$

3 m

6 m

8 m

5   Find the area of a path 2 m wide round a rectangular lawn 11 m by 6 m.

1st method

The complete rectangle is 15 m long and 10 m wide.

Total area of lawn and path $= lb$
$$= 15 \times 10\,\text{m}^2$$
$$= 150\,\text{m}^2$$
Area of lawn $= 11 \times 6\,\text{m}^2$
$$= 66\,\text{m}^2$$
Area of path $= (150 - 66)\,\text{m}^2 = 84\,\text{m}^2$

6 m   10 m

11 m

15 m

2nd method

Split the path into 4 rectangles, which are all 2 m wide.

Area of (1) $= 15 \times 2\,\text{m}^2 = 30\,\text{m}^2$
Area of (2) $= 15 \times 2\,\text{m}^2 = 30\,\text{m}^2$
Area of (3) $= 6 \times 2\,\text{m}^2 = 12\,\text{m}^2$
Area of (4) $= 6 \times 2\,\text{m}^2 = 12\,\text{m}^2$
Total area $= (30 + 30 + 12 + 12)\,\text{m}^2$
$$= 84\,\text{m}^2$$

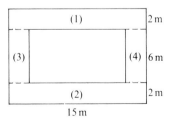

Exercise 14.1

1. Find the area of these figures.

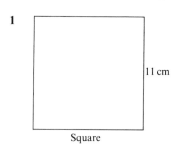

Square

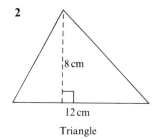

Triangle

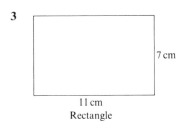

Rectangle

2. **1** Find the area and perimeter of a rectangular lawn 7 m long and 4 m wide.
   2 If the perimeter of a square is 36 cm, what is its area?
   3 A rectangle $9\frac{1}{2}$ cm by 6 cm is cut out of the corner of a square piece of paper of side 12 cm. What area is left? What is the perimeter of the piece that is left?
   4 There is a path 1 m wide all round a rectangular lawn of size 10 m by 8 m. Find the area of the path.

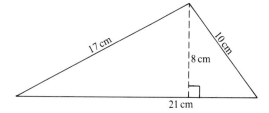

3. Find the area and the perimeter of this triangle.

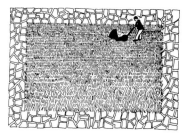

4. Find the perimeters of these figures. All angles are right angles.
    By dividing the figures into rectangles, find their areas.

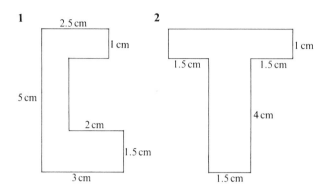

5. Find the area of this trapezium, by considering it as a rectangle + a right-angled
    triangle.

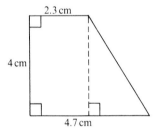

6. A room 8 m by $7\frac{1}{2}$ m contains a carpet 6 m by $5\frac{1}{2}$ m.

    1 What is the area of the uncarpeted floor?
    2 What is the cost of buying floor-covering for the uncarpeted floor at a cost
       of £4 per m²?

7. A floor 12 m long and 7.5 m wide is to be covered by tiles 30 cm square. How
    many tiles will be needed?

8. Find the areas of the following figures. They are drawn full size. Make any measurements you need, measuring in cm, to the nearest $\frac{1}{2}$ cm.

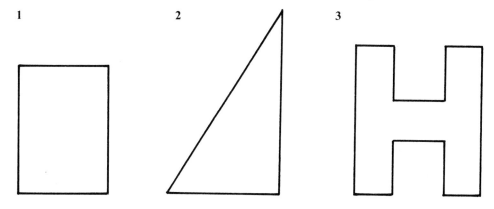

1   2   3

9. Find the perimeters of the figures in question 8. Make any measurements in cm, to the nearest mm, and give final answers to the nearest cm.

10. Find the total area of the quadrilateral *ABCD*.

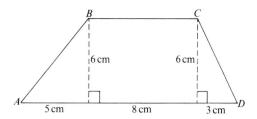

11. *ABCD* is a square. Find its area and the areas of the 3 corner triangles and hence find the area of △*AEF*.

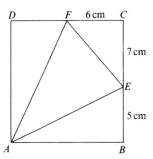

12. Draw these figures full-size

    (a) a triangle base 5 cm, height 2.2 cm,
    (b) a square side 2.4 cm,
    (c) a rectangle length 3.6 cm, breadth 1.4 cm.
    Decide by estimation which of these 3 shapes has **1**   the largest area,
    2   the smallest area. Calculate the areas to verify your estimate.

13. Find the areas of these figures, assuming that they are drawn on a grid of squares of edge 1 cm.

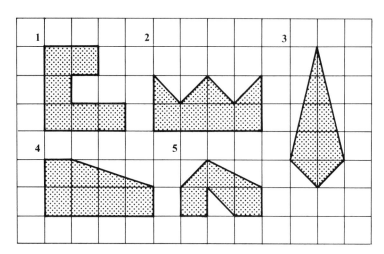

14. Find the area of the square *ABCD* by finding the area of square *EFGH* and subtracting the areas of the 4 triangles.
(Assume the lines on the grid are 1 cm apart.)

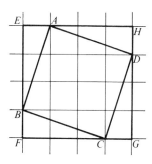

Exercise 14.2

1. How many tiles of size 9 inches square are needed to tile a wall 15 feet long to a height of 6 feet? (There are 12 inches in 1 foot.)
If the tiles are sold in boxes of 24 how many boxes must be bought?

2. What is the length in metres of a side of a square lawn which has an area of 144 m²? What is the perimeter of the lawn?

3. In this rhombus, *AC* = 7 cm, *BD* = 12 cm.
∠*AXB* = 90° and *X* is the mid-point of *BD*.

   1 what is the length of *BX*,
   2 what is the area of △*ABC*?
   3 Find the area of the rhombus.

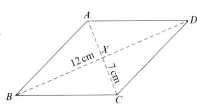

4. Find the area of the floor of this room in square feet. (All the angles are right angles.) (18′ means 18 feet.)

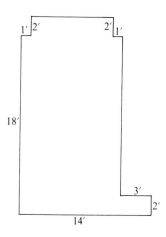

5. A floor 6 m long and 5 m wide is to be covered by carpet which is sold in rolls 1 m wide. How many metres of carpet will be required?
What will be the cost at £12 per metre?

6. The formula to find the area of a kite is
Area = $\frac{1}{2} \times AC \times BD$

Find the area of this kite if $AC = 150$ cm and $BD = 80$ cm.

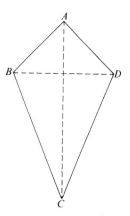

7. Construct a triangle ABC with $AB = 9$ cm, $BC = 7.5$ cm and $AC = 6.5$ cm. Draw and measure an additional line needed to calculate the area of $\triangle ABC$, and find this area.

8. $ABCD$ is a square of side 8 cm. Find the areas of the four triangles, and hence find the area of the quadrilateral $PQRS$.

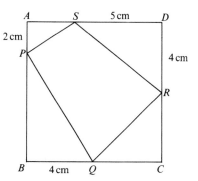

9. Find the shaded area by finding the areas of
   $\triangle ADE$ and $\triangle BCE$.

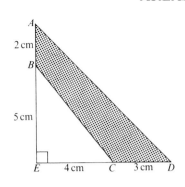

10. Find the area of the rectangle *ABCD*.
    (Assume the lines on the grid are 1 cm apart.)

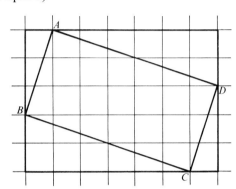

PUZZLE

43. **The 3, 4, 5 problem**

    See how many whole numbers you can represent using the figures 3, 4 and 5 once each.
    Make further rules, such as:
    In every number 3 and 4 and 5 must all be used.
    Signs such as $+ \times - \div \sqrt{}$ and brackets can be used.
    Are you going to allow the sign ! It is called 'factorial'.
    5! means $5 \times 4 \times 3 \times 2 \times 1$ which equals 120. $4! = 4 \times 3 \times 2 \times 1 = 24$ and
    $3! = 3 \times 2 \times 1 = 6$.
    Are you going to allow decimals such as .5, and recurring decimals such as $\dot{.3}$ which
    equals $\frac{1}{3}$?
    Examples: $23 = (5 \times 4) + 3$,
              $90 = 5! - 4! - 3!$

    $$10 = \frac{\sqrt{4} + 3}{.5}$$

    Perhaps you had better begin with numbers up to 100, but you will not be able to
    represent all of them.

15 *Percentages*

Percentages

'Per cent' means 'per hundred', so 17% means $\frac{17}{100}$ or 0.17.

Example 1

Express 45% as a fraction.

$$45\% = \frac{45}{100} = \frac{9}{20}$$

Example 2

Express 63% as a decimal.

$$63\% = \frac{63}{100} = 0.63$$

To change a fraction or decimal to a percentage, multiply by 100 and write the % sign.

Example 3

$$\frac{2}{5} = \frac{2}{5} \times 100\% = \frac{200}{5}\% = 40\%$$

$$0.57 = 0.57 \times 100\% = 57\%$$

It is useful to learn the percentages corresponding to simple fractions or decimals.

Fraction	Decimal	Percentage
$\frac{3}{4}$	0.75	75%
$\frac{1}{2}$	0.5	50%
$\frac{1}{4}$	0.25	25%
$\frac{1}{5}$	0.2	20%
$\frac{1}{10}$	0.1	10%
$\frac{1}{100}$	0.01	1%

Also, $33\frac{1}{3}\%$ is equivalent to the fraction $\frac{1}{3}$, and $66\frac{2}{3}\%$ is equivalent to the fraction $\frac{2}{3}$.

To find a percentage of a sum of money

Change the percentage into a fraction, if it is a simple fraction such as $\frac{1}{2}, \frac{1}{4}, \frac{1}{5}, \frac{1}{10}, \frac{1}{20}$, or change it into a decimal and use your calculator.

Examples

4   Find 20% of £360.

$$20\% = \frac{20}{100} = \frac{1}{5}, \text{ so find } \frac{1}{5} \text{ of £360.}$$

$$\frac{1}{5} \text{ of £360} = £72.$$

5   Find 27% of £250.

27% is 0.27 so find 0.27 × £250.

0.27 × £250 = £0.27 × 250 = £67.50

Use a similar method to find a percentage of a quantity.

Example 6

Find 24% of 60 cm.

24% is 0.24 so find 0.24 × 60 cm, which is 14.4 cm.

Increase or decrease by a percentage

Example 7

Increase £50 by 15%.

Find 15% of £50, which is £0.15 × 50 = £7.50.
Add this to the original £50, making £57.50.

Example 8

Decrease £900 by 12%

Find 12% of £900, which is £0.12 × 900 = £108.
Subtract this from the original £900, leaving £792.

Profit and Loss

Example 9

A dealer buys an article for £60 and wants to make a profit of 25% on it. What price must he sell it for?

$25\% = \dfrac{25}{100} = \frac{1}{4}$, so he wants to make $\frac{1}{4}$ of £60 profit.

$\frac{1}{4}$ of £60 is £15 so he adds £15 onto the cost price of £60.
He sells it for £75.

Example 10

A dealer buys a car for £480 and has to sell it making a loss of 5%. How much does he sell it for?

$5\% = \dfrac{5}{100} = \dfrac{1}{20}$ so he loses $\dfrac{1}{20}$ of £480.

$\dfrac{1}{20}$ of £480 (or $0.05 \times £480$) = £24 so he loses £24.

He sells it for £$(480 - 24)$ = £456.

Simple Interest

If you invest money, this money earns money which is called Interest. e.g. If you invested money in a Building Society which was paying interest at 8% (per year), then for every £100 invested you get £8 every year.

Example 11

If £600 is invested at 8% per annum for 4 years, what is the Simple Interest? ('per annum' means 'for a year'. It is sometimes abbreviated to 'p.a.')

Every £100 invested gains £8 interest per year.
So £600 invested gains £48 interest per year.
£600 invested for 4 years gains £48 × 4 = £192.
The Simple Interest is £192.

This can also be worked out using the formula

$$I = \frac{PRT}{100}$$ where I is the Simple Interest
                                              P is the Principal, (the money invested)
                                              R is the rate per cent (per annum)
                                              T is the time (in years)

In this example, P = £600, R = 8, T = 4

$$I = \frac{PRT}{100} = £\frac{600 \times 8 \times 4}{100} = £192$$

Compound Interest

If the interest earned on money invested is added to the investment, then that money earns interest in future years. This is called Compound Interest.

Suppose £600 is invested at 8% per annum for 2 years and the interest is added to the investment.
In the first year the interest is 8% of £600.
This is £0.08 × 600 = £48.
This is added to the £600 so the account now holds £648.
In the second year the interest is 8% of £648.
This is £0.08 × 648 = £51.84.
This is added to the £648 so after 2 years the account holds £699.84.
If you need to find the total interest for the 2 years, it is £48 + £51.84 (or £699.84 − £600) and is £99.84.

Loans

If you borrow money then you probably have to pay interest on the loan. Usually you agree to make repayments at so much per month or per week and these amounts include the interest, so that you pay back more than you borrowed. The sooner you repay a loan the less the interest will be. The bank, finance company or other lender must tell you the true rate of interest. In advertisements look for the letters **APR** (Annual Percentage Rate), for instance APR 24.6% means that you will pay at that rate of interest over the period of the loan. It might be possible to find another source from which you could borrow money at a cheaper rate of interest.

VAT. Value Added Tax

This tax is added to the cost of many things you buy. In most shops the price marked includes the tax so you do not have to calculate it.

Occasionally, however, the prices are given without VAT and it has to be added to the bill.

The present rate of this tax is 15%.

Example 12

A builder says he will charge £80 for doing a small job. To this, VAT at 15% is added. What is the total cost?

The VAT is 15% of £80.
This is £0.15 × 80 = £12
The total cost is £80 + £12 = £92.

The rate of tax might be changed. If it has, work out this example using the up-to-date rate.

Income Tax

This is tax taken as a proportion of any money you earn. Most employees pay tax as PAYE which means 'Pay as you earn', so the tax is deducted from the pay by the employer, and the amount depends on how much is earned.

You are allowed a Personal Allowance, and maybe other Allowances. These give an amount you can earn without paying tax on it, then any income above that is taxed at a Basic Rate. There is also a Higher Rate tax so that people with high incomes pay more.

Example 13

Mr Taylor earns £12 000 a year. How much income tax will he pay?

(We will imagine that the Personal Allowance is £3000 and the Basic rate of tax is 25%. The questions in this book use imaginary rates, since every year, on Budget Day, the tax rates can be altered and we cannot forsee what they will be when you are reading this book. Also, Allowances vary according to whether you are single or married, or if you have children.)

Income	£12 000
Personal Allowance	£3 000
Taxable Income	£9 000

Tax. 25% of £9000 = £2250   (This is $\frac{1}{4}$ of £9000 or £0.25 × 9000)

Mr Taylor pays £2250 income tax in that year. That leaves him with £9750. (The tax will be deducted in equal amounts each week, if he is paid weekly, or each month if he is paid monthly. In addition to having tax deducted from his earnings he will also have National Insurance contributions deducted.)

If you know the up-to-date tax rates, work out this example using them.

Exercise 15.1

1. Express these percentages as fractions in their simplest forms.

   1 30%   **2** 35%   **3** 15%   **4** 40%   **5** 60%

2. Express as decimals.

   1 47%   **2** 95%   **3** 22%   **4** 6%   **5** 99%

3. Change these fractions or decimals to percentages.

   1 $\frac{3}{4}$ **2** $\frac{4}{5}$ **3** 0.15   **4** $\frac{7}{10}$ **5** 0.87

4. **1** Find 72% of £5   **4** Find 75% of £3.20
   2 Find 80% of 75 p   **5** Find 20% of 65 p
   3 Find 15% of £4.20

5. **1** Find 48% of 200   **4** Find 10% of 50 cm
   2 Find 30% of 400 g   **5** Find 62% of 50 litres
   3 Find 5% of 40 minutes

6. **1** Increase £6 by 4%   **4** Decrease £75 by 20%
   2 Increase £2.60 by 15%   **5** Increase £300 by 12%
   3 Decrease £120 by 10%

7. **1** Find the selling price of an article which cost £2.50 to make, and is sold making a profit of 20%.

   2 Find the selling price of an article which was bought for £4 and sold making a loss of 25%.

   3 Find the selling price of a car which was bought for £800 and sold making a profit of 12%.

   4 Find the selling price of some furniture which a dealer bought for £600 and had to sell making a loss of 12%.

   5 William bought a bike for £40. Later on he sold it, making a gain of 5%. How much money did he gain on the sale?

8. **1** A dealer bought a car for £1200 and made 40% profit when he sold it. What price did he sell it for?

2 To clear goods during a sale a shopkeeper reduced the prices by 10%. What would you pay for a vase previously priced at £3.60?

3 A bottle of shampoo normally holds 300 ml of liquid. A special bottle marked '10% extra' is put on sale. What quantity should it hold?

4 Miss Scott earned £9000, then she was given an 8% pay-rise. What was her new salary?

5 A meal in a restaurant cost £15. To this a service charge of 10% was added. What was the total cost?

9. Find the Simple Interest, using the formula $I = \dfrac{PRT}{100}$, or otherwise, if

1 £250 is invested for 3 years at 8% per annum,

2 £600 is invested for 4 years at 11% p.a,

3 £840 is invested for 2 years at 10% p.a.

10. If £360 is invested at 5% p.a., find the interest paid at the end of the first year. If this interest is added to the money invested, find the interest which will be paid at the end of the second year.

11. If £1000 is invested at 9% per annum, find the interest paid at the end of the first year.
    If the interest is added to the money invested, find the interest which will be paid at the end of the second year.
    What is the total interest paid for the 2 years?

12. Mrs Evans wants to borrow some
    money to finance a special project.
    Four firms are willing to lend her the
    money.

    A  B

    1 Which firm charges the cheapest
       rate of interest?

    2 Which firm charges the dearest rate
       of interest?

    C  D

13. Mr Parmar buys some DIY materials marked at £24. VAT at 15% is added to
    this price. What is the total cost, including the tax?

14. Mr Kent employed a firm to do some repairs and the bill, excluding VAT, came
    to £184. How much extra had to be paid for VAT at 15%? What was the total
    bill?

15. Mr Yates had a taxable income of £8800. How much income tax did he pay if
    the tax rate was 25%?

16. Assuming that the income tax rates were: Personal Allowance £2200, Basic rate
    of tax 30%; find how much tax Miriam Kirby paid in the year if her salary was
    £9000. If this tax was paid in equal monthly instalments, how much did she pay
    per month?

    (Taxable income = salary − personal allowance. Tax paid in the year = 30% of
    taxable income.)

17. A firm owns machinery which was worth £2000 last year. During the year the
    value of the machinery has been reduced by 5%. What is it worth today?
    If during the coming year it loses 5% of today's value, what will it be worth in
    a year's time?

Exercise 15.2

1. Write down the percentages equivalent to these fractions.

   $\frac{1}{2}$, $\frac{1}{4}$, $\frac{1}{5}$, $\frac{1}{10}$, $\frac{1}{20}$, $\frac{1}{100}$

2. Write down the fractions equivalent to these percentages.

   30%, $33\frac{1}{3}$%,   40%, $66\frac{2}{3}$%,   75%

3. In an election 40 000 people voted. Of the 3 candidates A, B, C; A got 25% of
   the votes, B got 35% and C got the rest.
   1 What percentage of votes did C get?
   2 Who won the election?
   3 How many votes did the winner get?

4. A grocer bought 10 cases of tinned fruit at £7.50 per case, each case containing 24 tins. He sold some tins at 42 p each but the remainder were damaged and unfit for sale. He made 12% profit on the sales.

    1 How much money did he take from the sales?
    2 How many tins did he sell?

5. In a school, pupils can learn either French or German or Spanish. In a year group of 150 pupils, 50% of the pupils learn French and 40% learn German. What percentage learn Spanish? How many pupils learn each language?
    If there are 25 pupils in each French class, 20 pupils in each German class and just 1 class for Spanish, how many classes are there altogether?

6. Debbie knits a jumper from 12 balls of wool costing 40 p per ball. In addition the pattern costs 20 p. She sells the jumper, making 60% profit on what it cost her. How much did she sell it for?

7. A car insurance premium is £195 but there is a deduction of 60% of this for 'no claims discount'. How much is deducted, and how much remains to be paid?

8. One firm will lend £800 at 10% per annum Simple Interest while another will lend it at 9% per annum Simple Interest. If the money is needed for 2 years, how much cheaper would it be to borrow from the second firm?

9. Mr Turner buys this car and is allowed a discount of 5%.

    1 What discount does he get?
    2 What does he actually pay for the car?

10. Machinery which cost £5600 when new was reduced in value by 20% in its first year and by 10% in the second year.

    1 How much did it lose in value in the first year?
    2 What was its value after 1 year?
    3 How much did it lose in value in the second year?
    4 What was its value after 2 years?

11. In one tax year Mr Burke's taxable income was £5200. He paid income tax at the rate of 30%. How much tax did he pay?
    The money was deducted from his wages weekly. How much tax was taken out per week? (In one year there are 52 weeks.)

12. A firm prints photographs on paper of size 10 cm square. If they decide to make larger prints, size 11.2 cm square,

    1 what is the new area?
    2 The firm have advertised their prints as being 25% larger. Is this correct?

13. A house was valued at £25 000. During the next year, due to a rise in house prices, its value increased by 10%. In the second year its value increased over the year by 8%. What was the house worth at the end of the 2 years?

14. Here is an advertisement for a loan.

Secured Loans Weekly Equivalent Payments				e.g. £8250 over 5 yrs = £227.98 per month Total cost of repayment = £13 678.80 APR 22.4% variable. Total cost greatly reduced on early settlement
LOAN	10 yrs	$7\frac{1}{2}$ yrs	5 yrs	
£2250	£10.52	£11.69	£14.34	
£3200	£14.96	£16.63	£20.40	
£5500	£25.71	£28.58	£34.89	

1 What does the advertisement quote for the annual percentage rate of interest?

Mr Parker wishes to borrow £3200 to buy a car and he decides he can afford to repay about £15 per week.

2 For how long will he take out the loan?
3 What will the total payment be?
4 Instead of this, he thinks he ought to pay more weekly, so as to repay the loan in 5 years. How much extra per week will this cost him, and what will the total payment be in this case?

15. Copy and complete this phone bill. (The rates are not up-to-date.)

Quarterly rate		£17.35
Previous reading 001501	Present reading 001622	
___ units at 5.0 p		___
Total (exclusive of VAT)		___
Add VAT at 15%		___
Total payable		___

(If you know the up-to-date rates you may prefer to use them.)

PUZZLE

44. Arrange (a) three 1's, (b) three 2's, (c) three 4's, without using any mathematical signs, so that you represent the highest possible number in each case.

Miscellaneous section C

Exercise C1   Aural Practice

If possible find someone to read these questions to you.
You should do questions 1 to 15 within 10 minutes.
Do not use your calculator.
Write down the answers only.

1. From London to Manchester is 184 miles. What is this distance to the nearest 10 miles?

2. If 1 gallon of petrol costs £1.70, how much will 2 gallons cost?

3. Pauline arrived at school at 13 minutes to 9. School begins at 5 minutes to 9. How many minutes early was she?

4. What is 7 less than one-quarter of 48?

5. The sides of a triangle have lengths 6 cm, 8 cm and 10 cm. What is its perimeter?

6. What fraction of 1 metre is 20 cm?

7. An old clock gains 5 minutes a day. If it is correct at noon on Sunday, what time will it show at noon on the following Wednesday?

8. If 20 equal packages weigh 60 kg, what is the weight of 1?

9. What is left when 0.9 is subtracted from 1?

10. A rectangular piece of paper measuring 30 cm by 20 cm is cut into squares with side 5 cm. How many squares can be made?

11. A girl was 5 years old in 1986. When will she be 16 years old?

12. Three parcels weigh 5 kg, 6 kg and 10 kg. What is their average weight?

13. I bought 3 similar tins of beans and received 67 pence change from £1. How much did one tin of beans cost?

14. If a car costing £500 is sold at a profit of 20%, what is the selling price?

15. There are two parcels with total weight 10 kg. One is 4 kg heavier than the other. What does the heavier one weigh?

Additional aural questions using data from other pages.

16. Turn to page 22. Use the insurance table, of question 15.

    What is the cost of insurance for a 14 day summer holiday in France?

17.   Turn to page 64. Use the bus timetable, of question 12.

Mrs Greene uses this bus service to go to Suntown on market days. How long does she spend in town, before catching the bus home?

18.   Turn to page 63. Use the rainfall graph of question 9.

In which month was a rainfall of 7.9 cm recorded?

19.   Turn to page 93. Use the table of prices for curtains, of question 14. Mrs Smith needs a pair of curtains either 90 by 90 inches or 108 by 90 inches. What is the difference in price?

20.   Turn to page 110. Use the table of postage rates, of question 7.

What is the cost of postage for a parcel weighing 1.5 kg which is sent at the area rate?

21.   Turn to page 198. Use the rectangle drawn round the table in question 15.

This rectangle is 10.5 cm long. Estimate its height (width).

22.   Turn to page 221. Use the diagram of question 14.

Estimate the size of the obtuse angle *AOB*.

Exercise C2   Multi-choice Exercise

Select the correct answer to each question.

1.   Which of the following has no axis of symmetry?

   A   right-angled isosceles triangle   **B**   equilateral triangle

   C   square   **D**   rhombus   **E**   parallelogram

2.   In this quadrilateral, the angles *a* and *b* are equal. The size of angle *a* is

   A   98°   **B**   110°   **C**   115°

   D   130°   **E**   140°

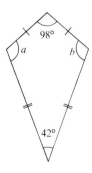

3.   Which one of the following statements referring to a parallelogram is **not** correct?

   A   opposite angles equal   **B**   sum of angles = 360°

   C   opposite sides equal   **D**   opposites sides parallel

   E   diagonals equal

4. The mean of the numbers 6, 5, 8, 11, 7, 6, 13 is

    A 6   **B** $6\frac{1}{2}$ **C** 7   **D** 8   **E** 11

5. The median of the numbers 6, 5, 8, 11, 7, 6, 13 is

    A 6   **B** $6\frac{1}{2}$ **C** 7   **D** 8   **E** 11

6. A length of 9060 mm is equal to

    A 9.06 m   **B** 9.06 km   **C** 90.6 cm   **D** 90 600 cm

    E 0.0906 km

7. Four goats are tethered to posts at *A*, *B*, *C* and
    D and the boundaries of the regions they can
    graze are shown. The regions which can be
    grazed by more than two goats are

    A 1, 2, 3, 5, 6, 7   **B** 1, 2, 3, 4, 5, 6, 7

    C 1, 3, 5, 7   **D** 2, 4, 6

    E 2, 6

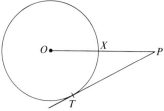

8. In the diagram, the line *PT* is called

    A a tangent   **B** a radius

    C a diameter   **D** a chord

    E an arc

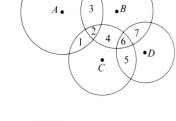

9. A bicycle wheel is 70 cm in diameter. How far has the bicycle travelled when the
    wheel has made 500 complete turns? (Take π as $\frac{22}{7}$)

    A 110 m   **B** 220 m   **C** 350 m   **D** 1100 m

    E 2200 m

10. A courtyard is 10 m long and 6 m wide. It is paved with flagstones which are $\frac{1}{2}$ m
    square. How many are needed?

    A 32   **B** 60   **C** 64   **D** 120   **E** 240

11. *ABCD* is a square with diagonal *BD*,
    $\triangle CDE$ is isosceles with $CD = DE$. What
    is the size of $\angle BDE$?

    A 80°   **B** 85°   **C** 90°

    D 95°   **E** 100°

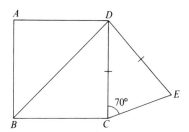

12. $\dfrac{19.5 \times 0.21}{5.1}$ is approximately equal to

A 0.0008   **B** 0.008   **C** 0.08   **D** 0.8   **E** 8

13. A man earns £7500, and he gets a pay-rise of 6%. The following year he get a pay-rise of 4%. What does he earn then?

A £7950   **B** £8250   **C** £8268   **D** £10 625   **E** £10 937.50

14. In $\triangle PQR$, the length of PQ is $\frac{3}{4}$ of the length of PR, and QR is 6 cm longer than PQ. The perimeter of the triangle is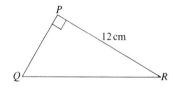

A 34 cm   **B** 36 cm   **C** 39 cm

D 48 cm   **E** 54 cm

15. Jack and Bill are partners in a business. Jack takes 65% of the profit and Bill gets the remainder. What fraction of the profit does Bill receive?

A $\frac{7}{20}$ **B** $\frac{13}{20}$ **C** $\frac{7}{13}$ **D** $\frac{3}{10}$ **E** $\frac{1}{3}$

16. Which of the numbers 71, 75, 77, 79 are prime numbers?

A 71, 77 only   **B** 77, 79 only   **C** 71, 79 only

D 71, 77, 79   **E** all of them

17. $4\frac{3}{4} - 2\frac{2}{3} + 1\frac{1}{6} =$

A $2\frac{1}{12}$ **B** $2\frac{11}{12}$ **C** $3\frac{1}{12}$ **D** $3\frac{1}{4}$ **E** $3\frac{4}{7}$

18. A shopkeeper buys an article for £2.70. His marked selling price is 10% more than the cost price. His marked selling price is

A £2.80   **B** £2.84   **C** £2.97   **D** £3.00   **E** £5.40

19. This figure consists of a square of side 10 cm and an isosceles triangle of height 8 cm. The area of the whole figure is

A 60 cm^2 **B** 80 cm^2 **C** 90 cm^2

D 140 cm^2 **E** 180 cm^2

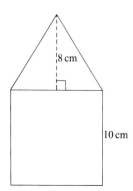

20. In △ABC, the mid-point of BC is M, and
     MA = MB = AB. The size of ∠BAC is

     A   More than 60° but less than 90°

     B   Exactly 90°

     C   Between 90° and 120°

     D   Exactly 120°

     E   More than 120°

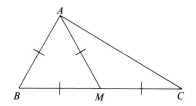

Exercise C3 Revision

1. Write correct to the nearest thousand.

    1 63912   **2** 26357   **3** 4781   **4** 9501   **5** 51499

2. Copy the diagram and

    1 reflect █ in the line AB,

    2 reflect █ in the line CD,

    3 rotate █ through 90° clockwise
         about the point E,

    4 rotate █ through 180° about
         the point G.

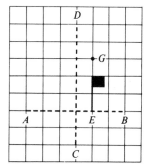

3. Find the total cost of the ingredients used in
    making a cake from 150 g of butter, 150 g of
    sugar, 3 eggs and 200 g of flour, when flour
    costs 40 p for a 2 kg bag, butter 50 p for 250 g,
    sugar 60 p for a kg bag and eggs 80 p per
    dozen.

4. How many square tiles of length 50 cm are needed to cover the floor of a
    rectangular room 5 m by 4 m?

5. $C = \dfrac{1000P}{V}$, where P is power in kilowatts, V is voltage in volts, C is current in
    amps. If the local voltage is 240 volts, what is the current for a 2 kW fire, to the
    nearest amp?

6. Simplify

    1 5.32×100 **4** $55 \div 0.11$

    2 0.07×0.5

    3 $2.8 \div 70$ **5** $\dfrac{6.3 \times 0.8}{0.56}$

7. Construct a triangle with sides 10 cm, 9 cm and 7 cm. Measure the largest angle. Draw a line from this angle perpendicular to the opposite side. Measure this line, to the nearest mm. Hence find the area of the triangle.

8. A woman has a salary of £12 000. If for income tax she has a personal allowance of £2200 and tax is paid on the remainder of her income at 27%, find how much tax she pays in the year. If her salary is raised by £1000, how much extra tax will she pay?

9. $ABCD$ is a square, BEC is an isosceles triangle and $\angle CED = \angle AEB = 90°$. $\angle BEC = 42°$. Find the size of $\angle CDE$.

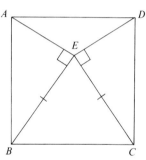

10. The marks of 12 students in a test are 5, 5, 6, 6, 6, 7, 8, 8, 10, 10, 14, 17. Find

    1 the mode,

    2 the median,

    3 the mean,

    4 the range, of the marks.

11. A square has a side of 1.7 cm and a circle has radius 1 cm. Which has the greater perimeter, and by how much? Take π as 3.14

12. In the diagram, AD bisects $\angle BAC$. Find the size of $\angle C$.

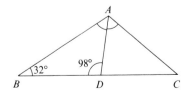

Exercise C4   Revision

1. 1 The marks on a
       harbour wall show
       the water level at
       −2 (feet). Where
       will it be when the
       water has risen 6
       feet?

    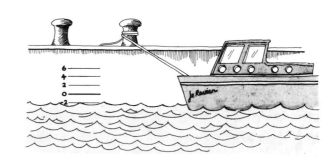

    2 At its highest point
       the water level was
       at 6 (feet), and
       several hours later
       it was at −6 (feet).
       What was the fall in
       the tide?

2. In a certain quarter the quarterly rental charge
    for a telephone was £14.20, and each unit used
    cost 4.30 pence. To the total amount, VAT
    was added at 15%. What was the telephone
    bill in that quarter if 600 units had been used?

3. Find the Simple Interest on £125 for 4 years at 8% per annum.

4. Find the size of angle d.

5. The probability of Amy winning a prize in a raffle is $\frac{7}{100}$, the probability of
    Barbara winning it is $\frac{1}{20}$ and the probability of Charles winning it is $\frac{2}{25}$. What is
    the probability that none of them will win it?

6. P is a point on the rim of
    a bicycle wheel. At the start,
    P touches the ground at A.
    The bicycle is moved forward
    until P touches the ground at B,
    the wheel having moved through
    one complete turn.

    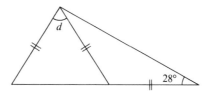

    If the diameter of the wheel is 35 cm, find the length of AB.
    How many metres will a cyclist have travelled when the wheel has made 100
    turns? Take π as 3.14.

7. Three men weigh 60 kg, 58 kg and 68 kg. What is their average weight? A fourth man joins them and the average weight of all four is 64 kg. What is the total weight of all four? What does the fourth man weigh?

8. Construct a quadrilateral $ABCD$ as follows:
    Draw a line AC, 10 cm long.
    Draw the perpendicular bisector of AC, cutting AC at M.
    Find points B and D on the bisector, such that $BM = MD = 3$ cm.
    Join AB, BC, CD, DA.
    Measure AB, to the nearest mm.
    Measure $\angle ABC$.
    What sort of quadrilateral is $ABCD$?

9. A soil sample is found to have the following composition.

    Air   25%
    Water   25%
    Mineral material   45%
    Organic material   5%

    Draw a bar chart showing this information.

10. In the diagram, the angle marked x is 52°. Find the size of the angle marked y. O is the centre of the circle.

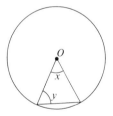

11. A fence is erected round a rectangular field which is 100 metres long and 80 metres wide. What is the total cost of the fence, if it costs £3 per metre of length?

12. 1 Express $\frac{2}{7}$ as a decimal, correct to 2 decimal places.

    2 Express 0.005 as a fraction in its lowest terms.

Exercise C5   Practical work and Investigations

1. **Ways of paying for goods and services**

    e.g. Cash, cheque, credit card, hire-purchase, bank loan, payments by instalments, tokens such as TV licence stamps, having an account at a shop.
    Find out details about each method. Consider the advantages and disadvantages of each.

2. **Planning for a Wedding**

This is a most important occasion in a couple's life and deserves proper planning. You can imagine it is your own wedding in a few years' time or the wedding of imaginary friends.

Decide what type of wedding. Church, other place of worship, Registry Office? It can be a very simple wedding with just two witnesses or a very grand one. Plan all the details of the wedding, and make a list of costs involved, with a separate note of who pays for each. Traditionally the bride's father paid for most things but that is not always the case nowadays. There are many small details to include, for instance, transport to the wedding, legal costs, wedding ring or rings. Plan the timetable for the day, so that the ceremony begins on time, and the couple leave for their honeymoon on time, especially if they have a train or plane to catch.

Illustrate your booklet with pictures, e.g. of the bride's dress.

(Magazines often have articles about weddings just before Easter, so that is a good time to find information for this topic.)

3. **Models of the main solid figures**

Make a set of models of the cube, cuboid, prism, etc., and display them.
As well as making models you could make a collection of tins and boxes of different shapes, arrange them in a display and take a photograph of them.
(These solid figures are shown on page 217.)

Plaited cubes

It is interesting to make a plaited cube. It has a different pattern to an ordinary net since faces have to overlap.

Copy the pattern. (It is useful to use the 2 cm squares on graph paper.)

Cut it out and crease all the lines, bending the paper away from the numbers so that the numbers stay on the outside. Now cover up number 1, by putting the square above number 5 sideways on top of it. Next cover up number 2, then 3 and so on. 5 is covered by 6, 7 is covered by 8. Finally there is one square left. Cut the corners off this one and tuck it in.

If you make several such cubes you can use them to investigate volumes and surface areas of different rectangular shapes. You can also use them as dice, but they may not give fair results. (You could investigate to see if the results were biased.)

Here also is a pattern for a plaited tetrahedron. The triangles are equilateral. Perhaps you can find out how to make other solid figures by plaiting.

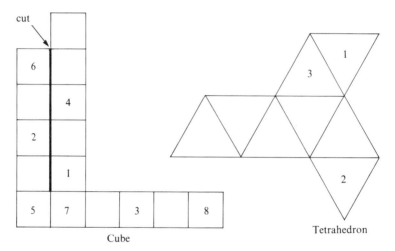

Cube

Tetrahedron

4. **Solid figures with pentagonal holes**

   These are easier to make than closed solid figures as you can get your fingers inside the solids to press the glued faces together.

   1   Rhombicosidodecahedron

   The basic figure is a square (of side 3 cm) with equilateral triangles on two opposite sides. You need 30 pieces like this. One way is to draw several squares in a line, on cardboard, then with compasses, radius 3 cm, find the points above and below for the third points of the equilateral triangles. When you have the pattern for some pieces, copy them by putting another piece of cardboard underneath, then prick through the main points using your compasses. (Put something underneath to protect the desk.) Then join these points.

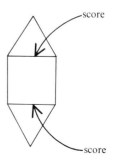

You must score the two lines by putting a ruler along them and then drag your compass point along so that it makes a nick in the lines. Always fold away from the side you scored on. Fold these lines slightly.

Now take 5 pieces and glue them together with triangles exactly on top of each other, to make a ring like this.

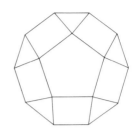

Then glue a third triangle on the top of each other two to start off 5 more rings like this.

Complete these rings with 2 more pieces each. (Every ring has an edge of 5 squares because it is a pentagonal hole. i.e. a hole with 5 edges.)
Continue in this way so that there are 3 triangles stuck together every time.

2 Snub dodecahedron

This is made in a similar way to the previous model.
The basic figure is 4 equilateral triangles.
Make the edges 3 cm long.
You need 30 pieces. As before, you can make a block of several pieces together and then copy them.
Score the 3 inside lines and bend slightly.
Glue together as for the last model, only using the triangles at the ends of the strips for glueing together.

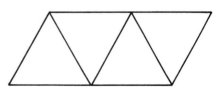

3   Spherical truncated icosahedron

The basic figure is a regular hexagon in a
circle. (See page 311 question 5 method 2.)
You need 20 pieces like this.
Cut off 3 alternate segments.
Score the other 3 lines and bend away from the
scored side.

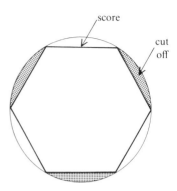

Glue 2 pieces together by the small curved segment. Add pieces until 5 hexagons
are joined together in a circle, with the curved segments on the outside.
Add other pieces to the unused segments and continue making pentagonal holes.

5.   Volumes

When we measure volume we compare it with a unit
volume. We can use the volume of a cube of side 1 cm
for the unit. This is called 1 cubic centimetre and written as
1 cm^3, sometimes as 1 cc.

Try to find 24 equal sized cubes.
Cubes of side 1 cm are rather small to make so you may prefer to use bigger ones
and imagine that they are 1 cm cubes. You could use child's building blocks, oxo
cubes, sugar lumps, dice, cubes made by your class or cubes cut out of wood.
You could make plaited cubes as shown on page 208, but put some blu-tack
inside to make them heavier and easier to handle.
Together these cubes make a volume of 24 cm^3 (or 24 cubic units). By arranging
them together, find some shapes which have a volume of 24 cm^3.
Some of these shapes are cuboids (rectangular blocks). What are the
measurements of cuboids which have a volume of 24 cm^3? If you had more
cubes, say 60 cubes, what sizes of cuboids could you make? Can you find the
formula for the volume of a cuboid?
How many cubes do you need to make a larger cube? What is the formula for
the volume of a cube?

If we are measuring larger volumes we will compare them with 1 m^3. Imagine
you are making a cube of edge 1 m with cubes of edge 1 cm. How many small
cubes will you need? This tells you how many cm^3 make 1 m^3.

You can extend your investigations to the volumes of other solid shapes such as
prisms, pyramids, cylinders, cones and spheres.

The Greek mathematician, Archimedes, who lived about 200 B.C., needed to find the volume of the King's crown. (When he knew the exact volume, he could prove that it was not made of solid gold, because it did not weigh the same as such a volume of gold would have weighed.) Can you find out the method he used to find the volume?

When you have finished investigating with the 24 cubes, if you can find 3 more, to make 27 altogether, stick them together to make these 6 pieces. Then see if you can rearrange the 6 pieces to form a larger cube.

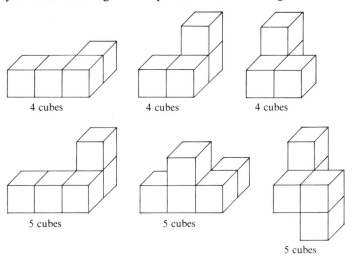

4 cubes   4 cubes   4 cubes

5 cubes   5 cubes

5 cubes

6. More experiments in statistics and probability

1 The average number of tosses of a coin needed to get a head

Before you begin, estimate

(1) what is the most likely number (mode number) of tosses made before you get a head,
(2) what is the average number (mean number) of tosses made before you get a head.

Toss a coin and count the number of tosses before you get a head.
e.g. tail, tail, head, counts as 3.
(You can use the results of a previous experiment if you have kept them.)
Repeat about 100 times.
Put the results in a tally chart, then find the mode number and the mean number of tosses.
How close were your estimates?

6.   **2   The average number of throws of a die needed to get a six**

Do this experiment in a similar way.

3   This experiment involves 8 beads in a bag. 6 are red and 2 are blue. You draw out the beads one at a time until a blue one appears.
Before you begin, estimate

(1) what is the most likely number (mode number) of beads drawn out,
(2) what is the average number (mean number) of beads drawn out.

Put the beads in a bag and shake them up and then draw out the beads one at a time until a blue one appears. If it is the third one out, count that result as 3. Replace the beads and repeat the experiment about 100 times.
Put the results in a tally chart, then find the mode number and mean number of draws.
How close were your estimates?
(If you have not got any beads, anything suitable will do, as long as the items feel the same and two of them are marked differently from the rest.)

4   To find the probability that two dominoes match each other

Before you begin, estimate how many times out of 100 trials two dominoes will match.

Put the set of dominoes in a bag and draw two out at random. Count it as a success (s) if the dominoes match and a failure (f) if they do not.
e.g. $2 - 4$ and $3 - 5$ have no number in common and do not match, (f),
      $2 - 4$ and $4 - 4$ have 4 in common and match, (s),
      $2 - 4$ and $1 - 2$ have 2 in common and match, (s),
      $0 - 0$ and $0 - 6$ have 0 in common and match, (s).
Repeat the experiment 100 times, recording your results.
How close was your estimate?
From your experiment, the probability that two dominoes will match each other

is $\dfrac{s}{100}$.

6. **5 Find π using probability and by tossing sticks.** If you toss sticks over a set of parallel lines then the sticks may either land touching or across a line, or land completely between the lines. The probability that a stick will touch a line is $\dfrac{2s}{\pi d}$, where the sticks are s cm long and the lines are d cm apart.

Use the floorboards of the room if they form parallel lines, otherwise draw lines on the floor. Find 10 thin sticks with length about $\frac{3}{4}$ of the distance between the lines. Toss the sticks randomly 50 times, and find the total number n, out of 500, which land touching or across a line. Then $\dfrac{n}{500}$ is an estimate of the probability.

So $\dfrac{n}{500} = \dfrac{2s}{\pi d}$. This formula rearranged gives $\pi = \dfrac{1000\,s}{nd}$. Put your numbers for s, n and d into this formula to find an experimental value for π. Is your result close to the true value of 3.14?

7. **Curve stitching and String Art**

Curve stitching is done with embroidery thread onto cardboard. Here is a basic pattern to get you started. Draw any lines and mark points on the wrong side of the cardboard so that only the thread shows on the right side.

Draw 2 lines AB, AC 9 cm long, meeting at A at an angle of about $50°$.

Mark 8 points along AB 1 cm apart and number them from 1 to 8 starting 1 cm from A. Mark 8 points along CA 1 cm apart and number them from $1'$ to $8'$ starting 1 cm from C.

3-strand embroidery thread is suitable to use. Choose a colour which shows up against the background of the cardboard.

Begin by making a knot then go through point 1 from the wrong side to the right side. Prick the hole at $1'$ so that you can find it from the right side and go through hole $1'$ from right side to wrong side. Go on the wrong side to $2'$ (because that is nearer than 2), go through $2'$ and then through 2. Then go through 3 and $3'$, and so on until you have used all the numbers. Fasten off the thread by looping under some on the wrong side, and tying it. On the right side the threads will make the outline of a parabola.

Now you can invent your own patterns. Perhaps start with two sides of a square, then the opposite two sides, then the other pairs of sides in another colour.

String Art is based on the same idea but it is done on a board with nails and thread. Paint the board or cover it with cloth, to contrast with the colour of the thread. Use nails $\frac{3}{4}$ inch long, with large heads so that the thread will not slip off. Draw the pattern above on paper, put it over the board and then knock nails in positions 1 to 8 and $1'$ to $8'$. Remember which is which and then tear off the paper.

Start by knotting the thread round nail 1, leaving a small end to tuck in later. Take the thread to $1'$ and go round the nail, then go to $2'$ and round the nail, then to 2, 3, $3'$, $4'$ and so on. Fasten off round nail 8 and try to tuck the end out of sight.

Now invent your own patterns using this basic design.

You may get further ideas from the next question.

8.   **Cardioids and other designs from circles**

Draw a circle and divide the circumference into 72 equal parts. (If you choose
a radius just larger than that of your protractor you can mark off points every
5° along the protractor edge.)

Number the points from 1 to 72 in order.

Join 1 to 2, 2 to 4, 3 to 6, 4 to 8, and so on, with straight lines. After joining 36
to 72 imagine the numbering continues past 72, or continue numbering, so that
the point numbered 2 is also number 74. Continue joining 37 to 74, 38 to 76, etc.
Number 72 will join to 144, which is the same point, so just make a dot there.
You can investigate similar ideas by joining 1 to 3, 2 to 6, 3 to 9 etc., then 1 to
4, and so on. You can also number points in a positive direction and a negative
direction and join 1 to -2, 2 to -4, etc.

For extended patterns, don't draw the circle, only mark the points, and manage
without numbering them. Draw another circle with the same centre and a radius
2 or 3 cm larger. When you join 2 points, extend the line in both directions until
it meets the outer circle.

These patterns could be done as curve stitching. Remember to do the drawing
on the wrong side of the work in this case.

A mystic rose pattern.

Divide the circumference into 20 equal parts. Join every point to every other one.
Try a mystic rose extended pattern, or try using different colours.

The mystic rose makes a good pattern for string art, but use a number of points
which is a prime number, such as 23. Get a large board and 1 inch nails. Start
by joining points which are nearly opposite so go 1 to 12, 12 to 23, and continue
going round missing out 10 nails each time. When you get back to 1 go 1 to 11,
11 to 21, 21 to 8, etc. missing out 9 nails each time. Eventually you go 1 to 2,
2 to 3, 3 to 4, etc., when you should wind the string firmly round each nail.

Patterns in squares.

Draw a square side 12 cm. Mark points round the perimeter every 2 cm, starting
at a corner. Join every point to every other point.

To make an extended design, don't mark the square, only put dots for the points.
Draw another square to surround them, with 2 cm of space in-between. Extend
all lines in both directions to meet the outer square.

Experiment with other designs.

You could also experiment with designs based on equilateral triangles or other
regular polygons.

9. **Cubes**

(a) Work out the cubes from 1^3 to 10^3.
Copy and complete this pattern.

natural numbers	sum	cubes of natural numbers	sum
1	1	1^3	1
$1 + 2$	3	$1^3 + 2^3$	9
$1 + 2 + 3$	6	$1^3 + 2^3 + 3^3$	36
...		...	
$1 + 2 + \cdots + 10$	55	$1^3 + 2^3 + \cdots + 10^3$	

What do you notice about the connection between the 2nd and 4th columns?
Double the numbers in column (2) and divide each by the largest number of the
same row in column (1). What do you notice? Can you use this pattern to find

(1) $1 + 2 + 3 + \cdots + 20$,

(2) $1^3 + 2^3 + 3^3 + \cdots + 20^3$?

(b) Several cubes of edge 1 cm are stacked together to form a larger cube. This
larger cube is then painted on the outside. Thus the small cubes may have some
of their faces painted. Make a table of results for the small cubes.

Edge of large cube	Number of small cubes	Number with these faces painted			
		0 faces	1 face	2 faces	3 faces
2 cm	8	0	0	0	8
3 cm	27				
4 cm					
5 cm					
...					

Do you notice any patterns? What would be the results for a large cube of edge
10 cm?

10. **For the Computer Programmer**

More suggestions for programs:

1 To find the mean of a set of numbers.
2 To calculate the circumferences of circles of
   different radii.
3 To calculate areas of various figures.
4 To work out Simple Interest, Compound
   Interest, VAT, Income Tax, etc.

To the student:

4   Making plans for revision

As the time of the examination draws nearer you should look back over your progress and see if you are satisfied with it, and make a plan of action for the future. If you have been working steadily from the beginning of the course, you may not need to make any extra effort. If you enjoy the challenge of Maths you are probably working well and learning everything as you go along. But if you find some of the work difficult and are feeling discouraged, perhaps a little extra effort at this stage, and perhaps a change in the way you approach your work, will help to improve your standard, and you will feel more confident.

In addition to lessons and set homework you should spend some time each week on individual study. Make a plan for this depending on how much time you have available and what you need to learn or practise. In addition to Maths, you will have work to do in all your other subjects, so take these into consideration. If you have to do a 'Project' in any subject, then start it in good time or you will find yourself at the last minute spending all your time on it, and your other work is neglected.

There is a revision checklist on page 358. You could copy this, and use it to decide what you are going to do. You could work through this book again in order, spending so much time on each chapter. Choose a suitable selection of questions to do, either straightforward ones if you need practice in these, or the more challenging questions if you are more confident with the topic. Alternatively, you could use the revision exercises in the miscellaneous sections A to E of the book. You might prefer to revise all the arithmetic, then the statistics, then the geometry, and so on. The important thing is that **you** should decide for yourself what **you** need to do, and then plan how you are going to do it.

Sort out your difficulties as you go along. Try to think things out for yourself as far as possible, rather than having to be shown how to do everything. But if you need extra help, then **ask** someone to help you, either your teacher, someone in your class or a higher class, a parent or a friend.

Keep a list of what you are doing. At first there will be a lot to do and not much done, but you will find it encouraging when after a few weeks you can see that you are making real progress.

About Chapters 16 to 20

The Geometry of solid figures, together with calculations of volumes, is in Chapter 16. (There is an introduction to volume in Exercise C5.) There is more Geometry in Chapter 19, dealing with similarity and enlargements and scale drawing. More Arithmetic, of ratio and rate, comes in Chapter 17. This includes some real-life applications which you will find useful to know later. Graphs are used in Chapter 18, and there are other graphs included with the work on time and speed in Chapter 20. Details about 'the calendar' are also included in this chapter.

16 *Solid figures*

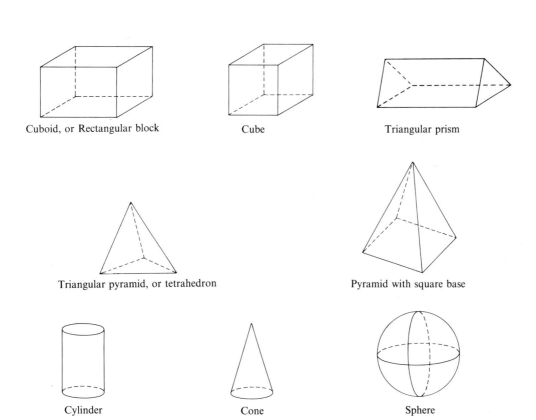

Cuboid, or Rectangular block

Cube

Triangular prism

Triangular pyramid, or tetrahedron

Pyramid with square base

Cylinder

Cone

Sphere

Nets of solid figures

These are the patterns which when cut out and folded will make the solid figures.

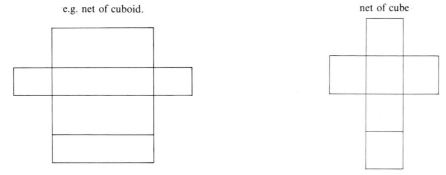

e.g. net of cuboid.

net of cube

net of pyramid with
square base

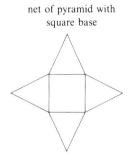

net of triangular prism

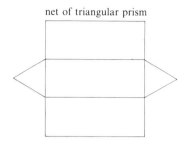

There are other arrangements possible, to make the same solid figures.

Volumes

There is a practical introduction to this section in Exercise C5, question 5.

Cuboid Volume = length × breadth × height = lbh

Cube Volume = (length)^3 = l^3

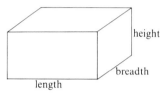

Surface areas

The surface area of a cuboid or cube is the sum of the areas of the 6 faces.

Example for a cuboid

To find the volume

Volume = lbh
$$= 10 \times 8 \times 5 \, cm^3$$
$$= 400 \, cm^3$$

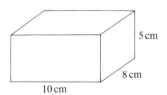

To find the total surface area

Area of front or back = 10 × 5 cm^2 = 50 cm^2
Area of a side = 8 × 5 cm^2 = 40 cm^2
Area of top or bottom = 10 × 8 cm^2 = 80 cm^2

Total area = 2 × (50 + 40 + 80) cm^2 = 340 cm^2

To find the total length of its edges

There are 4 edges of length 10 cm, 4 of 8 cm and 4 of 5 cm.
Total length = 4 × (10 + 8 + 5) cm = 92 cm

Exercise 16.1

1. Find the volumes of these figures, if they are built with cubes of edge 1 cm, by finding how many cubes are used.

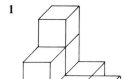

2
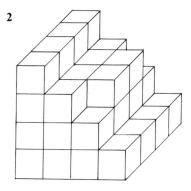

2. Find the volumes of these figures.

   1 A rectangular box 12 cm by 10 cm by 5 cm.
   2 A cube of edge 5 cm.
   3 A rectangular room 5 m by 4 m with height $2\frac{1}{2}$ m.
   4 A matchbox 7.5 cm by 4 cm by 1.5 cm.
   5 A case 50 cm by 30 cm by 18 cm.

3. Find the total surface areas of these figures.

   1 A rectangular box 12 cm by 5 cm by 3 cm.
   2 A cube of edge 3 cm.

4. A room is 4 m wide, 3 m long and $2\frac{1}{2}$ m high. What is the total area of the four walls?

5. This swimming pool is 1.8 m deep. Find the volume of water which it will hold.

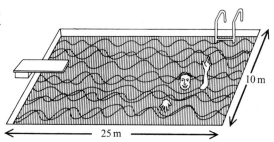

10 m

25 m

6. How many cubic metres of concrete will be needed to make a path 25 metres long, 1.6 metres wide, if the concrete is to be laid to a depth of 0.1 m?

7. A rectangular tank is 4 m long, $2\frac{1}{2}$ m wide and 3 m deep. How many cubic metres of water does it contain when it is half-full?

8. A box measures 10 cm by 6 cm by 4 cm.

   1 Find its volume.
   2 How many cubes of edge 2 cm will fit in the box?

9. Count the number of faces, edges and vertices (corners) on a cuboid, triangular prism, tetrahedron and pyramid on a square base.
    Copy and complete this table.
    F = number of faces, E = number of edges, V = number of vertices.

	F	E	V	$F + V - E$
cuboid				
triangular prism				
tetrahedron				
pyramid				

The relationship between F, E and V applies to all solids with plane faces (i.e. no curved faces).
If a solid figure has 15 plane faces and 12 vertices, how many edges will it have?

10. The net of a cube can be arranged in several different ways. Which of these drawings of arrangements of six equal squares, if cut out and folded, would make a cube?

(a)

(b)

(c)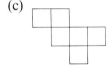

(d)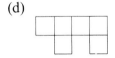

(e)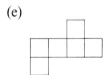

11. A solid consists of a triangular pyramid fitted exactly on top of a triangular prism. State how many faces, edges and vertices the solid figure has.

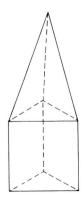

12. This net can be folded to make a
     triangular prism.
     Which letter(s) will point *A* join?

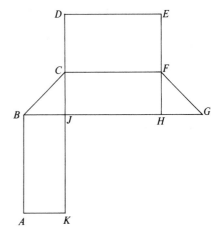

13. **1** The circular cylinder has an axis of
         symmetry. Sketch 3 other solid figures which
         have an axis of symmetry.

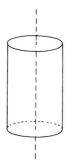

     2 The cylinder has a plane of symmetry. How
         many planes of symmetry has a cuboid?

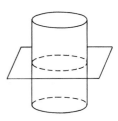

14. The curved surface of a cone is made from a
     sector of a circle. Draw a circle centre *O*, radius
     8 cm. Cut out the sector *AOB*, bend it round
     and join *OA* to *OB*. (The shape of the cone will
     depend on the size of ∠*AOB*.)
     What shape is needed to make the curved
     surface of a cylinder?

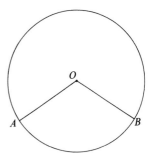

15. Some cylindrical tins have radius $3\frac{1}{2}$ cm and height 10 cm.
     The tins are packed in a rectangular box of length 28 cm, width 21 cm and height
     10 cm. How many tins will fit in a box?

Exercise 16.2

1. A child's sandpit is rectangular in shape, 2 m long and $1\frac{1}{2}$ m wide. What weight
    of sand is needed to fill it to a depth of $\frac{1}{2}$ m? (Assume 1 m³ of sand weighs
    1500 kg.)

2. A new road 4 km long and 25 m wide is to be constructed.
    1 How many square metres of land will be required?
    2 If the soil has to be removed to a depth of 0.3 m how many cubic metres of
       soil will have to be removed?

3. The internal dimensions of the base of a rectagular tank are 3 m by 2 m and it
    can contain water to a depth of 1.5 m. How long will it take to fill the tank by
    means of an inlet pipe delivering water at the rate of 50 litres per minute?
    $(1 \text{ m}^3 = 1000 \, l)$

4. Ice 0.1 m thick covered a rectangular paddling pool 20 m long and 15 m wide.
    Find the weight of ice, if 1 m³ of ice weighs 920 kg.

5. A square sheet of cardboard has sides length 17 cm.
    Out of each corner a square of side 4 cm is cut, and
    the flaps remaining are turned up to form an open
    box of depth 4 cm.
    What are the measurements of the box?
    Find its volume.

    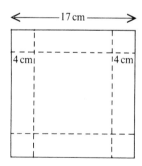

6. 1 If a large rectangular room has length 9 m, breadth 8 m and its volume is
       360 m³, what is its height?
    2 What is the surface area of a solid cube whose volume is 27 cm³?

7. The volume of a hemisphere can be found by
    using the approximate formula
    Volume = 2.1 × (radius)³
    This hemispherical dome has a radius of 2 m.
    Find its volume, correct to the nearest m³.

    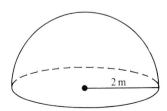

8. Two identical pyramids with square bases have their bases glued together to make a solid figure with 8 triangular faces (an octahedron). How many edges and vertices does this solid figure have?

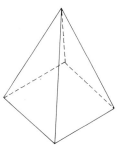 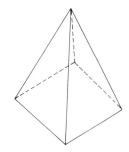

9. If small triangular pyramids are sliced off all the corners of a cube, how many faces, edges and vertices has the remaining solid?

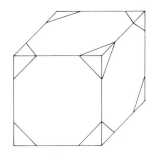

10. If the ends of a triangular prism are equilateral triangles and the other faces are rectangular, how many planes of symmetry has the prism?

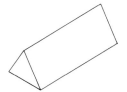

PUZZLES

45. Decode this bill. Each capital letter stands for a figure and each figure stands for the corresponding letter.

R	6480	at	LI pence each	UI
I	6489520	at	BI pence each	UI
L	372430	at	BN pence each	RP
L	3711430	at	C pence each	BN
				£L.SE

46. What is the next symbol in this sequence?

17 *Ratio and rate*

Ratio and Proportion

Examples

1   Express $25\,\text{cm} : 1\tfrac{1}{2}\,\text{m}$ as a ratio in its simplest form.

$\dfrac{25\,\text{cm}}{1\tfrac{1}{2}\,\text{m}} = \dfrac{25\,\text{cm}}{150\,\text{cm}} = \dfrac{25}{150} = \dfrac{1}{6}$. Ratio is $1:6$

2   Divide £24 in the ratio $3:5$

$3:5$ gives 8 parts. 1 part is $\dfrac{£24}{8} = £3$

Shares are $3 \times £3$ and $5 \times £3$, i.e. £9 and £15.

3   The angles of a triangle are in the ratio $4:5:6$. Find their sizes.
$4:5:6$ gives 15 parts.   The sum of the angles is $180°$.

1 part is $\dfrac{180°}{15} = 12°$

The angles are $4 \times 12°$, $5 \times 12°$, $6 \times 12°$, i.e. $48°$, $60°$ and $72°$.

4   Children aged 12 years, 9 years and 4 years share £1 in proportion to their ages. How much does the youngest child get?

Shares are in the ratio $12:9:4$, i.e. 25 parts.

1 part is $\dfrac{£1}{25} = 4\,\text{p}$

The youngest child gets $4 \times 4\,\text{p}$, i.e. 16p.

5   Increase $12\,\text{kg}$ in the ratio $5:3$

New weight is $\dfrac{5}{3}$ of $12\,\text{kg} = \dfrac{5}{3} \times 12\,\text{kg} = 20\,\text{kg}$

6   Decrease £120 in the ratio $9:10$

New amount is $\dfrac{9}{10}$ of $£120 = £\,\dfrac{9}{10} \times 120 = £108$

Exercise 17.1

1. Express as ratios in their simplest forms

    1   12 cm : 15 cm

    2   25 p : 60 p

    3   20 minutes : 32 minutes

    4   50 g : 240 g

    5   60 ml : 20 ml

2. 1   Divide £2.25 in the ratio 2 : 3

    2   Divide £1.54 in the ratio 4 : 7

    3   Divide 60 p in the ratio 7 : 3

    4   Divide £1.75 in the ratio 6 : 1

    5   Divide £4 in the ratio 7 : 3

3. 1   Increase £270 in the ratio 5 : 3

    2   Increase £37.50 in the ratio 9 : 5

    3   Decrease £280 in the ratio 4 : 7

    4   Decrease £12 in the ratio 5 : 8

    5   Increase £25 in the ratio 11 : 10

4. Two circles have diameters 8 cm and 10 cm. What is the ratio of their radii?

5. The angles of a quadrilateral are in the ratio 2 : 3 : 5 : 8. Find their sizes.

6. A line AB of length 9 cm is divided at P so that $AP : PB = 3 : 7$. Find the length of AP.

7. The costs of manufacture of an article are divided among labour, materials and overheads in the ratio 8 : 4 : 1. If the materials for 1000 articles cost £640, what are the costs for labour, and for overheads? What is the total cost of these articles?

8. Three men invest £2000, £3500 and £4500 respectively into a business and agree to share the profits in the ratio of their investments. The profits in the first year were £8000. How much did they each receive?

9. A shade of paint is made up of 3 parts blue and 4 parts purple. How many litres of blue are needed to make up 10.5 litres of this paint?

10. To make gunmetal, copper, tin and zinc are used in the ratio 43 : 5 : 2. What quantities of tin and zinc are used with 21.5 kg of copper?

11. Two boys share some apples in the ratio 4 : 3. The boy with the larger share took 56 apples. How many did the other boy take?

12.   What is the ratio of $75\,g : 2\,kg$ in its simplest form?

13.   A concrete mixture is made by mixing cement, sand and gravel by volume in the ratio $1:2:4$. How much sand and gravel must be added to $0.5\,m^3$ of cement?

14.   For these cylinders, find the ratio of

      1   their base-radii,

      2   their heights.

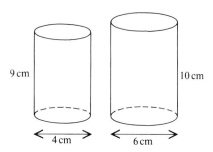

9 cm   10 cm

4 cm   6 cm

15.   Two spheres have radii 15 cm and 20 cm. What is the ratio of their diameters?

Direct and Inverse Proportion.

Quantities which increase in the same ratio are in **direct proportion**.

Example 7

      If 21 notebooks cost £7.56, what do 28 similar notebooks cost?

      1st method

      (7 is a factor of both 21 and 28 so we find the cost of 7 notebooks first.)
      21 notebooks cost £7.56
      7 notebooks cost £2.52   (dividing by 3)
      28 notebooks cost £10.08   (multiplying by 4).

      2nd method

      The price is in direct proportion to the quantities.
      Ratio of quantities, new : old $= 28:21 = 4:3$
      Ratio of prices $= 4:3$

      New price $= \dfrac{4}{3}$ of £7.56 $= £\,\dfrac{4}{3} \times 7.56 = £10.08$.

Quantities which vary so that one increases in the same ratio as the other decreases are in **inverse proportion**.

Example 8

      If there is enough food in an emergency pack to last 12 men for 10 days, how long would the food last if there were 15 men?

1st method

(3 is a factor of both 12 and 15, so we first find how long the food would last if there were 3 men.)
The food lasts 12 men for 10 days
The food lasts 3 men for 40 days   (multiplying by 4 because it would last four times as long)
The food lasts 15 men for 8 days   (dividing by 5).

2nd method

As the number of men increases, the time the food will last decreases.
Ratio of number of men, new : old $= 15 : 12 = 5 : 4$
Ratio of times, new : old $= 4 : 5$

New time the food lasts for $= \dfrac{4}{5}$ of 10 days $= 8$ days.

Which method do you prefer to use?

Exercise 17.2

1. If 24 parcels weigh 60 kg, what is the weight of 36 similar parcels?

2. If 32 bars of chocolate cost £6.40, what is the cost of 24 similar bars?

3. If 9 men can build a wall in 10 days, how long would 6 men take, working at the same rate?

4. A carpet to cover a floor of area 18 m² cost £270. How much would it cost for a similar carpet to cover a floor of area 24 m²?

5. If a store of emergency food would last 36 men for 20 days, how long would the same food last if there were 45 men?

Rate

The word **rate** is used in many real-life situations.

For example:
A man is paid for doing a job at the rate of £6.75 per hour.

Grass seed is sown to make a lawn at the rate of 2 oz per square yard.

Income tax is paid at the standard rate of 25 p in the £ (or whatever the current rate is).

A car uses petrol at the rate of 40 miles to the gallon.

Wallpaper paste powder is added to water at the rate of 1 packet to 6 pints of water.

Rateable Value

The local council needs money to run its own services such as Education, Health, Leisure, Police.

It assesses the value of each property and gives it a **rateable value**. Thus the rateable value of a particular house could be £245. A bigger or better house would have a greater rateable value.

The council then decides how much money it will need to collect for the next year, and it sets a **rate** such as 84 p in the £.

This means that for every £1 of rateable value the householder or property owner would pay 84 p in rates.

For the house with a rateable value of £245 the annual rates bill would be 245 × 84 p = £205.80.

Exercise 17.3

Use the data from the previous page in questions 1 to 5.

1. How much will the man be paid if the job takes 6 hours?

2. How many lbs of grass seed will be needed to make a rectangular lawn, 8 yards by 7 yards? (16 oz = 1 lb.)

3. In addition to his normal work, a man did a part-time job and earned £120. How much tax at the standard rate had to be paid out of this?

4. If I use half the packet of wallpaper paste, how much water must I mix it with?

5. How much petrol will the car use on a journey of 100 miles, approximately?

6. A plumber charges £143 for a job taking 22 hours. What rate does he charge per hour?

7. A car used 12 litres of petrol on a journey of 150 km. What is the petrol consumption in km per litre?

8. Two bottles of detergent are shown. What is the cost per litre of the two brands? Which one is the better value for money if the two brands are equally effective in use?

9. Water flows from a tap at the rate of 20 litres per minute. How long will it take to fill a tank holding 240 litres?

10. A firm offers a discount of 5p in the £. What will you actually pay for goods which are priced at £7.00?

11. How much would the rates bill be on a house with rateable value £320 if the rate was 92p in the £?

12. How much would the rates bill be on a house with rateable value £465 if the rate was £1.32 in the £?

Foreign Currency

In USA the currency is in dollars and cents, with 100 cents = 1 dollar. The symbol for dollar is $.

In France, Switzerland and Belgium, the currency is in francs and centimes, with 100 centimes = 1 franc.

Many other countries have a similar system, where the main unit of currency is divided into 100 smaller units.
Calculations in such currencies are carried out in a similar way to calculations in £'s and pence.

Rate of Exchange

At Banks and a few other places you can change money into different currencies. The Banks make a small charge (commission) for changing the money. The rate of exchange varies slightly from day to day and may change considerably at times, depending on the financial situations in the countries concerned. In order to attract customers, some banks may offer slightly better rates than others.
Here are some of the rates quoted on one particular day. These amounts are equivalent to £1.

Australia	2.18 dollars
Austria	19.70 schillings
Belgium	58.60 francs
Canada	1.95 dollars
Denmark	10.67 kroner
France	9.24 francs
Germany	2.81 marks
Greece	189 drachmae
Holland	3.18 guilders
Ireland	$1.04\frac{1}{2}$ punts
Israel	2.30 shekels
Italy	1955 lire
Japan	221 yen
Malta	0.5180 lire
New Zealand	2.70 dollars
Norway	10.34 kroner
Portugal	209 escudos
Spain	188.25 pesetas
Switzerland	2.31 francs
United States	1.41 dollars
Yugoslavia	648 dinars

For example,
£10 will be worth 10 × 9.24 French francs

$$= 92.4 \text{ francs}$$

£15 will be worth 15 × 1.95 Canadian dollars

$$= 29.25 \text{ dollars}$$

1500 Spanish pesetas will be worth

$$£\frac{1500}{188.25} = £7.97$$

10 Irish punts will be worth $£\dfrac{10}{1.04\frac{1}{2}}$

$$= £\frac{10}{1.045} = £9.57$$

Exercise 17.4

1. Find the total cost of articles bought in New York costing $1.25, $2.80 and $5.15.

2. If 3 dollars is shared among 3 children in the ratio $3:4:5$, how much do they each get?

3. Find the total cost of 5 books at $4.95 each.

4. In Switzerland a packet of sweets cost 0.45 francs. What is the total cost of 12 packets?

5. Find the total cost of food bought in Switzerland costing 9.50 f, 12.30 f, 4 f, 7.90 f. How much change is there from 50 francs?

6. In a market, 5 pairs of tights are sold for 3.90 francs. How much is this per pair?

Using the rates of exchange given in the list, say how much you get if you change these amounts.

7. £100 into Greek money.
8. £150 into Swiss francs.
9. £12 into U.S. dollars.
10. £3000 into Japanese money.
11. £200 into Yugoslavian money.

Using the rates of exchange given in the list, change this money into British currency, to the nearest penny.

12. 5000 Australian dollars.
13. 2000 Belgian francs.
14. 4000 German marks.
15. 1000 Portuguese escudos.
16. 200 Norwegian kroner.

If you know the up-to-date exchange rates, repeat questions 7 to 16 using them.

17. Whilst on holiday, Mr Wood bought a carton containing 10 packets of cigarettes for 1260 pesetas. On returning home he sold these packets to his friends for £1 each. How much profit (in £'s) did he make?
    The rate of exchange at the time was 210 pesetas = £1.

18. Two tourists, Alan and Bill, returned to England, each with 300 francs to change back into British money. When Alan changed his the rate was 12.0 francs to the £, and a week later when Bill changed his the rate was 12.5 francs to the £. Who got more British money, and how much more?

19. If the rates of exchange are £1 = 1.75 dollars and £1 = 11.9 francs, how much is 14 dollars worth

    1   in British currency,
    2   in francs?

Exercise 17.5

1. £900 is raised and is divided among 3 charities, A, B and C in the proportion $4:5:6$. Find the amount each charity receives.

2. The measurements of two rectangles are (a) length 12 cm and width 9 cm. (b) length 24 cm and width 7 cm.
   Find

   1 the ratio of their perimeters,

   2 the ratio of their areas.

   3 If all the sides are increased by 3 cm, find the new ratio of their areas.

3. The edge of two cubes are 4 cm and 6 cm. Find the ratio of their volumes.

4. A firm buys petrol and diesel oil in the ratio $5:7$, spending £2700 altogether per week. How much is spent on each?
   If the price of petrol is increased by 5% and the diesel oil by 3%, find the increase in the total cost.

5. A man gave £500 to his four children in the ratio $2:4:5:9$. What was the difference between the largest and the smallest shares?

6. The insurance for the contents of a house are charged at £6.50 per £1000 of value. How much will the insurance cost for contents valued at £8500?

7. If the rates rise by 12 p in the £, how much extra would be paid by a householder whose house had a rateable value of £260?

8. For a car journey of 120 miles I need to buy 4 gallons of petrol. How much will I need for a journey of 150 miles?

9. A firm allows a discount of 5 p in the £ for prompt payment of a bill. If the bill is for £480, how much should be paid, if it is paid quickly?

10. A tin of paint holding 2.5 litres will cover an area of 45 m². What is the rate in square metres per litre?

11. The weekly wages paid by a firm to 8 workers total £760. What will be the weekly wages if they employ 2 extra women and pay them all at the same rate?

12. Mrs Robins and Mrs Webb both do a similar part-time job. Mrs Robins works for 9 hours and earns £24. Mrs Webb earns £32. How many hours does she work?

13. A recipe for 12 small cakes uses 75 g butter, 75 g castor sugar, 100 g flour and 2 eggs.

    1 How much flour is needed to make 30 of these cakes?
    2 How many eggs are needed to make 30 of these cakes?

14. Mrs Modi wants to buy some toothpaste. What is the cost for 25 ml of toothpaste in each size? Which size is the best value for money?

15. Maureen went on holiday to Belgium taking £120 which she changed into francs at the rate of 61 francs to the £. She spent on average 500 francs each day for 12 days on holiday expenses, and also she bought for presents a watch costing 599 francs, a doll for 30 francs, perfume for 49 francs and a necklace for 215 francs.
    How many francs had she left?
    On her return home she changed this money back into British currency at the same rate as before. How much did she get?

16. Brian is spending 10 days holiday in Austria. On the first day he changed his spending money of £220 into schillings at the rate of 20 schillings to the £.
    He spent 335 schillings, 195 schillings, 265 schillings and 295 schillings in the first four days. Then he saw a camera which he would like to buy, costing 1480 schillings.
    If he buys the camera, how much will he have left to spend each day, on average, for the next 6 days?
    What is the value of the camera in British currency?

Copy and complete this ready reckoner for Brian to use in Austria.

1 sch =	6 sch =	20 sch = £1.00	70 sch =
2 sch =	7 sch =	30 sch =	80 sch =
3 sch =	8 sch =	40 sch =	90 sch =
4 sch =	9 sch =	50 sch =	100 sch =
5 sch =	10 sch =	60 sch =	1000 sch =

PUZZLE

47. Using the figures 1 to 7 and the multiplication sign, as in these examples, $6 \times 325\,714$, 341×5276, $21 \times 56 \times 473$, which arrangement gives the largest product?

18 *Graphs*

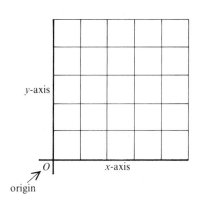

Coordinates

A point on a graph can be specified by giving its coordinates, i.e. its *x*-value and *y*-value.

Example 1

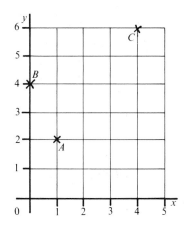

Point *A* has *x*-value 1 and *y*-value 2. This can be written as the point (1, 2). (The *x*-value is always written first.)

A is (1, 2)
B is (0, 4)
C is (4, 6)

Copy this diagram and plot the point *D* (5, 4).

Join *AB*, *BC*, *CD*, *DA*.
What sort of figure is *ABCD*?

Graphs extended to negative numbers

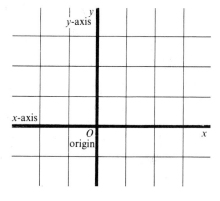

Example 2

Point *P* has *x*-value −3 and
y-value 2.
P is (−3, 2)
Q is (−1, −2)
R is (4, −3)

Copy the diagram and mark the
point *S*(2, 1).
Join *PQ, QR, RS, SP.*
What sort of figure is *PQRS*?

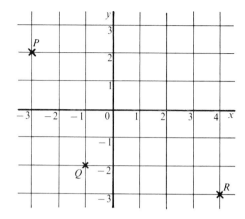

Exercise 18.1

1. Draw the *x*-axis from 0 to 10 and the *y*-axis from 0 to 7 using equal scales on both
    axes.
    Plot points *A* (6, 3) and *B* (10, 5), and join *AB.*
    Plot the point *C* (9, 7) and join *BC.*
    Find the point *D* such that *ABCD* is a rectangle. Join *AD* and *DC.*
    What are the coordinates of *D*?

2. Draw the *x*-axis from 0 to 8 and the *y*-axis from 0 to 10 using equal scales on both
    axes. On this graph

    1 Plot the points *A* (1, 7), *B* (4, 8), *C* (5, 10), *D* (2, 9).
       Join *AB, BC, CD, DA.*
       What sort of quadrilateral is *ABCD*?

    2 Plot the points *P* (4, 3), *Q* (5, 6), *R* (8, 5). Join *PQ* and *QR.*
       Mark a point *S* and join *PS* and *RS*, such that *PQRS* is a square.
       What are the coordinates of *S*?

    3 Plot the points *J* (0, 2), *K* (2, 4), *L* (3, 6), *M* (8, 10). Three of these points
       lie on a straight line. Draw this line.
       Write down the coordinates of 4 more points which lie on the line.
       What is the connection between the *x* and *y* values for all points on the line?
    4 Complete this pattern.

       (0, 6), (1, 5), (2, 4), (3, _), (4, _), (5, _), (6, _).

       Plot these points and join them with a line.
       What are the coordinates of the point where this line crosses the line drawn
       in 3?

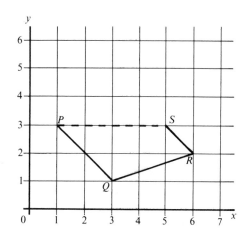

3. Copy and complete the figure *PQRSTU* so that *PS* is a line of symmetry.
   State the coordinates of *T* and *U*.

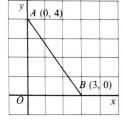

4. Find the area of $\triangle AOB$, assuming that the squares have edge 1 cm.

5. On a graph, draw the *x*-axis from −3 to 5 and the *y*-axis from −1 to 6, using equal scales on both axes.
   Plot the points *A* (3, 2), *B* (5, 6) and *C* (0, 4). Join *AB* and *BC*.
   Plot point *D* such that *AD* is parallel and equal in length to *BC*.
   What are the coordinates of *D*?
   Join *AD* and *DC*. What kind of quadrilateral is *ABCD*?

6. On a graph draw the *x*-axis from −3 to 4 and the *y*-axis from −3 to 4, using scales of 1 cm to 1 unit on both axes.
   Plot points *A* (4, 0), *B* (1, 4), *C* (−3, 1) and *D* (0, −3). Join *AB*, *BC*, *CD*, *DA*.
   What kind of quadrilateral is *ABCD*?
   Plot the point *E* (−1, 0) and join *BE*. Find the area of $\triangle ABE$.

7. On a graph, draw the *x*-axis from −7 to 3 and the *y*-axis from 0 to 6, using a scale of 1 cm to 1 unit on both axes.
   Plot the points *A*, *B*, *C* where *A* is (−7, 1), *B* is (3, 1) and *C* is (1, 6).
   Join *AB*, *BC*, *CA*.
   Find the area of $\triangle ABC$.

Conversion Graphs and other graphs

Example 3

Draw a graph to convert kilometres into miles, given that 1 km ≈ 0.62 miles.

Draw the 'kilometres' axis horizontally, label from 0 to 100.
Draw the 'miles' axis vertically, label from 0 to 70.
You know that 0 km = 0 miles so plot a point at (0, 0).
Also 100 km = 100 × 0.62 miles = 62 miles, so plot a point at (100, 62).
A third point would be useful as a check.
50 km = 50 × 0.62 miles = 31 miles, so you can plot a point at (50, 31).
Join the points with a straight line.
You can use this graph to convert km into miles or miles into km.

1 Convert 23 km into miles.

2 Convert 50 miles into km.

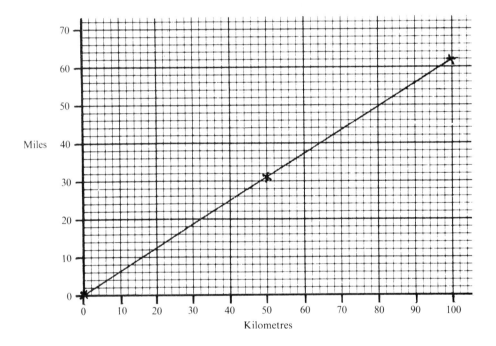

For 1, draw a dotted line up from the horizontal axis where the reading is 23 km, to the graph.
Then draw a dotted line sideways from this point on the graph to the vertical axis, where its value can be read. (It is 14 miles.)

For **2**, start with a dotted line sideways from the vertical axis where the reading is 50 miles, to the graph. Then draw a dotted line downwards from this point on the graph to the horizontal axis, where its value can be read. (It is 81 km.)

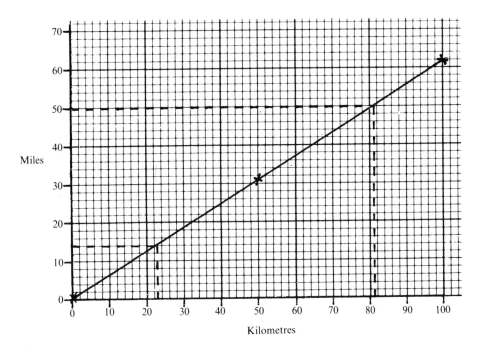

Exercise 18.2

1. Draw a graph to convert U.S. dollars into £'s at a time when the rate of exchange was 1 dollar = £0.69. Draw the 'dollars' axis horizontally, label from 0 to 100. Draw the £'s axis vertically, label from 0 to 70. Plot the point representing 100 dollars on the graph and join it to the origin (0, 0) with a straight line.
    Use your graph to convert

    1 75 dollars into £'s,
    2 £22 into dollars.

    (If you know the up-to-date rate of exchange you may prefer to use that.)

2. Draw a graph to convert gallons into litres.
    Draw the 'gallons' axis horizontally, label from 0 to 10.
    Draw the 'litres' axis vertically, label from 0 to 50.
    10 gallons is equivalent to 45.5 litres.
    Plot this point on the graph and join it to the origin (0, 0) with a straight line.
    Use your graph to convert 6.5 gallons into litres, and to convert 10 litres into gallons.

3. Draw a graph to convert metres/second into km/hour for speeds up to 50 m/s. Label the horizontal axis from 0 to 50 (m/s) and the vertical axis from 0 to 180 (km/hour). Use the information that 0 m/s = 0 km/hour and 50 m/s = 180 km/hour to draw the straight-line graph.
    What speed is equivalent to   **1**   13 m/s,   **2**   100 km/hour?

4. The diameter and circumference of different-sized circular objects were measured, with the following results:

Diameter, in cm	2.6	5.4	8.2	13.2	15.8
Circumference, in cm	7.8	17.5	26.2	41.0	49.5

    Draw the horizontal axis for diameter from 0 to 16 (or 20) cm and the vertical axis for circumference from 0 to 50 cm. Plot the points representing these results and show that they lie approximately on a straight line.
    Draw this line. It should pass through the origin (the point (0, 0)).
    Use the graph to find
    1   the circumference of a circle with diameter 10 cm,
    2   the diameter of a circle with circumference 20 cm.

    (You can check these results using the formula $C = \pi d$.)

5. The temperature of water in a jug is shown in this table.

Time in minutes	0	2	4	6	8	10	12
Temperature in °C	100	60	40	30	25	23	21

    Plot the points on a graph with time on the horizontal axis, from 0 to 12 minutes, and temperature on the vertical axis, from 0° to 100°.
    Join the points with a smooth curve.
    Use the graph to estimate the temperature of the water after 7 minutes.

6. A paddock is rectangular in shape and it is three times as long as it is wide. Copy and fill in this table showing its area for different widths.

    (Area = length × width, where length = 3 × width.)

Width in m	0	10	20	30	40	50
Area in m²	0	300				

    Draw axes for width, horizontally, from 0 to 50 m and for area, vertically, from 0 to 8000 m², and plot the points corresponding to the values in the table. Join the points with a smooth curve.
    Use the graph to find the measurements of the paddock when its area is 6000 m², giving them to the nearest metre.

Exercise 18.3

1. Draw axes for x and y from -8 and 8 using equal scales on both axes.

   1 Plot points $A(0, 1)$, $B(6, 4)$, $C(8, 8)$, $D(2, 5)$. Join AB, BC, CD, DA.
   What sort of quadrilateral is $ABCD$?
   Mark the point of symmetry, E, and state its coordinates.

   2 Plot points $F(-8, 5)$, $G(-6, 2)$, $H(-3, 4)$. Join FG and GH.
   Find a point J such that $FGHJ$ is a square. Complete the square.
   What are the coordinates of J?
   Draw the axes of symmetry of the square on your diagram. How many axes
   of symmetry are there?

   3 Plot points $K(-7, -6)$, $L(-4, -8)$, $M(-1, -6)$, $N(-4, -4)$.
   Join KL, LM, MN, NK.
   What sort of quadrilateral is $KLMN$?
   Draw its axes of symmetry.

2. Draw the x-axis from -6 to 10 and the y-axis from -4 to 11 using equal scales
   on both axes. Draw triangles labelled A to F by plotting and joining the 3 points
   given in each case.
   Triangle A $(2, 6)$, $(2, 9)$, $(3, 10)$
   Triangle B $(5, 3)$, $(6, 6)$, $(7, 6)$
   Triangle C $(9, 0)$, $(6, -2)$, $(6, -3)$
   Triangle D $(-5, 7)$, $(-3, 10)$, $(-2, 10)$
   Triangle E $(-5, 4)$, $(-2, 4)$, $(-1, 5)$
   Triangle F $(-4, -2)$, $(-4, -3)$, $(-1, -1)$
   Which pairs of triangles are exactly the same shape and size? (They may need to
   be turned over to fit.)

3. Draw the x-axis from the 0 to 6 and the y-axis from 0 to 4 using a scale of 1 cm
   to 1 unit.

   1 Plot the points A $(6, 0)$, B $(6, 4)$ and C $(0, 4)$. O is the origin.
   Join AB and BC.
   What is the area of the rectangle $OABC$?

   2 Plot the points D $(6, 2)$ and E $(2, 4)$. Join OD and OE. What are the areas of
   $\triangle OAD$ and $\triangle OCE$?

   3 What is the area of the quadrilateral $ODBE$?

4. Draw a graph to convert temperatures from °F to °C.
   Draw the °F axis horizontally, label from 0 to 240, and draw the °C axis
   vertically, label from 0 to 120.
   When the temperature is 32°F, it is 0°C. (Freezing point.)
   When the temperature is 212°F, it is 100°C. (Boiling point.)
   Plot these two points on the graph, and join them with a straight line.
   Use your graph to convert 70°F into °C, and to convert 80°C into °F.
   A person's 'normal' temperature is 98.4°F. What is the approximate value in °C?

5. These times are taken from a table of 'lighting-up times for vehicles', on the Sunday of each week.

Week number	1	2	3	4	5	6	7	8
Time of day	16.32	16.40	16.50	17.02	17.14	17.26	17.39	17.52

Plot these values on a graph. Draw the 'week number' axis horizontally with 2 cm to each unit. Draw the 'time of day' axis vertically, from 16.00 hours to 18.00 hours taking 1 cm to 10 minutes. Join the plotted points with a smooth curve. These lighting-up times are worked out as half-an-hour after sunset. On the same axes draw the graph showing times of sunset during the same weeks.

6. Rectangular plots of land of area $600 \, \text{m}^2$ are to be sold.

Copy and fill in this table showing the relationship between the length and breadth of the plots.

(Breadth $= \dfrac{600}{\text{length}}$, in metres.)

Length in m	10	15	20	30	40	50	60
Breadth in m	60					12	

Draw axes for length (horizontally) and breadth (vertically) from 0 to 60 m. Plot the corresponding values for length and breadth from the table. Join the points with a smooth curve.
Use the graph to find the breadth of a plot with length 35 m, to the nearest metre.

7. Three workmen charge for doing a job as follows:
    Mr *A* charges £120 for the 1st 40 hours and £5 an hour for any hours over 40.
    Mr *B* charges a flat-rate of £6 per hour.
    Mr *C* charges £150 for the job regardless of how long it will take.

    Copy and fill in this table showing the charges by the three men for jobs up to
    50 hours.

Number of hours	1	10	20	30	40	50
Mr A	£120					
Mr B	£6					
Mr C	£150					

Draw a graph with time on the horizontal axis, from 0 to 50 hours, and cost on
the vertical axis from £0 to £300.
Plot the points in the table for Mr B, and join them with a straight line.
Draw the straight line representing the costs for Mr C.
For Mr A the graph consists of two straight lines, one to the point (40, 120) and
one past that point. Draw this graph.
Label the graphs for Mr A, Mr B and Mr C.
From your graphs find

1 which man charges least for a job taking 15 hours,
2 which man charges least for a job taking 25 hours,
3 which man charges least for a job taking 48 hours.

8. Draw a graph to convert between British and Yugoslavian currency at a time
    when the rate of exchange was £1 = 580 dinars.
    On the horizontal axis, for £, label from 0 to 10 with 1 unit to 1 cm.
    On the vertical axis, for dinars, label from 0 to 6000 with 500 units to 1 cm.
    Plot the point representing £10 in dinars and join this to the origin with a straight
    line.
    From your graph find

1 the amount you would get if you changed £3 into dinars,

2 the value in British money of a present which cost you 4500 dinars.

    (If you know the up-to-date rate of exchange you may prefer to use that.)

PUZZLE

48. Mark, the racing driver, did his first practice lap at 40 miles per hour. What speed would
     he have to average on his second lap if he wanted to produce an average for the two laps
     of 80 miles per hour?

19 Similarity

Similar figures

Similar figures have the same shape.
All corresponding lengths are in proportion.
All corresponding angles are equal.

Enlargement

A figure and its enlargement are similar figures.
The ratio $\dfrac{\text{length of line on enlargement}}{\text{length of line on original}}$ is called the **scale factor** of the enlargement.
So length of line on enlargement = scale factor × length of line on original.
Corresponding lines on the two figures are parallel.

Examples

1 Enlargement with scale factor 2

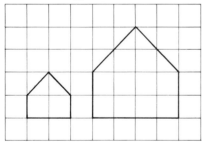

2 Enlargement with scale factor 3

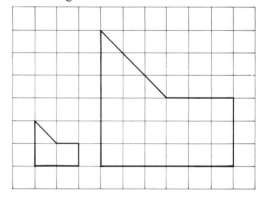

3 The lengths of these rectangles are in the ratio $4:10 = 2:5$
The breadths of these rectangles are in the ratio $3:7.5 = 6:15 = 2:5$
(All angles are 90°)
Since the sides are in the same proportion, the rectangles are similar.

Note that the **areas** are not in the same proportion as the lengths.
Ratio of areas $= 3 \times 4 : 7.5 \times 10 = 12:75 = 4:25$

4   Two similar cylinders have heights of 6 cm and 10 cm. If the smaller one has a radius of 4.2 cm, what is the radius of the larger one?

Ratio of heights $= 6 : 10 = 3 : 5$
Because the cylinders are similar, the radii are in the same ratio as the heights. The larger radius is $\frac{5}{3}$ of the smaller radius $= \frac{5}{3} \times 4.2$ cm $= 7$ cm.

Similar triangles

Similar triangles have the same shape.
(If they have the same size also, they are called congruent triangles.)

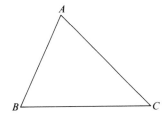

If the triangles ABC, DEF are similar then they have the same shape, so
$\angle A = \angle D$
$\angle B = \angle E$
$\angle C = \angle F$

Their sides are in proportion, so the ratios $\dfrac{AB}{DE}$, $\dfrac{AC}{DF}$ and $\dfrac{BC}{EF}$ are equal.

Example 5

Find the lengths of AC and EF in these triangles.

The triangles have the same shape so they are similar.

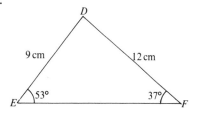

$\dfrac{AB}{DE} = \dfrac{6}{9} = \dfrac{2}{3}$

So AC is $\frac{2}{3}$ of $DF = \frac{2}{3} \times 12$ cm $= 8$ cm

$\dfrac{DE}{AB} = \dfrac{3}{2} = 1\frac{1}{2}$ so $EF = 1\frac{1}{2} \times BC$
$\qquad\qquad\qquad\qquad = 1\frac{1}{2} \times 10$ cm $= 15$ cm

Exercise 19.1

1. Copy these figures and for each one draw an enlargement with scale factor 2.

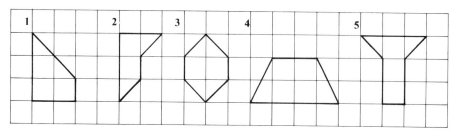

2. What is the scale factor of the enlargement which transforms figure *A* into figure *B*?

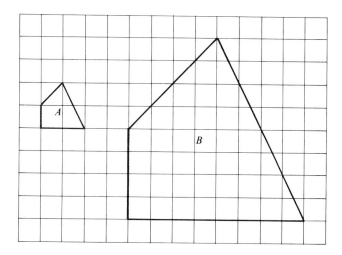

3. 1 In what ratio, in its simplest form, are the lengths of these rectangles?
    2 In what ratio, in its simplest form, are the breadths of these rectangles?
    3 Are these rectangles similar?

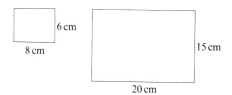

4. 1 What is the ratio of the heights of these cylinders?
    2 What is the ratio of the radii of these cylinders?
    3 Are these cylinders similar?

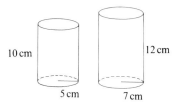

5. These pyramids have square bases with edges 4 cm and 6 cm. Their heights are 6 cm and 9 cm.

    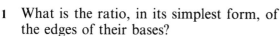

    1   What is the ratio, in its simplest form, of the edges of their bases?
    2   What is the ratio, in its simplest form, of their heights?
    3   Are the pyramids similar?

6. These triangles are similar.

    1   What is the ratio $AB:DE$?
    2   What is the length of DF?

    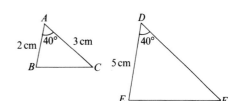

7. These triangles are similar.

    1   What is the ratio $AB:DE$?
    2   What is the length of DF?
    3   What is the length of BC?
    4   Name an angle equal to $\angle B$.

    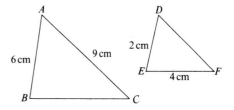

8. Triangles ABC, ADE are similar.
    1   What is the ratio $AD:AB$?
    2   What is the ratio $ED:CB$?
    3   If $DE = 4\frac{1}{2}$ cm, what is the length of BC?

    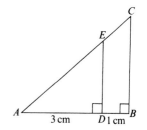

9. Two similar cones have heights in the ratio $3:7$. If the base radius of the larger one is 14 cm, what is the base radius of the smaller one?

Scale Drawing

Scales can be given in various ways, such as
    1 cm represents $\frac{1}{2}$ m
or 2 cm represents 1 m
or Scale 1 : 50

or $\dfrac{1}{50}$ scale.

The symbol $\equiv$ can be used for 'represents', e.g. 2 cm $\equiv$ 1 m.

In any scale drawing, the scale should be stated.

Example 6

This diagram shows a sketch of one end of a
building. Draw an accurate scale drawing,
using a scale of 1 : 100.
By measurement, find how high the highest
point is from ground level.

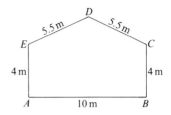

1 : 100 means that 1 cm will represent 1 m.
Begin by drawing the line *AB*, 10 cm long. Make accurate right angles at *A* and
B, and draw the lines *AE* and *BC*, both 4 cm long.
To find point *D*, use compasses. With centre *E*, radius 5.5 cm, draw an arc, and
with centre *C*, same radius, draw an arc which will cut the first arc at *D*. Join
CD and *ED*.
To find the height of *D* above *AB*, construct a perpendicular line from *D* to *AB*.
(By symmetry, this will be the line from *D* to the mid-point of *AB*.) This
distance is 6.3 cm on the scale drawing.
So the highest point is 6.3 m above ground level.

Exercise 19.2

1. A hall is 20 m long and 15 m wide. What measurements should be used on a plan
    to a scale of 1 cm to represent 2 m?

2. Draw an accurate scale drawing of a rectangular field, 80 m long and 55 m wide.
    By measurement on your drawing, find the actual distance from a corner of the
    field to the opposite corner, to the nearest metre.

3. A surveyor who wishes to find the
    width of a river stands on one
    bank at a point *X* directly opposite
    a tree *T*. He then walks 80 m along
    the river bank to a point *C*. The
    angle *XCT* is found to be 52°. By
    scale drawing find the width of the
    river.

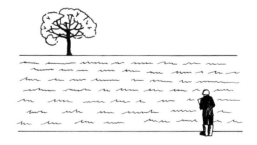

4. The diagram shows a church
    steeple seen from a point *A* 120 m
    away, on level ground. The angle
    at *A* is 32°. Draw a scale drawing
    to find the height of the steeple.

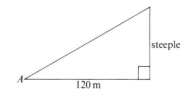

5. The diagram shows a rectangular field. There is a path in a straight line from A to C. Treasure is buried on this path 30 m from A. Draw a scale drawing of the field and show the path.
   Find and mark the position of the treasure. How far is it from C?

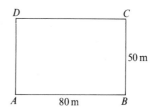

6. This plan of the ground floor of a house is drawn to a scale of 1 cm represents 1 m.
   What are the measurements of

   1 the lounge,   2 the dining-room,   3 the kitchen?
   4 What is the area of the lounge? A carpet for this room costs £18 per m². What is the cost of the carpet?

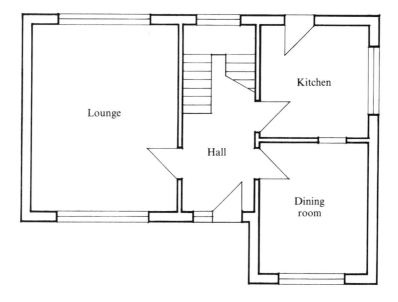

7. The diagram shows two trees in a field, drawn to scale. If the smaller one is 15 m tall, estimate the height of the other one.

Exercise 19.3

1. Squared paper has been used to draw a figure representing a cuboid.
   Copy the figure onto squared paper and then draw an enlargement with scale factor 2.

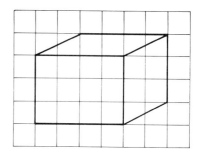

2. Triangle *ABC* has been enlarged into triangle *A′B′C′*. What is the scale factor of the enlargement?

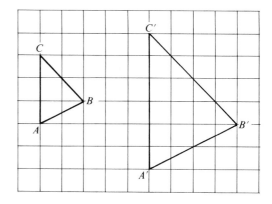

3. Copy these diagrams onto squared paper.

   Using a scale factor of 3, transform triangle *T* into a triangle *T′*.

   1 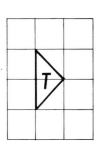 **2** 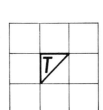 **3**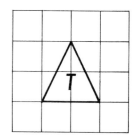

4. A triangle is transformed by enlargement with scale factor 3 into a similar triangle.

   1 One side of the new triangle has length 4.5 cm. What is the length of the corresponding side of the original triangle?
   2 One angle of the new triangle has size 66°. What is the size of the corresponding angle of the original triangle?

5. Two model boats are similar in shape. Their lengths are in the ratio $2:5$. The smaller one is 10 cm wide. How wide is the larger one?

6. Two rectangular boxes are similar in shape. The smaller one has length 20 cm, width 16 cm and height 10 cm.

   1 The larger one has height 15 cm. What are its other measurements?
   2 Find the volumes of these boxes and hence find the ratio of the volumes, in its simplest form.

7. A stick 2 m long is placed vertically so that its top is in line with the top of a cliff, from a point A on the ground 3 m from the stick and 120 m from the cliff. (This makes triangles ABC and ADE similar.) How high is the cliff?

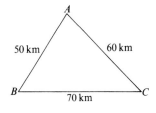

8. A model of a hall of rectangular shape is made to a scale of 2 cm to 1 m. The height of the model is 16 cm and its floor measurements are 25 cm by 32 cm. Find the height and floor measurements of the hall and hence calculate its volume.

9. There are radio stations at 3 places A, B, C. Broadcasts from A can be heard within a distance of 30 km, those from B within a distance of 40 km, and those from C within a distance of 45 km.
   Draw a scale drawing of the triangle ABC, using a scale of 1 cm to represent 10 km.
   With centre A, draw a circle radius 3 cm to represent the region where broadcasts from A can be heard.
   Similarly, draw circles with the necessary radii with centres B and C.
   On your diagram, shade in the region where all three stations can be heard.

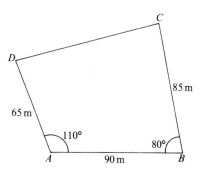

10. The diagram represents a field $ABCD$. Make a scale drawing using a scale of 1 cm to represent 10 m.
    Find the length of DC, in metres.
    What is the perimeter of the field?
    There are straight paths in the field from A to C and from B to D. Draw these paths and measure their lengths.
    The paths cross at point T. A boy runs from A to T and then to D. How much further does he run than if he had gone directly from A to D?

11. The diagram shows a tower seen from a point A 100 m away on level ground. The angle at A is 38°.
     By scale drawing, find the height of the tower.

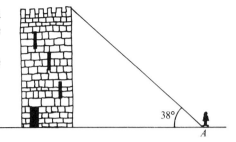

12. Draw an accurate scale drawing of this garden which is 25 m long and 15 m wide, using a scale of 1 cm to represent 2 m.
     The lawn is 17 m long and 11 m wide and the path round three sides of it is 1 m wide.
     In the centre of the lawn, draw in a circular pond of diameter 5 m.
     Find the area of the vegetable plot.

PUZZLES

49. There are two discs; one is red on both sides, the other is red on one side and green on the other, but they are otherwise identical. Without looking, one is picked at random and placed flat on the table. If the top side of this disc is red, what is the probability that the hidden side is also red? Is it $\frac{1}{4}$, $\frac{1}{3}$, $\frac{1}{2}$, $\frac{2}{3}$ or $\frac{3}{4}$?

50.   S H A R O N
      + S A R A H
     ———————
       S A N D R A

     Each figure is represented by a different letter.
     Find which figure each letter represents.
     There are three different solutions, so begin with the one where $A = 9$.

20 *Time and speed*

Speed

The rate at which distance is travelled is called **speed** and it is found from the formula

$$\text{speed} = \frac{\text{distance}}{\text{time}}$$

It is measured in units such as miles per hour, km per hour, metres per second. The abbreviation for metres per second is m/s or ms^{-1}.

The formula rearranged gives $\text{time} = \dfrac{\text{distance}}{\text{speed}}$, distance = speed × time.

The units have to correspond, e.g. metres, seconds, metres per second or km, hours, km per hour.

If the speed is variable, these formulae will give or use the **average speed**.

Average speed

Example 1

A car travels 45 km at an average speed of 30 km/hour and then travels 175 km at 70 km/hour. What is the average speed for the whole journey?

(Do **not** just average the two speeds 30 and 70, getting 50, since this is wrong.)

$$\text{Average speed} = \frac{\text{total distance}}{\text{total time}}$$

The total distance is (45 + 175) km = 220 km.
To find the time for the first part of the journey,

$$\text{time} = \frac{\text{distance}}{\text{speed}} = \frac{45}{30} \text{ hours} = 1\tfrac{1}{2} \text{ hours}.$$

For the second part of the journey,

$$\text{time} = \frac{\text{distance}}{\text{speed}} = \frac{175}{70} \text{ hours} = 2\tfrac{1}{2} \text{ hours}.$$

Total time = $(1\tfrac{1}{2} + 2\tfrac{1}{2})$ hours = 4 hours.

$$\text{Average speed} = \frac{220}{4} \text{ km/hour} = 55 \text{ km/hour}.$$

Exercise 20.1

1. Find the time taken to travel 72 km at an average speed of 48 km/hour.

2. Find the distance travelled by a train going for 3 hours at an average speed of 66 miles/hour.

3. Mrs Owen travels 21 miles to work and the journey normally takes 30 minutes. What is her average speed?

4. On a journey to work, Mr Davies travelled 5 miles through town in 40 minutes and then 16 miles along the motorway in 20 minutes. What was his average speed over the whole journey?

5. A train travels 50 km at a speed of 100 km/hour and then another 96 km at a speed of 64 km/hour.

    1 What is the total distance travelled?
    2 What is the total time taken?
    3 What is the average speed?

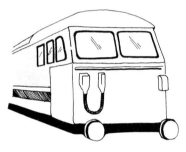

6. A boat travels for 3 hours at 10 km/hour and for the next 7 hours at 15 km/hour.

    1 What is the total distance travelled?
    2 What is the total time taken?
    3 What is the average speed?

7. A train travels for 2 hours at 100 km/hour and then for 1 hour at 85 km/hour. Find its average speed for the whole journey.

8. Two motorists, Mr Bowen and Mr Crane, set off at 9 a.m. to travel to a town 120 km away. Mr Bowen arrives there at 11.30 a.m. and Mr Crane arrives there at noon.

    1 How long did they each take?
    2 What is the ratio of their times taken?
    3 What is the ratio of their average speeds?

Time-distance graph

Example 2

This graph represents a boy's journey from a town P.
He leaves at 12 noon and walks for 30 minutes at a steady speed. This is represented by the line AB.
At what speed does he walk?
The line BC represents the next stage, where he cycles.

For how long does he cycle?
What distance does he travel?
The line CD represents a rest of 30 minutes.
How far is he away from P?
The line DE represents his journey home by bus.
What time does the bus journey begin?
How long is the bus journey?
What is the average speed of the bus?

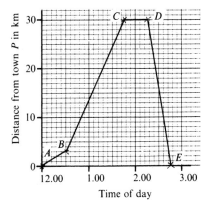

Exercise 20.2

1. The graph shows the journeys of 2 girls, Pam and Ruth.
   Pam cycles from town A to village B, stopping for a rest on the way. Ruth cycles from village B to town A.

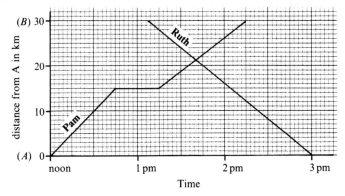

1 For how long did Pam rest?

2 What was Pam's average speed on the part of her journey after her rest?

3 When did the two girls pass each other and how far from B were they at this time?

4 How far apart were the girls at 2.00 p.m.?

5 How far did Ruth travel between 2.00 p.m. and 3.00 p.m.?

6 What was Ruth's average speed?

2. The diagram represents the
    journeys of 4 trains, 3 of them
    travelling from town A to
    town B, 100 km away, and
    one going in the opposite
    direction.

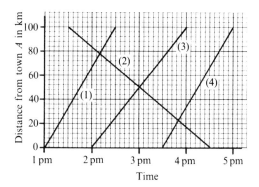

    1 Which two trains travel at
       the same speed?

    2 Which train has the slowest
       speed? What speed is it?

    3 At what speed does train (3) travel?

    4 Train (2) should have been travelling at a speed of 40 km/hour. How many
       minutes late was it on reaching town A?

3. A train leaves town A for town B at 1 p.m. and maintains a steady speed of
    60 km/hour. At 2 p.m. another train leaves B for A maintaining a steady speed of
    60 km/hour. The distance between A and B is 180 km. Draw the time-distance
    graphs for these two trains using the same axes. Draw the time axis with times
    from 1 p.m. to 5 p.m. and the distance axis with distances from A from 0 to 180 km
    with A at 0 and B at 180. When do the trains pass one another and how far are
    they from A at this time?

Sketch of the graph

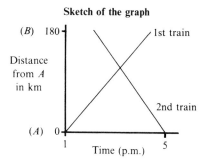

4. The table shows the distances reached by a train at different times after leaving
    a station.

Time in minutes	0	10	20	30	40	50	60
Distance in km	0	4	13	15	22	33	50

    Show the data on a time–distance graph, joining the points by a curve.
    Draw the time axis from 0 to 60 minutes and the distance axis from 0 to 50 km.
    Find from your graph

    1 the distance travelled in the first 45 minutes,

    2 the time when the train was 10 km from the station.

5. An object moves from rest so that its distance travelled at different times is shown in this table.

Time in seconds   0   0.5   1   1.5   2   2.5   3

Distance in metres   0   0.8   3.3   7.4   13.2   20.6   29.7

Draw a time-distance graph, joining the points with a smooth curve.
Draw the time axis from 0 to 3 seconds and the distance axis from 0 to 30 m.
Estimate the time needed to travel 25 m.

Time−Speed Graph

Example 3

Draw a graph to represent the journey of a car which starts from rest and increases its speed uniformly for 10 seconds, reaching a speed of 30 m/s. It maintains this speed for 30 seconds and then decreases its speed uniformly at the rate of 2 m/s per second until it comes to rest.

Put time on the horizontal axis, from 0 to 55 s.
Put speed on the vertical axis, from 0 to 30 m/s.
For the first part of the journey, join the point (0, 0) to the point (10, 30) with a straight line.
Then draw a straight line with the speed 30 for the next 30 seconds.
Finally, the slowing-down period from 30 m/s to 0 at the rate of 2 m/s per second will take 15 seconds. Draw in the line to represent this.

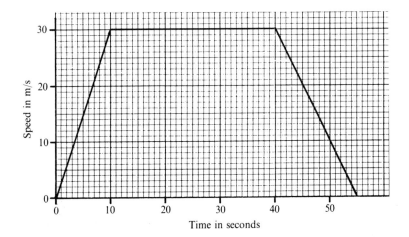

Use your graph to find the speed of the car at time 6 seconds, and at time 42 seconds.

Exercise 20.3

1. A train starts from rest at a station *A* and increases speed at a steady rate for 2 minutes until it reaches a speed of 100 km/hour. It maintains this steady speed for 12 minutes, and then slows down at a steady rate of 20 km/hour per minute until it comes to a stop at station *B*.
    Represent this information graphically on a time–speed graph.
    Draw the time axis from 0 to 20 minutes and the speed axis from 0 to 100 km/hour.

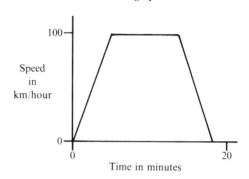

Sketch of the graph

    1 How far does the train travel at its highest speed?

    2 What is its speed after $\frac{1}{2}$ minute, and at what time is it next travelling at this speed?

2. The table shows the speed of a train at various times as it travels between two stations.

Time from start, in seconds	0	15	30	45	60	75	90	105	120
Speed, in m/s	0	9	14	18	21	21	18	11	0

    Draw a time–speed graph, joining the points with a smooth curve.
    Draw the time axis from 0 to 120 seconds and the speed axis from 0 to 24 m/s (or 25 m/s).
    Find from the graph

    1 the greatest speed,

    2 the two times when the train was travelling at half its greatest speed.

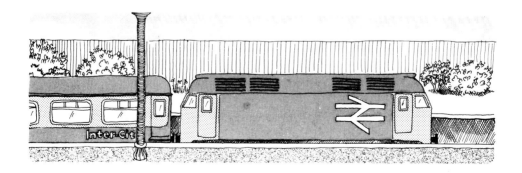

The calendar

A year has 365 days.
Every 4th year is a leap year and has an extra day, 29th February.

There are 52 weeks (+ 1 extra day) in a year.
There are 52 weeks (+ 2 extra days) in a leap year.

There are 12 months in a year:–
January, February, March, April, May, June, July, August, September, October, November, December.

April, June, September and November have 30 days.
February has 28 days, and 29 days in leap years.
All the other months have 31 days.

Thirty days hath September,
April, June and dull November,
All the rest have 31,
Excepting February alone,
Which has 28 days clear,
And 29 in each leap year.

FEBRUARY 1988

Sun	Mon	Tu	Wed	Th	Fri	Sat
	1	2	3	4	5	6
7	8	9	10	11	12	13
14	15	16	17	18	19	20
21	22	23	24	25	26	27
28	29					

Leap years are years whose dates are divisible by 4, e.g. 1988 and 2000.

(A number divides by 4 if its last 2 figures divide by 4.
e.g. to check if 1992 divides by 4, just check if 92 divides by 4. Does it? If so, 1992 is a leap year, if not, 1992 is not a leap year.)

The exceptions to the leap year rule were the years 1700, 1800 and 1900 which were not leap years. However, 2000 will be a leap year.
(The reason for these exceptions is that the actual length of a year is nearly $365\frac{1}{4}$ days, but not precisely.)

There are 4 weeks (+ usually some extra days) in a month.
There are 7 days in a week:–
Sunday, Monday, Tuesday, Wednesday, Thursday, Friday, Saturday.

Exercise 20.4

1. Find a calendar of the present year and use it to answer these questions.

   1 On what day of the week is 29th October?

   2 How many weeks are there from 1st July to 9th September?

   3 The financial year (for income tax purposes) begins on 6th April. What day of the week is this?

   4 George went to the doctor today. He has to make another appointment to return six weeks today. What date will that be?

   5 Is this year a leap year?

   6 How many 'shopping days' are there from 1st September to Christmas Day. (Sundays and Christmas Day, 25th December, are not counted.)

2. Use the calendar of February, 1988 on page 257 to answer these questions.

   1 Sandra works a 5-day week (Mondays to Fridays). She was taken ill and off work on Tuesday, 2nd February and was fit to return to work on Thursday, 18th February. How many days was she away from work?

   2 On which day of the week is/was 6th March, 1988?

   3 Patrick did a temporary job for which he earned £4.50 a day. He started work on 4th February (1988) and his last day at work was 21st February. He did this work on Thursdays, Fridays, Saturdays and Sundays. How much did he earn?

3. How many days are/were there in February in these years?

   1 1992   2 1946   3 1808   4 2012   5 1994

4. Name these months.

   1 It begins with the letter J and has only 30 days.

   2 It follows two months which have 31 days.

   3 It ends with the letter y and has less than 31 days.

Exercise 20.5

1. If a train is travelling at 90 miles/hour, how far does it go in 1 minute?

2. When Ron visits his mother, the journey takes $2\frac{1}{2}$ hours if he goes at an average speed of 30 miles per hour. If he reduces his average speed to 25 miles per hour in wet weather, how much longer will his journey take?

3. A main road through a village has a speed limit of 40 miles per hour. A motorist covers the $1\frac{1}{2}$ mile section in 2 minutes. Did he break the speed limit?

4. A car passes a point A at 3.58 p.m. and reaches a point B $3\frac{1}{2}$ km distant at 4.03 p.m. What is the average speed of the car?

5. Dhiren leaves village A on his bicycle at noon and cycles at a speed of 15 km/hour towards a town B, 33 km away. After an hour he has 30 minutes rest and then continues at a speed of 12 km/hour. His father leaves town B by car at 1.45 p.m., driving towards A at a steady speed, and arrives at A at 2.30 p.m.
Represent this information on a time-distance graph, drawing the time axis from noon to 3 p.m. and the distance axis showing distances from A from 0 to 33 km.

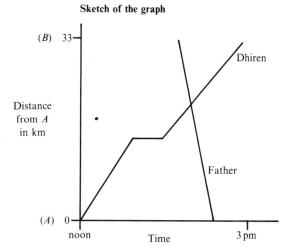

Sketch of the graph

1   At what time does Dhiren reach town B?

2   How far from B, and at what time, did his father pass Dhiren?

6. On a holiday journey the car mileage indicator readings and times were as follows:

Time	9.05 a.m.	11.35 a.m.	12.15 p.m.	2.15 p.m.
Mileage indicator reading	16335	16455	16455	16525

(I had stopped to visit a place of interest from 11.35 a.m. to 12.15 p.m.)

1   What was the average speed for the part of the journey up to 11.35 a.m.?

2   What was the average speed for the part of the journey from 12.15 p.m.?

3   I estimate that my car used 5 gallons of petrol on the journey. What is the approximate fuel consumption in miles per gallon?

7. The table gives the heights of an object projected vertically upwards from ground level.

Time in seconds	0	1	2	3	4	5
Height in metres	0	20	30	30	20	0

    Draw a horizontal axis from 0 to 5 (for time, in seconds) and a vertical axis from 0 to 40 (for height, in metres). Plot the points and join them with a smooth curve. Estimate the height the object attains. At what times is the object 10 m above the ground?

8. The following values of the speed of an object at different times are obtained by experiment. Plot the values on a graph with time on the horizontal axis and speed on the vertical axis, and show that the plotted points lie approximately on a straight line.
    Draw this line and use it to estimate the speed at time 3.5 seconds.

Time in seconds	1	2	3	4	5	6
Speed in m/s	2.0	2.7	3.6	4.4	5.3	5.9

9. If today is April 24th, what will be the date this day next week?

10. In a particular year, August 1st is on a Monday. On which day of the week are these dates in that year?

    1   August 9th

    2   August 25th

    3   July 25th

    4   What date will it be on the Monday 5 weeks after Aug 1st?

PUZZLES

51. How far would someone have to travel to get to 'the opposite end of the Earth' assuming that the Earth is a sphere of diameter 12 750 km?
    If instead of travelling over the surface, the person went by plane which travelled at a height of 10 km over the earth, how much further would the journey be?

52. A practical test. You are given 27 packages and told that 26 of them are of equal weight but 1 is slightly lighter. You are also given a balance-type weighing scale so that you can weigh some on one side against some on the other. However, you are only allowed to make 3 weighings. How can you find the lighter one?

Miscellaneous section D

Exercise D1   Aural Practice

If possible find someone to read these questions to you.
You should do questions 1 to 15 within 10 minutes.
Do not use your calculator.
Write down the answers only.

1. There are 12 eggs in a box. One-quarter of them are cracked. How many are whole?

2. What is the total cost of 100 badges at 8 pence each?

3. How many minutes are there from 11.25 a.m. to 12 noon?

4. If £1 is equal to 1.3 dollars, how many dollars will I get for £10?

5. How many pieces of ribbon of length 50 cm can be cut from a piece 2 metres long?

6. Write in figures 'Two million, thirty-five thousand'.

7. A rectangle 4 cm by 5 cm is cut out of a square piece of paper of side 6 cm. What area is left?

8. 6 men can build a wall in 8 days. How long would 3 men take?

9. How many faces has a cube?

10. If 5 similar books weigh 2.5 kg, what will 2 of them weigh?

11. What is the length of the perimeter of a square of edge 9 cm?

12. What is the smallest number which must be added to 40 in order to make it exactly divisible by 6?

13. A purse contained 3 pound coins and 3 fifty-pence coins. How much money was left after spending £1.50?

14. How many minutes will it take to travel 12 km when driving at an average speed of 48 km per hour?

15. What is 6% of £200?

Additional aural questions using data from other pages.

16. Turn to page 109. Use the chart of question 12.

     In the distance chart, which of the places listed is furthest away from London, and how many kilometres away is it?

17. Turn to page 229. Use the list of exchange rates.

     I have 6000 Italian lire. How many £'s are these worth, approximately?

18. Turn to page 236. Use the graph of example 3.

     How many kilometres are approximately equal to 20 miles?

19. Turn to page 240. Use the 'lighting-up times', of question 5.
     How many minutes later is lighting-up time in week 4 than it was in week 2?

20. Turn to page 343. Use the table of question 3.

     What is the cost of sending 3 packets each weighing just under 200 grams, by 2nd class post?

21. Turn to page 283. Use the rectangle enclosing the map in question 7.

     The length across this rectangle is 10 cm. Estimate the length from top to bottom.

22. Turn to page 243. Use the 1st triangle *ABC*.

     Estimate the size of angle *C*.

Exercise D2   Multi-choice Exercise

Select the correct answer to each question.

1. How many cubic centimetres are there in 1 cubic metre?

    A 100   **B** 1000   **C** 10 000   **D** 100 000   **E** 1 000 000

2. A cube has edges of length 2 cm. The surfce area of the cube, in cm^2, is

    A 4   **B** 8   **C** 16   **D** 24   **E** 30

3. Express 50 g : 20 kg as a ratio in its simplest form.

    A 1 : 400   **B** 1 : 4000   **C** 5 : 2

    D 250 : 1   **E** 2500 : 1

4. In a cuboid, the number of faces + the number of edges =

    A 12   **B** 14   **C** 18   **D** 20   **E** 24

5. A man travelled by car for 30 km at an average speed of 45 km/hour and then, on the motorway, another 100 km at an average speed of 80 km/hour. If he started his journey at 9 a.m., he finished at

  A   10.55 a.m.   **B**   11.00 a.m.   **C**   11.15 a.m.

  D   11.18 a.m.   **E**   11.55 a.m.

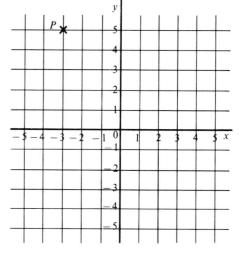

6. If the point *P* with coordinates (−3, 5) is reflected in the *y*-axis its image point is

  A   (−3, 5)   **B**   (−3, −3)

  C   (3, −5)   **D**   (3, 5)

  E   (5, 5)

7. A triangular field has sides 40 m, 50 m and 60 m. Which of these triangles makes a correct scale drawing of the field?

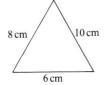
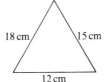

  A   1 and 2 only   **B**   2 only   **C**   2 and 3 only   **D**   3 only

  E   1, 2 and 3

8. A shortbread recipe uses flour, butter, sugar and nuts in the ratio, by weight, of 9 : 6 : 3 : 2. How much butter is used in making 1 kg of the mixture?

  A   30 g   **B**   100 g   **C**   150 g   **D**   300 g   **E**   450 g

9. ∠*BAC* =

  A   12°   **B**   23°

  C   35°   **D**   47°

  E   67°

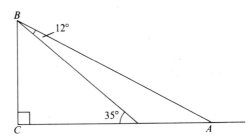

10. What is the circumference of a circle of radius 5 cm? (Take π as 3.14)

 A 15.7 cm **B** 31.4 cm **C** 62.8 cm **D** 78.5 cm

 E 314 cm

11. Raffle tickets are numbered from 1 to 50. What is the probability that the winning ticket is a multiple of 7 or includes a figure 7?

 A $\frac{4}{50}$ **B** $\frac{7}{50}$ **C** $\frac{8}{50}$ **D** $\frac{11}{50}$ **E** $\frac{12}{50}$

12. A car travels for $2\frac{3}{4}$ hours at an average speed of 60 km/hour and then for $2\frac{1}{4}$ hours at an average speed of 80 km/hour. What is its average speed for the whole journey?

 A 69 km/hour **B** 70 km/hour **C** 75 km/hour

 D 80 km/hour **E** 140 km/hour

13. The volume of this rectangular box, in cm³, is

 A 40 **B** 50 **C** 80

 D 340 **E** 400

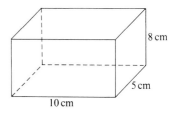

14. Triangles *ABC*, *DEF* are similar.

 The length of *DE* is

 A $6\frac{3}{4}$ cm **B** $10\frac{1}{3}$ cm **C** 12 cm

 D 13 cm **E** $21\frac{1}{3}$ cm

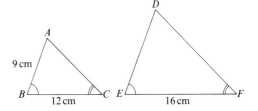

15. A group of men invested money in a business and shared the profits in the same ratio as their investments. One man invested £2000 and received £750 from the profits. What did another man invest if he received £300 from the profits?

 A £112.50 **B** £750 **C** £800 **D** £1550 **E** £5000

16. The graph represents the journey of a boy who cycles from a town *A* to a town *B*, and after a rest there, cycles back to *A*. How far did he cycle altogether between 2 p.m. and 4.30 p.m.?

 A 12 km **B** 18 km

 C 24 km **D** 30 km

 E 36 km

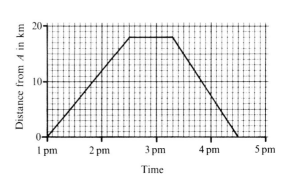

17. A salesman is paid a commission of 8% on the value of goods he sells. If he sells goods worth £800, what commission does he get?

    A £64   **B** £100   **C** £736   **D** £864   **E** £900

18. These circles with the same centre have radii 11 cm and 9 cm.
    The difference between the lengths of the circumferences of the two circles is

    A 0 cm   **B** 2 cm   **C** 2π cm

    D 4 cm   **E** 4π cm

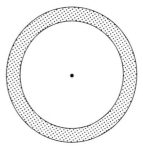

19. If $m = \dfrac{3a + 2b + c}{6}$, then the value of m when $a = 12$, $b = 9$ and $c = 6$ is

    A $5\frac{1}{3}$ **B** 6   **C** 9   **D** 10   **E** 30

20. If a team of 8 volunteers estimate that it will take 12 hours for them to do a certain project task, how long should it take them if two people drop out of the scheme, and the remainder all work at the same rate?

    A 9 hours   **B** 12 hours   **C** 14 hours   **D** 15 hours

    E 16 hours

Exercise D3   Revision

1. On a small photograph, a building is 4 cm high and its width is 10 cm. On an enlargement, if the building is 10 cm high, what is its width?

2. State how many axes of symmetry these figures have.

    1 Isosceles triangle   **4** Circle
    2 Equilateral triangle   **5** Kite
    3 Parallelogram

    State the order of rotational symmetry of these figures.

    6 Square   **9** Rhombus
    7 Rectangle   **10** Outline of a 50 pence coin
    8 Equilateral triangle

3. Draw a graph to convert kg to lbs, given that 1 kg is equivalent to 2.2 lb. Draw the kg axis horizontally from 0 to 20 kg, and the lb axis vertically from 0 to 50 lb. Use your graph to find

    1 how many lbs are equivalent to 15 kg,
    2 how many kg are equivalent to 15 lb.

4. These diagrams represent the nets of solid figures. Give the names of the solid figures.

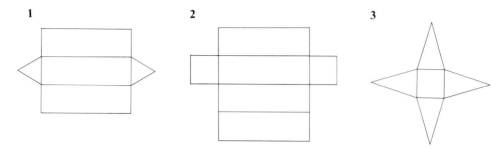

1   2   3

5. A man buys a painting as an investment. He pays £2000 for it and estimates that its value should increase by 10% each year. He plans to sell it in 3 years time. If it increases as he hopes, how much will it be worth at the end of the first year? How much will its value increase during the second year? How much will it be worth at the end of the second year? How much will its value increase during the third year? How much will it be worth at the end of the third year?
    How much profit does he hope to gain on this investment?

6. A train starts at 2.30 p.m. and reaches the next stop at 3.45 p.m. If its average speed is 52 km/hour, what is the distance it has travelled?

7. A lawn-mower has blades 35 cm wide and it is used to cut a lawn 35 metres by 21 metres. Find, in km, the least distance travelled by the mower in covering the ground once over, ignoring the turns made at each end.

8. A trader buys 20 sacks of potatoes at £5 a sack and 100 sacks of potatoes at £3.80 a sack. What is the total cost? What is the average price per sack?

9. The rateable value of a house was £200. The water authority charged for water and services as follows:- a standing charge of £15 plus a charge of 30 p in the £ on the rateable value. How much did it cost the householder in water rates that year?

10. The profits on a business were £4800. The three partners divided this amount amongst themselves in the ratio 3 : 5 : 7. How much did each receive?

11. Find the perimeter and area of $\triangle ABC$.

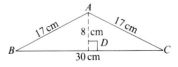

12. $ABCD$ is a rhombus with $\angle ABC = 60°$.
    What sort of triangles are

    1 $\triangle ABC$,
    2 $\triangle ABD$,
    3 $\triangle ABX$?

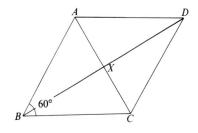

Exercise D4   Revision

1. Three years ago the cost of an article was £24, made up of charges for labour, materials and other expenses in the ratio $9 : 4 : 3$. Find the cost of each item. Since then labour costs have increased by one-third, the price of materials has increased by one-fifth and the cost of other expenses has increased by one-tenth. What is the cost of the article now?

2. A spherical wire cage for holding a plant-pot is formed by fastening together 3 circular hoops of diameter 30 cm and one smaller hoop of diameter 20 cm. Find the total length of wire needed. Take π as 3.14 and give the answer to the nearest cm.

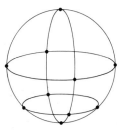

3. Find the values of

    1 $0.07 + 0.05$

    2 0.07×0.05

    3 $0.07 \div 0.05$

4. 1 What is the probability of getting a six when a fair die is thrown? In 120 throws, what is the approximate number of sixes you would expect to get?
   2 What is the probability of getting an ace if a card is dealt to you from a full pack of 52 cards? If a card was dealt in this way 120 times, what is the approximate number of times you would expect to get an ace?
   3 If the probability that the bus to take you to school is late on any one morning is reckoned to be $\frac{1}{10}$, how many times approximately would you expect to be late out of 120 mornings?

5. On graph paper, plot the points $A(-3, -2)$, $B(2, -1)$, $C(4, 5)$, $D(-1, 4)$. Join AB, BC, CD, DA. What sort of figure is $ABCD$? If its diagonals intersect at E, write down the coordinates of E.

6. A shop allows a discount of 10% on all purchases during a sale. What was the sale price of an article which was originally marked at £39?

7. Name the solid figures with the shape of

   1 a cricket ball,
   2 a tin of soup,
   3 a clown's hat,
   4 a match box,
   5 a child's building block.

8. When travelling abroad a man bought 15 watches for 700 francs. Use your calculator to find the average cost per watch, in £'s to the nearest 10p, if the rate of exchange was 3.4 francs to the £.

9. It is estimated that 5 men can lay a pipeline in 16 days. To do the work in 10 days, how many extra men should be used (assuming that all men work at the same rate)?

10. A rectangular water tank is 120 cm long, 60 cm wide and 50 cm high. How many litres of water will it hold?

11. The diagram shows a woman walking under a motorway bridge. Estimate the height AB of the bridge above the ground. (You can assume the woman is 1.6 m tall.)

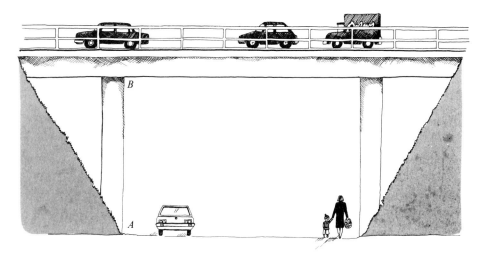

12.   The triangles are similar.
      Find the lengths of *DE* and *DF*.

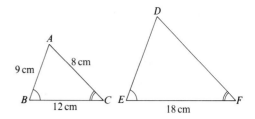

Exercise D5   Practical work and Investigations

1.   **My House**

     Imagine that it is a few years into the future and you are about to buy a house.
     Design the house and draw a plan of each floor.

     Then draw the plan of each room, showing where the doorways and windows
     are, and where each item of furniture will go.

     Find the approximate cost of each item of furniture (by looking in shops,
     catalogues or advertisements).

     For each room make a list of the furniture and fittings you will need and find
     the total cost. Find the total cost for all the rooms in the house.

     If you intend to have a garden you could include a plan for this, and add on the
     costs of garden tools and garden furniture.

     Find the up-to-date price of a similar house by looking at advertisements, and
     find the total cost of everything.

     Cut pictures from magazines and catalogues to illustrate your booklet, and
     make an attractive cover for it.

     This is your dream house so you need not be too practical about being able to
     afford it, if you wish to design a really luxurious one, on the other hand you may
     prefer to be practical and plan for an inexpensive one. You may prefer to choose
     a flat, or a bungalow, instead of a house.

2. **Savings**

Investigate the different places or ways in which money can be saved or invested, such as banks, building societies, shares, savings certificates, life insurance policies, or hidden in the house.

Consider the advantages and disadvantages of each, such as

1 safety of your money,
2 interest gained (a) if you are a taxpayer or (b) if you are not,
3 easy access to your money.

Does it make any difference if you have

(a) only a small amount of money,
(b) quite a large sum of money?

If someone saves regularly out of his or her wages, e.g. saving £10 per week for several years, make a table or graph to show how this money would grow if invested in a regular savings' scheme.

3. **Make your own Maths Magazine**

Or at least, issue No. 1. for a beginning.

Don't be too ambitious. Use a plain sheet of A4 paper and fold it down the middle to make a leaflet.

On the first page you need a title in the top half, and then an article or a puzzle.

On the next three pages you need further articles, puzzles, cartoons or jokes. You could make up a Maths cross-figure, similar to a crossword but with numbers instead of words for the answers. Articles could be about something you have learnt recently, or you could use library books to find out about great Mathematicians and their discoveries. You could describe how to do paper folding or how to make Maths models.

Try to keep some variety in your magazine. Keep your writing neat and perhaps use plenty of colour, unless you intend to make photocopies, when you should use black ink only.

You could have a display in your class if you all made magazines.

Alternatively you could combine together as a class and all produce articles, puzzles, etc, which could be sorted out and put together as a class Maths magazine.

4. **The cost of keeping a pet**

Make a survey of your friends and relatives to find out the sort of pets people have. You could also work out the average number of pets per family. Then ask these people about the costs of keeping their various pets. Here are some of the costs to consider:

Somewhere for the pet to live—hutch, cage, fish tank, stable.

Weekly food bill, including different sorts of food for a healthy diet.

Costs of cleaning out—cat litter, sawdust for cage, straw for stable.

Necessary Vet's bills, for inoculations, etc.

Unexpected Vet's bills, an average cost of treatment for illnesses.

Insurance, and any other costs.

You could also make a survey asking people what sort of pet they would like to own.

You could also ask about the amount of time people spend each week on looking after their pets, from the goldfish which needs very little attention to the dog or pony which need regular exercise.

5. **A snowflake curve**

Draw an equilateral triangle with sides 8.1 cm long (or 10.8 cm, 13.5 cm or 16.2 cm. A multiple of 2.7 is useful.)

Divide each side into 3 equal parts. Use compasses to construct an equilateral triangle on the outside of the middle third of each side, then rub out that middle third.

(Now the figure is a 6-pointed star and has 12 sides.)

Repeat the last instruction for each of the 12 sides.

(The figure is beginning to look like a snowflake. It has 48 sides.)

Repeat the last instruction for each of the 48 sides as accurately as you can.

This process should go on for ever. You may be able to take it one stage further if you started with a large enough triangle. Now colour the snowflake and this will hide the traces of the rubbing-out.

For an anti-snowflake curve the triangles are drawn on the inside of the existing figure, so that the area shrinks. Try drawing it.

6. **Planning a Day's Sightseeing Trip**

Choose an interesting place which you have never visited, but which is near enough to your school or home for a day's outing. Suggestions include London, Stratford-on-Avon or York, but there are many more possibilities, depending on where you live.

Find a guide book of that city, town or area, and decide what you would like to see. If you can find a street map you can make your own sketch map and mark on it where these places are, and then plan your route for visiting them in a sensible order.

Decide how you are going to get to the place, by train, bus, coach or other means. Make a timetable for the day, including the times of the journeys there and back, and approximate times of visiting each place. Remember to allow time for getting from one site to another, and include time for a lunch break. Will you take a packed lunch, and if so, where will you eat it, or will you buy a meal? Calculate an approximate cost for the day, including fares, admission charges and possibly refreshments and pocket money for souvenirs.

Instead of a sightseeing trip in a city or town you could plan a similar outing to an outdoor region such as Snowdonia. You might prefer to make a plan for a trip lasting more than one day, in which case you will have to plan for overnight accommodation, and include the cost of it.

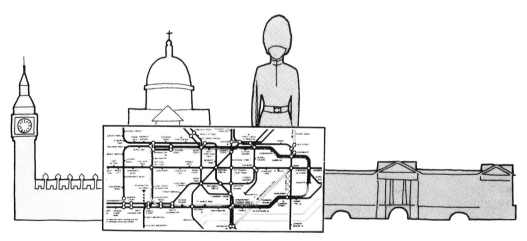

7. **Estimation**

It is useful to be able to make good estimates of weights and measurements. Here are some suggestions to improve your skill. You should think of others.

Lengths. Find out the measurements of your thumb as far as the knuckle, the width of your hand across four fingers, the length of your hand-span, the length of your foot with a shoe on, your height, the distance you can reach with arms stretched out, the height you can reach on tiptoe, and so on. Use a measured distance of 100 m to find the length of your pace when you walk normally, and how long your stride is. Practise estimating distances by comparing them with these lengths.

Time. See how many times you take a breath normally, in 1 minute, and then practise estimating 1 minute by counting your breathing.

Weight. Get used to the weight of 1 kg (a bag of sugar) and 2.5 kg (a bag of potatoes). Find your own weight in kg and the weight of a small child. Estimate other weights by comparing them with these known weights.

Capacity. Estimate how much water various containers hold and check by using a measuring jug, a litre bottle (or a pint bottle for British measures). A bucket or a watering can may have measuring lines marked on it. It is useful to remember that 1 litre of water weighs 1 kg. In British measures 1 gallon of water weighs 10 lb.

Area. Find the area of a local football pitch and compare other large areas with that. For smaller areas, compare with 1 m^2 or 1 cm^2.

Angles. Practise drawing an angle of 45° by eye by cutting a right angle in half. Then practise making angles of 30° and 60° by cutting a right angle into 3 equal parts. Practise guessing the sizes of angles, then check with your protractor.

If you cannot find a measurement directly, there are various methods you could use, relying on scale drawing or similar triangles.

A clinometer

Make one of these to measure angles of elevation and depression. Mark the angles as on a protractor edge but put 0° in the centre and 90° at each end.
When you look at an object through the tube the string will hang vertically and measure the angle of elevation or depression.

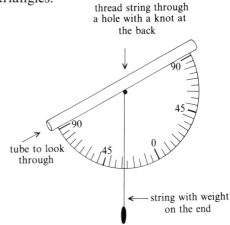

Here are some practical problems. There are several possible solutions. See how many you can think of. Make up similar problems to solve.

1 An explorer in unknown territory discovers a deep gorge. He needs to report on its width but it is too wide to get across to measure it. How can he estimate its width?

2 He can see the bottom and wants to estimate its depth. How can he do this?

3 On the other side of the gorge is a very tall unusual tree. How can he estimate its height?

4 He has been travelling from his base camp in a north-easterly direction so he knows he has to go in a south-westerly direction to return to camp. Unfortunately, he has dropped his compass down the gorge. How can he find out which direction to go in?

8. **Pascal's Triangle**

```
                        1
                    1       1
                 1      2      1
              1     3      3     1
           1     4     6      4     1
        1     5    10     10     5     1
        .     .     .      .      .     .     .
```

Pascal was a French Mathematician who lived in the 17th century. See if you can find out more about him from library books.

This triangle of numbers is named after him, although it was known long ago in Ancient China.

Decide how each number is formed from the numbers in the row above, and copy the triangle and continue it for a few more rows. (As a check, a later row is 1 8 28 56 70 56 28 8 1)

What do you notice about the sum of each row?

What do we call the numbers in the diagonal which begins 1, 3, 6, 10?

Diversions:

1   If you toss three coins in turn, there are 8 possible results, HHH, HTH, etc. which can be summarised like this.

	0 heads	1 head	2 heads	3 heads
Number of ways	1	3	3	1

Investigate the results when 4, or more, coins are tossed.

2   Suppose there are 7 people and 3 of them have to be selected for some purpose. How many ways are there of making the selection? First select 3 from 3, (1 way), then 3 from 4, (4 ways) and so on.
    See how this connects with Pascal's triangle.

3   The diagram shows the railway station and the roads to the beach. From the station, how many ways are there of getting to each access point A, B, C, D, E or F?
    How does this link with Pascal's triangle?
    Why is the beach more crowded in the centre?

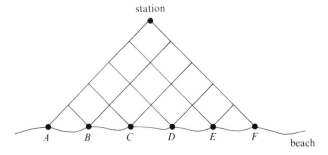

9. **Curves of pursuit**

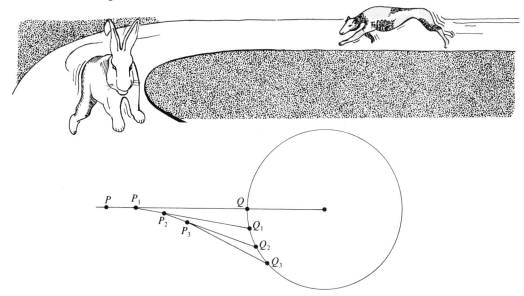

e.g. A dog at P chases a rabbit at Q, which is running along a circular track. Mark PQ to represent the dog's intended path. The rabbit runs to Q_1 whilst the dog reaches P_1. Mark P_1Q_1 which is the dog's new direction. In the next interval the rabbit reaches Q_2 and the dog reaches P_2, and so on.

Decide on their speeds, e.g. represent the dog's speed by 1 cm so that $PP_1 = P_1P_2 = P_2P_3 = \cdots = 1$ cm. If you want the rabbit to be slower choose a length such as 0.7 cm. Mark $QQ_1 = Q_1Q_2 = Q_2Q_3 = \cdots = 0.7$ cm, using compasses to mark off the distances along the circle.

When the rabbit is caught, or the dog gives up the chase, go over PP_1, P_1P_2, P_2P_3, ... in colour as this is the curve of pursuit.

What happens if (1) the dog goes faster, or slower, (2) the rabbit starts from a different part of the circle, (3) the dog starts nearer to the circle, (4) the rabbit runs along a line instead of a circle?

Try the curve of pursuit for 3 dogs A, B, C starting from the 3 corners of an equilateral triangle with equal speeds, if A is chasing B, B is chasing C and C is chasing A.

Make up some other investigations for yourself.

10. **For the Computer Programmer**

More suggestions for programs:

1   To calculate volumes and surface areas of cuboids.
2   To make tables for converting to and from foreign currency, into which you can input different exchange rates.
3   To draw a figure and an enlargement of the figure.
4   To draw a scale drawing of a figure.
5   To draw travel graphs or conversion graphs.

To the student:

5.   Practice Exams

You may have a Practice Exam at school. This will give you some idea of your present standard. It will show you that you can do well if you have learnt the work. It will give you practice in working to time and working under pressure.

After the exam, you will be told your marks or grade and given back your paper. Perhaps your teacher will go through all the questions with the class or you may have to correct them yourself. Ask about anything you do not understand.

If you get a low mark, do not be too discouraged if you know that you can do better next time. But decide what you are going to do to improve your standard.

In an exam it is the marks which count. Could you have got more marks if you had spent less time on some questions and more on others? Should you have revised some topics more thoroughly?

Did you throw away any marks by:
not reading a question carefully enough,
not showing the necessary working with the answer,
writing so badly that the marker could not read it,
writing so badly that **you** could not read it and copied it wrongly on the next line,
not checking an answer that was obviously wrong,
not giving an answer to the accuracy asked for, e.g. to the nearest cm?

Since this was a practice exam, having made some of these mistakes, you can see that by avoiding them in future you can gain more marks.

Make a list of topics you still need to revise, and plan how you will use the remaining time before the proper examination.

Your teacher may give your further practice papers to do at home. If not, you may like to give yourself some. You can use the revision papers in this book, doing 10 of the 12 questions in each. Try to do them as in a proper exam, spending the correct time on them and working in a quiet room without referring to books or notes.

About Chapters 21 to 25

You may not need all the work of these last 5 chapters, so check your own syllabus, so that you can concentrate on what you need for your own examination, at this stage.
There is work on bearings, compass directions and maps in Chapter 21.
Chapter 22 is an easy chapter, about number patterns. Pythagoras' theorem is here, too.
There is more Statistics in Chapter 23.
Geometry patterns are included in Chapter 24, together with other geometry which you may need to know about.
In Chapter 25, just to finish the course, there is a section to make sure that you have no problems with calculations.
After these chapters you will have covered everything. Well done!

21 *Bearings*

Horizontal and vertical lines

A spirit level shows whether lines are horizontal.
A plumb line (a heavy weight on a thin string) shows whether lines are vertical.

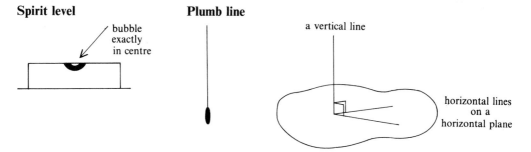

Spirit level

bubble
exactly
in centre

Plumb line

a vertical line

horizontal lines
on a
horizontal plane

Compass Directions

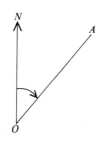

North

West ← → East

South

N

NW   NE

W   E

SW   SE

S

Bearings. 3-figure bearings

Bearings (directions) are measured from the North, in a clockwise direction. They are given in degrees, as 3-figure numbers.

N

A

O

N

O

B

Examples

1 Show the directions given by the bearings 060°, 300°.

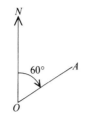

Direction *OA* has a bearing of 060°   Direction *OB* has a bearing of 300°

To find the bearing of a reverse direction, add 180°. If this comes to 360° or more, subtract 180° instead.

2 Find the bearings of *AO* and *BO* from example 1.

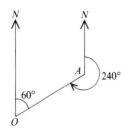

Bearing *OA* was 060°.   Bearing *OB* was 300°.
Bearing *AO* is 060° + 180° = 240°   Bearing *BO* is 300° − 180° = 120°

Exercise 21.1

1. Find the bearings given by *OA*, *OB*, *OC*, *OD* and *OE*.

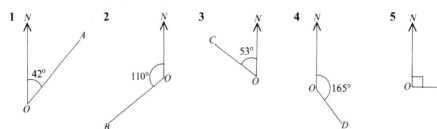

2. Draw sketches to show the directions given by the bearings

   1 200°   **2** 020°   **3** 290°   **4** 135°   **5** 002°

3. Find the bearings of the directions *AO*, *BO*, *CO*, *DO* and *EO* in question 1.

4. **1** The bearing of *OA* is 033°.
The bearing of *OB* is 123°.
Find the size of ∠*AOB*.

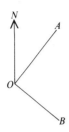

2 The bearing of *OA* is 040°.
The bearing of *OB* is 310°.
Find the size of ∠*AOB*.

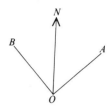

5. **1** Through how many degrees do you turn when facing South-East and turning clockwise to West?

   2 Through how many degrees do you turn when facing North-West and turning anticlockwise to South-West?

   3 In which direction are you facing if you start facing South and then turn through 135° anticlockwise?

   4 In which direction are you facing if you start facing North-East and then turn through 90° clockwise?

   5 If you are facing North-East after having turned 135° clockwise, in which direction were you facing originally?

Bearings, Alternative Notation

In this notation, bearings are measured from North or South, whichever is the nearer direction, and they are measured towards the East or towards the West.

Examples:

N 20°E   N 30° W   S 40°W   S 5° E

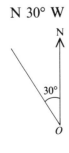

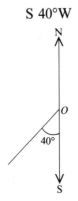

Exercise 21.2

1. Using this notation, find the bearings given by *OA*, *OB*, *OC*, *OD*, *OF*.

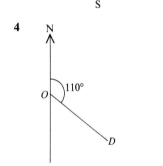

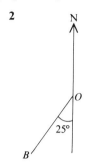

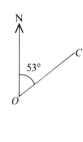

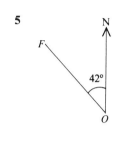

2. Draw sketches to show the directions given by the bearings

   1 N 40° E   **2** S 15° W   **3** N 80° W   **4** N 4° E   **5** S 10° E

Scale drawing and scales of a map

Scale Drawing
Scales can be given in various ways, such as
   1 cm represents $\frac{1}{2}$ m
or 2 cm represents 1 m
or Scale 1 : 50
or $\frac{1}{50}$ scale.

The symbol ≡ can be used for 'represents', e.g. 2 cm ≡ 1 m.

The scale of a map
Some possible scales are 1 : 1250, 1 : 2500, 1 : 10 000, 1 : 25 000, etc.

The scale 1 : 100 000 means that
1 unit represents 100 000 units, so
1 cm represents 100 000 cm, which is 1 km.

The scale 1 : 250 000 means that
1 unit represents 250 000 units, so
1 cm represents 250 000 cm, which is 2.5 km.

Example 3

An explorer walks 1000 m on a bearing of 070° and he then walks 2000 m on a bearing of 160°. Draw an accurate scale drawing of his route. By measurement, find how far he has to go to return directly to his starting point.

First draw a sketch map.
Begin with a direction for North. Usually this is towards the top of the page although this is not essential.

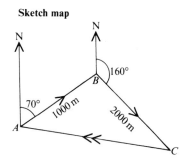

Sketch map

Use the sketch map to see how the drawing is going to fit on the page. Choose a suitable scale. 1 cm to represent 200 m will mean that the first line is 5 cm long and the second line is 10 cm long. 1 mm represents 20 m. If this will fit on your paper this is a suitable scale.

Draw a line at A in the direction of North. Measure an angle of 70° clockwise from the North direction and draw the line AB making it 5 cm long. Then at B draw another line pointing North. (Draw a line parallel to the first North line.)

At B, draw a line at an angle of 160° with the North line and mark point C on this line 10 cm from B.

The line CA is the line showing the return journey. Join CA and measure the line.

The line CA is 11.2 cm long, so the actual distance is 11.2×200 m $= 2240$ m.

Note. The method for drawing parallel lines with a set-square is explained on page 115.

If you use a protractor instead, the two angles in the position of a and b in this diagram add up to 180°.
If $a = 70°$, $b = (180 - 70)° = 110°$.

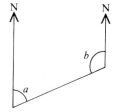

Exercise 21.3

1. The scale of a map is 1 : 25 000. What is the actual distance in km between two points which are 8 cm apart on the map?

2. A and B are points on two mountain peaks. The distance between A and C on a map is 12 cm. The scale of the map is 1 : 50 000. Find the horizontal distance AC, in km. The heights of A and B are given as 2900 m and 3650 m respectively. How much higher is B than A?

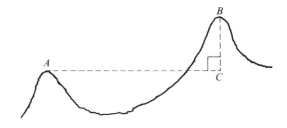

In questions 3 to 6, draw accurate scale drawings using suitable scales.

3.

A speedboat travels 8 km North and then 3 km East. On what bearing must it be steered to go directly back to the starting point?

4. A man walks 10 km North-East and then 7 km South-East. How far is he from his starting-point, and on what bearing must he walk to go directly back to his starting-point?

5. In a sailing race the boats go round a triangular course ABC, with AB = 4 km, BC = 5 km and CA = 6 km. If the direction of AB is due North, on what bearing do the boats head from B to C?
    (Draw the line representing AB first, then find the position of C using compasses.)

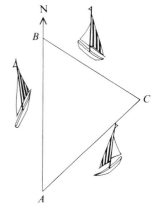

6. *P* and *Q* are places 900 m apart on a coastline running East-West.
   A ship *S* is at sea on a bearing of 341°
   from *P*, and on a bearing of 071° from *Q*.

   Find

   1 *SP*,

   2 *SQ*,

   3 the distance of *S* from the nearest
      point on the coast.

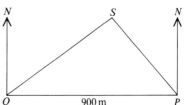

7. A boat is just off the cape at *A* and it wants to reach the harbour at *B*. On what
   bearing must the boat sail?
   The distance *AB* is actually 10.8 km. What is the scale of the map?
   After reaching *B*, the boat then sails to a bay at *C*. What is the actual distance
   from *B* to *C*?
   From *C*, on what bearing must the boat sail to return round the cape at *A*?

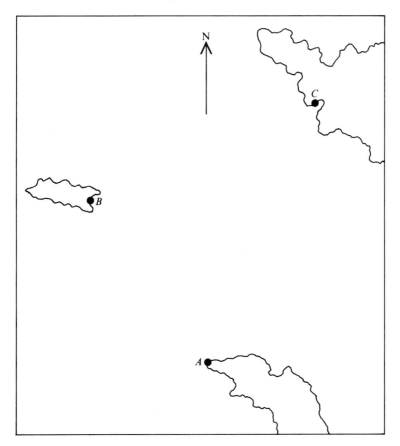

Exercise 21.4

1. The bearing of *OA* is 240°.
    The angle *OAB* is 80°.
    OA = *AB*.
    What is the size of ∠*AOB*?
    Find the bearing of *OB*.

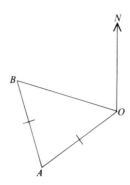

2. A map has a scale of 2 cm to represent 1 km. What is this scale in ratio form?
    If two villages are 8.4 cm apart on the map, what is the actual distance between
    them?

3. There are four towns *A, B, C, D*.
    B is 100 km North of *A*, *C* is
    90 km on a bearing of 140° from
    A, *D* is 120 km on a bearing 260°
    from *A*.
    Draw an accurate scale drawing
    and find the distances between
    the towns *B* and *C*, *C* and *D*,
    B and *D*.

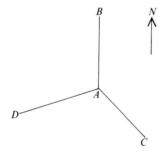

4. A fishing boat is 20 km due North of its harbour. It
    sails on a bearing of 110° at an average speed of
    12 km/hour for 2 hours. Show this information on a
    scale drawing.
    After 2 hours there is a gale warning on the radio. In
    what direction should the boat be headed to get
    straight back to the harbour, and how far has it to
    go? If it increases its speed to 15 km/hour, how long
    will it take?

Sketch map

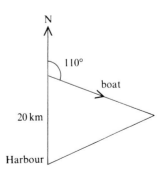

5. The map shows the positions of 4 towns *A*, *B*, *C*, *D*.

This table shows the distances by road between the towns, in km.

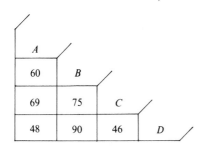

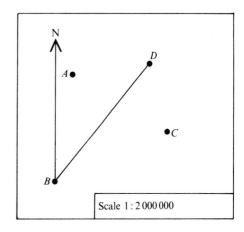

Scale 1 : 2 000 000

1 A helicopter must fly directly from *B* to *D*. On what bearing must it fly?

2 How much further is it for a motorist to travel from *B* to *D* than for the helicopter?

PUZZLE

53. Jill has lost her timetable. She remembers that tomorrow's lessons end with Games, but she cannot remember the order of the first 5 lessons. She asks her friends, who decide to tease her.
Alison says, 'Science is 3rd, History is 1st'.
Brenda says, 'English is 2nd, Maths is 4th'.
Claire says, 'History is 5th, Science is 4th'.
Denise says 'French is 5th, English is 2nd'.
Emma says 'French is 3rd, Maths is 4th'.
Naturally, Jill is very confused by all this. Then her friends admit that they have each made one true statement and one untrue one.
When is Maths?

22 *Number patterns*

There are many patterns in numbers which you can notice.

For example $3 \times 37 = 111$
$\qquad\qquad 6 \times 37 = 222$
$\qquad\qquad 9 \times 37 = 333$
$\qquad\qquad \cdots$

Copy and continue this pattern to 27×37.

Sequences of numbers

Whole numbers 1, 2, 3, 4, . . .

Odd numbers 1, 3, 5, 7, . . .

Even numbers 2, 4, 6, 8, . . .

Multiples of 5.   5, 10, 15, 20, . . .

Prime numbers   2, 3, 5, 7, 11, . . . (These do not follow a regular pattern, but apart from 2 and 5 they all have unit figures of 1, 3, 7 or 9.)

Square numbers 1, 4, 9, 16, . . . from 1^2, 2^2, 3^2, 4^2, . . .
(What are the differences between successive numbers, 1 and 4, 4 and 9, 9 and 16, etc? Another pattern emerges.)
Square numbers can be represented by dots arranged in the form of squares.

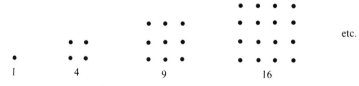

Triangular numbers 1, 3, 6, 10, 15, . . .
These can be represented by dots in the form of triangles.

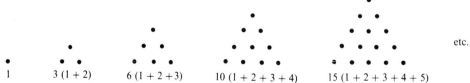

(What do you notice about the sum of two successive triangular numbers? Can you show why this is so, using a dots pattern?)

Cube numbers 1, 8, 27, 64, . . . from 1^3, 2^3, 3^3, 4^3, . . .

There are many other sequences of numbers.

The Fibonacci Sequence

Every term of this sequence is obtained from the sum of the previous two terms. The sequence is 1, 1, 2 (1 + 1), 3 (2 + 1), 5 (3 + 2), 8 (5 + 3), and so on.

Other sequences could be made in the same way, e.g. 10, 3, 13, 16, 29, 45, 74, . . .

Other sequences can go in pairs, e.g. 14, 10, 20, 16, 32, 28, 56, . . .
Here the rule is: 1st time subtract 4, next time multiply by 2, and repeat these two operations in order.

Making number patterns with your calculator

Press 2 $\boxed{\times}$ $\boxed{=}$ $\boxed{=}$ $\boxed{=}$ . . . and see what you get.

(On some calculators you may have to

press 2 $\boxed{\times}$ $\boxed{\times}$ $\boxed{=}$ $\boxed{=}$ $\boxed{=}$ . . .)

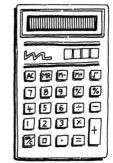

Try 7 $\boxed{+}$ $\boxed{=}$ $\boxed{=}$ $\boxed{=}$ . . . (or 7 $\boxed{+}$ $\boxed{+}$ $\boxed{=}$ $\boxed{=}$ $\boxed{=}$ . . .)

Try 1 $\boxed{+}$ 7 $\boxed{=}$ $\boxed{=}$ $\boxed{=}$ . . . (or 7 $\boxed{+}$ $\boxed{+}$ 1 $\boxed{=}$ $\boxed{=}$ $\boxed{=}$ . . .)

Try 100 $\boxed{-}$ 6 $\boxed{=}$ $\boxed{=}$ $\boxed{=}$ . . . (or 6 $\boxed{-}$ $\boxed{-}$ 100 $\boxed{=}$ $\boxed{=}$ $\boxed{=}$ . . .)

There are other patterns and suggestions for patterns in the practical exercises. There is unlimited scope for discovery, investigation and invention with number patterns.

If you have to identify a sequence and continue it, see if you can recognise anything special about it. Also look at the differences between successive terms.

e.g. 8, 17, 26, 35, . . .
You might notice that the difference between successive numbers is always 9. You get the next term by adding on 9.
You might notice that the unit figures go down in 1's and the ten's figures go up in 1's, so the next term is 44. This will give you terms up to 80, although the sequence continues beyond that.
You might notice that the digits add up to 8 each time.

e.g. 6, 12, 24, 48, 96, . . .
The differences between successive terms are 6, 12, 24, 48. These are the same numbers as in the sequence, so the sequence is a doubling one. The next term is $96 \times 2 = 192$.

e.g. $\frac{1}{2}, \frac{1}{4}, \frac{1}{6}, \frac{1}{8}, \ldots$
These are fractions which are getting smaller. The numerators are all 1. The denominators in turn go 2, 4, 6, 8 so they increase by 2 each time and the next one is 10. So the next number in the sequence is $\frac{1}{10}$.

e.g. 2, 3, 5, 9, 17, 33, . . .
The sequence is growing more and more rapidly and after 2 the numbers are all odd. Investigate the differences between successive terms. They are 1, 2, 4, 8, 16. These are always doubled, the next difference is 32 and the next number in the sequence is $33 + 32 = 65$.

Exercise 22.1

1. Find the next 2 numbers in these sequences.

   1 4, 10, 16, 22, 28, . . .   **6** 3, 4, 6, 9, 13, . . .

   2 3, 6, 9, 12, 15, . . .   **7** 3, 1, $\frac{1}{3}$, $\frac{1}{9}$, $\frac{1}{27}$, . . .

   3 5, 10, 20, 40, 80, . . .   **8** 3, 7, 15, 31, 63, . . .

   4 3, 9, 27, 81, 243, . . .   **9** 3, 8, 18, 38, 78, . . .

   5 3, 0, -3, -6, -9, . . .   **10** 1, 2, 6, 24, 120, . . .

2. Find the missing terms in these sequences.

   1 7,   9,   *,   13,   15,   17.

   2 2,   *,   10,   17,   26,   37.

   3 *, $\frac{2}{3}$, $\frac{3}{4}$, $\frac{4}{5}$, $\frac{5}{6}$.

   4 2,   4,   8,   *,   32,   64.

   5 2,   6,   12,   20,   *,   42,   56.

3. Find the 10th number in these sequences.

   1 1, 3, 5, 7, 9, . . .

   2 1, 8, 27, 64, 125, . . .

   3 1, $\frac{1}{2}$, $\frac{1}{3}$, $\frac{1}{4}$, $\frac{1}{5}$, . . .

   4 2, 8, 14, 20, 26, . . .

   5 100, 95, 90, 85, 80, . . .

4. There is one mistake in this pattern. Copy the pattern, replacing the wrong number by the correct one.

   $$1 = 1$$
   $$1 + 3 = 4$$
   $$1 + 3 + 5 = 8$$
   $$1 + 3 + 5 + 7 = 16$$

   Fill in the next 3 rows of the pattern.
   What do you notice about the totals?
   If this pattern was continued, what would be the total of numbers in the 20th row?

5. Copy and complete this number pattern to the row which begins 123456789

   $$1 \times 8 + 1 = 9$$
   $$12 \times 8 + 2 = 98$$
   $$123 \times 8 + 3 =$$
   $$1234 \times 8 + 4 =$$

   . . .

6. Copy these sequences, correcting the mistake in each one.

   1 $1, 3\frac{1}{2}, 6, 8\frac{1}{2}, 10, 13\frac{1}{2}$.

   2 $1, 4, 9, 16, 24, 36$.

   3 $1, 3, 6, 27, 81, 243, 729$.

7. **Magic Squares**

   Rearrange these numbers so that each row, each column and
   each diagonal add up to 15.
   (Leave 5 in the centre and put 4 in a corner.)

1	2	3
4	5	6
7	8	9

8. This is a multiplication table pattern using the
   numbers 1, 3, 5, 7 only.
   Make a similar table but instead of writing the
   answer down, for numbers greater than 7, divide
   them by 8 and just write the remainder down.
   e.g. $5 \times 7 = 35$ and $35 \div 8 = 4$ remainder 3, so
   write down 3.
   Do you notice any patterns?

	1	3	5	7
1	1	3	5	7
3	3	9	15	21
5	5	15	25	35
7	7	21	35	49

   Make a similar table for the numbers 1, 3, 7, 9 just
   writing the units figures down, and another one for the numbers 2, 4, 6, 8 just
   writing the units figures down.

   Make a similar table for the numbers 1, 2, 3, 4, dividing the answers by 5 and just
   writing the remainders down.

   Do you notice any similarities?

9. Copy and complete the table, of the number of lines needed to join 2, 3, 4, . . .
   points. (The diagrams may help you to discover the pattern.)

Number of points	2	3	4	5	6	7	8	9	10
Number of lines needed	1	3	6						

2 points
1 line

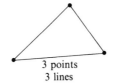

3 points
3 lines

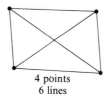

4 points
6 lines

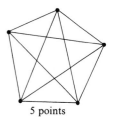

5 points

10. **Number chains** These change a number into another number by a certain rule. Then the new number is changed and the process is repeated.
    Rule For 2-figure numbers, multiply the 10's digit by 4 and add to the units digit. Stop the chain when you get a single figure.

    e.g. $29 \rightarrow (2 \times 4) + 9 = 17 \rightarrow (1 \times 4) + 7 = 11 \rightarrow (1 \times 4) + 1 = 5.$

    $94 \rightarrow (9 \times 4) + 4 = 40 \rightarrow (4 \times 4) + 0 = 16 \rightarrow (1 \times 4) + 6 = 10 \rightarrow (1 \times 4) + 0 = 4.$

    Carry out this rule for some 2-figure multiples of 6. What do you notice?
    Try it out for other 2-figure numbers.
    Make other number chains using different rules.

Square roots

number	square root
1	1
4	2
9	3
16	4
25	5
36	6
49	7
64	8
81	9
100	10

The numbers 1, 4, 9, . . . have exact square roots. Other numbers have square roots which can be found approximately.

Numbers between 1 and 4 have square roots between 1 and 2.
Using your calculator you will find that
$\sqrt{2} = 1.4$
$\sqrt{2.5} = 1.6$
$\sqrt{3} = 1.7$, correct to 1 decimal place.

Numbers between 4 and 9 have square roots between 2 and 3.
Use your calculator to find the square roots of 5, 6, 7 and 8, correct to 1 decimal place.

Similar rules work for other numbers. e.g. 45 is between 36 and 49 so its square root is between 6 and 7, so you know it begins with 6.
Find its value correct to 1 decimal place, using your calculator.

Pythagoras' Theorem

In a right-angled triangle the area of the square on the hypotenuse is equal to the sum of the areas of the squares on the other two sides.
(The side opposite the right angle is called the hypotenuse.)

$$a^2 = b^2 + c^2$$

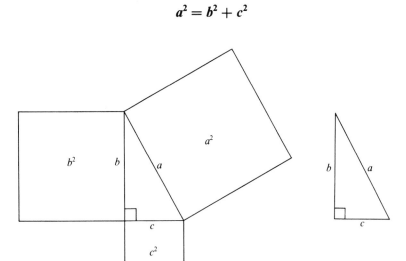

Examples

1 To find a

$$a^2 = b^2 + c^2$$
$$= 8^2 + 5^2$$
$$= 64 + 25 = 89$$
$$a = \sqrt{89}\,\text{cm}$$
$$= 9.4\,\text{cm (to the nearest mm)}$$

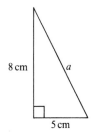

2 To find b

$$a^2 = b^2 + c^2$$
$$30^2 = b^2 + 10^2$$
$$900 = b^2 + 100$$
$$b^2 = 800$$
$$b = \sqrt{800}\,\text{cm}$$
$$= 28.3\,\text{cm (to the nearest mm)}$$

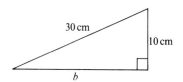

There are certain groups of numbers which give exact answers.

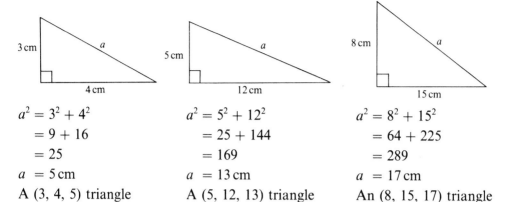

$$a^2 = 3^2 + 4^2$$
$$= 9 + 16$$
$$= 25$$
$$a = 5\,cm$$
A (3, 4, 5) triangle

$$a^2 = 5^2 + 12^2$$
$$= 25 + 144$$
$$= 169$$
$$a = 13\,cm$$
A (5, 12, 13) triangle

$$a^2 = 8^2 + 15^2$$
$$= 64 + 225$$
$$= 289$$
$$a = 17\,cm$$
An (8, 15, 17) triangle

There are many others, including multiples of these numbers such as 6, 8, 10; 10, 24, 26;   30, 40, 50; . . .

Exercise 22.2

1. Without using your calculator, find the whole number part of the square roots of these numbers. Then use your calculator to find the square roots, correct to 1 decimal place.

   1 57   **5** 12.1   **8** 89

   2 28.2   **6** 21   **9** 5.5

   3 80   **7** 60   **10** 65

   4 96

2. Use your calculator to find the square roots of these numbers. If they are not exact, give them correct to 1 decimal place.

   1 500   **5** 169   **8** 576

   2 625   **6** 220   **9** 316

   3 160   **7** 225   **10** 289

   4 300

3. Find the hypotenuse, a, in these triangles. (If the answer is not exact, give it correct to 1 decimal place.)

   1 $b = 5\,cm$, $c = 10\,cm$
   2 $b = 6\,cm$, $c = 8\,cm$
   3 $b = 1\,cm$, $c = 2\,cm$
   4 $b = 7\,cm$, $c = 4\,cm$
   5 $b = \sqrt{7}\,cm$, $c = 3\,cm$ (Note that $b^2 = 7$)

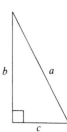

4. Find the third side in these triangles. (If the answer is
    not exact, give it correct to 1 decimal place.)

    1 $b = 8\,\text{cm}, \quad a = 17\,\text{cm}$

    2 $b = 6\,\text{cm}, \quad a = 9\,\text{cm}$

    3 $c = 24\,\text{cm}, \quad a = 25\,\text{cm}$

    4 $c = 5\,\text{cm}, \quad a = 6\,\text{cm}$

    5 $c = \sqrt{7}\,\text{cm}, \; a = \sqrt{11}\,\text{cm}$

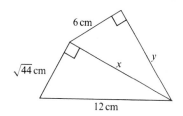

5. **1** The longer side of a rectangular field is 40 m and a footpath crossing the field
    along a diagonal is 50 m long. Find the length of the shorter side of the field.

    2 Find the length of sides x and y.

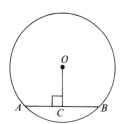

6. AB is a chord 24 cm long, in a circle centre O. The
    radius is 13 cm. C is the mid-point of AB.
    Find the length of OC.

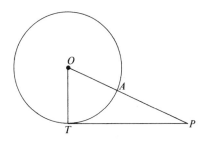

7. O is the centre of the circle. The
    tangent PT is 15 cm long. The radius is
    8 cm. $\angle OTP = 90°$. Find the length of
    OP and hence find the length of AP.

8. Find the lengths of

    1 AB,

    2 BC,

    3 AC.

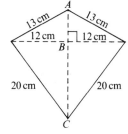

Exercise 22.3

1. Find the next 2 numbers in these sequences.

   1 1, 2, 5, 10, 17, . . .   **6** $\frac{1}{3}, \frac{1}{6}, \frac{1}{9}, \frac{1}{12}, \ldots$

   2 288, 144, 72, 36, . . .   **7** 45, 36, 27, 18, . . .

   3 0, 4, 8, 12, . . .   **8** 2, 5, 8, 11, . . .

   4 81, 27, 9, 3, . . .   **9** 1, 10, 100, 1000, . . .

   5 3, 7, 11, 15, . . .   **10** 100, 91, 82, 73, . . .

2. Copy and complete the 1st 9 rows of this pattern.

   $$1 \qquad\qquad = \frac{1 \times 2}{2} = 1$$

   $$1 + 2 \qquad\quad = \frac{2 \times 3}{2} = 3$$

   $$1 + 2 + 3 \quad\;\; = \frac{3 \times 4}{2} = 6$$

   $$1 + 2 + 3 + 4 = \qquad =$$

   . . .

   Now using the method of this pattern, work out the sum of the numbers from 1 to 40.

3. Three coins are to be arranged in a row in as many different ways as possible. Three examples in which **H** represents heads and **T** tails are shown.

   T H T   H T T   H H H

   Write down the other 5 possible arrangements in the same way.
   List the number of arrangements when this investigation is done with different numbers of coins.

Number of coins	1	2	3	4	5	6
Total number of arrangements	2		8			

   If there were 1024 different arrangements how many coins would be used?

4. Copy and complete this magic square which uses numbers 1 to 16.
   All rows, columns and the main diagonals add up to 34.

			12
3	16		
15		14	

5. Write down the next term of these sequences.

    1 2, 4, 8, 16, 32, . . .   **4** 21, 25, 29, 33, 37, . . .

    2 100, 93, 86, 79, 72, . . .   **5** 3, 12, 27, 48, 75, . . .

    3 $\frac{1}{2}, \frac{2}{3}, \frac{3}{4}, \frac{4}{5}, \ldots$

6. 6 is called a **perfect number** because its factors are 1, 2, 3 and when you add them up their sum equals 6.

    12 has factors 1, 2, 3, 4, 6 and their sum equals 16, not 12, so 12 is not a perfect number.

    However, there is one other number less than 50 which is a perfect number. Which is it?

7. Copy and complete this number pattern.

    $142857 \times 1 = 142857$

    $142857 \times 5 =$

    $142857 \times 4 =$

    $142857 \times 6 =$

    $142857 \times 2 =$

    $142857 \times 3 =$

    What do you notice about the answers?

8. Continue the pattern of numbers:

    $(0, 0), (1, 1), (2, 4), (3, 9), (4, 16), (\ \ ), (\ \ ), (\ \ )$.

    If the first number in the bracket is x, and the second one y, what is the connection between x and y in any bracket?

    On graph paper, use a scale of 2 cm to 1 unit on the x-axis, with x from 0 to 7, and a scale of 2 cm to 10 units on the y-axis, with y from 0 to 50.

    Plot the 8 points given above and also the 2 points $(5\frac{1}{2}, 30\frac{1}{4})$, $(6\frac{1}{2}, 42\frac{1}{4})$.

    Join all these points to form a smooth curve.

    On the curve, what is the value of y when $x = 4\frac{1}{2}$?

9. **1** Find the length of AC.
    2 Find the length of DC.
    3 Find the perimeter of $ABCD$.
    4 Find the area of $ABCD$.

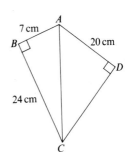

10. A patrol boat goes 8 km South, then 6 km East. Find how far it is from its starting point.

11. Plot the points $A\,(-1, 3)$ and $B\,(2, -1)$. Find the length of the line AB.

12. A gardener is making a rectangular concrete base for a greenhouse 5 feet wide and 12 feet long. Having measured out the edges he checks that it is truly rectangular by measuring both diagonals. How long should these diagonals be?

13. Find the lengths of
   1 BD, (using $\triangle ABD$),
   2 BC,
   3 AC.

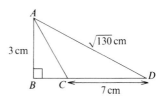

14. In the diagram, O is the centre of the circle and the radius is 8.5 cm. $BC = 8$ cm. $\angle ABC = 90°$.

   1 What is the length of AB?

   2 What is the perimeter of $\triangle ABC$?

   3 What is the area of $\triangle ABC$?

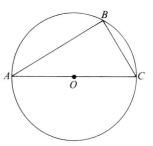

PUZZLES

54. Make 12 pieces like this (with 3 squares) out of cardboard.

Colour them red (R), yellow (Y), blue (B) as follows.

3 of these	2 of these	3 of these	2 of these	1 of this	1 of this

Rearrange the pieces to form a rectangle. How many different-sized rectangles can you make?

Now rearrange the pieces to form a rectangle such that only two of the three colours appear on the perimeter.

55. See how many of the numbers from 1 to 100 you can represent using three 9's, and the usual signs.
   e.g. $78 = (9 \times 9) - \sqrt{9}$
   (You will not be able to represent them all.)

23 *Further statistics*

Pie chart

Example 1

A family with a weekly income of £90 spend it as follows:

	£
Rent	20
Fuel	14
Food	30
Clothing	10
Household goods	6
Other expenses	10
	90

Spending by a family

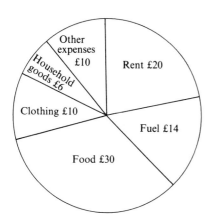

(Working for the pie chart)

Since £90 is represented by 360°,
    £1   is represented by 4°.

Rent	20 × 4° = 80°
Fuel	14 × 4° = 56°
Food	30 × 4° = 120°
Clothing	10 × 4° = 40°
Household goods	6 × 4° = 24°
Other expenses	10 × 4° = 40°

(It is not necessary to mark the sizes of angles on the diagram if you show your working clearly as above. The diagram shows the statistical figures and is clearer without the angle markings.)

Which diagram to draw

A bar chart shows clearly the different frequencies. It is easy to compare them. You can see at a glance which of two similar bars is longer.

A pie chart shows more easily the fraction of the total which each item takes. A sector using more than half of the circle represents more than half of the total, a sector with a small angle represents a small part of the total, and so on. It is not so easy to compare sectors with each other if they are nearly the same size.

A pictogram shows information in a similar way to a bar chart, but by making attractive drawings it makes it look more interesting than a bar chart, so people are more likely to look at it.

Misleading bar charts or line graphs

1. Because the scale does not start at 0, there seems to be a rapid increase. Sometimes the scale is distorted, also.

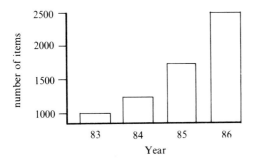
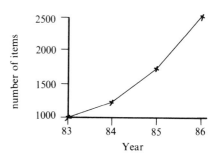

This gives the true picture.

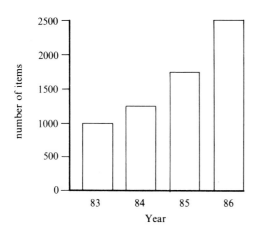
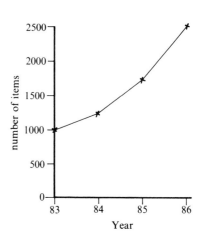

2. Although the profits have increased, the dotted block or line suggests a greater increase to follow in the future.

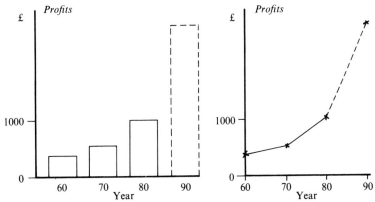

3. These are meaningless as there are no scales or units given. It gives the impression that 'ours is best'.

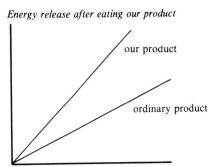

Misleading pictograms

If  represents a house, use to represent 2 houses.

If you double the measurements of the house instead, the proportion is all wrong. (In fact the new house has eight times the volume of the other one and should represent 8 houses.)

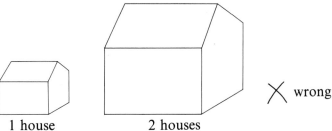

People might use this method when they want to give a misleading impression. The method is acceptable if the measurements are calculated properly so that the volumes, or areas in a two-dimensional picture, are in the correct proportion.

Notice the effect of colour or shading. On a diagram the parts with brighter colours seem to be more important than the others.

Look out for examples of misleading statistics.

Exercise 23.1

1. A camping holiday cost £36. This pie chart shows how the money was used.

   Measure the angles with your protractor
   to the nearest 5° in each case.
   Find how much was spent on each of the
   four items.

2. Of 24 school leavers, 9 went to the Further Education College, 8 found employment in a local factory, 5 found other employment and the others joined a training scheme.

   1 How many joined the training scheme?

   2 Represent the data on a pie chart.

3. 18 children are asked about their pets.
   3 have a dog.
   5 have a cat.
   2 have a budgie.
   1 has a guinea-pig.
   The others have no pets.

   1 How many children do not have a pet?

   2 Represent the data on a pie chart.

4. Mrs Harris puts aside £12 a week from her wages as personal spending money.

   In one particular week she spent £5 on a restaurant meal, £2 on tights and make-up and £3 on a birthday present. She gave 50 p to a charity collection, and saved the rest for her holidays.

   1 How much did she save?

   2 What fraction of the £12 did she save?

   3 Represent the data on a pie chart.

5. The diagram represents the milk sold by a dairy in 1985 and 1986.

   1 Why is the diagram rather misleading?

   2 Draw a more suitable diagram.

1985
1000 gallons

1986
2000 gallons

6. This bar chart shows the takings at the local fete for 3 years.

   1 Why is the diagram misleading?

   2 Draw a more suitable bar chart.

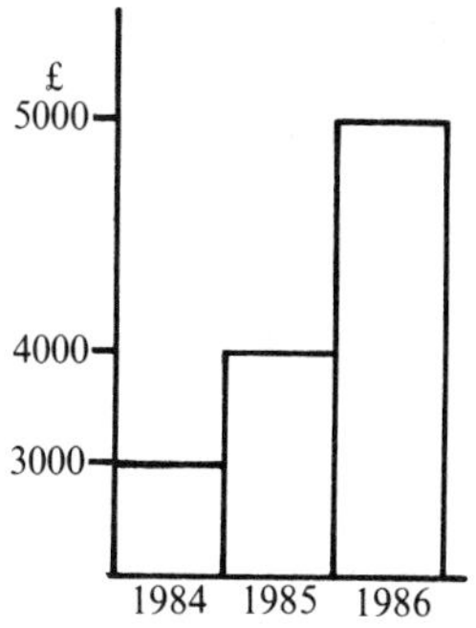

Frequency Distributions

Example 2

The numbers of children in 50 families (with at least 1 child) are as follows:

4 5 2 2 3 4 4 3 5 4 7 3 3 4 2 2 2 2 2 6
3 2 3 3 1 2 3 2 2 6 5 5 3 2 4 4 2 4 1 2
2 2 1 3 3 2 2 4 5 3

Tally chart

Number of children	Number of families	f
1	|||	3
2	𝍸 𝍸 𝍸 |||	18
3	𝍸 𝍸 ||	12
4	𝍸 ||||	9
5	𝍸	5
6	||	2
7	|	1
		50

(Remember the 5th tally mark goes through the other 4.)

f is short for **frequency**, the number of times each item occurs.

Histogram

This is a vertical bar chart with no gaps between the bars.
The tallest column shows the mode (the value which has the greatest frequency).

Children in 50 families

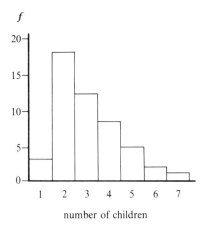

Averages

Mode There are 18 families with 2 children, so the mode is 2.

Median If the numbers were arranged in order of size

1 1 1 2 2 2 . . . 5 6 6 7

the middle value would be halfway between the 25th and 26th numbers, and these are both 3, so the median is 3.

To find the mean you must first find the total number of children.

```
1 child    in  3 families =   3
2 children in 18 families =  36
3 children in 12 families =  36
4 children in  9 families =  36
5 children in  5 families =  25
6 children in  2 families =  12
7 children in  1 family   =   7
               50            155
```

There are 155 children in 50 families.

$$\text{Mean number of children per family} = \frac{\text{total number of children}}{\text{number of families}}$$

$$= \frac{155}{50}$$

$$= 3.1$$

If the range of data is wide we can put it into convenient groups, called class intervals.

Example 3

The distribution of examination marks of 120 students.

Mark	0–9	10–19	20–29	30–39	40–49	50–59	60–69
f (number of students)	5	14	22	29	27	19	4

The data can be represented by a histogram.

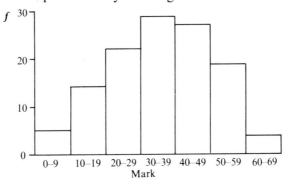

The tallest column shows the **modal class** (the class interval which has the greatest frequency).
The modal class here is 30–39 marks.

Exercise 23.2

For the frequency distributions in questions 1 to 4, draw a histogram (bar chart) of the distribution. State the mode of the distribution.

1. Number of people per household in a sample of 50 households.

size of household	1	2	3	4	5	6
number of households	10	18	9	7	4	2

2. Number of goals scored by 30 teams in a league.

goals	0	1	2	3	4	5
f (number of teams)	8	9	5	4	2	2

3. Number of heads when 8 coins were tossed together 60 times.

number of heads	0	1	2	3	4	5	6	7	8
f (number of times)	1	2	7	15	17	11	5	2	0

4. Number of pupils per class in 30 classes in a school.

number in class	29	30	31	32	33
f (number of classes)	6	10	5	5	4

5. With the data of question 1,

    1 what is the total number of people in the households,

    2 what is the mean (average) number of people in the households? (Give your answer correct to 1 decimal place.)

6. A girl plays a computer game in which she can score from 0 to 10 in each game.
    The scores she achieved in several games are shown here.
    Draw a histogram (bar chart) of the distribution.

Score	0	1	2	3	4	5	6	7	8	9	10
Frequency	2	3	0	4	3	8	5	9	3	1	2

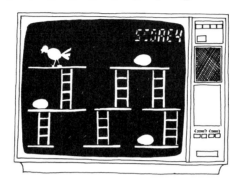

7. The goals scored by 20 football teams were as follows:
    8 teams scored no goals, 4 teams scored 1 goal each, 3 teams scored 2 goals, 1
    team scored 3 goals, 3 teams scored 4 goals, 1 team scored 5 goals.
    Draw a histogram (bar chart) of the distribution.

8. In a year-group of 60 pupils, the number of subjects each pupil passed in an
    examination, was as follows:

    5 8 8 7 8 7 6 4 8 7 8 7 7 8 5 6 6 3 6 6
    8 7 9 5 7 8 7 7 8 6 7 9 4 7 8 9 6 5 9 8
    3 8 7 4 5 8 4 5 6 9 9 9 9 7 8 8 5 6 7 6

    Tally the results to form a frequency distribution.
    Draw a histogram (bar chart) of the distribution.
    What is the mode (most frequent) number of subjects passed?

9. The number of matches in 50 boxes of matches was as follows:

    34 36 40 37 37 38 37 42 36 41 37 38 38 39 39 37 36
    41 36 39 37 32 36 38 37 38 40 41 37 38 38 33 34 35
    37 41 40 37 42 39 35 35 37 32 37 35 37 41 41 41

    Make a tally chart and frequency distribution table of the data.
    Draw a histogram (bar chart) of the distribution.
    What is the mode (most frequent) number of matches per box?

10. The marks of 25 children in an examination were as follows:

    68 78 64 67 73 94 69 86 62 67 82 69 61
    87 71 81 79 82 77 73 81 84 74 76 66

    Tally these data in classes 60–64, 65–69, 70–74, etc.
    Draw a histogram (bar chart) of the grouped distribution.
    What is the modal class (class with the greatest frequency)?

11. The histogram shows the times taken by
    a group of boys to run a race.

    (The times are to the nearest minute.)

    1 How many boys were there altogether?
    2 What fraction of boys took less than
       7 minutes, to the nearest minute?
    3 What is the modal class of the
       distribution?

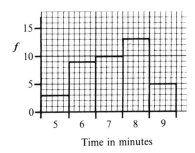

Time in minutes

Exercise 23.3

1. The diagram is a pie chart showing the expenses
   of a catering firm. The total expenses were
   £54 000.

   What amount is represented by 1°?
   If the angles at the centre of each sector were
   Wages, 150°; Food, 120°; Fuel, 40°; Extras, 50°;
   find the cost of each item. In the following year
   the cost of food rose by 6%, fuel increased by
   10% and wages increased by 8%. The cost of
   the extras decreased by 10%. Find the new total
   cost.

2. This line graph shows the profits of a
   company.
   Give two reasons why the diagram is
   misleading.

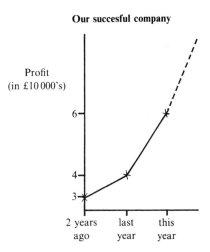

Our succesful company

Profit
(in £10 000's)

3. The number of seeds germinating in 40 pots when 6 seeds were planted in each pot was as follows:

    number of seeds   0   1   2   3   4   5   6
    frequency (number of pots)   0   1   3   12   10   11   3

    1 Draw a histogram (bar chart) of the distribution.

    2 What is the total number of seeds germinating?

    3 What is the mean (average) number of seeds germinating per pot?

    4 If you pick a pot at random from this batch what is the probability that it will have 4 or more germinating seeds.?

4. The weights of a group of children are given in this frequency distribution.

    (Weights are given to the nearest kg.)

    1 How many children are there altogether?
    2 What is the modal class?
    3 How many children are there in the modal class?
    4 What fraction of the children weigh less than 10 kg (to the nearest kg)?

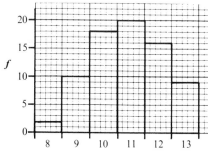

Weight in kg

5. The number of goals scored in the 1st 4 divisions of the football league were written down in order as they were heard on the radio.
    Results:

    0 2 0 2 2 2 0 3 1 4 1 0 1 0 2 1 4 1 5 1 5 0 3
    2 2 1 1 4 2 0 3 0 1 1 2 1 0 1 1 2 2 1 2 0 1 1
    1 2 0 0 2 2 1 2 0 3 2 0 1 0 0 0 1 0 1 2 1 0 2
    2 3 0 2 0 3 1 1 2 1 2 2 2 1 3

    Make a frequency table to show these results.
    Draw a histogram (bar chart) of the distribution.
    What is the mode (most frequent) number of goals scored?

6. 30 students were asked in a survey
    to say how many hours they spent
    watching television in the previous
    week. Their answers, in hours to
    the nearest hour, are as follows:

    12   20   13   15   22   3   6   24

    30   7   12   14   25   2   6   12

    20   15   9   12   5   6   8   20

    20   18   3   18   8   9

    Tally these data in classes 1 – 5,
    6 – 10, 11 – 15, etc.
    Draw a histogram (bar chart) of
    the distribution.

7. Throw two dice and note the total score shown, and repeat this 180 times. (If you
    have already recorded the results of throwing 1 die, as on page 80, question 9,
    part **2**, use the results in pairs, as if you had thrown two dice together.

    e.g. if the results were 1 6   5 5   4 6   6 2 . . .

              the scores are   7   10   10   8   )

    Before you begin it is interesting to estimate the most likely score (the mode) and
    the average score (the mean).
    Make a frequency table of the results.
    Draw a histogram (bar chart) of the distribution, and find the mode score.
    (You can compare your results with the theoretical frequencies. As on page 100,
    question 18, find the theoretical probabilities of scoring each total from 2 to 12.
    Multiply each of these by 180, the total number of throws in this experiment, to
    get a list of theoretical frequencies. Your experimental results should not match
    completely.)

8. Use 5 cards with numbers 1, 2, 3, 4, 5 printed, one number on each. Draw 3 cards
    at random and add the numbers together to get the 'score'. Mix the cards again
    and repeat this several times, putting the scores in a tally chart.

    Make a frequency distribution of the results and show this in a histogram (bar
    chart). Find the mode score.
    Make a list of all the possible different outcomes of the experiment, with their
    'scores', e.g. 1, 3, 4; score 8. (Disregard the order so that 3, 1, 4 is not counted
    as a different outcome.) Since these are equally likely outcomes you can find the
    theoretical probability of each score. Multiply each probability by the number of
    times you did your experiment to get a theoretical frequency distribution.
    Compare this with your experimental results.

9. See the lists of suggestions for collecting statistical data on pages 54 and 173. If you have collected data, you can draw histograms of the results. You can collect further data at this stage, including some data suitable for representation in pie charts.

PUZZLES

56. A group of six children have to send a team of four of them to take part in a quiz. But they all have their own views on whether they will take part or not.
Laura won't be in the team unless Michelle is also in it.
Michelle won't be in the team if Oliver is.
Naomi won't be in the team if both Laura and Michelle are in it.
Oliver won't be in the team if Patrick is.
Patrick will be in the team with any of the others.
Robert won't be in the team if Laura is, unless Oliver is in it too.
Which 4 took part in the quiz.?

57. Here is the final table in the local league. Every team has played every other team once. What was the score in the match between the Allsorts and the Dribblers?

	played	won	drawn	lost	goals for	goals against	points
Allsorts	3	3	0	0	4	0	6
Buskers	3	1	1	1	4	4	3
Cobblers	3	0	2	1	3	4	2
Dribblers	3	0	1	2	0	3	1

58. Write the numbers from 100 to 200 as the sum of consecutive integers.
e.g. $100 = 18 + 19 + 20 + 21 + 22$
$101 = 50 + 51$
$102 = 33 + 34 + 35$
$104 = 2 + 3 + 4 + \cdots + 13 + 14$
It is possible to do this for every number except one of them. Which number is this?

59. How many triangles are there in this figure?

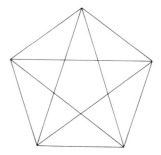

24 *Further geometry*

Polygons

A polygon is a figure with straight sides.

Number of sides	Name
3	triangle
4	quadrilateral
5	pentagon
6	hexagon
7	heptagon
8	octagon

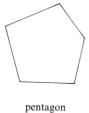

pentagon

hexagon

octagon

Regular Polygons

A regular polygon has all sides equal and all angles equal.

Number of sides	Name
3	equilateral triangle
4	square
5	regular pentagon
6	regular hexagon
7	regular heptagon
8	regular octagon

Regular polygons

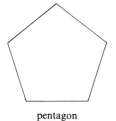

pentagon

hexagon

heptagon

octagon

Exercise 24.1

1. Sketch these figures and mark any lines or points of symmetry: equilateral triangle, square, regular pentagon, regular hexagon, regular heptagon, regular octagon.
   Copy and complete this table.

name of figure	number of axes of symmetry	Has it a point of symmetry?	order of rotational symmetry
equilateral triangle			
square			
. . .			

Is there a pattern in your answers?

2. Sketch this regular hexagon and join points as necessary.
   What sort of quarilaterals are

   1 *ABCD*, **2** *ABDE*?

   What sort of triangles are

   3 △*ABC*, **4** △*ABD*, **5** △*ACE*?

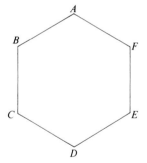

3. Three regular polygons fit exactly together at a point *P*.

   1 If they are all exactly alike, what are the sizes of the angles at *P*?

   2 If one polygon is a square and the other two are exactly alike, what are the sizes of the angles at *P*?

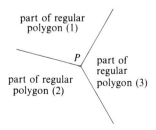

4. **To construct a regular pentagon *ABCDE***

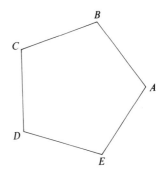

Starting at a point *O*, draw 5 lines *OA*, *OB*, *OC*, *OD* and *OE*, each 5 cm long, with an angle of 72° between each one and the next. Join *AB*, *BC*, *CD*, *DE*, *EA* and measure these lines (which should be equal in length).

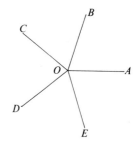

5. **To construct a regular hexagon *ABCDEF***

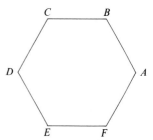

Method 1 is similar to the method for a pentagon, shown above. Make angles of 60° between the lines. There are 6 lines.

Method 2
With compasses mark a centre *O* and draw a circle, radius 6 cm.
Take 1 point on the circumference to be *A*.
With compasses, radius 6 cm, centre *A*, mark off an arc to cut the circumference at *B*.
Repeat with centre *B* to get point *C*.
Continue this method to get points *D*, *E* and *F*.
As a check, *FA* = 6 cm.
Join the sides *AB*, *BC*, *CD*, *DE*, *EF* and *FA*.

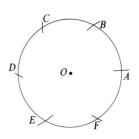

Translation

The dotted lines show the translation of the triangles when every point has been moved an equal distance in the same direction.

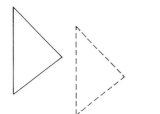 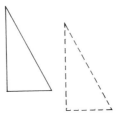

distance and direction

e.g. the translation 4 units in the *x*-direction,
1 unit in the *y*-direction.

A (2, 1) is transformed into *A*′ (6, 2)
B (3, 2) is transformed into *B*′ (7, 3)
The line *AB* is translated into the line *A*′*B*′.

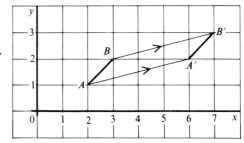

Exercise 24.2

1. Draw *x* and *y* axes from −8 to 8. Draw the triangle *ABC* where *A* is (1, 1), *B* is (4, 2) and *C* is (3, 7).
    A is translated to A_1 (−5, −6). Describe this translation. Using the same translation, translate *B* and *C* and draw the new triangle $A_1 B_1 C_1$.

2. Describe the transformations (reflection, rotation or translation) which map the triangles

    1 *A* onto *B*

    2 *A* onto *C*

    3 *B* onto *C*

    4 *C* onto *D*.

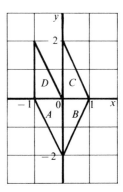

Congruent figures are the same shape and the same size.

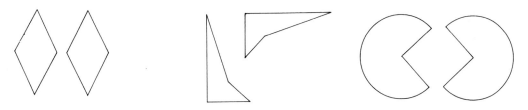

Congruent triangles

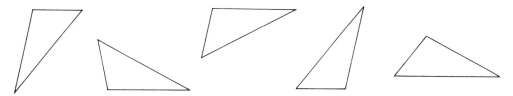

If one triangle can be reflected into the position of a second triangle, then the triangles are congruent.

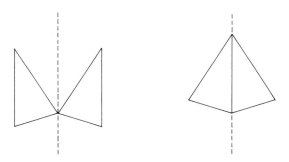

If one triangle can be rotated into the position of a second triangle, then the triangles are congruent.

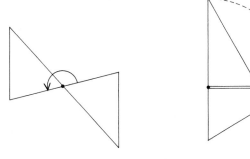

Exercise 24.3

1. Name the pairs of congruent figures in the diagram.

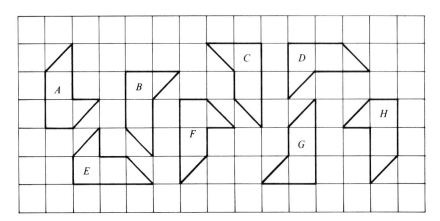

2. Name the pairs of congruent triangles in the diagram.

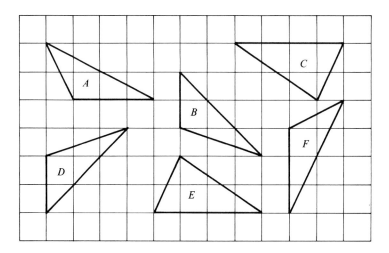

Geometric Patterns

We see many examples of patterns in our daily lives.
Notice the patterns on wallpaper and fabric and see how they involve reflections, rotations and translations.
Look for symmetry in buildings and in natural objects such as flowers.

Tessellations

These are congruent shapes arranged in a pattern to cover an area.
At every point where shapes join, for them to fit exactly, the sum of the angles is 360°.

examples

triangles covering a surface   hexagons   rhombuses

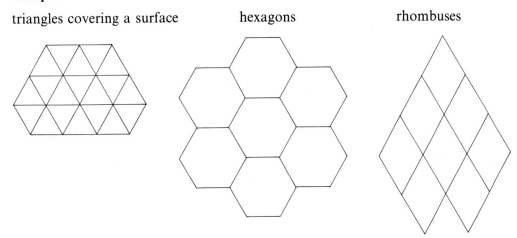

If we take triangles or other
shapes out of 2 sides of a
square

and add them to the
other 2 sides

the shapes will still fit together, and make a more interesting pattern.

The second pattern takes out equal curved shapes.

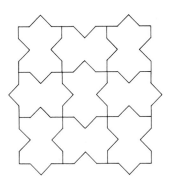   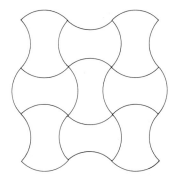

Tessellations can also be made using combinations of regular polygons.

examples

equilateral triangles and   regular octagons
regular hexagons   and squares

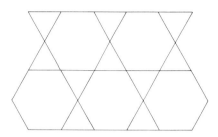

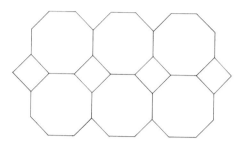

The possibilities are endless. Notice any tessellations you see, for example, on tiled floors.
Make up your own designs.

Exercise 24.4

1. Patterns made with triangles. Copy and continue these patterns and design others.

    1   Reflection and translation.

    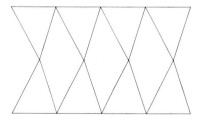   or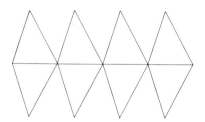

    2   Rotation and translation.

    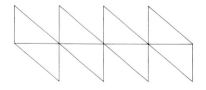   or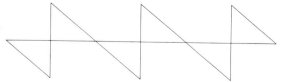

2. Patterns made with circles. Copy these patterns and design others.

   1 Keep the same radius   **2** Extend to outer circles

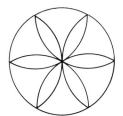

3. Copy and continue these patterns, or design similar patterns for yourself.

   1

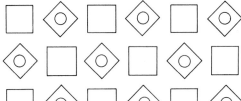

   2

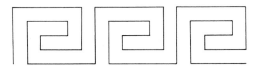

   3

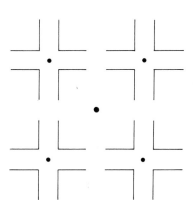

4. Start with a square with sides divided into 4 equal parts. By joining points make
    a symmetrical pattern.
    Here is one idea.

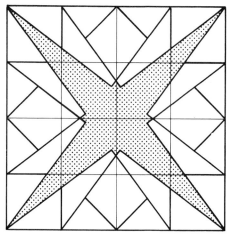

5. Start with a circle and mark 12 equally-spaced points round the circumference.
    By joining some of these points make a symmetrical pattern.
    Here is one idea.

6. Draw on squared paper and cut out several pieces of each of these shapes. Draw
    outlines on squared paper to show how each shape can be used to tessellate an
    area.

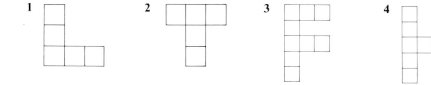

7. Draw a regular hexagon with side 4 cm on thick card. Cut it out. By drawing round the outside, make several more hexagons. Also make some equilateral triangles and some squares of side 4 cm.
Draw sketches of these tessellated areas.

   1 Use equilateral triangles and regular hexagons, so that every point is the join of 1 hexagon and 4 triangles.

   2 Use equilateral triangles, regular hexagons and squares. How many of each meet at every point?

   3 Use equilateral triangles and squares.

Exercise 24.5

1. Sketch the regular pentagon *ABCDE* and join points as necessary.

   1 What sort of triangle is △*BCD*?

   2 What sort of figure is *ABDE*?

   3 If *CE* cuts *BD* at *K*, what sort of figure is *ABKE*?

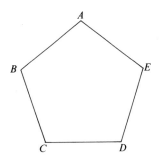

2. Here are 2 flow charts for finding the size of each interior angle of a regular polygon.

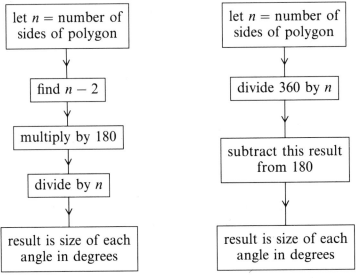

Use each flow chart to find the size of an interior angle in

1 a hexagon   2 an octagon.

Which flow chart do you prefer to use?

3. Draw x and y axes from -4 to 8 using equal scales on both axes. Draw the
    triangle ABC where A is $(1, 1)$, B is $(4, 2)$ and C is $(3, 7)$.
    Translate triangle ABC to triangle $A_1B_1C_1$ by moving each point 3 units in the
    x direction and then -2 units in the y direction. What are the coordinates of the
    image points A_1, B_1, C_1?
    Translate triangle $A_1B_1C_1$ to triangle $A_2B_2C_2$ by moving each point -8 units in
    the x direction and then 3 units in the y direction.
    What are the coordinates of the image points A_2, B_2, C_2?
    What single transformation would map triangle ABC onto triangle $A_2B_2C_2$?

4. $ABCD$ is a rectangle and M and N
    are points on AB and DC such that
    $AM = DN$.

    Which triangle is congruent to $\triangle AMC$?

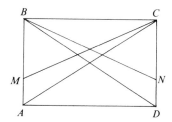

5. Start with an equilateral triangle of
    side 8 cm.
    Mark points every 2 cm along each
    side.
    By joining points, design a pattern.
    Here is one idea.

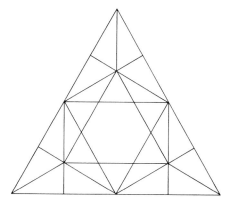

6. Draw a regular octagon as follows:
    From a point O draw 8 lines OA, OB, OC, OD, OE, OF, OG, OH each 4 cm long
    with an angle of 45° between each two adjacent lines.
    Join AB, BC, CD, DE, EF, FG, GH, HA. Measure these lines which should be
    equal.
    Cut out the octagon, and make several more of the same size.
    Make several squares with sides the same length as AB.
    Arrange the octagons and squares to make a tessellated area and show your
    design on a sketch.

25 *Calculating*

As you have worked through this book you have had a great deal of practice in doing arithmetic mentally, and you must continue to maintain the standards you have achieved as you will need to work out simple sums all your life.

For more complicated calculations you have had practice in using a calculator, and you should be very efficient in its use. This simple, cheap tool has made a great difference to our lives. Answers which would have taken too long to work out twenty years ago can now be found at the touch of a few keys. Do not lose your skills with a calculator. Whether you need to use it in your future work, or just use it to keep track of your personal finances, you will need to keep it available, and use it.

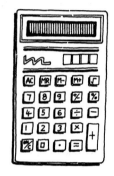

The computer is also making a great impact on our lives. Here the changes are coming so rapidly that machines which were so special a few years ago may now be out-of-date as they have been replaced by better ones. If you have access to a computer, do make use of it, either to run programs designed by someone else, perhaps teaching programs on some aspect of Maths, or try to write some of your own programs, or amend existing ones to improve them.

Here are some ideas to improve your speed and accuracy in mental arithmetic. First read the beginning of Chapter 1 again and work through Exercise 1.1.

1. **Multiplying pence by 100**

    Since $100 \times 1 p = £1$, multiplying by 100 changes pence into £'s.
    If a packet of sweets cost 12 p, then 100 packets cost £12.
    If the coach fare per child is 75 p, then for 100 children it is £75.
    If 1 pencil costs 6 p, then 100 cost £6, so 200 cost £12.

2. **Multiplying grams by 1000**

    Since $1000 \times 1 g = 1 kg$, multiplying by 1000 changes grams into kg.
    If 1 article weighs 12 g, then 1000 of them weigh 12 kg.

3. **Articles costing 99 p, £1.99, £2.99, etc**

    To find the cost of 7 articles at 99 p each, this is 7 at £1 less 7×1 p
    $= £7 - 7p = £6.93$.
    To find the cost of 4 articles at £5.99 each, this is 4 at £6 less 4×1 p
    $= £24 - 4p = £23.96$.

4. **Multiplying by 5**, especially for even numbers. Halve the number and then multiply by 10.

    $82 \times 5 = 41 \times 10 = 410$
    $38 \times 5 = 19 \times 10 = 190$
    $23 \times 5 = 11\frac{1}{2} \times 10 = 11.5 \times 10 = 115$

    Some other numbers can be multiplied more quickly by halving one number and doubling the other.

    12×15 (halve 12, double 15) $= 6 \times 30 = 180$
    30×18 (double 30, halve 18) $= 60 \times 9 = 540$

    Multiplying by 25. Divide by 4 and multiply by 100.

    $28 \times 25 = 7 \times 100 = 700$
    $63 \times 25 = 15\frac{3}{4} \times 100 = 15.75 \times 100 = 1575$

5. **Multiplying 2-figure numbers by 11**

    Add the 2 figures together and put the total in the middle of the 2 figures.

    $32 \times 11 = 3\ 5\ 2$ Put $3 + 2 = 5$ in the middle of 3 and 2.
    $63 \times 11 = 693$

    If the figures add up to 10 or more, you must carry 1 onto the left-hand figure.

    $87 \times 11 = 9\ 5\ 7$ $8 + 7 = 15$. Put 5 in the middle, carrying 1 changes 8 into 9.
    $68 \times 11 = 748$.

6. **Subtraction** by the method of adding on. This is useful when subtracting from a number such as 100, 200, . . .
    $100 - 63$. To make 63 into 70 you need 7, then to make 70 into 100 you need 30. The answer is 37.
    $300 - 51$. To make 51 into 60 you need 9, to make 60 into 100 you need 40 and to make 100 into 300 you need 200. The answer is 249.

    This is the way a shopkeeper would count out the change.
    $£5 - £1.83$. £1.83 and 7 p makes £1.90, and 10 p makes £2, and £3 makes £5. You receive £3.17 in change.

7. **Learn the equivalent fractions** for simple percentages, especially that 10% is $\frac{1}{10}$. (But 5% is $\frac{1}{20}$, not $\frac{1}{5}$, of course.)

Learn the fractions equivalent to 50%, 25%, 75%, $33\frac{1}{3}$%, $66\frac{2}{3}$%, 20%, 40%, 60%, 80%, 5%, $12\frac{1}{2}$%.

$33\frac{1}{3}$% of $123 = \frac{1}{3}$ of $123 = 41$

$12\frac{1}{2}$% of $56 = \frac{1}{8}$ of $56 = 7$

Money. 1% of £1 is 1 p so 6% of £1 is 6 p.
To find 8% of £8.50.
1% of £8.50 is $8\frac{1}{2}$ p so 8% is $8 \times 8\frac{1}{2}$ p $= 4 \times 17$ p $= 68$ p

VAT. (If it is at 15%)
Find the VAT on £7.
1% of £7 $= 7$ p so 15% of £7 $= 15 \times 7$ p $=$ £1.05.
Another way to do this is to find 10%, then 5%, and add these together.
10% of £7 $= \frac{1}{10}$ of £7 $= 70$ p
5% is $\frac{1}{2}$ of 10% $= 35$ p
Tax at 15% $=$ £1.05, and price + tax $=$ £7 + £1.05 $=$ £8.05.

8. When adding a long list of small numbers, look for pairs of numbers making 10 and add these together.

$9 + 2 + 5 + 8 + 1 = (9 + 1) + (2 + 8) + 5 = 10 + 10 + 5 = 25$

9. 20 articles at 7 p + 20 articles at 23 p

1 article at 7 p + 1 article at 23 p $= 30$ p, so 20 of each $= 20 \times 30$ p $=$ £6.

10. **Practise taking numbers from 180** as you use this when finding the 3rd angle of a triangle. Use the method of adding on.

$180 - 57$. To make 57 into 60 you need 3, then to make 60 into 80 you need 20, then to make 80 into 180 you need 100. The answer is 123.

Practise dividing numbers into 360 as this is used in pie charts and polygons. Divide 360 by 2, 3, 4, 5, 6, 8, 10 and 12.

Practise squaring numbers mentally up to 12^2.
Note that all square numbers end with unit figures of 0, 1, 4, 5, 6, or 9, never 2, 3, 7 or 8.

Practise cubing numbers mentally up to 10^3.

Learn the 13 times table up to 13×4. This is needed for probability questions involving a pack of 52 cards, with 13 in each suit.

Practise recognising simple fractions as decimals and vice versa.

$\frac{1}{2} = 0.5$, $\frac{1}{4} = 0.25$, $\frac{3}{4} = 0.75$, $\frac{1}{5} = 0.2$, . . .

Practise multiplying decimals

$0.1 \times 0.2 = 0.02$.
$0.35 \times 10 = 3.5$

Use of a Calculator

Here are some further points about using your calculator. Read the details given in Chapter 1 and Chapter 6 again, and make sure you can do the basic operations with your calculator.

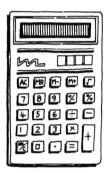

Different makes of calculators work in slightly different ways. Read the instruction booklet of your own calculator and try the examples shown there. You may find there are quicker ways than you normally use to do some calculations. But you will not be allowed to use the instruction booklet in an examination so you must be really sure that any method you use is correct.

Practise using the **memory** keys. It is useful to know how to store a number in the memory, to add numbers to it or to take numbers from it, and then to recall the contents of the memory for further use.

Mixed operations

Not all calculators work in the same way in a calculation where plus and minus operations are mixed with multiplication and division operations. Some calculators deal with the operations in the order in which they are entered, some do the multiplication and divison operations first, as if they were in brackets.

Try a simple question such as $3 \boxed{\times} 4 \boxed{+} 5 \boxed{\times} 6 \boxed{=}$ to see how your calculator reads this.

If it gives the answer 102, it is doing each operation in order.

$3 \times 4 = 12$, $12 + 5 = 17$, $17 \times 6 = 102$.

If it gives the answer 42, it is reading the question as $(3 \times 4) + (5 \times 6)$.

When you have found out how your calculator works, you can decide on the sequence of keys you need to do questions of the types

$$33 - (4 \times 5), (3 + 4) \times 5, \frac{3 + 4}{5}, 3 - \frac{4}{5}, (3 \times 4) - (2 \div 6).$$

You may have to use brackets, or enter partial answers into the memory.

To find the remainder in a division sum

e.g. $79 \div 19$.

Press 79 $\boxed{\div}$ 19 $\boxed{=}$ getting 4.157 . . .
So 19 divided into 79 goes 4 times.
Now find out what 4×19 equals.
$4 \times 19 = 76$ and $79 - 76 = 3$, so the remainder is 3.
A simpler way to do this is:

79 $\boxed{\div}$ 19 $\boxed{=}$ 4.157 . . .

Keeping this number on the calculator, subtract 4 to leave the decimals, then multiply by 19.
This should give the remainder, 3, but due to rounding errors it may not give 3 exactly.
So count a number such as 2.999 . . . . or 3.000 . . . . as 3.

Percentages

There may be a $\boxed{\%}$ key on your calculator, but unless you use it a great deal for the different kinds of percentage calculations so that you know exactly what you are doing, it may be safer to stick to the methods shown in Chapter 15, rather than use this key.
If you do want to use this $\boxed{\%}$ key, find out from your instruction booklet how to use it in the different types of calculations, and always make a rough estimate to see if the answer seems correct.

Accuracy of Measurements

If we were measuring the width of a field to the nearest metre and it came to between 66.5 m and 67.5 m then we would give the answer as 67 m. The boundaries of the range of measurement if the result is 67 m are 66.5 m and 67.5 m. So if we measure to the nearest metre we are accurate to within $\frac{1}{2}$ metre above or below.
If we were measuring the length of a room, for most purposes it would be sufficient to give it to the nearest 0.1 m (that is, to the nearest 10 cm). However, if we were measuring it to buy a fitted carpet, we would need the measurement to the nearest cm.
If we were timing someone in running 200 m we would give the time to the nearest second, but a more serious runner would want his time to the nearest 0.1 second and in an important race he would be timed to 0.01 second.
When weighing ingredients for baking, precise measurements are not needed. If we need 250 g of sugar, it is sufficient to weigh this on scales to the nearest 50 g, that is to within 25 g above or below, but if we were doing a chemical experiment we would use a more accurate balance.

If we are using exact numbers then we can give an exact answer,
e.g. $4.1 \times 3.2 = 13.12$. But if the numbers are measurements correct to 1 decimal place then we are not justified in giving more decimal places in the answer, so an answer of 13.1 would be sensible and even that is only an average answer. (4.1 could be anywhere between 4.05 and 4.15, 3.2 between 3.15 and 3.25 and the product could be as small as 12.76 or as large as 13.49.)

Accuracy of Answers

When you are doing calculations for practical purposes you will give answers to a sensible degree of accuracy.

'It will take me about 20 minutes to get there, I will spend about £10 on food, there are about 800 pupils in our school, the car is travelling at about 50 miles an hour.'

However, if you are giving an answer in an examination, the examiner will want to check that you can do an accurate calculation, so first you must give that answer before you correct it up to a sensible degree of accuracy.

So, as a general guide,

1 Give the exact answer if there is one, but if the answer fills the calculator, give the answer correct to 4 figures at this stage.
2 **Read the question** to see if there are any instructions about giving the answer to the nearest whole number, 2 decimal places, etc, and **carry these out**.
3 If there are no instructions, then you will have to decide on how many figures it is sensible to leave in your final answer. Make sure you leave the answer from 1 legible as well, in case it is needed.

Exercise 25.1

Questions 1 to 15 are for practice in quick calculations, without using a calculator.

1. If 1 article costs 4 p, what do 100 cost?

2. Find the cost of 6 articles at 99 p each.

3. If 1 washer weighs 3 g, what do 1000 weigh?

4. Multiply these numbers by 5.

    28, 62, 96, 17, 89.

5. Multiply these numbers by 25.

    24, 32, 46, 81, 39.

6. Subtract these numbers from 100.

    55, 22, 76, 87, 18.

7. Find the change from £5 if I spend

    84 p, £2.33, £4.61, £1.11, £3.30.

8. State the fractions which are equivalent to

    10%, 75%, $33\frac{1}{3}$%, 60%.

9. Find 12% of £1, and 23% of £2.

10. Give the squares of these numbers.

    7, 9, 12, 1, 6.

11. Give the cubes of these numbers.

    3, 5, 1, 10, 2.

12. By changing the decimals into fractions, find the values of

    0.5×18, 0.75×44, 0.25×32, 0.2×55, 0.05×80.

13. Find the total cost of 20 cups at 48 p and 20 saucers at 32 p.

14. Find the total amount if **VAT** at 15% is added to £12.

15. Find the 3rd angle in a triangle if the other 2 angles add up to

    $163°$, $121°$, $55°$, $97°$, $101°$.

Questions 16 to 18 are for practice in using a calculator.

16. These numbers are approximations of the numbers used in question 17. Find the answers, if possible without using your calculator. Keep the answers to use in question 17.

1	$3 + 2 + 8$	6	4×300
2	0.1×2	7	$1 \div 2$
3	$7 \div 0.2$	8	$400 + 800 - 600$
4	$13 - 3$	9	$2 + 2 + 2$
5	$(20 \times 20) + (10 \times 10)$	10	$1000 \div 5$

17. Work out the following, using your calculator. Compare each answer with the corresponding answer from question 16. If they are very different, check your work again.

1	$3.17 + 2.4 + 7.73$	6	3.63×280
2	0.09×2.1	7	$1.32 \div 2.4$
3	$6.8 \div 0.17$	8	$379 + 821 - 560$
4	$13.3 - 2.84$	9	$2.35 + 2.4 + 1.85$
5	$19^2 + 11^2$	10	$1008 \div 4.8$

18. Use your calculator to find the numbers represented by □ in these statements.

1	$\square + 22.5 = 103.1$	6	$1760 - \square = 990$
2	$\square \times 13 = 22.1$	7	$12.6 \times \square = 10.08$
3	$\square - 5.3 = 12.7$	8	$136.8 \div \square = 15.2$
4	$\square \div 2.4 = 1.5$	9	$2 \times (\square + 5.3) = 17.8$
5	$1967 + \square = 1988$	10	$(5.1 \times 7.3) - \square = 27.23$

19. For these statements 4 alternatives are given in brackets. Which one makes the most sensible statement?

   1 Jim's 20-year old brother is   (1.2) (1.8) (2.4) (6)   metres tall.
   2 Mary's baby sister weighs (35 g) (3½ kg) (35 kg) (350 lb). Her other young sister weighs   (35 g) (3½ kg) (35 kg) (350 lb).
   3 Tessa measured one of the other angles of a right-angled triangle and it was (72°) (99°) (100°) (108°).
   4 Sam's car does 40 miles to the gallon. On his holiday he expects to drive about 600 miles, and he estimates that he will need about (£3) (£20) (£30) (£300)   for petrol, which costs £1.90 per gallon.
   5 The height of the oak tree in the field is   (1.5) (20) (50) (75)   metres.

20. The radius of a circle, measured to the nearest metre, is 11 m. Find

   1 the largest possible length of the radius,
   2 the smallest possible length of the radius,
   3 the smallest possible length of the circumference,
   4 the largest possible length of the circumference.

   For **3** and **4**, take π as 3.14 and give answers correct to the nearest metre.

Exercise 25.2

Questions 1 to 15 are for practice in quick calculations, without using a calculator.

1. If 1 article costs 11 p, what do 200 cost?

2. Find the cost of 5 articles at £3.99 each.

3. If 1 cm³ of liquid weighs 1.1 g, what will 1000 cm³ of the liquid weigh?

4. Multiply these numbers by 11.

    26,   61,   83,   45,   29.

5. Multiply these numbers by doubling the first one and halving the second one.

    6×14, 15×16, 30×24.

6. Find the value of $3^2 + 4^2$.

7. Work out the values of $300 - 51$, $200 - 45$, $500 - 92$.

8. Find the change from £1 if I spend

    87 p,   62 p,   56 p,   13 p,   47 p.

9. Subtract these fractions by the method of adding on.

    $1 - \frac{3}{5}$, $3 - \frac{7}{10}$, $3 - \frac{1}{6}$, $2 - \frac{3}{8}$, $5 - \frac{5}{12}$.

10. Find the values of the following by turning the percentages into fractions.

    10% of £9.60,   25% of £5.20, $66\frac{2}{3}$% of £1.50,   80% of £2.50.

11. Work out these decimal questions.

    0.3×0.4, $\quad 0.71 \times 10$, $\quad 0.03 \times 0.1$, $\quad 0.7 \times 0.8$, $\quad 1.4 \div 10$, $\quad 0.2^2$, $\quad 0.5 \times 0.6$, 0.03×100, $\quad 0.6^2$, $\quad 4.2 \div 100$.

12. Find the total cost of 12 bags of crisps at 13 p and 12 bottles of lemonade at 17 p.

13. Give the square roots of these numbers.

    64, 121, 49, 1, 100.

14. Which of these numbers are cube numbers?

    64, 6, 1000, 125, 81.

15. Find these fractions of 360°.

    $\frac{1}{2}$, $\frac{1}{10}$, $\frac{1}{12}$, $\frac{1}{8}$, $\frac{1}{5}$.

16. Work out the following. (If you use your calculator, take care with the mixed units.)

    1 2 hr 56 min + 1 hr 23 min + 5 hr 48 min

    2 12 hr 18 min − 5 hr 42 min

    3 12 yr 9 mths × 5

    4 40 yr 3 mths ÷ 7

    5 (2 hr 14 min × 5) + (7 hr 12 min × 4)

17. These questions are approximations of the numbers used in question 18. Find the answers, if possible without using your calculator. Keep the answers to use in question 18.

    1 $\dfrac{200 \times 0.1}{10}$

    2 $(35 - 30) \times 60$

    3 $2 + (\frac{1}{4} \times 8)$

    4 $20 \div (3 + 2)$

    5 $(5 \times 3) - 5$

    6 $(6 \times 7) - (3 \times 4)$

    7 $\dfrac{30 + 60}{20}$

    8 $\frac{30}{4} + \frac{8}{2}$

    9 $(20 \times 3) - (10 \times 3)$

    10 $\frac{3}{4}$ of 28 + $\frac{1}{4}$ of 32

18. Work out the following, using your calculator. Compare each answer with the corresponding answer from question 17. If they are very different, check your work again.

    1 $\dfrac{216 \times 0.084}{9.6}$

    2 $(35 - 29.7) \times 61.3$

    3 $1.93 + (0.25 \times 7.64)$

    4 $23.75 \div (2.8 + 2.2)$

    5 $(4.7 \times 3.1) - 5.07$

    6 $6.5^2 - 3.5^2$

    7 $\dfrac{33.6 + 61.8}{21.2}$

    8 $\dfrac{28.7}{3.5} + \dfrac{8}{1.6}$

    9 $(19 \times 3.14) - (9 \times 3.14)$

    10 $\frac{3}{4}$ of 29.6 + $\frac{1}{4}$ of 31.2

19. Find the remainders when

1 371 is divided by 12
2 827 is divided by 23
3 1024 is divided by 13
4 7 is divided into 2000
5 60 is divided into 400

20. Find approximate answers to the following, then use your calculator to work out the exact answers.

1 1.4×2.32 **4** 6.3^2

2 $203.7 - 114.9$ **5** $319.2 + 97.5$

3 $8.74 \div 3.8$

21. Write down the number and the unit which together make the most sensible statement.

1 To knit a pair of gloves you will need (2, 10, 60)   (g, kg) of wool.
2 A good runner can run a mile in about (4, 20, 60)   (seconds, minutes, hours).
3 If 200 new pencils were placed end-to-end to make a long straight line, the line would stretch for about (2, 10, 30)   (cm, m, km).

22. The sides of a rectangle, each measured to the nearest cm, are 6 cm and 4 cm. Find

1 the largest possible length of the rectangle,
2 the largest possible breadth,
3 the largest possible length of the perimeter,
4 the largest possible area of the rectangle,
5 the smallest possible length of the rectangle,
6 the smallest possible breadth,
7 the smallest possible length of the perimeter,
8 the smallest possible area.

23. Find the results of these calculations without using your calculator. Then repeat the questions using your calculator, making sure that you get the same results.

1 $\dfrac{5 \times 3}{2}$ **6** $10^2 - 7^2$

2 $(6 - 2) \times 3$ **7** $\dfrac{15 + 13}{4}$

3 $7 + (5 \times 4)$ **8** $\frac{12}{4} + \frac{15}{3}$

4 $20 \div (3 + 2)$ **9** $(12 \times 4) - (10 \times 3)$

5 $(5 \times 7) - 29$ **10** $\sqrt{64} - \sqrt{36}$

24. In each of these calculations a mistake has been made. Find the correct answers. Can you also discover what mistake was made in each case?

   1   $1.32 + 2.5 + 3.79 = 7.09$ 4 $5.32 \times 6.15 = 34.6332$

   2   $10 - 0.918 = 0.82$ 5 $1234 \div 0.032 = 3856.25$

   3   $(13.1 + 17.9) \times 1.2 = 34.58$

PUZZLES

60. What is the area of a square of side 21 cm? Draw a square of side 21 cm on cardboard and divide it into 4 pieces as shown. Cut the pieces out and rearrange them to form a rectangle.
What are the measurements of the rectangle?
What is the area of the rectangle?
Where has the extra 1 cm² come from?

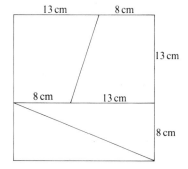

61. Mary is the eldest of five children and she is responsible for bringing her brothers, Tony and James, and her sisters, Patricia and Wendy, home from school. This journey includes crossing a river by a small rowing-boat, which only holds two of them at a time, and only Mary and Tony can row this. Usually they all get across quite quickly, but one particular afternoon the children were quarrelsome and Mary did not want to leave the two boys together, or the two girls together, unless she was with them to keep them in order. She usually sent Wendy across the river first, with Tony, but on this afternoon Wendy refused to go with Tony and insisted she would only go in the boat with Mary. Then James said it was his turn to go across before Wendy did.
How did Mary get them all across the river peacefully?

62. Whilst Mr Mercer's car was being repaired, he travelled to and from work either by train or by bus. When he went to work on the train, he came home on the bus. If he came home on the train, he had taken the bus to work. During this time he travelled on the train 9 times and travelled on the bus 10 times going to work and 15 times coming home from work. For how many days was his car off the road?

63. Mrs Richards left her umbrella on the bus so she went into the local gift shop to buy a new one at £6.75. She paid with a £20 note, but since it was early in the morning, Mr Jenkins who owned the gift shop had no change so he took the £20 note next door to Mrs Evans at the confectioner's, and got £20 in change. Then he gave Mrs Richards her £13.25 change and she went on her way.
Later on, Mrs Evans came in, very worried, because she had just discovered that the £20 note was a forgery. Mr Jenkins had to give her a cheque for £20, and give the forged note to the police. Later on he told his wife the sad tale—that he had lost a good umbrella, £13.25 in change and a cheque for £20, total value £40.
Was he correct?

Miscellaneous section E

Exercise E1   Aural practice

If possible find someone to read these questions to you.
You should do questions 1 to 15 within 10 minutes.
Do not use your calculator.
Write down the answers only.

1. What is the smallest number into which both 4 and 10 divide exactly?
2. When 15% tax is added to £1, what is the total price?
3. A rectangular lawn is 10 metres long and 8 metres wide. What is its perimeter?
4. What is the total cost of 4 articles at 99 pence each?
5. A water tank is 5 m long, 3 m wide and 2 m deep. How many cubic metres of water does it hold?
6. What is the change from £1 after buying 2 grapefruits at 34 pence each?
7. If today is May 24th, what will be the date this day next week?
8. How many packets of sweets at 12 pence each can be bought for £1, and how much change is there?
9. What is 0.25 as a fraction in its lowest terms?
10. If 1 kg of a mixture costs 12 pence, what will 100 kg cost?
11. A train which was due at 3.50 p.m. arrived 20 minutes late. At what time did it arrive?
12. The base of a triangle is 10 cm and the height is 6 cm. What is its area?
13. A man buys a bicycle for £40 and sells it to gain 10%. What is the selling price?
14. What is the next prime number after 31?
15. Find the total cost of 10 pencils at 6 pence each and 10 notebooks at 14 pence each.

Additional aural questions using data from other pages.

16. Turn to page 20. Use the fares table, of question 6.

    What is the total cost for 3 adults to travel from Long Lane to Victoria Road?

17. Turn to page 111. Use the thermometer shown in question 11.

    What is the approximate Celsius temperature equivalent to a temperature of 80° Fahrenheit?

18. Turn to page 198. Use the repayments table, of question 14.

    What are the weekly payments on a loan of £5500 taken out for 10 years?

19. Turn to page 343. Use the timetable of question 2.

I am in Kereva, wanting to go to Veefield, and I miss the train which leaves just after half-past one in the afternoon. At what time is the next train?

20. Turn to page 306. Use the graph of question 4.

How many children weigh 12 kg, to the nearest kg?

21. Turn to page 98. Use the picture of question 5.

The ace of diamonds in the picture is drawn to scale. The longer edge of the card measures 9 cm. Estimate the length of its shorter edge.

22. Turn to page 122. Use the larger triangle of question 4.

Estimate the size of angle B in the triangle.

Exercise E2 Multi-choice Exercise

Select the correct answer to each question.

1. The number 2749 when written to the nearest 100 is

   A 2700 **B** 2800 **C** 2740 **D** 2750 **E** 3000

2. The line OP is reflected in the y-axis and the image line OP_1 is then rotated in an anticlockwise direction through $90°$ about the origin. The coordinates of the final position P_2 of P are

   A $(2, -1)$ **B** $(1, 2)$ **C** $(-1, 2)$

   D $(-1, -2)$ **E** $(-2, -1)$

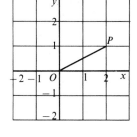

3. The area of $\triangle PQR$ is

   A $36\,\text{cm}^2$ **B** $54\,\text{cm}^2$ **C** $67\frac{1}{2}\,\text{cm}^2$

   D $90\,\text{cm}^2$ **E** $108\,\text{cm}^2$

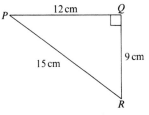

4. The diagram shows the goals scored by some football teams. The total number of goals was

   A 15 **B** 16 **C** 21

   D 28 **E** 32

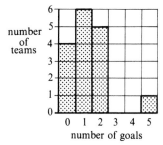

5. The area of a square is $900 \, \text{cm}^2$. What is its perimeter?

    A 30 cm   **B** 120 cm   **C** 900 cm   **D** 1200 cm   **E** 3600 cm

6. How many axes of symmetry has a regular octagon?

    A 0   **B** 2   **C** 4   **D** 8   **E** 16

7. Three men invest £2000, £3000 and £4000 in a business. They share the profits in the same ratio as their investments. If the total profit is £2700, what does the man who invested £2000 receive?

    A £600   **B** £900   **C** £1200   **D** £1350   **E** £2000

8. On a map a distance of 48 km is represented by a line of 2.4 cm. What is the scale of the map in ratio form?

    A $1:200$ **B** $1:2000$ **C** $1:20\,000$

    D $1:200\,000$ **E** $1:2\,000\,000$

9. The graph shows the speed of a train which starts from A and increases speed steadily until it reaches 20 m/s. After keeping a steady speed for some time it then decreases its speed steadily until it stops at B. For how long altogether was its speed greater than 12 m/s?

    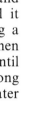

    A 12 s   **B** 30 s   **C** 50 s

    D 55 s   **E** 62 s

10. What is 12% of £90?

    A £1.08   **B** £7.50   **C** £10.80   **D** £13.33   **E** £75

11. Three cylinders have measurements as follows:-

    P: radius 24 cm, height 40 cm

    Q: radius 36 cm, height 48 cm

    R: radius 27 cm, height 45 cm

    The cylinders which are similar are

    A P and Q only   **B** P and R only   **C** Q and R only

    D P, Q and R **E** no two are similar

12. What is the value of $0.08 \div 0.2$?

    A 0.0004   **B** 0.004   **C** 0.04   **D** 0.4   **E** 4

13. What is the Simple Interest on £1250 invested for 3 years at 8% per annum?

    A £10   **B** £30   **C** £100   **D** £300   **E** £1000

14. Two angles of a triangle are 65° and 50°. Which of the following accurately describes the triangle?

    A isosceles triangle   **B** equilateral triangle

    C right-angled triangle   **D** right-angled and isosceles triangle

    E none of these

15. In the pie chart, the angle representing *B* should be

    A 90°   **B** 100°   **C** 110°

    D 120°   **E** 150°

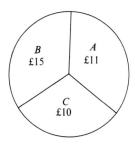

16. Which of these triangles are congruent to each other?

    A I and II only

    B I and III only

    C II and III only

    D I, II and III

    E no two of them

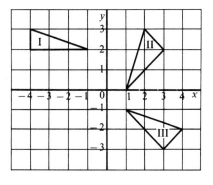

17. If you face North-West and turn 135° clockwise, you will then be facing

    A East   **B** South   **C** SE   **D** SW   **E** NE

18. A card is drawn from a pack of 52 cards. What is the probability that it is a heart or a picture card (Jack, Queen or King)?

    A $\frac{12}{52}$ **B** $\frac{13}{52}$ **C** $\frac{19}{52}$ **D** $\frac{22}{52}$ **E** $\frac{25}{52}$

19. The direction with a bearing of 303° is

    A *OA*   **B** *OB*   **C** *OC*

    D *OD*   **E** *OF*

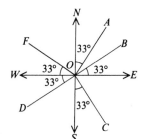

20. The length of *PR* is

    A   8 cm   **B**   9 cm

    C   10 cm   **D**   12 cm

    E   14 cm

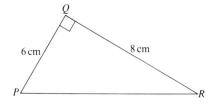

Exercise E3   Revision

1.   **1**   Find 36% of $2\frac{1}{2}$ hours.

    2   Find 8% of 5 m.

2. One number in each of these sequences is incorrect. Copy them, replacing the wrong number by the correct number.

    1   1,   3,   6,   9,   15,   21,   28.
         What is this sequence of numbers called?
         Write down the next 3 numbers in the sequence.

    2   1,   1,   2,   3,   5,   8,   13,   22,   34.
         (Each number is connected to the previous two numbers.)
         Write down the next 3 numbers in the sequence.

    3   1,   6,   27,   64,   125,   216.
         Is 1000 a member of this sequence?

    4   100,   93,   86,   79,   72,   66,   58,   51.
         Write down the next 3 numbers in the sequence.

3. Divide £14.85 in the ratio 4 : 5.

4. Calculate the length of *AB*.

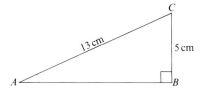

5. Simplify

    1 $2\frac{1}{2} + 1\frac{2}{3}$

    2 $3\frac{1}{2} - 1\frac{2}{3}$

    3 $1\frac{2}{3} \times 6$

6. 35 packets of sweets cost £3.15. What will be the cost of 42 similar packets?

7. A rectangular lawn 9 m by 8 m has a path $\frac{1}{2}$ m wide surrounding it. Find the area of the path.

8. A boy, John, goes jogging and leaves his home *A* at 6 p.m. on a straight run of 8 km to a village *B*, which he reaches at 6.45 p.m. Assuming that he jogs at a steady speed, draw a time-distance graph to represent his journey. Another boy, Ken, leaves *B* at 6 p.m., cycling towards *A*, at a steady speed of 24 km/hour. Draw on the same graph a line to represent his journey.

When and where do the two boys pass each other?

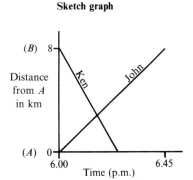

Sketch graph

Distance from *A* in km

(*B*) 8

Ken   John

(*A*) 0

6.00   6.45

Time (p.m.)

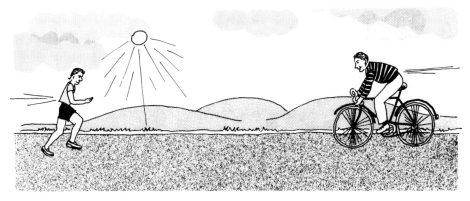

9. A boat sails from a port *A* for 10 km on a bearing of 135° to an island *B* and then 14 km on a bearing of 070° to a port *C*. Choose a suitable scale and draw an accurate scale drawing of the course sailed. If the boat then sails directly back to *A*, how far is the return journey and in what direction?

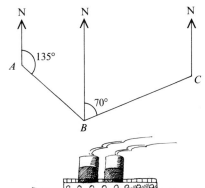

N   N   N

A   135°

C

70°

B

10. On graph paper draw x and y axes from 0 to 6.
    Plot the points $A(3, 1)$, $B(3, 2)$, $C(6, 1)$, $D(6, 5)$. Join AB and CD.
    What is the scale factor of the enlargement which maps AB onto CD?

11. This table shows the number of children in 100 families.

Children in family	0	1	2	3	4	5	6
Number of families	15	20	30	21	8	5	1

   1 Draw a histogram (bar chart) to illustrate the data.
   2 What is the mode number of children per family?
   3 What is the total number of children in the families?
   4 What is the mean (average) number of children in the families? (Give your answer correct to 1 decimal place.)

12. In the diagram, $AB = BC = AC$.
    Calculate the size of angle d.

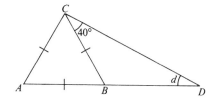

Exercise E4   Revision

1. Write in order of size, smallest first, $\frac{3}{8}$, 0.4, $\frac{3}{10}$, $\frac{1}{3}$, 38%.

2. A hair shampoo is sold in two sizes costing 46 p and 67 p. The cheaper bottle is marked as holding 100 ml and the other one holds 150 ml. Which bottle is the better value for money?
   (Explain how you get your answer.)

3. Find the Simple Interest on £220 invested for 5 years at 9% per annum, using the formula $I = \dfrac{P \times R \times T}{100}$, or otherwise.

4. Use your calculator to find the price of fuel in pence per litre, to the nearest penny, when it is £2 per gallon. (Take 1 gallon as equivalent to 4.55 litres.)

5. An explorer setting out from his base camp C walks due West for 8 km and then due North for 5 km. Use scale drawing to find on what bearing he must now travel to go directly back to camp.

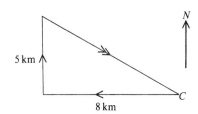

6. A rectangular shallow tray is 120 cm long, 80 cm wide and 5 cm high. How many litres of water will it hold? ($1000 \text{ cm}^3 = 1$ litre).

7. The following numbers were written on pieces of paper, put into a hat, and drawn out at random.

10, 13, 16, 17, 21, 25, 30, 36, 39, 49, 110, 121.

What is the probability of drawing out

1 a number greater than 100,

2 a number less than 20,

3 a prime number,

4 a number which is not a square number?

5 If an odd number is drawn out and not replaced, what is the probability of drawing out a second odd number?

8. A certain estate of 720 hectares consists of ploughed land, pasture land and woodland. This is represented in the pie chart shown.

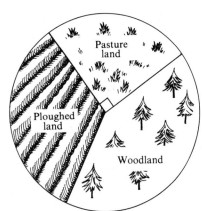

1 The angle in the pasture land sector is 90°. How many hectares are pasture land?

2 There are 240 hectares of ploughed land. The angle in this sector has not been drawn accurately. What should it be?

3 How many hectares are woodland?

9. Name the solid figures made from these nets.

1

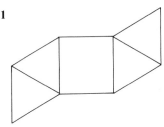

2

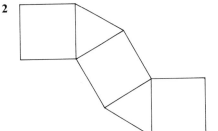

10. Triangles *AXY*, *ABC* are similar.
If $AX = 4\,cm$, $XB = 2\,cm$ and $AY = 5\,cm$, find the length of *YC*.

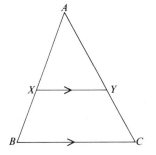

11. Find the mean, the median and the mode of this set of numbers.

1   2   2   2   5   7   8   10   14   17   20

12. A vegetable plot is rectangular in shape, 20 m long and 18 m wide. A hedge is to be planted round the boundary, except at the gateway which is 2 m wide. The hedging plants cost £1.20 per metre. Find the cost of the hedge.

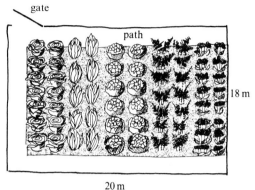

Inside the plot, there is a path 1 m wide round 3 sides, as shown. The remaining area is to be fertilized at the rate of 75 g per m². How much fertilizer is needed?

Exercise E5   Revision

1. 3 kg of fertilizer costing 22 p per kg is mixed with 7 kg of fertilizer costing 12 p per kg. What is the cost per kg of the mixture?

2. There are 7 discs in a bag numbered from 1 to 7. A disc is drawn (and not replaced) and a second disc is drawn. Show the sample space of all possible pairs of results and find the probability that

    1 the sum of the numbers drawn is odd,
    2 the 1st disc drawn has a higher number than the 2nd one.

		1st disc						
		1	2	3	4	5	6	7
2nd disc	1							
	2							
	3							
	4							
	5							
	6							
	7							

3. *A* and *B* are two harbours 15 km apart on a straight coastline running West–East. A ship *C* out at sea is seen from *A* on a bearing of 056° and from *B* on a bearing of 288°. Use scale drawing to find the distance of the ship from *B*, to the nearest 0.1 km.

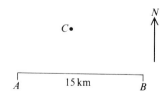

4. A television set costs a total of £81 if bought
    on a hire-purchase agreement. The same set
    costs £72 if bought for cash.

    1 If the hire-purchase agreement is for a
       deposit of £12 followed by 12 equal monthly
       payments, how much would be paid each
       month?
    2 During a sale the cash price of all goods is
       reduced by 5%. How much is deducted
       from the cash price of the television set?

5. This shows the reading when Bert had
    filled his car with some petrol.

    1 How many litres had he bought?
    2 He paid for the petrol with a £20
       note. How much change did he get?
    3 What is the price per gallon, to the
       nearest penny, if 1 gallon = 4.546
       litres?

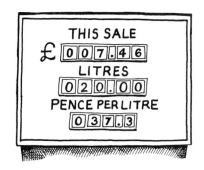

6. In a road survey, the cars passing a certain point in 1 minute intervals were
    counted, for 30 minutes. Here are the results.

    9   11 3   15 11   1   13 12   1   10 15   0   9   11   0
    10   5   5   4   5 11   7   13   7   9   12   5   9   10   6

    Show the results in a tally chart in classes 0–3, 4–7, 8–11, 12–15.

7. Calculate the sizes of the angles
    marked with small letters.

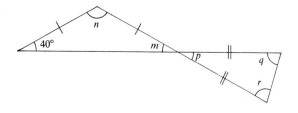

8. Draw a graph to convert inches to centimetres, given that 1 inch is equivalent
    to 2.54 cm. Draw the inches axis horizontally, from 0 to 10 inches, and the
    centimetre axis vertically, from 0 to 30 cm.
    Use your graph to find

    1 how many cm are equivalent to 8 inches,
    2 how many inches (and tenths) are equivalent to 10 cm.

9. In the sunshine, a stick which is 1 m high has a shadow of length 0.8 m on the horizontal ground. At the same time a flagpole has a shadow which is 4.8 m long. How high is the flagpole?

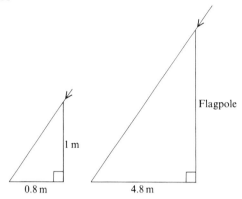

10. A motorist normally made a journey of 90 km in $1\frac{1}{2}$ hours. On one occasion road works reduced his average speed to 40 km/hour. How much longer than usual did the journey take?

11. The diagram represents an octagon formed by cutting equal isosceles triangles with short sides 3 cm from the corners of a square of side 12 cm.
    Find the total area of the four corners.
    Hence find the area of the octagon.
    Find the perimeter of the octagon, correct to the nearest mm.

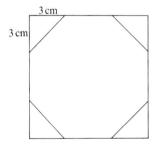

12. On graph paper draw the x-axis from -3 to 6 and the y-axis from -8 to 8.
    Draw the triangle ABC where A is $(-2, 2)$, B is $(-3, 3)$ and C is $(-1, 6)$.
    The triangle ABC is translated 7 units parallel to the x-axis and 2 units parallel to the y-axis to form triangle $A_1 B_1 C_1$. State the coordinates of A_1, B_1 and C_1.
    The triangle $A_1 B_1 C_1$ is transformed into triangle $A_2 B_2 C_2$ by reflection in the x-axis. State the coordinates of A_2, B_2 and C_2.

Exercise E6   Revision

1. A man went abroad taking £200 which he changed into francs at the rate of 12.5 francs to the £. He stayed 7 days in a hotel for 180 francs per day, and his other expenses averaged 60 francs per day. In addition he spent 340 francs on presents. After 7 days how many francs had he left? On his return he changed his remaining money back into £'s but the rate this time was 12 francs to the £. How much did he get?

2. The air service between London and 'Kereva', together with connecting train services to 'Veefield', are given in a time-table as follows:

London dep.	23.00	10.20	11.20	15.25	16.55
Kereva airport arr.	00.30	11.40	12.50	16.45	18.10
Kereva station dep.	04.30	13.31	15.17	17.55	20.01
Veefield arr.	06.13	14.43	16.25	19.03	21.09

1 What is the time of departure from London of the fastest service to Kereva?

2 What is the time taken for the slowest journey from London to Veefield?

3 The single fare from London to Kereva is £95, and the distance is 760 km. How much is the cost per km?

4 From Kereva to Veefield is 84 km. What is the average speed of the 13.31 train.

3. The costs for inland mail are as follows.

Not over	1st class	2nd class
60 g	18 p	13 p
100 g	26 p	20 p
150 g	32 p	24 p
200 g	40 p	30 p

(Note that these rates may not be up-to-date.)

A firm has the following items to post.
50 letters weighing less than 60 g, 20 letters weighing over 60 g but less than 100 g, 1 packet weighing 120 g and 1 packet weighing 130 g.
Find the costs of sending these items by 1st class, and by 2nd class post.
How much extra does it cost to send them all by 1st class instead of 2nd class post?

4. A plumber does three repair jobs as follows:— the first from 9.35 a.m. to 11.15 a.m., the second from 11.45 a.m. to 12.50 p.m. and the third from 2.05 p.m. to 3.50 p.m. Find the average time taken for a job.

5. Copy this drawing of a prism on your own squared paper, then using the squares to help you, draw an enlargement of your prism with scale factor 2.

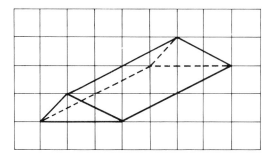

6. Draw axes as shown and show the journey of a boy on his bicycle and his father in the car. The boy starts from A at 1 p.m. and cycles at a steady speed of 10 km/hour for 2 hours. He then rests for $\frac{1}{2}$ hour and then continues cycling to B, which is 40 km from A, and he arrives at 6 p.m.

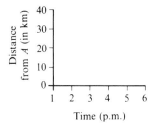

His father starts from A at 4 p.m. and arrives at B at 5.20 p.m., travelling at a steady speed.

1 On the second part of the journey the boy travelled at a steady speed. What was his speed?
2 What was his father's speed?
3 When and where did the father overtake his son?

7. A boy is playing near a circular pool of diameter 20 m. He sends his toy boat across the centre of the pool from *A* to *B* at a speed of 2.5 m/s, and at the same time as the boat leaves *A* he starts to run round the edge of the pool from *A* to *B* at a speed of 4 m/s.

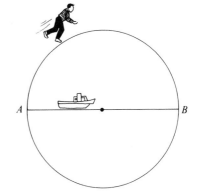

   1 How long does the boat take to go from *A* to *B*?
   2 How far is it from *A* to *B* round the edge of the pool? Take π as 3.14.
   3 How long will the boy take to run from *A* to *B*?
   4 Which gets to *B* first, the boy or his boat?

8. The rule for a number chain for 2-figure numbers is:
   Square the tens digit and add the units digit. Stop the chain when you get a single figure.
   e.g. $36 \rightarrow 3^2 + 6 = 9 + 6 = 15 \rightarrow 1^2 + 5 = 1 + 5 = 6$
   Carry out this rule for the numbers 52, 84 and 92.

9. A farmer wants to make a rectangular paddock by bounding three sides by fences, the fourth side being bounded by a river. He has 160 m of fencing available. He wants to enclose as large an area as possible.

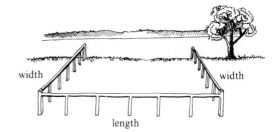

   Copy and complete this table.

length (m)	20	40	60	80	100	120	140
width (m)	70	60	50				
area (m²)	1400						

   Draw a graph with length on the horizontal axis from 0 to 160 m and area on the vertical axis from 0 to 3500 m².
   Plot the points for length and area given in the table, e.g. (20, 1400), and plot also (0, 0) and (160, 0). Join the points with a curve.
   Find the highest point on the graph.
   What is the largest area the farmer can enclose? What measurements should his paddock have to enclose this area?

(map for question 12 on facing page)

10. In congruent triangles *ABC* and *DEF*, $\angle A = \angle F$ and $\angle B = \angle E$. Name the three pairs of equal sides.

11. In the diagram, $\triangle APQ$ has been enlarged into $\triangle ABC$.

    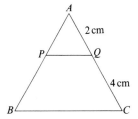

    1 What is the scale factor of the enlargement?
    2 If $PQ = 2.5\,$cm, what is the length of *BC*?

12. Use the map of England and Wales to answer these questions.
    Find which places are given by these approximate directions and say how far away they are, in miles, (to the nearest 10 miles) from the place mentioned.

    (The scale of the map is 1 cm represents 40 km, but assume that 1 cm represents 25 miles.)

    1 North of Liverpool,
    2 South of Hull,
    3 North-east of Manchester,
    4 West of Bristol,
    5 South-west of London

    Give the approximate direction (North, north-east, etc.) from the 1st place to the 2nd place mentioned and give the approximate distance between them.

    6 Manchester to Liverpool,
    7 Southampton to Dover,
    8 Hull to Cardiff,
    9 London to Birmingham,
    10 Carlisle to Hull.

Exercise E7 Practical work and Investigations

1. **An ABC book**
   You know many Mathematical facts now. You could make a 'Maths ABC' book. Put one letter on each page and choose a mathematical word beginning with that letter, e.g. A is for Angle. Then illustrate that page with an angle, if you want a simple, attractive book, or with facts about angles, such as types of angles, with illustrations, if you want to do more research. Even letters like Q, X, Y and Z give no difficulty. The most difficult letter to find a suitable word for seems to be J. There is 'join', as in 'Join the points', or 'Joule', whose name is used for a unit of work.

2. **A budget for a year**

Imagine that in a few year's time you have moved away from home into your own flat.

You have your wages from your work or your grant as a student and you plan ahead how you are going to manage.

Total income for the year . . .

Total spending for the year . . .

Firstly, there is necessary spending on the flat—rent, rates, water rates, gas, electricity and other fuel, insurance, TV licence, phone bills, etc.

Then there is the necessary spending on yourself—food, travelling expenses (including car expenses if you have one), clothes, etc.

Then there are all the extras such as HP or loan repayments, things for the flat, holidays, presents, entertainment, sports or hobbies, etc.

Make a complete list with estimated costs.

If the spending total exceeds the income total you will have to decide what you can do about it.

(If you prefer, instead of this do a similar budget for a family.)

3. **Palindromes**

A palindrome is a number which is the same when written down backwards such as 22, 353, 1441, 70607, etc.

In this investigation you are turning numbers into palindromes.

Write down the 2-figure numbers which are palindromes.

For the other numbers, e.g. 25,

Write the number down backwards and add to the number.

25

$\underline{52}$

77   This is a palindrome, so stop.

Make a list of the 2-figure numbers which form palindromes after this one stage.

For the others, keep repeating the process and see how many stages are needed.
e.g. 69

69

$\underline{96}$

165   Now write 165 backwards and add to 165

$\underline{561}$

726   Now write 726 backwards and add to 726, and repeat until you get a palindrome.

(If the process seems to go on indefinitely you may have to abandon that particular number when it gets very big, unless you can program a computer to carry the investigation further.)

You can also investigate for 3-figure numbers.

4. **A scale model**

Design a study-bedroom suitable for a teenager and make a scale model of the room, showing the door, windows and heating source. Make scale models of the furniture and include those. Show where the lighting is and where the power points are. Paint your model to show the colour scheme.

A more ambitious project would be to make a model of a house, a famous building or a village.

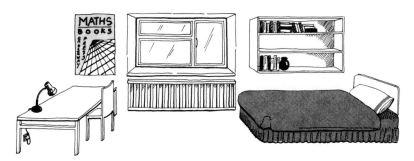

5. **The Fibonacci Series**

1,   1,   2,   3,   5,   8,   13,   21,   . . .

Discover how each number in the series is linked to the previous numbers and continue the series for several terms.

(As a check, 377 is a member of the series.)

Fibonacci was an Italian who lived in the 13th century. See if you can find out more about him.

1   His series is usually linked to 'the rabbit problem'.

'How many pairs of rabbits can be produced from a single pair in a year assuming that every month each pair gives birth to a new pair, which starts breeding from the second month?'

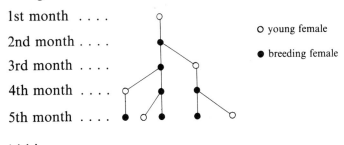

1st month . . . .

2nd month . . . .

3rd month . . . .

4th month . . . .

5th month . . . .

    . . . .

○ young female

● breeding female

2   If you are paying out money using only 10 pence coins and 20 pence coins, and you take into account the order in which you pay the coins, then, for example, 50 pence can be paid in these ways

| 10, 10, 10, 10, 10 | 10, 10, 10, 20 | 10, 10, 20, 10 | 10, 20, 10, 10 |
| 20, 10, 10, 10 | 20, 20, 10 | 20, 10, 20 | 10, 20, 20 |

Altogether there are 8 ways. Investigate for other amounts.

3 Many natural objects have links with Fibonacci numbers. Count the number of petals on a daisy-type flower. Count the spirals on a pine cone, a pineapple or the centre part of a sunflower, and then count the spirals in the opposite direction.

4 Divide each number of the series by the preceding number, and then divide each number by the next one.

$\frac{1}{1} = 1$ $\frac{1}{1} = 1$

$\frac{2}{1} = 2$ $\frac{1}{2} = 0.5$

$\frac{3}{2} = 1.5$ $\frac{2}{3} = 0.667$

$\frac{5}{3} = 1.667$ $\frac{3}{5} = 0.6$

. . .   . . .

Continue these for about 20 terms. What do you notice?
Investigate the relationships between each number and the next alternate number.

5 Draw a regular pentagon and draw its diagonals.

Find the ratios $\frac{AB}{BC}$, $\frac{AC}{AB}$ and $\frac{AD}{AC}$, by measuring.

$\left(\text{These equal 1.618 or } \frac{\sqrt{5} + 1}{2} \text{ exactly.}\right)$

Find the ratios $\frac{BC}{AB}$, $\frac{AB}{AC}$ and $\frac{AC}{AD}$.

$\left(\text{These equal 0.618 or } \frac{\sqrt{5} - 1}{2} \text{ exactly.}\right)$

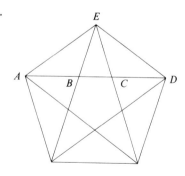

Is there a link with the Fibonacci series?
The ratio 1.618 : 1 or 1 : 0.618 is known as The Golden Section.
It is often used in Art and Architecture.

6 Golden section spiral

Start with a large rectangle with sides 25.9 cm and 16 cm.

Mark off a square.

Starting from A, with centre A_1, draw a quarter circle, going to B.

Now join XY and A_1Z as guidelines as a corner of each following square lies on one of these lines.

Mark off a square including point B.

Starting from B, with centre B_1, which is on A_1B and on XY, draw a quarter circle, going to C.

Mark off a square including point C.

Starting from C, with centre C_1, which is on B_1C and on A_1Z, draw a quarter circle going to D.

Continue until the squares get too small to go any further. Where does it end?

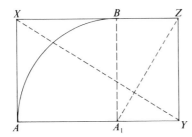 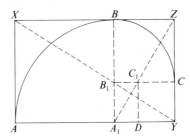

7 Pascal's Triangle

Start with Pascal's Triangle (see Exercise D5), move the numbers along so that the first number starts one column further along each time, and add the column totals.

1										
	1	1								
		1	2	1						
			1	3	3	1				
				1	4	6	4	1		
					1	5	10	10	.	
						.	.	.	.	
1	1	2	3	5	8	.	.	.	.	

8 Number patterns

Take every three consecutive numbers of the series. Multiply the two outside ones and square the middle one. What do you notice?

Investigate consecutive numbers 4 at a time, then 5 at a time.

Find the sums of 1, 1 + 1, 1 + 1 + 2, 1 + 1 + 2 + 3, etc. What do you notice if you add 1 to each?

Investigate sums of squares of 2 consecutive numbers, and differences of squares of alternate numbers.

Investigate number patterns such as

$$8 = 8 \times 1 + 5 \times 0 = 8 \times 1 - 3 \times 0$$
$$13 = 8 \times 1 + 5 \times 1 = 8 \times 2 - 3 \times 1$$
$$21 = 8 \times 2 + 5 \times 1 = 8 \times 3 - 3 \times 1$$
$$34 = 8 \times 3 + 5 \times 2 = 8 \times 5 - 3 \times 2$$
$$55 = 8 \times 5 + 5 \times 3 = 8 \times 8 - 3 \times 3$$
$$89 = \ldots$$
$$\ldots$$

6. **Geometrical models**

There are 5 regular solids so you could begin by making these.
Equilateral triangles stuck together, 3 at a point, will make a regular tetrahedron.
Equilateral triangles stuck together, 4 at a point, will make a regular octahedron.
Equilateral triangles stuck together, 5 at a point, will make a regular icosahedron.
Why are these the only regular solids which can be made with equilateral triangles?
Another regular solid is made with squares. What is it?
The 5th regular solid is made by sticking together regular pentagons. It is a dodecahedron.

If you have the plans of the nets of these solids you can make them from their nets. Put a tab on each alternate edge of the net. Score all lines before you bend them.

There are 13 semi-regular solids, made with combinations of regular polygons. You could try to make these.
With 6 squares and 8 equilateral triangles, with the same length of edge, putting 2 of each alternately at each point, you get a cuboctahedron. With 18 squares and 8 triangles, with 3 squares and 1 triangle meeting at a point, you can make a rhombicuboctahedron. With 6 squares and 32 triangles, with 4 triangles and a square meeting at a point, you can make a snub cube. Other solids use different combinations of equilateral triangles, squares and regular pentagons, hexagons, octagons and decagons. Can you discover them all?
There are 4 other regular solids called the Kepler-Poinsot Polyhedra, which are interesting models.
To make the great stellated dodecahedron, first make a regular icosahedron as a base. Then make 20 triangular pyramids to stick on the 20 faces of the icosahedron. The long slant edges of these pyramids must be 1.62 times the length of the base edges, which are the same length as the edges of the icosahedron. If you are interested in making maths models you can find details of many others from library books.

7. **Regular Polygons**

1 Sketch a regular pentagon *ABCDE* and draw all its diagonals. (A diagonal is a line which joins two non-adjacent points, e.g. *AC* and *AD* are diagonals.) How many diagonals are there?

Sketch a regular polygon with 10 sides. From one point, how many diagonals can be drawn? To find the total number of diagonals, multiply this number by 10, because you can draw diagonals from each of the 10 points, then divide by 2 because using this method you have counted every diagonal twice. Can you find a formula for the number of diagonals of a regular polygon with *n* sides?

If so, use your formula to find the number of diagonals of a regular polygon with 20 sides.

2 When all the diagonals are drawn, how many regions are there inside the polygon?

3 Paper knots. Use strips of paper of uniform width. Practise with narrow strips first. Tie an ordinary knot to get a pentagon. Go round an extra turn to get a heptagon. Tie a reef knot in two strips of paper for a hexagon. By bending the paper in a different way you get an octagon.

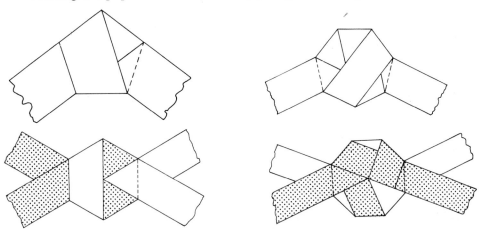

4 You probably can construct a hexagon using ruler and compasses. Here is how to find the arc length to construct a regular pentagon or decagon, without measuring the angles.

Draw a circle centre *C*, radius *r* and mark a point *A* on the circumference. Construct a tangent at *A*. Mark a point *D* on the tangent such that $AD = \frac{1}{2}r$. (Measure or bisect *AC* to get this length.) With centre *D*, radius *DC*, mark a point *E* on the tangent on the other side of *A* to *D*. Then *AE* is the radius you need to step out arcs on the circle to make the vertices of a regular decagon. Joining alternate arcs will give a pentagon.

5 Draw a regular pentagon and join its diagonals. Find in the figure an acute-angled isosceles triangle, an obtuse-angled isosceles triangle, an isosceles trapezium, a rhombus, a kite, a pentagon. Find non-regular polygons with different numbers of sides. How many triangles are there altogether in the figure?

Do a similar investigation for a regular hexagon and a regular octagon.

8. **Planning a party for children**

Your party can be in your own home, for a younger brother or sister, or it may be a party for members of a children's club, held in the clubroom, or a party for the junior classes at your school. It can be a birthday party, a party at Christmas or some other festival time, or an end-of-term party.

First decide on what sort of party you are planning, how many children there will be, the ages of the children involved, when and where it will be held.

Decide how much you can spend on the party, perhaps as an over-all total or as 'so much a head'.

Plan a menu and decide how much of each item must be bought. Don't forget to include soft drinks.

Plan a timetable for the party with time of beginning and the time it will end, times for various activities such as games and entertainment, and time for eating. Decide what other things must be bought, other than food, e.g. balloons, decorations, small prizes. Are there any other expenses such as hire of a disco or hire of a room? Find the total cost of everything.

Everything for the party has to be ready in time. Who is doing the shopping, and when? Who is making the sandwiches, and how long will this take? Plan the timetable for the time leading up to the party. (There are also details for tidying up after the party.)

Make a topic booklet about all this. Include a sample invitation, a copy of the menu, and illustrate it with pictures.

You might prefer to plan your party for a different age-group, a teenage party, a surprise party for your parents, or a party for the handicapped or for senior citizens living locally.

9. **To find the day of the week for any date (1800–2099)**

By using this method you will be able to find the day of the week for any date without looking at a calendar for that year.
On which day of the week does your 18th birthday fall?
On which day of the week were you born?
On which day of the week does 1st January, 2001 fall?
Work out these and other dates.

e.g. 12th September, 1987. This is written as 12.9.87
You are going to write down 5 numbers, add them up, divide by 7 and find the remainder.

(a) Add the three numbers for day, month and year together.   108
(b) Double the number of the month.   18
(c) Write down the special number (see below).   2
(d) Divide the last two figures of the year by 4, ignoring any remainder.   21
(e) Write down the century number. (For years 1800–1899 this is 6, for 1900–1999 it is 4, for 2000–2099 it is 3.)

$$\underline{4}$$
$$153$$

$153 \div 7$ gives remainder 6.
This remainder gives the day of the week, using this list.

Remainder	0	1	2	3	4	5	6
Day	Sun	Mon	Tues	Wed	Thur	Fri	Sat

So 12th September, 1987 is a Saturday.

The special number is found by counting how many of the following list of imaginary dates would occur **after** the date you are using.

Feb 29,   Feb 30,   Feb 31,   Apl 31,   Jun 31,   Sep 31,   Nov 31.

(Do not count Feb 29 in a leap year as it is not an imaginary date.)

(In our example, after 12th September there are 2 imaginary dates, Sep 31 and Nov 31, so the special number is 2.)

10. **For the Computer Programmer**
More suggestions for programs:

1   To make number patterns and investigate them.
2   To find the 3rd side of a right-angled triangle.
3   To find the mean of a frequency distribution.
4   To draw a histogram for given data.
5   To find the size of an interior angle of a regular polygon, for any number of sides.
6   To make geometric patterns.

These lists contain ideas related to the work in the main chapters of this book. In many investigations you do, you could make use of the computer.

PUZZLES

64. What is this? On graph paper label the x and y axes from 0 to 55, using the same scale
     on both axes. Mark these points. Join each point to the next one (working downwards
     in columns) except where there is a cross after the point. Add a circle, centre (17, 42),
     radius 1 unit. Also add shading or any other lines you think necessary.

(6, 41)	(15, 33)	(16, 6)	(20, 8)	(30, 8)	(30, 31)	(16, 45)
(7, 42)	(13, 30)	(17, 6)	(21, 8)	(26, 7)	(26, 34)	(14, 46)
(7, 43)	(12, 27)	(17, 7)	(21, 9)	(26, 5)	(15, 33)×	(15, 45)
(6, 43)	(11, 25)	(18, 7)	(22, 12)	(48, 5)	(15, 35)	(14, 44)
(5, 42)	(10, 20)	(18, 8)	(23, 10)	(51, 7)	(26, 36)	(7, 43)×
(6, 41)	(12, 23)	(19, 10)	(24, 11)	(55, 14)	(26, 34)×	(21, 47)
(6, 39)	(11, 19)	(20, 11)	(24, 9)	(55, 17)	(26, 36)	(22, 55)
(7, 35)	(12, 21)	(21, 11)	(26, 11)	(52, 21)	(27, 39)	(23, 51)×
(7, 33)	(13, 16)	(25, 15)	(26, 9)	(52, 16)	(27, 43)	(16, 42)
(8, 36)	(14, 19)	(24, 18)	(28, 11)	(51, 12)	(25, 46)	(16, 44)
(8, 34)	(15, 15)	(25, 20)×	(29, 9)	(47, 8)	(24, 55)	(17, 43)
(9, 36)	(15, 18)	(16, 5)	(31, 10)	(46, 10)	(22, 47)	(17, 44)
(10, 34)	(16, 13)	(18, 5)	(30, 13)	(46, 13)	(20, 47)	(18, 43).
(11, 37)	(14, 8)	(18, 6)	(30, 16)	(45, 16)	(18, 46)	
(12, 35)	(11, 7)	(19, 6)	(32, 20)×	(42, 20)	(17, 47)	
(13, 36)	(11, 5)	(19, 7)	(31, 10)	(39, 22)	(17, 45)	
(15, 35)	(16, 5)	(20, 7)	(33, 8)	(35, 27)	(15, 47)	

65. An explorer wants to estimate the width of a river, flowing East-West. She stands due
     South of a tree growing on the opposite bank, and then walks due West, counting her
     paces, until the tree is in the North-East direction. If by that time she has taken 120 paces,
     and her usual pace-length is 90 cm, what estimate can she make of the width of the river?

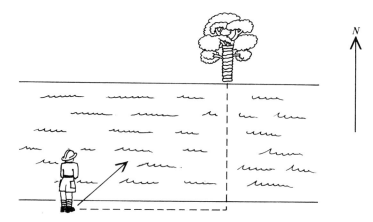

66. The ages of my father, my son and myself total 85 years. My father is just twice my age,
     and the units figure in his age is equal to the age of my son. How old am I?

67. Copy and complete this magic square. All rows, columns and the main diagonals should add up to 111, and when complete all numbers from 1 to 36 are used.

1		24			31
35	8			26	
34		15	21		4
3		16		10	33
	11	14	20		
	7		18	25	36

68. By crossing out just SIX LETTERS in the following, leave the name of a topic in this book.

P S R I O X B L A E B T I T L E I R T S Y

69. A farmer has 70 m of fencing available and he wants to enclose a rectangular area of 300 m^2. What measurements will his rectangle have?

70. Is it correct to say 'Half of 13 **is** $7\frac{1}{2}$' or 'Half of 13 **are** $7\frac{1}{2}$'?

Revision Checklist

If you will find this list helpful in planning your revision, then copy it out and tick off
the topics when you are satisfied with them.

If you prefer to keep to the order of the textbook, use the list of contents of the book
as your checklist.

You could also make your own checklist by using the printed syllabus of your
Examination Board.

Tick when satisfied		Chapters
	Numbers, prime numbers, factors, number patterns	1, 22
	Fractions	4
	Decimals	6
	Percentages	15
	Ratio and proportion	17
	Metric and British tables, money and time	2, 6, 8
	Time, distance, speed, travel graphs	20
	Conversion graphs and other graphs	18
	Use of calculator	2, 6, 25
	Applications of arithmetic to everyday life	1, 2, 4, 6, 8, 15, 17, 18, 20, 25
	Algebraic expressions	10
	Formulae	10
	Directed numbers	10
	Inequalities	10
	Coordinates	18
	Symmetry, reflection, rotation	3
	Angles	3
	Lines, parallel lines	9
	Triangles	9
	Quadrilaterals	11
	Circles	13
	Solid figures	16
	Similar figures, similar triangles, enlargement	19
	Scale drawing	19, 21
	Compass directions and bearings	21
	Pythagoras' theorem	22
	Polygons	24
	Translation	24
	Congruent figures, congruent triangles	24
	Geometric patterns, tessellations	24

Tick when satisfied		Chapters
	Perimeters of plane figures, circumference of a circle Areas of plane figures Volumes and surface areas of solid figures	9, 11, 13 14 16
	Statistics, collection of data and diagrams Averages: mean, median and mode Dispersion: range Frequency distributions and histograms	5, 23 12, 23 12 23
	Probability	7

Checklist for formulae, facts and methods

I   This is a list of the more important formulae. Copy it, complete and check the
    formulae, and learn the ones you do not know.

Perimeters, Areas and Volumes

1.   Perimeter of a rectangle =
2.   Area of a rectangle =
3.   Area of a square =
4.   Area of a triangle =
5.   Volume of a cuboid =
6.   Volume of a cube =

Circle

7.   Circumference =

Probability and Statistics

8.   Probability of a successful outcome =
9.   Mean of a set of numbers =
10. Range of a set of numbers =

Angles

11. Sum of angles of a triangle =
12. Sum of angles of a quadrilateral =

Time, distance, speed

13. Speed =
14. Time =
15. Distance =
16. Average speed =

II Here are some questions to remind you of the more important mathematical
    facts. You could answer these questions orally, or in some cases draw quick
    sketches. Find out the answers to those you do not know.

17. What different kinds of numbers do you know?
18. What is an even number?
19. What is an odd number?
20. What is a prime number?
21. What is a factor of a number?
22. What is a multiple of a number?

23. What is a square number?
24. What is the square root of a number?
25. What are the main metric measures of length? How are they connected with each other?
26. What are the main metric measures of weight? How are they connected with each other?
27. What are the main metric measures of capacity? How are they connected with each other?
28. Name some British measures of length.
29. Name some British measures of weight.
30. Name some British measures of capacity.
31. In which units do we measure time? How are these units connected with each other?
32. Name some kinds of statistical diagrams and describe them.
33. Name 3 kinds of averages and say how you would find each of them.
34. What do we mean by the probability of an event happening?
35. When we give the probability as a number, what range of numbers do we use?
36. What does it mean if the probability of an event happening is $\frac{1}{2}$?
37. What does it mean if the probability of an event happening is $\frac{1}{3}$?
38. What does it mean if the probability of an event happening is 0.99?
39. How do you calculate the probability of an event happening?
40. What is an angle? How do we measure angles?
41. What kinds of angles are there?
42. What are parallel lines?
43. What are perpendicular lines?
44. What is a triangle?
45. What kinds of triangle are there?
46. What do you know about the angles of a triangle?
47. What is an isosceles triangle?
48. What do you know about the angles of an isosceles triangle?
49. What is an equilateral triangle?
50. What do you know about the angles of an equilateral triangle?
51. What is a quadrilateral?
52. What do you know about the angles of a quadrilateral?
53. What special kinds of quadrilateral do you know? What is special about each one?
54. What is a diagonal of a quadrilateral?
55. What names of parts of a circle do you know? Describe each one.
56. What kinds of solid figures do you know? Describe each one.
57. What is a polygon?
58. What is special about a regular polygon?
59. What are the names of some polygons?
60. What are similar figures?
61. What are congruent figures?
62. What is Pythagoras' theorem?
63. What is the perimeter of a figure?

64. How would you find the perimeter of a triangle?
65. How would you find the perimeter of a rectangle?
66. What is the area of a figure?
67. How would you find the area of a rectangle?
68. How would you find the area of a square?
69. How would you find the area of a triangle?
70. What is the height of a triangle?
71. What is the circumference of a circle?
72. How would you calculate the circumference of a circle?
73. What is π?
74. What is the volume of a solid figure?
75. How would you find the volume of a cuboid?
76. How would you find the surface area of a cuboid?
77. What is the net of a solid figure?
78. How many faces, edges and vertices (corners) has a cuboid?
79. How many faces, edges and vertices has a triangular prism?
80. How many faces, edges and vertices has a pyramid on a square base?
81. What is a horizontal line?
82. What is a vertical line?
83. What are the 8 main compass directions?
84. How are bearings measured?
85. What is an axis of symmetry?
86. What is a point of symmetry?

III   Here is a list of some of the methods you should know. Make sure you can do all these.

87. Use a calculator efficiently.
88. Calculate with decimals, using a calculator if necessary.
89. Add and subtract fractions.
90. Calculate with money, and with metric units.
91. Calculate with time and with common British units.
92. Find a percentage of a sum of money.
93. Use directed numbers in practical situations.
94. Express 2 quantities as a ratio.
95. Substitute numbers into a formula.
96. Use drawing instruments. Construct diagrams, including scale drawings.
97. Construct graphs from given data. Make readings and deductions from graphs.

To the student:

6   The examination.

The day before

Get all your equipment ready:
Pen (and spare cartridges),
Pencil and sharpener,
Rubber,
Ruler,
Compasses, protractor, set square,
Calculator,
Watch.

For your calculator, buy new batteries and make sure they work. Spend a few minutes playing with your calculator to recall what functions you can get with the various keys. How do you find $\sqrt{40}$, 40^2, $\frac{1}{40}$, $(2 \times 40) - 3$, $\frac{20 + 40}{3}$? Remove the instruction booklet which you must not take into the examination room.

Although there should be a clock in the examination room, you may not be able to see it from where you are sitting so it is advisable to wear your watch. Does it also need new batteries? If you have not got a watch, then borrow one or buy a cheap one.

You want to be comfortable in the exam room so plan to wear a jacket or pullover to keep you warm if it is cold, but which you can take off if you get too hot. (If it gets very stuffy during the exam, ask the invigilator if a window can be opened. If you are in a chilly draught, ask him if it can be closed.)

Check your exam timetable. If you think the exam is in the **afternoon**, check very carefully, because you will be too late if you turn up in the afternoon for an exam that actually took place that morning. Check with someone else in your class to make sure.

Have a last-minute glance at last year's paper or a practice paper. See what instructions were given on that. Plan ahead as to how you will allocate your time. Have a final look at your revision checklist and maybe do just a little more revision, but not too much, as this should be a time for relaxation. Get out into the fresh air and have some exercise. Then go to bed at a reasonable time.

The examination

Get to the exam room in good time, with all your equipment, and have nothing on your desk or in your pockets which you are not supposed to have with you.

When the exam begins, make a note of the time shown on your own watch, and note the time it is due to end.

Check the instructions at the beginning of the paper so that you know whether you must answer all the questions or whether you have to make a choice from one section. Note any other important points.

Do not rush into the first question too quickly. Read it very carefully. Decide how to answer it, then do so. If you have to show your working, set it down neatly. You have plenty of time. It is so easy to make a mistake at this stage as you have not settled down, so don't be in too much of a rush.

When you have finished this question, and this applies to all the other questions as well, read the printed question again. Have you done what you were asked to do? Have you answered all of it? Is the answer reasonable? (Should you check your calculations again?) Is the answer given to the accuracy required, e.g. to the nearest whole number, and have you given the units, e.g. cm^2?

Continue answering questions carefully until you have done a few. Then check the time. If you are going very slowly it might be sensible to leave out any long questions so as to do a few quick ones at this stage. Remember it is the marks which count so spend the time on what will gain you the most marks.

If you can't do a question, read it again carefully. What is it about? Are you using all the information given? Is there a diagram? Is there any other information you could deduce from the diagram? If there is not a diagram, would a sketch diagram help? If so, draw one. What facts or formulae do you know about this topic? Do they help? If the question is in several parts, often an answer to an earlier part may be needed in working out a later part. Even if you can't finish the question, put something down on paper because your attempt might be worth some marks and it cannot be marked if it is not written down. If you can't do part (1) of a question but can do part (2), then do part (2) so that you will get the marks for that. You can always go back to thinking about part (1) later if you want to, and have the time. If you cannot get any further on any part of the question then abandon it and try a different one.

If the numbers in a question turn out to be complicated it is possible that you have made a simple mistake. Check that you have copied the numbers or expression correctly, and check your calculations again.

Keep your writing clear. Show all necessary working with your answer as you cannot gain marks for it if it is in a jumbled mess at the bottom of the page. You can do rough work at the side of the page near the answer, and then cross it out if you wish, but cross it out neatly so that it can still be read, in case it is worth some marks.

Do not use white paint correction fluid to blot out your mistakes. Some Examination Boards do not allow you to use this, but even if allowed, it wastes time, and if you write over it the new writing might get soaked up and be illegible by the time your script has reached the examiner.

Once the examination is over, forget it, until the results come out. You have done your best and that is all that matters. We hope you will be satisfied with your final grade. GOOD LUCK!

Index

This index refers to topics in the main chapters of the book.

Answers

Some answers have been given corrected to reasonable degrees of accuracy, depending on the questions.
There may be variations in answers where questions involve drawings or graphs.

Page 4   **Exercise 1.1**

1. 56, 24, 20, 60, 120, 15, 121, 8, 15, 6, 600, 12, 72, 0, 8, 13, 20, 106, 0, 144

2. 8, 6, 8, 7, 3, 12, 10, 12, 11, 8, 12, 5, 6, 5, 7, 12, 3, 7, 9, 9

3. **1** 3   **6** 4
    2 4   **7** 8
    3 2   **8** 5
    4 0   **9** 3
    5 4   **10** 19

4. **1** 265 384
    2 12 040
    3 1500
    4 $30\frac{3}{4}$
    5 4 440 404
    6 One hundred thousand, five hundred, sixty
    7 Two million, eight thousand

5. **1** 15   **6** 188
    2 0   **7** 36
    3 19   **8** 12
    4 8000   **9** 90
    5 250   **10** 110

6. **1** 4, 9   **6** 9, 8
    2 5, 6   **7** 8, 3
    3 2, 50   **8** 11, 7
    4 1, 15   **9** 2
    5 4, 12   **10** 4

7. **1** 4   **4** 106
    2 1024   **5** 105
    3 8

8. **1** 8   **2** 4   **3** 10

9. 200, 9901, 220, 4010, 1000

10. **1** 19   **4** 15
    2 7   **5** 16
    3 9

11. **1** 21   **2** 6   **3** 7

Page 10   **Exercise 1.2**

1. 23, 29

2. **1** 31, 37   **2** 41, 43

3. **1** $2^2 \times 3^2$ **6** $2^3 \times 3$
    2 $3^2 \times 11$ **7** $2 \times 5 \times 7$
    3 $2^2 \times 13$ **8** $2 \times 3 \times 11$
    4 $2^2 \times 3 \times 5$ **9** $2^3 \times 5$
    5 11^2 **10** $2^2 \times 5^2$

4. **1** 132, 156, 400
    2 135, 225, 400
    3 132, 135, 156, 225

5. **1** 11   **6** 8
    2 9   **7** 3
    3 5   **8** 8
    4 3   **9** 2
    5 4   **10** 7

6. **1** 15   **6** 22
    2 24   **7** 18
    3 20   **8** 6
    4 24   **9** 10
    5 20   **10** 21

7. **1** 8   **4** 90
    2 72   **5** 88
    3 140

8. **1** $2 \times 3 \times 5$
    2 $2 + 11 + 17$ or $2 + 5 + 23$

9. **1** 33   **6** 65
    2 48   **7** 121
    3 39   **8** 33
    4 55   **9** 9
    5 3   **10** 33

10. **1** 121, 36, 4, 100, 1
    2 8, 12, 7, 3, 5
    3 5, 6
    4 9, 10
    5 3, 4, 5

11. **1** 15   **5** 75   **8** 44
    2 42   **6** 14   **9** 65
    3 33   **7** 21   **10** 101
    4 16

12. **1** 50, 7690, 30, 1530, 100
    2 700, 9700, 300, 3800, 2000
    3 7000, 3000, 86 000, 12 000, 254 000

13. **1** 19   **4** 12
    2 16   **5** 16, 20
    3 20   **6** 8, 19

14. **1** 19, 23   **4** 27
    2 25   **5** 19, 25
    3 18, 27

15. **1** 81   **5** 8
    2 8   **6** 360
    3 37, 73   **7** 81
    4 91   **8** 50

16. 41

17. 66

18. 45

Page 12   Exercise 1.3

1. 1089 or 198

2. 99

3. **1** 31   **2** 30

4. 7225

6. **1** even number   **4** even number
    2 even number   **5** odd number
    3 even number

---

7. **1** 1st one, by 6
    2 60, 13, 17
    3 196, 676

8. David

9. **1** 23   **2** 48

10. **1** 81, 121   **6** 216, 343
    2 21, 28   **7** 40, 35
    3 32, 64   **8** $\frac{5}{6}, \frac{6}{7}$
    4 65, 58   **9** 14, 17
    5 $\frac{1}{6}, \frac{1}{7}$ **10** 35, 48

11. 15

12. **1** 3200, 5700, 10 500, 2800
    2 3000, 6000, 10 000, 3000

13. **1** 7   **2** 3   **3** 3

14. 9 miles

Page 17   Exercise 2.1

1. **1** 100   **4** £30
    2 16 p   **5** £3.96
    3 10 p

2. $3\frac{1}{2}$ p

3. £12

4. 4 p

5. 20

6. £54

7. £149

8. £1.60

9. £49.95

10. 40

11. £37.80

12. **1** 1 of 5 p, 4 of 2 p
    2 3 of 5 p, 2 of 2 p or 1 of 5 p, 7 of 2 p

13. 10 inches

14. 12 lb

15. 864

16. 171 yards

17. 120

18. 1995

19. 4.05, 14.00, 15.15, 18.05, 23.55, 1.10 a.m., 5.18 a.m., 10.30 a.m., 5.05 p.m., 9.50 p.m.

20. 4 hrs 43 min

21. 4.05 p.m.

22. 5 hrs 10 min, 01.20

23. 40 min

24. 5°C, 104°F

25. 91 p

26. 72 lb

27. £14.40

28. 18 days

29. 18 days

30. £300

Page 19   Exercise 2.2

1. £3.34

2. 1 lb 12 oz

3. 6 gallons

4. £3.52, £16.48

5. **1** 1 hour 35 min
   2 4 hours 55 min

6. **1** 74 p   **3** 84 p

7. £2.72, £2.22

8. 24

9. 1 hour 24 min

10. £735

11. **1** 4.16 p.m. (1616), 25 minutes
    2 1608 (4.08 p.m.), 36 minutes

12. £5.64, £67.68, £90, £118.50

13. £2.65

14. 20 min

15. **1** £3.65

    2 £29.75 each, total £59.50

    3 £74.20

Page 25   Exercise 3.1

2. **1** yes   **2** yes   **3** yes

3. **1** A M T U Y   **4** N S Z
   2 B C   **5** H I X
   3 H I X

Page 29   Exercise 3.2

1. **1** acute   **3** obtuse
   2 obtuse   **4** acute

4. **1** 25°   **2** 118°   **3** 73°

5. **1** $a = 136°, b = 78°, c = 50°, d = 96°$
   2 $e = 154°, f = 26°$
   3 $g = 112°, h = 68°, j = 112°, k = 68°$

6. **1** 160°   **2** 40°
   3 $c = 35°, d = 145°, e = 145°$

7. **1** 80°
   2 67°
   3 $c = 125°, d = 55°, e = 40°$

Page 31   Exercise 3.3

1. **1** E **2** H **3** S

7. **1** 3   **2** 6   **3** 7

8. **1** 4   **2** 1   **3** 2   **4** 3

9. **1** $a = 126°, b = 126°$
   2 $c = 30°, d = 30°$
   3 $e = 62°, f = 118°$

10. **1** $a = 40°, b = 140°$
    2 $a = 28°, b = 332°$
    3 $a = 137°, b = 223°$

11. **1** $a = 142°$
    2 $b = 47°, c = 133°, d = 133°$
    3 $e = 30°$

12. **1** $a = 30°$
    2 $b = 36°$
    3 $c = 28°, d = 62°, e = 62°$

13. **1** 72°   **2** 75°

Page 39   Exercise 4.1

1. **1** $\frac{2}{5}$ **4** $\frac{1}{4}$
   2 $\frac{1}{6}$ **5** $\frac{1}{3}$
   3 $\frac{2}{3}$

2.
  1 44, 9, 4, 7, 30, 12, 21, 26, 45, 48
  2 6, 33, 20, 8, 15, 9, 1, 7, 13, 25
  3 2, 7, 20, 25, 13, 11, 1, 6, 40, 9
  4 12, 4, 9, 2, 20, 3, 7, 15, 11, 40
  5 4, 10, 16, 6, 20, 40, 22, 60, 50, 12

3.
  1 $\frac{2}{3}$ **5** $\frac{3}{10}$ **8** $\frac{7}{12}$
  2 $\frac{5}{6}$ **6** $\frac{2}{5}$ **9** $\frac{4}{9}$
  3 $\frac{1}{6}$ **7** $\frac{5}{8}$ **10** $\frac{3}{4}$
  4 $\frac{3}{10}$

4.
  1 $\frac{14}{18}$ **3** $\frac{15}{18}$ **5** $\frac{6}{20}$
  2 $\frac{12}{20}$ **4** $\frac{21}{24}$

5.
  1 $\frac{7}{4}$ **5** $\frac{23}{8}$ **8** $\frac{15}{2}$
  2 $\frac{7}{3}$ **6** $\frac{22}{5}$ **9** $\frac{10}{3}$
  3 $\frac{37}{10}$ **7** $\frac{9}{8}$ **10** $\frac{23}{10}$
  4 $\frac{11}{6}$

6.
  1 $4\frac{3}{5}$ **5** $2\frac{3}{4}$ **8** $4\frac{1}{4}$
  2 $2\frac{5}{6}$ **6** $6\frac{2}{3}$ **9** $8\frac{1}{3}$
  3 $3\frac{1}{10}$ **7** $2\frac{3}{5}$ **10** $3\frac{1}{4}$
  4 $2\frac{5}{8}$

7.
  1 $\frac{5}{6}$ **5** $\frac{3}{4}$ **8** $5\frac{1}{3}$
  2 $\frac{19}{24}$ **6** $8\frac{1}{24}$ **9** $4\frac{5}{12}$
  3 $1\frac{3}{10}$ **7** $6\frac{1}{2}$ **10** $6\frac{1}{5}$
  4 $1\frac{11}{20}$

8.
  1 $\frac{3}{8}$ **5** $\frac{3}{10}$ **8** $1\frac{5}{8}$
  2 $\frac{1}{4}$ **6** $1\frac{5}{8}$ **9** $2\frac{1}{12}$
  3 $\frac{1}{9}$ **7** $\frac{11}{20}$ **10** $1\frac{2}{3}$
  4 $\frac{1}{2}$

9.
  1 $\frac{3}{4}$ **5** $1\frac{4}{5}$ **8** $10\frac{1}{2}$
  2 $4\frac{1}{6}$ **6** $10\frac{1}{2}$ **9** 20
  3 6 **7** $10\frac{2}{3}$ **10** $6\frac{2}{5}$
  4 $3\frac{3}{4}$

10.
  1 $\frac{1}{3}$ **5** $\frac{3}{5}$ **8** $\frac{1}{9}$
  2 $\frac{2}{9}$ **6** $\frac{2}{3}$ **9** $\frac{1}{5}$
  3 $\frac{1}{6}$ **7** $\frac{1}{4}$ **10** $\frac{1}{3}$
  4 $\frac{3}{4}$

11.
  1 £2.70   **6** 15°
  2 8 inches   **7** 6 pints
  3 60 p   **8** 4 inches
  4 1 hour   **9** 9 lb
  5 15 oz   **10** 2 feet 11 inches

12.
  1 $\frac{5}{6}$ **4** $\frac{5}{6}$
  2 $\frac{1}{3}$ **5** $\frac{3}{4}$
  3 $\frac{2}{3}$

13. $5\frac{1}{2}$ inches

14. $\frac{5}{12}$

15. $\frac{1}{3}$

16. $3\frac{3}{4}$ feet

17. 150

18. 126

19. $\frac{5}{12}$, Mr A, 400

20. 60, $\frac{1}{4}$

21. 27

22. $\frac{2}{5}$

23. 180 gallons

Page 43   Exercise 4.2

1. 32

2. **1** $\frac{1}{12}$, 30°   **2** 105°   **3** 105°

3. £300

4. $\frac{1}{20}$ s

5. £3

6. $\frac{1}{6}$

7. 360

8. £60.50

9. £146.20, 48 hours

10. £63

Page 46   Example 2

$\frac{4}{9}$, $\frac{37}{90}$

Page 49   Example 5

  1 week 9   **2** weeks 1 and 2

Page 50   Exercise 5.1

2. $\frac{3}{10}$

5. 13 p

7. 1 Sun, 1st week, 1000
    2 Fri, 2nd week, 5400
    3 Tues.

9. 1 Mon, 1st week
    2 3
    3 Thurs, 1st week
    4 6

10. 1 1489   2 Sunday   3 13

11. £10

12. $\frac{1}{4}$

13. A 14, B 4, C 22, D 10

14. a 14, e 11, i 7, o 8, u 5

Page 57   Exercise A1

1. 41
2. 6
3. £1.50
4. 8600
5. 67 (1987),
    68 (1988),
    etc
6. 400
7. $\frac{1}{6}$
8. £5
9. 14.15
    (or 1415)
10. 8
11. 40 p
12. 3406
13. 13, 17, 19
14. 10
15. $\frac{3}{4}$

16. £1.06
17. 16.12 (or 4.12 p.m.), 15 min
18. 11.5 cm to 14.5 cm (13.1 cm)
19. 4 million
20. £62.22
21. 3400
22. 50° to 65° (58°)

Page 58   Exercise A2

1.	B	6.	D	11.	B	16.	E
2.	E	7.	C	12.	D	17.	D
3.	C	8.	C	13.	A	18.	D
4.	C	9.	B	14.	E	19.	A
5.	A	10.	D	15.	A	20.	D

Page 61   Exercise A3

1. 1506 miles

2. £72

5. 1 $2^2 \times 3^2$ 2 150   3 41, 43, 47

6. 5; 50 p, 20 p, 10 p, 2 p, 1 p;
    3; 10 p, 5 p, 2 p

7. 1 45°, clockwise
    2 90°, anticlockwise
    3 180°, either
    4 140°, clockwise
    5 60°, anticlockwise

8. 1 £25   2 $\frac{1}{20}$

9. 1 Jan, 10.7 cm,
    2 Feb, 2.7 cm,
    3 Apl

10. 20, £760.60

11. 1 $c = 94°$, $d = 35°$, $e = 145°$

    2 $a = 45°$, $d = 45°$, $e = 135°$

12. 1 1 hour 25 min   2 10 min
    3 4 hours 35 min

Page 64   Exercise A4

1. 2

2. $a = 40°$, $b = 48°$, $c = 26°$, $d = 18°$,
    $e = 66°$

3. 1 Thurs   2 £76.20

4. 1 21 lb 3 oz   2 7 lb 11 oz

6. $\frac{1}{6}$, £240 000

8. 1 U, M   2 B, E   3 N, S

9. Your age

10. 1 £130   2 50

11. 1 Hotel Marti, £444
    2 £273, £819
    3 £596.40

12. R 16, S 10, T 23, U 11

Page 90   Exercise 6.1

1. 1 7.61   4 10.02
    2 7   5 7.86
    3 0.63

2. 1 20.96   4 9.09
    2 6.95   5 4.88
    3 0.37

3. **1** 15.48   **4** 9.42
    2 0.6   **5** 9.6
    3 5.6

4. **1** 0.97   **4** 2.2
    2 0.007   **5** 5.9
    3 0.16

5. **1** 0.75   **4** 0.37
    2 0.4   **5** 0.6
    3 0.7

6. **1** 13.2   **4** 2.7
    2 250   **5** 62
    3 1030

7. **1** 0.379   **4** 0.0031
    2 0.0015   **5** 0.17
    3 0.0213

8. **1** 0.072   **4** 0.63
    2 0.003   **5** 0.02
    3 0.012

9. **1** 8.792   **4** 0.24
    2 0.0798   **5** 0.001 271
    3 198.38

10. **1** 39   **4** 300
    2 83   **5** 0.8
    3 31

11. **1** 2.86   **4** 0.97
    2 51.67   **5** 1.14
    3 0.09

12. **1** 0.67   **4** 0.17
    2 0.71   **5** 0.73
    3 0.44

13. **1** 29.71   **4** 4.68
    2 1.63   **5** 0.04
    3 202.92

14. 0.7, 0.75, 0.778, 0.8, 0.81

15. 60.9, 62.49, 62.5, 63.7, 63.72

16. **1** 20   **4** 10
    2 3   **5** 40
    3 16

17. **1** 20   **4** 10
    2 3   **5** 41
    3 15

18. **1** 107   **4** 36
    2 28   **5** 47
    3 13

19. £10.20, £9.80

20. 20 p

21. 55, 10 p

22. £15.79

23. £55.80

Page 92   Exercise 6.2

1. 2150   5. 0.625
2. 1.44   6. 0.054
3. 0.006   7. 10.688
4. 3.5   8. 1
9. 0.299, 0.3, 0.35
10. **1** 22.149   **2** 0.0514   **3** 81.6
11. 1
12. **1** 9877   **2** 9876.52
13. $\frac{5}{8}, \frac{7}{10}, \frac{3}{4}, \frac{7}{9}, \frac{5}{6}$
14. **1** £150   **2** £149.97
15. £4227, £773
16. £38.46
17. 60

Page 97   Exercise 7.1

1. **1** $\frac{1}{6}$ **2** $\frac{1}{3}$

2. **1** $\frac{1}{4}$ **2** $\frac{11}{20}$ **3** $\frac{3}{10}$

3. **1** $\frac{1}{2}$ **2** $\frac{1}{6}$

4. $\frac{1}{8}$

5. **1** $\frac{1}{13}$ **2** $\frac{1}{4}$ **3** $\frac{5}{26}$

6. **1** $\frac{2}{11}$ **2** $\frac{4}{11}$ **3** $\frac{3}{11}$

7. **1** $\frac{11}{25}$ **2** $\frac{3}{5}$ **3** $\frac{6}{25}$ **4** $\frac{3}{7}$

8. **1** $\frac{6}{25}$ **2** $\frac{1}{25}$ **3** 0

9. **1** $\frac{4}{7}$ **2** $\frac{2}{7}$

10. $\frac{4}{15}$

11. **1** 40   **2** 60   **3** $\frac{1}{6}$

12. 0.3

13. $\frac{1}{6}$

14. $\frac{7}{8}$

15. $\frac{1}{10}$

16. $\frac{1}{3}$

17. $\frac{7}{8}$

18. **2** 7
19. **1** Graham   **2** 0.24

Page 100   Exercise 7.2

1. $\frac{1}{12}$

2. **1** $1\frac{5}{8}$ **2** $\frac{4}{7}$

3. $\frac{1}{5}, \frac{1}{4}$

4. **1** $\frac{1}{16}$ **2** $\frac{3}{16}$ **3** $\frac{3}{16}$

5. **1** $\frac{6}{11}$ **2** $\frac{3}{11}$ **3** $\frac{3}{11}$ **4** $\frac{2}{5}$

6. **1** $\frac{1}{25}$ **2** $\frac{1}{5}$

7. **1** $\frac{1}{12}$ **2** $\frac{1}{10}$

8. **1** $\frac{4}{9}$ **2** $\frac{2}{9}$

9. **1** $\frac{1}{12}$ **2** $\frac{1}{6}$ **3** $\frac{1}{6}$ **4** $\frac{1}{9}$

10. **1** $\frac{1}{15}$ **2** $\frac{1}{5}$ **3** $\frac{1}{5}$

11. **1** $\frac{1}{4}$ **2** $\frac{4}{17}$

12. **1** $\frac{1}{16}$ **2** $\frac{5}{16}$ **3** $\frac{3}{8}$

Page 106   Exercise 8.1

1. **1** 50   **11** 10 000
   2 3000   **12** 135
   3 1000   **13** 150
   4 50   **14** 2000
   5 365   **15** 3000
   6 4000   **16** 52
   7 48   **17** 1000
   8 6000   **18** 30
   9 8000   **19** 1 000 000
   10 21   **20** 1000

2. **1** 920
   2 4
   3 £15
   4 2.5 kg
   5 50

3. 50

4. 7

5. 54 kg

6. 48 km/hour

7. £9

8. 6 g, 0.14 mm

9. **1** 10.64 kg   **3** 1.250 kg
   2 101.4° F   **4** 4 ml

10. **1** 1356   **2** 6239   **3** 7804

11. 1185 units, £63.99, £70.49

12. **1** Dover and Exeter
    2 124 km
    3 77 miles

Page 109   Exercise 8.2

1. **1** 2.38 kg   **6** 3100 g
   2 0.2 m   **7** 2.8 cm
   3 5000 ml   **8** 5.12 m
   4 120 mm   **9** 32 litres
   5 260 cm   **10** 250 g

2. 17, 24 cm

3. 5

4. 250 g size

5. 37 p

6. 12 oz

7. **1** £2.55   **2** 20 p   **3** £1.55

8. **1** C   **6** D
   2 D   **7** B (11 days $13\frac{3}{4}$ hours)
   3 C   **8** A (nearly 2740 years ago)
   4 A   **9** C
   5 D   **10** E

9. 4 kg

10. 40 100 km

11. **1** 46°F, 8°C   **2** 95°F   **3** 20°C

12. **1** 7.0 cm   **2** $1\frac{1}{2}$ inches

13. **1** 8429   **2** 79

14. **1** 4.50 p.m.   **2** 16.50

15. 250 units, 258 therms, £95.46, £104.96

Page 115   Exercise 9.1

2. $AB = 5.0$ cm, $CD = 9.8$ cm,
   $EF = 4.1$ cm, $GH = 12.1$ cm

3. $BC = 6.0$ cm, $DC = 10.0$ cm,
   $\angle C = 57°$

Page 118   Exercise 9.2

1. **1** $\angle A = 81°$, $\angle B$ 54°, $\angle C = 45°$
   2 $\angle A = 116°$, $\angle B = 37°$, $\angle C = 27°$

2. **1** $AB = 2.8$ cm, $BC = 3.9$ cm,
   $CA = 3.3$ cm, perimeter $= 10.0$ cm
   2 $AB = 2.6$ cm, $BC = 5.1$ cm,
   $CA = 3.4$ cm, perimeter $= 11.1$ cm

3. **1** $\angle A = 28°$, $\angle B = 76°$, $\angle C = 76°$
   2 $\angle A = 18°$, $\angle B = 144°$, $\angle C = 18°$

4. **1** $AB = 4.6$ cm, $BC = 2.2$ cm,
   $CA = 4.6$ cm, perimeter $= 11.4$ cm
   2 $AB = 4.4$ cm, $BC = 4.4$ cm,
   $CA = 8.4$ cm, perimeter $= 17.2$ cm

5. **1** $72°$ **4** $30°$
   2 $48°$ **5** $26°$
   3 $24°$

6. **1** $14°$, obtuse-angled
   2 $72°$, acute-angled isosceles
   3 $90°$, right-angled
   4 $60°$, equilateral
   5 $120°$, obtuse-angled

9. B

10. **1** $a = 141°$ **3** $c = 28°$
    2 $b = 50°$ **4** $d = 36°$

11. $\angle ACB = 48°$, $\angle DCB = 70°$

12. **1** $a = 30°$, $b = 75°$, isosceles
    2 $58°$

13. $a = 60°$, $b = 60°$, $c = 30°$

14. $a = 45°$, $b = 45°$

15. $b = 60°$, $c = 60°$, equilateral,
    perimeter 20.4 cm

Page 121   Exercise 9.3

5. $BC = 7.6$ cm, $\angle B = 34°$,
   $\angle C = 88°$, perimeter 21.6 cm

6. $\angle A = 58°$, $\angle B = 47°$, $\angle C = 75°$

7. $AC = 7.5$ cm, $\angle B = 43°$,
   $\angle C = 47°$, perimeter 26.5 cm

8. $CD = 6.6$ cm

9. $DE = 3.5$ cm

Page 123   Exercise 9.4

1. **1** DE **2** $\angle EDC$

2. **1** $\angle ADC$ **2** DX

3. **1** $30°$ **2** $38°$ **3** $60°$ **4** $35°$

4. $\angle ACD = 32°$, $\angle CDB = 64°$,
   $\angle DBC = 64°$, $\angle BCD = 52°$

6. $\angle B = \angle ACB$, $\angle ACD = 32°$,
   $\angle CDB = 90°$, $\angle DBC = 61°$,
   $\angle BCD = 29°$

7. $\angle A = 34°$, $d = 52°$

8. $93°$, 3.8 cm

9. **1** $71°$ **2** $35\frac{1}{2}°$ **3** $109°$

10. $\angle CED = 56°$, $\angle CDE = 64°$

11. $AC = 7.1$ cm, perimeter $= 24.1$ cm

Page 128   Exercise 10.1

1. **1** $5a$ pence
   2 $120b$ **7** $\dfrac{m}{3}$ pence
   3 $c - d$ **8** $180n$
   4 $(3e + 2f)$ pence
   5 $(50 - gh)$ pence   **9** $\dfrac{x}{q}$ pence
   6 $12k$ pence   **10** st

2. **1** c **6** m
   2 0 **7** a^2
   3 $8e$ **8** b^3
   4 $3g - 4h$ **9** 1
   5 $6j + 4k$ **10** $4d$

3. **1** $2a + 6b$ **3** $20e - 30f$
   2 $15c - 5d$

4. **1** 18 **6** 36
   2 10 **7** 12
   3 12 **8** 4
   4 12 **9** 16
   5 2 **10** 2

5. **1** 32 **6** 18
   2 25 **7** 27
   3 5 **8** 0
   4 24 **9** $2\frac{1}{2}$
   5 2 **10** 4

6. **1** 23 **4** 0
   2 34 **5** 5
   3 50

7. **1** 210 **4** 150
   2 $2\frac{1}{2}$ **5** 14
   3 880

8. 1 900   4 10
    2 6   5 300
    3 10

9. 1 £100   2 £180

Page 131   Exercise 10.2

1. 1 $+1°$ 6 $-5°$
    2 $-7°$ 7 $-7°$
    3 $+9°$ 8 $-3°$
    4 $0°$ 9 $-1°$
    5 $-2°$ 10 $+6°$

2. 1 risen 3°   6 fallen 27°
    2 fallen 9°   7 risen 10°
    3 risen 6°   8 risen 3°
    4 risen 2°   9 fallen 4°
    5 fallen 6°   10 fallen 3°

3. 1 7 minutes past 1
    2 12 minutes to 2
    3 6 minutes to 3

4. 1 17   2 20   3 15

5. 1 £150   3 £70
    2 £260   4 £30

6. 1 $+6$ 6 -3
    2 $+3$ 7 $+2$
    3 -2 8 -3
    4 -4 9 $+2$
    5 $+3$ 10 0

7. 1 -2 6 -20
    2 -8 7 -5
    3 2 8 -8
    4 2 9 -1
    5 0 10 -2

Page 133   Exercise 10.3

1. 1 x is greater than 7
    2 x is less than 8
    3 x is not equal to 1
    4 x is greater than 1 and less than 4
    5 x is greater than -5

2. 1 $x < 6$ 4 $-3 < x < 10$
    2 $x > -2$ 5 $x < 5$
    3 $x \neq 0$

4. 1 $a < c < b$ 4 $a < b < c$
    2 $c < b < a$ 5 $b < c < a$
    3 $c < a < b$

5. 1 4, 5, 6   4 $-7, -6, -5$
    2 5   5 1, 2, 3, 4
    3 $-1, 0, 1$

Page 134   Exercise 10.4

1. 1 $2a, 0, a^2, 1$
    2 $7a, a$
    3 $16x$

2. 1 8   2 29   3 4

3. 1 $(20y - 20x)$ pence
    2 £$8x$
    3 $1000x$
    4 $x - 5$

4. 1 14   6 770
    2 300   7 360
    3 50   8 30
    4 56   9 10
    5 84   10 5

5. 30

6. 1 1   2 13   3 4

7. 20, 3, 0

8. 3

9. 78

10. £85, £110, £135, £$(60 + 25n)$, £360

11. 40 min, 60 min, 80 min, $(20 + 20c)$ min

12. 1 0   4 -1
    2 4   5 3
    3 -12

13. 1 9   2 36

14. 1 $-7°$ 4 $-8°$
    2 $13°$ 5 $-5°$
    3 $15°$

Page 137   Exercise B1

1. 5   10. 90 p
2. 20   11. $7\frac{1}{2}$ km
3. £20   12. 15 p
4. 10   13. 24 litres
5. £180   14. 7.11 p.m.
6. 800 (or near)   15. $\frac{1}{3}$
7. 21 min   16. 20 miles
8. 90 cm   17. 7
9. 31

18. £162
19. 2 hours 10 min
20. 6 to 7 cm (6.4 cm)
21. 16°C
22. 12° to 25° (18°)

Page 138   Exercise B2

1.	B	8.	E	15.	D
2.	C	9.	D	16.	B
3.	C	10.	B	17.	D
4.	B	11.	B	18.	E
5.	A	12.	C	19.	B
6.	C	13.	C	20.	A
7.	E	14.	B		

Page 140   Exercise B3

1. **1** 47   **4** 21, 24
    2 15, 51   **5** 27, 15
    3 47, 57

2. **1** 690   **2** 530   **3** 270

3. $\frac{1}{2}$

4. £4.77, £5.23

5. **1** 100   **6** 100
    2 1000   **7** 1000
    3 60   **8** 60
    4 1000   **9** 100
    5 1000   **10** 1 000 000

6. **1** pf **3** $12 - x$, $x(12 - x)$
    2 $\frac{y}{x}$pence   **4** $(x - 2)$ years
                               5 £$(12x + 52y)$

7. **1** 4.73   **6** 0.09
    2 490   **7** 0.8
    3 0.0063   **8** 0.18
    4 0.024   **9** 0.506
    5 0.09   **10** 2.3

8. -4°C, 6°C

9. **1** $a = 89°$
    2 $b = 73°$, $c = 36°$
    3 $d = 123°$, $e = 57°$

10. **1** 12   **4** 9
    2 59   **5** 5
    3 0

11. 2.7 cm

12. **1** 3600   **3** C
    2 B and D **4** 14 000

Page 142   Exercise B4

1. $\frac{3}{4}$

3. $\frac{1}{6}$

4. **1** 563   **4** 10
    2 323   **5** 7
    3 3728

5. $a = 60°$, $b = 40°$, $d = 80°$

6. **1** £9   **2** 8

7. 6.9 cm

8. 36, 35.6

9. 600, £33.10

10. **1** 116   **4** 720
    2 240   **5** 9
    3 10

12. **1** (6)
    2 (4)
    3 (7)
    4 reflection in BH
    5 rotation through 180° about E
    6 reflection in GC

Page 158   Exercise 11.1

2. **1** $\angle A = 106°$, $\angle B = 106°$,
        $\angle C = 74°$, $\angle D = 74°$
    2 $\angle E = 93°$, $\angle F = 54°$,
        $\angle G = 93°$, $\angle H = 120°$
    3 $\angle J = 66°$, $\angle K = 114°$,
        $\angle L = 66°$, $\angle M = 114°$

3. **1** $AB = 3.6$ cm, $BC = 2.9$ cm,
        $CD = 5.2$ cm, $DA = 2.9$ cm,
        perimeter $= 14.6$ cm
    2 $EF = 4.5$ cm, $FG = 4.5$ cm,
        $GH = 2.4$ cm, $HE = 2.4$ cm,
        perimeter $= 13.8$ cm
    3 $JK = 4.8$ cm, $KL = 3.5$ cm,
        $LM = 4.8$ cm, $MJ = 3.5$ cm,
        perimeter $= 16.6$ cm

4. 112°

5. 85°

6. **1** $a = 60°$, $b = 30°$
    2 rectangle 22 cm, $\triangle ABX$ 15 cm

7. $a = 115°$, $b = 65°$, $c = 115°$

8. 110°

9. 1 right-angled
   2 right-angled isosceles
   3 isosceles

10. $AD = 5.4$ cm, trapezium

11. 1 parallelogram, rectangle
    2 kite
    3 rhombus, square

12. 1 $AC = 8.1$ cm, $BD = 13.0$ cm, no
    2 $AX = CX = 4.1$ cm,
      $BX = DX = 6.5$ cm, yes
    3 115°, no

13. 1 $AC = BD = 10.8$ cm, yes
    2 $AX = CX = BX = DX = 5.4$ cm,
      yes
    3 113°, no

14. 1 $AC = 6.2$ cm, $BD = 10.3$ cm, no
    2 $AX = CX = 3.1$ cm,
      $BX = DX = 5.1$ cm, yes
    3 90°, yes

15. 1 $AC = BD = 8.5$ cm, yes
    2 $AX = CX = BX = DX = 4.2$ cm,
      yes
    3 90°, yes
    4 45°

Page 162   Exercise 11.2

1. 1 2   2 4

2. 1 $a = 57°$, $b = 108°$, $c = 133°$
   2 $d = 95°$, $e = 85°$, $f = 105°$

3. 1 84°   2 48°   3 isosceles

4. 1 85°   2 76°

5. 1 both equal to DC
   2 isosceles
   3 $g = 90°$, $h = 60°$, $j = 15°$, $k = 45°$

7. 1 X
   2 $\angle BCD$
   3 $AX = XC$, $BX = DX$

8. 1 kite   2 rhombus   3 square

9. 9.6 cm

10. 6.9 cm, 51°, BD is axis of symmetry

11. 141°, 4.3 cm, perimeter 19.3 cm
12. $AC = BD = 7.1$ cm, angles all 90°

Page 169   Exercise 12.1

1. 1 9   4 40.7
   2 44   5 1.9
   3 8

2. 1 8   4 35
   2 39   5 1.95
   3 7

3. 1 9   2 28   3 4.5

4. 1 12   2 27   3 5

5. 1 64.4   4 2.5 cm
   2 £917.40   5 2.9 kg
   3 2 hrs 1 min

6. 1 mean 57 kg, median 55 kg
   2 12 yrs 2 mths
   3 164 g
   4 22°C
   5 10 min 25 sec

7. 1 13   4 76
   2 73   5 0.7
   3 12

8. 1 57.4   4 2.5 cm
   2 £122   5 2.1 kg
   3 1 hr 57 min

9. 352 runs, 32 runs

10. 94 years 5 months, 8 years 7 months

11. 43 kg, 38.4 kg, 4.6 kg

12. £264, 8.8 p

13. 1240, 62

14. £1320, £8.25

Page 171   Exercise 12.2

1. 1 mean 4.9, median 5, mode 5
   2 mean 5.6, median 6, mode 6
   3 A, 6; B, 4
   4 B
   5 A

2. 2.8, 3.0, North-west

3. 28 hours, 4 hours

4. £1.70, 17 p

5.   £1320, £110

6.   180 years, 9 years

7.   15, 14.5

8.   **1** 30   **2** 1.5

9.   11.6, the mean

10. 3, the mean

Page 176   Exercise 13.1

1.   **1** 31.4 cm   **4** 126 cm
     2 56.5 cm   **5** 47.1 cm
     3 34.5 cm

2.   **1** 44 cm   **2** 220 cm   **3** 132 cm

3.   **1** 50 m   **4** 81 m
     2 12 m   **5** 56 m
     3 22 m

5.   **1** OT **2** $\angle TOQ$

6.   **2** $\angle DOC$ **3** yes

7.   **2** isosceles
     3 $e = 20°, f = 140°$

8. $AC = 9.9$ cm, square

10. 6 cm, 9 cm, 16 cm, 22 cm, 25 cm

Page 178   Exercise 13.2

1.   **1** 88 cm   **3** 6.28 cm
     2 37.7 cm

2.   **1** 6 cm   **2** 18.8 cm

3.   **1** 113 m   **2** 20 m   **3** 126 m

4.   1100 m

5.   47 m

6.   411 cm

7.   1600 m

8.   377 inches, 15 inches

9.   **1** OT **3** $\angle QXT$
     2 QX **4** 90°

10. both isosceles, $\angle BCO = 20°$,
     $\angle ACO = 25°, \angle ACB = 45°$

Page 183   Exercise 14.1

1.   **1** 121 cm²   **2** 48 cm²   **3** 77 cm²

2.   **1** 28 m², 22 m   **3** 87 cm², 48 cm
     2 81 cm²   **4** 40 m²

3.   84 cm², 48 cm

4.   **1** 19 cm, 9.5 cm²
     2 19 cm, 10.5 cm²

5.   14 cm²

6.   **1** 27 m²   **2** £108

7.   1000

8.   **1** 8.75 cm²   **3** 9.5 cm²
     2 7.5 cm²

9.   **1** 12 cm   **2** 14 cm   **3** 21 cm

10. 72 cm²

11. 144 cm², $\triangle ABE$ 30 cm², $\triangle ADF$ 36 cm²,
     $\triangle FCE$ 21 cm², $\triangle AEF$ 57 cm²

12. **1** b
     2 c, a 5.5 cm², b 5.76 cm², c 5.04 cm²

13. **1** 6 cm²   **3** 5 cm²   **5** 4 cm²
     2 6 cm²   **4** 6.5 cm²

14. 10 cm²

Page 186   Exercise 14.2

1.   160, 7

2.   12 m, 48 m

3.   **1** 6 cm   **2** 21 cm²   **3** 42 cm²

4.   222 square feet

5.   30 m, £360

6.   6000 cm²

7.   24 cm²

8. $\triangle APS$ 3 cm², $\triangle BPQ$ 12 cm²,
     $\triangle CRQ$ 8 cm² $\triangle DRS$ 10 cm²,
     $PQRS$ 31 cm²

9.   14.5 cm²

10. 20 cm²

Page 194   Exercise 15.1

1.   **1** $\frac{3}{10}$ **4** $\frac{2}{5}$
     2 $\frac{7}{20}$ **5** $\frac{3}{5}$
     3 $\frac{3}{20}$

2. 1 0.47   4 0.06
    2 0.95   5 0.99
    3 0.22

3. 1 75%   4 70%
    2 80%   5 87%
    3 15%

4. 1 £3.60   4 £2.40
    2 60 p   5 13 p
    3 63 p

5. 1 96   4 5 cm
    2 120 g   5 31 litres
    3 2 min

6. 1 £6.24   4 £60
    2 £2.99   5 £336
    3 £108

7. 1 £3   4 £528
    2 £3   5 £2
    3 £896

8. 1 £1680   4 £9720
    2 £3.24   5 £16.50
    3 330 ml

9. 1 £60   2 £264   3 £168

10. £18, £18.90

11. £90, £98.10, £188.10

12. 1 A   2 C

13. £27.60

14. £27.60, £211.60

15. £2200

16. £2040, £170

17. £1900, £1805

Page 196   Exercise 15.2

1. 50%, 25%, 20%, 10%, 5%, 1%

2. $\frac{3}{10}, \frac{1}{3}, \frac{2}{5}, \frac{2}{3}, \frac{3}{4}$

3. 1 40%   2 C   3 16 000

4. 1 £84   2 200

5. 10% Spanish; 75 French, 60 German, 15 Spanish; 7 classes

6. £8

7. £117, £78

8. £16

9. £400, £7600

10. 1 1120   3 £448
     2 £4480   4 £4032

11. £1560, £30

12. 1 125.44 cm^2 2 yes

13. £29 700

14. 1 22.4% variable
     2 10 years
     3 £7779.20
     4 £5.44, £5304

15. 121 units, £6.05, £23.40, £3.51, £26.91

Page 199   Exercise C1

1. 180 miles   6. $\frac{1}{5}$ 11. 1997
2. £3.40   7. 12.15   12. 7 kg
3. 8   8. 3 kg   13. 11 p
4. 5   9. 0.1   14. £600
5. 24 cm   10. 24   15. 7 kg
16. £13.25
17. 3 hr 15 min
18. August
19. £25
20. £1.70
21. 4 cm to 5 cm (4.6 cm)
22. 106° to 120° (113°)

Page 200   Exercise C2

1. E   6. A   11. B   16. C
2. B   7. E   12. D   17. D
3. E   8. A   13. C   18. C
4. D   9. D   14. B   19. D
5. C   10. E   15. A   20. B

Page 203   Exercise C3

1. 1 64 000   4 10 000
    2 26 000   5 51 000
    3 5000

3. 63 p

4. 80

5. 8 amps

6. 1 532   4 500
    2 0.035   5 9
    3 0.04

7. 76°, 6.1 cm, 31 cm^2

8. £2646, £270

9. 69°

10. **1** 6   **2** $7\frac{1}{2}$ **3** 8.5   **4** 12

11. Square, by 0.52 cm

12. 48°

Page 205   Exercise C4

1. **1** 4(feet)   **2** 12 feet

2. £46.00

3. £40

4. 68°

5. $\frac{4}{5}$

6. 110 cm, 110 m

7. 62 kg, 256 kg, 70 kg

8. $AB = 5.8$ cm, $\angle ABC = 118°$, rhombus

10. 64°

11. £1080

12. **1** 0.29   **2** $\frac{1}{200}$

Page 219   Exercise 16.1

1. **1** 8 cm³   **2** 42 cm³

2. **1** 600 cm³   **4** 45 cm³
    2 125 cm³   **5** 27 000 cm³
    3 50 m³

3. **1** 222 cm²   **2** 54 cm²

4. 35 m²

5. 450 m³

6. 4 m³

7. 15 m³

8. **1** 240 cm³   **2** 30

9. 25 edges

10. (b), (c), (e)

11. 7, 12, 7

12. *E, G*

13. **2** 3

14. rectangle

15. 12

Page 222   Exercise 16.2

1. 2250 kg

2. **1** 100 000 m²   **2** 30 000 m³

3. 3 hours

4. 27 600 kg

5. 9 cm by 9 cm by 4 cm, 324 cm³

6. **1** 5 m   **2** 54 cm²

7. 17 m³

8. 12, 6

9. 14, 36, 24

10. 4

Page 225   Exercise 17.1

1. **1** 4 : 5   **4** 5 : 24
    2 5 : 12   **5** 3 : 1
    3 5 : 8

2. **1** 90 p, £1.35   **4** £1.50, 25 p
    2 56 p, 98 p   **5** £2.80, £1.20
    3 42 p, 18 p

3. **1** £450   **4** £7.50
    2 £67.50   **5** £27.50
    3 £160

4. 4 : 5

5. 40°, 60°, 100°, 160°

6. 2.7 cm

7. £1280, £160, £2080

8. £1600, £2800, £3600

9. 4.5 *l*

10. 2.5 kg, 1 kg

11. 42

12. 3 : 80

13. 1 m³, 2 m³

14. **1** 2 : 3   **2** 9 : 10

15. 3 : 4

Page 227   Exercise 17.2

1. 90 kg
2. £4.80
3. 15 days
4. £360
5. 16 days

Page 228   Exercise 17.3

1. £40.50
2. 7 lb
3. £30
4. 3 pints
5. $2\frac{1}{2}$ gall
6. £6.50
7. 12.5 km/litre
8. x 88 p, y 84 p, Brand y
9. 12 min
10. £6.65
11. £294.40
12. £613.80

Page 230   Exercise 17.4

1. $9.20
2. 75 cents, $1.00, $1.25
3. $24.75
4. 5.40 francs
5. 33.70 francs, 16.30 francs
6. 0.78 francs
7. 18 900 drachmae
8. 346.50 francs
9. 16.92 dollars
10. 663 000 yen
11. 129 600 dinars
12. £2293.58
13. £34.13
14. £1423.49

15. £4.78
16. £19.34
17. £4
18. Alan, £1
19. £8, 95.20 francs

Page 231   Exercise 17.5

1. £240, £300, £360
2. **1** 21 : 31   **2** 9 : 14   **3** 2 : 3
3. 8 : 27
4. petrol £1125, diesel £1575, £103.50
5. £175
6. £55.25
7. £31.20
8. 5 gallons
9. £456
10. 18 m²/litre
11. £950
12. 12 hours
13. **1** 250 g   **2** 5
14. normal 17.5 p, large 12 p, family size 11 p; family size
15. 427 francs, £7.00
16. 305 schillings, £74

Page 233   Example 1

rectangle

Page 234   Example 2

parallelogram

Page 234   Exercise 18.1

1. (5, 5)
2. **1** parallelogram
   2 (7, 2)
   3 $y = x + 2$
   4 (3, 3), (4, 2), (5, 1), (6, 0), meet at (2, 4)

3. T (6, 4), U (3, 5)

4. $6\,\text{cm}^2$

5. $(-2, 0)$, parallelogram

6.   square, $10\,\text{cm}^2$

7. $25\,\text{cm}^2$

Page 237   Example 18.2

1.   **1**   £52   **2**   32 dollars

2.   29.6 litres, 2.2 gallons

3.   **1**   47 km/hour   **2**   28 m/s

4.   **1**   31 cm   **2**   6.4 cm

5.   27°C

6.   length 135 m, width 45 m

Page 239   Exercise 18.3

1.   **1**   parallelogram, E $(4, 4\frac{1}{2})$
     2 J $(-5, 7)$, 4 axes
     3   rhombus

2. A and E, B and F, C and D

3.   **1** $24\,\text{cm}^2$
     2 $\triangle OAD$ $6\,\text{cm}^2$, $\triangle OCE$ $4\,\text{cm}^2$
     3 $14\,\text{cm}^2$

4.   21°C, 176°F, 37°C

6.   17 m

7.   **1**   Mr B **2**   Mr A **3**   Mr C

8.   **1**   1700 (1740) dinars
     2   £7.80 (£7.76)

Page 244   Exercise 19.1

2.   4

3.   **1**   2:5   **2**   2:5   **3**   yes

4.   **1**   5:6   **2**   5:7   **3**   no

5.   **1**   2:3   **2**   2:3   **3**   yes

6.   **1**   2:5   **2**   7.5 cm

7.   **1**   3:1   **3**   12 cm
     2   3 cm   **4** $\angle E$

8.   **1**   3:4   **2**   3:4   **3**   6 cm

9.   6 cm

Page 246   Exercise 19.2

1.   10 cm, 7.5 cm

2.   97 m

3.   102 m

4.   75 m

5.   64 m

6.   **1**   5 m by 4 m
     2   3.5 m by 3 m
     3   3 m by 3 m
     4 $20\,\text{m}^2$, £360

7.   20 m (or near)

Page 248   Exercise 19.3

2.   2

4.   **1**   1.5 cm   **2**   66°

5.   25 cm

6.   **1**   length 30 cm, width 24 cm
     2 $3200\,\text{cm}^3$, $10\,800\,\text{cm}^3$, 8:27

7.   80 m

8.   8 m, 12.5 m by 16 m, $1600\,\text{m}^3$

10. $DC = 100$ m, perimeter 340 m,
     $AC = 113$ m, $BD = 128$ m, 37 m further

11. 78 m

12. $90\,\text{m}^2$

Page 252   Exercise 20.1

1. $1\frac{1}{2}$ hours

2.   198 miles

3.   42 miles per hour

4.   21 miles per hour

5.   **1**   146 km   **2**   2 hours   **3**   73 km/hr

6.   **1**   135 km   **2**   10 hrs   **3**   13.5 km/hr

7.   95 km/hr

8.   **1** $2\frac{1}{2}$ hrs, 3 hrs   **2**   5:6   **3**   6:5

Page 253   Example 2

     Walk 6 km/hour
     cycle $1\frac{1}{4}$ hours, 27 km
     rests 30 km
     bus 2.15 p.m., $\frac{1}{2}$ hour, 60 km/hour

Page 253   Exercise 20.2

1. **1** $\frac{1}{2}$ hour   **4** 10 km
    2 15 km/hour   **5** 16 km
    3 1.40 p.m., 9 km   **6** 16 km/hr

2. **1** (1) and (4)   **3** 50 km/hr
    2 (2), 33 km/hr   **4** 30

3. 3.00 p.m., 120 km

4. **1** 27 km   **2** 17 min

5. 2.75 s

Page 255   Example 3

18 m/s, 26 m/s

Page 256   Exercise 20.3

1. **1** 20 km
    2 25 km/hour, 17.75 min after leaving *A*

2. **1** 22 m/s
    2 20 s, 105 s from the start

Page 258   Exercise 20.4

1. **2** 10   **6** 98 or 99

2. **1** 12   **2** Sunday   **3** £54

3. **1** 29   **4** 29
    2 28   **5** 28
    3 29

4. **1** June   **2** Sept   **3** Feb

Page 258   Exercise 20.5

1. $1\frac{1}{2}$ miles

2. $\frac{1}{2}$ hour

3. yes, average speed 45 miles per hour

4. 42 km/hour

5. **1** 3 p.m.   **2** 11.8 km, 2.01 p.m.

6. **1** 48 miles per hour
    2 35 miles per hour
    3 38 miles per gallon

7. 31.25 m, 0.45 s, 4.55 s

8. 4.0 m/s

9. May 1st

10. **1** Tues   **3** Mon
    2 Thurs   **4** Sept 5th

Page 261   Exercise D1

1. 9   6. 2 035 000   11. 36 cm
2. £8   7. 16 cm^2 12. 2
3. 35   8. 16 days   13. £3
4. 13   9. 6   14. 15
5. 4   10. 1 kg   15. £12
16. Penzance, 452
17. £3 to £3.20
18. 32 or 33
19. 22
20. 90 p
21. 10.5 cm to 12 cm (11 cm)
22. 37° to 52° (45°)

Page 262   Exercise D2

1. E   6. D   11. D   16. C
2. D   7. C   12. A   17. A
3. A   8. D   13. E   18. E
4. C   9. B   14. C   19. D
5. A   10. B   15. C   20. E

Page 265   Exercise D3

1. 25 cm

2. **1** 1   **6** 4
    2 3   **7** 2
    3 0   **8** 3
    4 infinite number   **9** 2
    5 1   **10** 7

3. **1** 33.0 lb   **2** 6.8 kg

4. **1** triangular prism
    2 cuboid
    3 pyramid on square base

5. £2200, £220, £2420, £242, £2662, £662

6. 65 km

7. 2.1 km

8. £480, £4.00

9. £75.00

10. £960, £1600, £2240

11. 64 cm, 120 cm^2

12. **1** equilateral
     2 obtuse-angled isosceles
     3 right-angled

Page 267   Exercise D4

1. labour £13.50, materials £6.00,
    other expenses £4.50, £30.15

2. 345 cm

3. **1** 0.12   **2** 0.0035   **3** 1.4

4. **1** $\frac{1}{6}$, 20   **2** $\frac{1}{13}$, 9   **3** 12

5. Parallelogram, $(\frac{1}{2}, 1\frac{1}{2})$

6. £35.10

7. **1** sphere   **4** cuboid
    2 cylinder   **5** cube
    3 cone

8. £13.70

9. 3

10. 360

11. 6 m to 7 m

12. $DE = 13.5$ cm, $DF = 12$ cm

Page 278   Exercise 21.1

1. **1** 042°   **4** 165°
    2 250°   **5** 090°
    3 307°

3. **1** 222°   **4** 345°
    2 070°   **5** 270°
    3 127°

4. **1** 90°   **2** 90°

5. **1** 135°   **4** SE
    2 90°   **5** W
    3 NE

Page 280   Exercise 21.2

1. **1** N 70°W   **4** S 70°E
    2 S 25°W   **5** N 42°W
    3 N 53°E

Page 282   Exercise 21.3

1. 2 km

2. 6 km, 750 m

3. 201°

4. 12.2 km, 260°

5. 097°

6. **1** 290 m   **2** 850 m   **3** 280 m

7. 323°, 1 : 200 000, 13 km, 205°

Page 284   Exercise 21.4

1. 50°, 290°

2. 1 : 50 000, 4.2 km

3. B–C 179 m, C–D 182 m, B–D 169 m

4. 242°, 25 km, 1 hr 40 min

5. **1** 040°   **2** 10 km

Page 288   Exercise 22.1

1. **1** 34, 40   **6** 18, 24
    2 18, 21   **7** $\frac{1}{81}$, $\frac{1}{243}$
    3 160, 320   **8** 127, 255
    4 729, 2187   **9** 158, 318
    5 −12, −15   **10** 720, 5040

2. **1** 11   **4** 16
    2 5   **5** 30
    3 $\frac{1}{2}$

3. **1** 19   **4** 56
    2 1000   **5** 55
    3 $\frac{1}{10}$

4. 8 should be 9, 400

6. **1** 10 should be 11
    2 24 should be 25
    3 6 should be 9

Page 292   Exercise 22.2

1. **1** 7.5   **6** 4.6
    2 5.3   **7** 7.7
    3 8.9   **8** 9.4
    4 9.8   **9** 2.3
    5 3.5   **10** 8.1

2. **1** 22.4   **6** 14.8
    2 25   **7** 15
    3 12.6   **8** 24
    4 17.3   **9** 17.8
    5 13   **10** 17

3. **1** 11.2 cm   **4** 8.1 cm
    2 10 cm   **5** 4 cm
    3 2.2 cm

4. **1** 15 cm   **4** 3.3 cm
    2 6.7 cm   **5** 2 cm
    3 7 cm

5. **1** 30 m   **2** $x = 10$ cm, $y = 8$ cm

6. 5 cm

7. 17 cm, 9 cm

8. **1** 5 cm   **2** 16 cm   **3** 21 cm

Page 294   **Exercise 22.3**

1. **1** 26, 37   **6** $\frac{1}{15}, \frac{1}{18}$
    2 18, 9   **7** 9, 0
    3 16, 20   **8** 14, 17
    4 1, $\frac{1}{3}$ **9** 10 000, 100 000
    5 19, 23   **10** 64, 55

2. 820

3. 10

5. **1** 64   **4** 41
    2 65   **5** 108
    3 $\frac{5}{6}$

6. 28

8. (5, 25), (6, 36), (7, 49), $y = x^2$, 20 $(20\frac{1}{4})$

9. **1** 25 cm   **3** 66 cm
    2 15 cm   **4** 234 cm^2

10. 10 km

11. 5

12. 13 feet

13. **1** 11 cm   **2** 4 cm   **3** 5 cm

14. **1** 15 cm   **2** 40 cm   **3** 60 cm^2

Page 300   **Exercise 23.1**

1. Food £15, transport £9.50,
    camp fee £7, extras £4.50

2. **1** 2

3. **1** 7

4. **1** £1.50   **2** $\frac{1}{8}$

Page 303   **Exercise 23.2**

1. 2

2. 1

3. 4

4. 30

5. **1** 133   **2** 2.7

8. frequencies for 3 to 9:
    2, 4, 7, 10, 14, 15, 8. Mode 8

9. frequencies for 32 to 42:
    2, 1, 2, 4, 5, 13, 7, 4, 3, 7, 2. Mode 37

10. frequencies 3, 6, 4, 4, 5, 2, 1.
    Modal class 65–69

11. **1** 40   **2** $\frac{3}{10}$ **3** 8 min

Page 305   **Exercise 23.3**

1. £150, wages £22 500, food
    £18 000, fuel £6000, extras £7500; £56 730

3. **2** 156   **3** 3.9   **4** $\frac{3}{5}$

4. **1** 75   **3** 20
    2 11 kg   **4** $\frac{4}{25}$

5. frequencies for 0 to 5: 21, 26, 25, 7, 3, 2.
    Mode 1

6. frequencies 4, 8, 8, 6, 3, 1

7. theoretical frequencies 2 to 12; 5, 10, 15,
    20, 25, 30, 25, 20, 15, 10, 5

8. 1 2 3,   1 2 4,   1 2 5,   1 3 4,   1 3 5,
    1 4 5,   2 3 4,   2 3 5,   2 4 5,   3 4 5;
    probabilities 6 to 12: 0.1, 0.1, 0.2, 0.2, 0.2,
    0.1, 0.1

Page 310   **Exercise 24.1**

2. **1** isosceles trapezium
    2 rectangle
    3 obtuse-angled isosceles
    4 right-angled
    5 equilateral

3. **1** 120°   **2** 90°, 135°, 135°

4. $AB = 5.9$ cm

Page 312   Exercise 24.2

1. − 6 units in *x*-direction,
   − 7 units in *y*-direction

2. **1** reflection (in the *y*-axis)
   2 rotation (about the origin through a half-turn)
   3 reflection (in the *x*-axis)
   4 translation (− 1 unit in *x*-direction)

Page 314   Exercise 24.3

1. *A* and *H*, *B* and *D*, *C* and *G*, *E* and *F*

2. *A* and *F*, *B* and *D*, *C* and *E*

Page 316   Exercise 24.4

7. **2** 1 hexagon, 1 triangle, 2 squares

Page 319   Exercise 24.5

1. **1** obtuse-angled isosceles
   2 isosceles trapezium
   3 rhombus

2. **1** 120°   **2** 135°

3. A_1 (4, − 1), B_1 (7, 0), C_1 (6, 5), A_2 (− 4, 2), B_2 (− 1, 3), C_2 (− 2, 8), translation − 5 units in *x*-direction and 1 unit in *y*-direction

4. $\triangle DNB$

6. $AB = 3.1$ cm

Page 326   Exercise 25.1

1. £4

2. £5.94

3. 3 kg

4. 140, 310, 480, 85, 445

5. 600, 800, 1150, 2025, 975

6. 45, 78, 24, 13, 82

7. £4.16, £2.67, 39 p, £3.89, £1.70

8. $\frac{1}{10}, \frac{3}{4}, \frac{1}{3}, \frac{3}{5}$

9. 12 p, 46 p

10. 49, 81, 144, 1, 36

11. 27, 125, 1, 1000, 8

12. 9, 33, 8, 11, 4

13. £16

14. £13.80

15. 17°, 59°, 125°, 83°, 79°

16. **1** 13   **6** 1200
    2 0.2   **7** 0.5
    3 35   **8** 600
    4 10   **9** 6
    5 500   **10** 200

17. **1** 13.3   **6** 1016.4
    2 0.189   **7** 0.55
    3 40   **8** 640
    4 10.46   **9** 6.6
    5 482   **10** 210

18. **1** 80.6   **6** 770
    2 1.7   **7** 0.8
    3 18   **8** 9
    4 3.6   **9** 3.6
    5 21   **10** 10

19. **1** 1.8   **4** £30
    2 $3\frac{1}{2}$ kg, 35 kg   **5** 20
    3 72°

20. **1** 11.5 m   **3** 66 m
    2 10.5 m   **4** 72 m

Page 328   Exercise 25.2

1. £22

2. £19.95

3. 1.1 kg

4. 286, 671, 913, 495, 319

5. 84, 240, 720

6. 25

7. 249, 155, 408

8. 13 p, 38 p, 44 p, 87 p, 53 p

9. $\frac{2}{5}, 2\frac{3}{10}, 2\frac{5}{6}, 1\frac{5}{8}, 4\frac{7}{12}$

10. 96 p, £1.30, £1, £2

11. 0.12, 7.1, 0.003, 0.56, 0.14, 0.04, 0.3, 3, 0.36, 0.042

12. £3.60

13. 8, 11, 7, 1, 10

14.   64, 1000, 125

15.   180°, 36°, 30°, 45°, 72°

16.   **1** 10 hr 7 min   **4** 5 yr 9 mth
      2 6 hr 36 min   **5** 39 hr 58 min
      3 63 yr 9 mth

17.   **1** 2   **6** 30
      2 300   **7** 4.5
      3 4   **8** 11.5
      4 4   **9** 30
      5 10   **10** 29

18.   **1** 1.89   **6** 30
      2 324.89   **7** 4.5
      3 3.84   **8** 13.2
      4 4.75   **9** 31.4
      5 9.5   **10** 30

19.   **1** 11   **4** 5
      2 22   **4** 40
      3 10

20.   **1** 3.248   **4** 39.69
      2 88.8   **5** 416.7
      3 2.3

21.   **1** 60 g   **2** 4 minutes   **3** 30 m

22.   **1** 6.5 cm   **5** 5.5 cm
      2 4.5 cm   **6** 3.5 cm
      3 22 cm   **7** 18 cm
      4 29.25 cm^2 **8** 19.25 cm^2

23.   **1** 7.5   **6** 51
      2 12   **7** 7
      3 27   **8** 8
      4 4   **9** 18
      5 6   **10** 2

24.   **1** 7.61   **4** 32.718
      2 9.082   **5** 38 562.5
      3 37.2

Page 332   Exercise E1

1.   20
2.   £1.15
3.   36 m
4.   £3.96
5.   30
6.   32 p
7.   May 31st
8.   8, 4 p
9. $\frac{1}{4}$
10. £12
11. 4.10 p.m.
12. 30 cm^2
13. £44
14. 37
15. £2
16. £1.20

17. 26° or 27°
18. £25.71
19. 15.17 (3.17 p.m.)
20. 16
21. 5.5 cm to 6.5 cm (6.1 cm)
22. 90° to 100° (93°)

Page 333   Exercise E2

1. A	6. D	11. B	16. C
2. D	7. A	12. D	17. A
3. B	8. E	13. D	18. D
4. C	9. C	14. A	19. E
5. B	10. C	15. E	20. C

Page 336   Exercise E3

1.   **1** 54 min   **2** 40 cm

2.   **1** 9 should be 10,
         triangular numbers, 36, 45, 55
      2 22 should be 21; 55, 89, 144
      3 6 should be 8, yes
      4 66 should be 65; 44, 37, 30

3.   £6.60, £8.25

4.   12 cm

5.   **1** $4\frac{1}{6}$ **2** $1\frac{5}{6}$ **3** 10

6.   £3.78

7.   18 m^2

8.   6.14 p.m., 2.5 km from A

9.   20.4 km, 276°

10. 4

11. **2** 2   **3** 206   **4** 2.1

12. 20°

Page 338   Exercise E4

1. $\frac{3}{10}$, $\frac{1}{3}$, $\frac{3}{8}$, 38%, 0.4

2.   larger one

3.   £99

4.   44 p

5.   122°

6.   48

7.   **1** $\frac{1}{6}$ **3** $\frac{1}{6}$ **5** $\frac{6}{11}$
      2 $\frac{1}{3}$ **4** $\frac{7}{12}$

8. **1** 180   **2** 120°   **3** 300

9. **1** pyramid on square base
    2 (triangular) prism

10. 2.5 cm

11. mean 8, median 7, mode 2

12. **1** £88.80   **2** 22.8 kg

Page 340   **Exercise E5**

1. 15 p

2. **1** $\frac{4}{7}$ **2** $\frac{1}{2}$

3. 10.6 km

4. **1** £5.75   **2** £3.60

5. **1** 20   **2** £12.54   **3** £1.70

7. $m = 40°$, $n = 140°$, $p = 40°$, $q = 70°$,
    $r = 70°$

8. **1** 20.3 cm   **2** 3.9 inches

9. 6 m

10. $\frac{3}{4}$ hour

11. 18 cm², 126 cm², 41.0 cm

12. A_1 (5, 4), B_1 (4, 5), C_1 (6, 8),
    A_2 (5, −4), B_2 (4, −5), C_2 (6, −8),

Page 343   **Exercise E6**

1. 480 francs, £40

2. **1** 16.55   **3** $12\frac{1}{2}$ p
    2 7 hr 13 min   **4** 70 km/hr

3. £14.84, £10.98, £3.86

4. 90 min

6. **1** 8 km/hr
    2 30 km/hr
    3 5.05 p.m., 33 km from A

7. **1** 8 s   **3** 7.85 s
    2 31.4 m   **4** the boy

8. $52 \to 2$, $84 \to 4$, $92 \to 1$

9. (80, 3200), 3200 m²; length 80 m,
    width 40 m

10. $AB = FE$, $BC = ED$, $AC = FD$

11. **1** 3   **2** 7.5 cm

12. **1** Carlisle, 100 miles
    2 London, 150 miles
    3· Leeds, 40 miles
    4 Cardiff, 30 miles
    5 Southampton, 70 miles
    6 West, 30 miles
    7 East, 110 miles
    8 South-west, 190 miles
    9 North-west, 100 miles
    10 South-east, 130 miles